APOCALYPSE, THE TRANSFORMATION OF EARTH

OTHER BOOKS IN ENGLISH BY FRIEDRICH BENESCH

Reverse Ritual
Spiritual Knowledge Is True Communion
(with Rudolf Steiner)

The Tourmaline
A Monograph

APOCALYPSE

The Transformation of Earth

an esoteric mineralogy

FRIEDRICH BENESCH

2015
Lindisfarne Books in association with Goldenstone Books
Lindisfarne Books is an imprint of SteinerBooks / Anthroposophic Press, Inc.
610 Main Street, Great Barrington, MA 01230
www.steinerbooks.org

Copyright © 2015 by SteinerBooks/Anthroposophic Press.
Foreword copyright © 2015 by Robert Sardello, PhD
This book was originally published in German as *Apokalypse: Die Verwandlung der Erde – eine okkulte Mineralogie* (Verlag Urachhaus, Stuttgart, 1994). Translation by Joseph Bailey.

All rights reserved. No part of this book may be reproduced, stored in a retrieval system, or transmitted in any form or by any means, electronic, mechanical, photocopying, recording, or otherwise, without the written permission of SteinerBooks.

Book and cover design: William Jens Jensen
Cover image: *The Fourth Angel Sounds His Trumpet* (Rev. 8) *Beatus escorial*, c. 950 (Real Biblioteca del Monasterio de San Lorenzo de El Escorial, Spain)

LIBRARY OF CONGRESS CONTROL NUMBER 2015931949

ISBN: 978-1-58420-165-6 (paperback)
ISBN: 978-1-58420-166-3 (eBook)

Contents

	Foreword by Robert Sardello, PhD	vii
	Preface	xi
PART 1: THE APOCALYPSE AND ITS IMAGES		1
1.	The Question	3
2.	Its Fundamental Structure	5
3.	The Series of Source Images	7
4.	Seven Images of God the Son	8
5.	Cosmic Source Images	12
6.	Mediator Entities Transit Images	19
7.	The Estuary (Mouth) Images	29
8.	Final Image of the Revelation	40
PART 2: SPIRIT IN THE MINERAL REALM		51
1.	Mineral and the Father-God	53
2.	Mineral as Soul Experience	54
3.	Esoteric Tradition	56
4.	Minerals and Natural Science	57
5.	Mineral as Entity	62
6.	Origin of the Mineral Realm	65
7.	Future of the Mineral Realm	70
8.	Minerals and the Fixed Stars	71
PART 3: HEAVENLY JERUSALEM AND MINERALS		79
1.	Forming the Question	82
2.	Minerals and Humanity	84
3.	Inner Life and Future Earth	88
4.	Minerals and the Human Body	91

5.	Cultic Action	95
6.	Four Questions from One	96
7.	The Human Being	98
8.	Minerals	103
9.	Earth and Macrocosm	107
10.	Evil and Minerals	109
11.	Summary	118

PART 4: BUILDING ELEMENTS OF HEAVENLY JERUSALEM — 121

1.	Water	125
2.	Crystal	155
3.	Jasper	176
4.	Jasper Experience	195
5.	Twelve Precious Stones	234
6.	Gold	295
7.	Pearl	327
8.	Wood	333
9.	Conclusion	340
10.	Retrospect and Outlook	346

APPENDICES	349
About the Author: A Note from the Publisher	439
Select Bibliography	453

Foreword

The Mineral World as a Spiritual Path

Robert Sardello, PhD

Crystals, mineral crystals, become wonderful objects of research and observation precisely for the person seeking entry into the spiritual worlds.... What we see down here as crystallized minerals is caused by the living spirit found in the expanse of the cosmos.
—Rudolf Steiner

In this book, with his exquisite descriptions of the twelve stones of the Apocalypse, Friedrich Benesch provides the basis for a completely new spiritual science of the mineral world. His work in these sections of the book holds the possibility of forming a spiritual path—the mineral world as a spiritual path. This summary of the essence of this book's mineral section is intended to highlight such a possibility.

The densest of matter holds the highest of mysteries. We know few details of the history of spiritual work in the mineral world. Spiritual initiates held the secrets of the material realms in deepest silence. They knew that knowledge of the spiritual nature of the mineral world had to be revealed gradually and according to one's spiritual development. Otherwise, misuse and destruction would ensue.

The many contemporary leaders, writers, and practitioners now working in the enticing area of metaphysical engagement with crystals and minerals were themselves once among the early initiates, and they rely heavily on semiconscious memories of those times. Nevertheless, with few exceptions, they all now follow a "new-age" approach to engaging with the mineral worlds. Sadly, this approach lacks inner soul and spirit intelligence.

There are currently many modern "compendiums" of the mineral world. They consist of long lists of minerals and give new-age, metaphysical descriptions of what the mineral or crystal and their "energy" are supposed to do—to enliven, to heal, to awaken new capacities, and to provide whatever the one with the stone wants. A complete absence of a spiritual science of stones exists, while interest in the mineral world now forms a very large new age business enterprise.

What comes to us from past spiritual initiates of spiritual paths of the mineral world is fragmentary and subject to much confusion, inflation, fantasy, and promises. Attempts to understand the power and magic of the mineral world seldom emanates from an understanding of the spiritual nature of the cosmos, and it never emanates from a coherent and sustained spiritual understanding of the Earth or the human being.

Present metaphysical work with crystals and minerals opens indiscriminately to all levels of stone presence—physical, etheric, astral, and spiritual. The spiritual path of the mineral world, however, requires the development of capacities to be present with the spiritual presences that transcend and yet also imprint and permeate the mineral world as creators, guardians, and caretakers of the ongoing, unfolding evolution of the complex of Earth-human spirit unity.

A contemporary spiritual path of the mineral world begins with sensitivity to the whole cosmos of spiritual beings. Such a path also begins with the sensed and felt presence of Earth as a being of body, soul, and spirit—some aspects being visible, and others invisible. In addition, such a path originates with inward presence to the essence of human beings as inherently spiritual. The difference between human beings doing spiritual acts and spiritual human beings acting according to their true nature can be discerned. The former always centers on self-interest; the latter always centers on being a reverent part of the whole.

The importance of spiritual work with the mineral world does not lie with mastering this world or using it only for our own benefit. Rather, the significance of such a path concerns the fact that ancient initiates were doing something for the future unity of the spiritual human with the spiritual Earth. The spiritual immortality of the human being—what is often called the "light-body"—is a human ideal. It is what the human being can become. Such spiritual immortality is inherently tied to unfolding the spiritual Earth's "light-body" in a similar manner.

All engagement with the mineral world holds this promise of spiritual completion. Every human interaction with the material world consists of combining the human spirit with the Earth spirit. Such knowledge formed the deepest esoteric wisdom of Freemasonry, now all but lost. Building the world, maintaining it, furthering it are all the result of interactions between the human spirit and the Earth spirit; it unites them, either in spiritual elevation or in spiritual degradation. Only when the interaction occurs consciously and reverently does the spiritual future of both unfold in proper unity.

In a similar manner, the living human body also consists of an ongoing, vital, relationship with the mineral world. All that we take in—not only through eating, but also in sensing and perceiving—combines the spirit of the mineral world with the human spirit through the body. All of our unending engagements with the spiritual human–spiritual Earth unity do not necessarily lead to the ideal of the immortality of both. This ideal cannot develop outside of conscious intent that is held deeply centered within the heart. We do not possess such a consciousness.

Modern consciousness splits us from Earth—our Mother—and elevates us to the false position of masters rather than workers with the mineral world, producing a world steeped in and motivated by fear. Individual spiritual work with the mineral world introduces a real and tangible current into the world as a healing force. Individual transformation through contemplative work with the mineral world indicates that such a current is activated.

Spiritual initiates have had one task—to be the holders, guardians, and inspirers of the future. The future of the earth-human ideal has been severed, and it is no longer possible to rely on culture to bear spiritual ideals. The present interest and fascination with the mineral realm exists today only as hanging on to a spiritual future by our fingernails. Moreover, in the context of our culture of fear, such interest understandably tends to be self-serving.

The very notion of attempting to develop a spiritual path of the mineral world breathes hope into the world. The very presence of such a path places something in the world that can serve as a balance to the prevailing forces of hubris and destruction. Such a path creates an ongoing prayer force. Having minerals as aesthetic objects or as collector's items can bring change and wake us up to accompanying spiritual beings of untold power. Working contemplatively with the mineral world goes a step further; it can become a life of working together with the spirits of *human spirit–Earth spirit* progress.

❦

Robert Sardello, PhD, is the cofounder and codirector of The School of Spiritual Psychology, which began in 1992, and coeditor of Goldenstone Press. His main professional emphasis has been to develop theoretical and practical approaches to perceiving and being in the right relationship with the Soul of the World—showing that human beings are being pulled from the time stream of the future rather than being pushed from the past—and developing the interior presence of heart with Earth, others, and the world. He is an independent teacher and scholar and a Fellow of the Dallas Institute of Humanities and Culture, and one of its founders. His books include *Money and the Soul of the World* (with Randolf Severson); *Facing the World with Soul: The Reimagination of Modern Life; Love and the Soul: Creating a Future for Earth; Love and the World: A Guide to Conscious Soul Practice, Freeing the Soul from Fear; The Power of Soul: Living the Twelve Virtues; Silence: The Mystery of Wholeness; Steps on the Stone Path: Working with Crystals and Minerals as Spiritual Practice;* and *Acts of the Heart: Culture-Building, Soul-Researching.*

Preface

The image handed down at the end of the Bible, in a few sentences of the Greek language of the first century AD, can be counted among the greatest riddles of world literature. It is the image of the Heavenly Jerusalem at the end of the final book of the New Testament, the "Revelation of St. John," the Apocalypse. For the suprasensory vision of the Apocalyptist John, a comprehensive image sets itself apart from the background of heaven: the imagination of a city, hovering and majestically luminous, slowly moving in its descent from heaven to the Earth. Among the elements of the image are geometric measures and figures, heavenly beings and substances, self-luminous manifestations, architectural structures, and writing on the building components that convey the names of persons and groups of people. Everything is bathed in a light that emanates from Divine Being itself. Moreover, the whole evokes an impression of originary, germinal virginity, the quality of a "bride" adorned for her groom. Its purpose, after all, is betrothal to the divine being called the "Lamb." Thus, the city is illuminated by the divine from three sides. It fills itself with the Godhead as a temple; in the light it interweaves with the Godhead; its intended purpose is to become impregnated by the Godhead in the form of an ongoing, most exalted nuptial ceremony. The whole, consisting of form, measure, color and light, is filled with the sound of the word *Come!*

All this proves to be perfect union, harmony and totality, interpenetration and transparency; but at the same time the strictest differentiation and arrangement by measure, number, and figure. It is constructed—and its construction followed through to conclusion—as a "city." Furthermore, it is plantlike in form: its components were autonomous parts that are now conjoined such that the whole is fully present in them, while each component nevertheless is autonomous.

To be sure: its substances are the materiality of light and of color; but also of mineral existence. What may previously have been something quite different has become a mineral here, which lends it the character of chastity, purity, constancy, and indestructible sterling quality—whereby the substance seems in diverse ways to correspond to what in our mineral world reminds us of the highest, noblest, purest sense appearance: gold, pearls, precious stones, crystals, glass. The substance of light and of minerals manifests as two sides of the One godly primal substance, which is the basis for all individual detail. In the motif of the wedding, this substantiality becomes evident as that of divine love.

It is this living essence of love that composes itself, amid the luminescent shapes and intoning, to become the word *Come!* In this *come*, there lives singing, music, word, and primal articulation of this whole mysterious essence.

In the document of the Revelation, this essence has a name: the city of Jerusalem. According to research that has been done, there is a whole series of derivations of this name. In general, it is translated as "city of peace." Appendix 30 of this book consists of an article from the *Biblisch-historisches Handbuch* on the etymology of this ancient city name, from which one can gain an impression of how research has struggled for this word's interpretation and its origin alike.

The actual mystery of this city-imagination is its "substance," its "construction material," the suprasensory mineral nature of which becomes the central question. The present book is an attempt to answer this question, which, in simplified form, reads as follows:

1. Are mineral substances pure matter or are they of spiritual nature?
2. Are there only material minerals that are perhaps also spiritual, or are there also "spiritual minerals" of non-material nature?
3. How are we to understand the concrete minerals used to build the Heavenly Jerusalem?

These three questions place us before the problem of an "esoteric mineralogy." For anything purely spiritual can only be the object of esoteric cognition, esoteric research, and science. Esoteric science presupposes, though, that not matter, but rather spirit is the actual, original, and essential reality of the world—hence of the mineral world as well. This fundamental question of knowledge, regarding our modern consciousness, can be structured into sub-questions in the following way:

1. The primacy of the spirit or of substance, of matter. Either the spirit is the origin and all that is material is a densified or condensed manifestation of the spirit, or else matter is what comes first and all that is spiritual but a function of matter, a product of material processes of sublimation.
2. The primacy of life or of death. Either life is the origin, and what is dead is a precipitation of the living; or the dead, mechanical is what comes first, and life a more complicated mechanism of the dead.
3. The primacy of the gestalt or of the atom. Either the gestalt—the living, organic structure, the whole, the unity—is the origin, and dust—the atom, the particle, the quantum—is a decimated gestalt, or the atom is the origin, and the whole is the mere result of mutual interaction of a sum of atoms according to structural laws, probabilities.
4. Primacy of the meaningful and harmonious or of the meaningless and coincidental. Either harmony, context and unison, the meaningful idea, the cosmic plan—including preestablished harmony in the Leibnizian sense—is the origin, or meaningless coincidence stands at the beginning (atomic theory's "Big Bang").
5. The primacy of the essential or of the objective. Beings, persons, and "I"-beings are the origin, or else objects and circumstances come first, and essences are merely appearance, or mere illusions of self-experience.

6. The primacy either of natural law as the actual law of the cosmos, or of the ethical world order proceeding from a soul and spiritual world that is the basis of the whole of world events and active within them, and through which natural law becomes provident—that is, assumes "higher meaning."

Of these two-times-six possibilities, one can take either the first or the second of each pair as a postulate and make it the premise for one's thinking about the world. If one takes spirit, life, unity, meaning, essence, and providence as the origin, one will find in matter, death, particle, coincidence, and object the appearance of the former in the latter. One will find the outer manifestation of something spiritual, living, and essential in every sensory phenomenon; and one will endeavor, based on this knowledge, to ascend through the veil of the sensory to an understanding of this essence.

However, one can also assume the second possibility as one's point of departure, in which case one will endeavor to find out how spirit is derived from matter, life from death, wholeness from particles, meaning from chance, and essence from objects. But one's view on the specifically spiritual, living, whole, meaningful and essential will always be obfuscated by the point of departure one has chosen, since one possesses organs and concepts for matter, mechanism, detail, chance and object. To be sure, for spirit, life, wholeness, and essence, one has organs as well; but one is equipped with them in seed-form only; they have to be awakened and developed. One has to do something for them. If in our thinking we support ourselves on substance, mechanism, particle, chance, object, we become untrue as human beings, for we live in both matter and spirit at the same time—in the material appearance of the outer world on the one hand, and in thinking, feeling, and willing within the inwardly manifesting thought and soul world on the other. However, since we ourselves are the latter, we have no self-knowledge to begin with; rather, we are blind for spirit, soul, and life. Like the eye that sees the world but not itself, we do not see ourselves. If by holding to the second series of presuppositions we interpret the first series away, we live with a fundamental alteration complex. This causes the human soul in its depths to be ground down; the mockery, ridicule, and contempt with which people treat the primacy of the spirit, in such a case, are the expression of this violent displacement into the unconscious; this is a contortion of the human essence that yearns for the primacy of the spirit.

One will always be confronted, however, by the difficulty of grasping that everything in the world that manifests sensorially, from stones up to the stars, passing over into the non-sensory in two opposite directions. For the path from the world of sense appearance to the fields researched by modern atomic physics—that is, elementary particles and the material fields of the laws of stasis, is completely different from the one leading to the realities of life. Life, the soul, and the conscious mind transition to a suprasensory area, quantum physics to a subsensory one. In either case, we are dealing with spiritual matters, each constituting the physical from a different side. Behind both the subsensory and the suprasensory manifestations, we seek something person-like, something ideal at work behind them. At first, we will be able to perceive not this personal nature itself, but only its effects in the form of influences from the one side, and of qualities and images from the other side. From the regularities and ideas specific to each respective side, we will be able to advance to the respective essence or entity.

An essence, or entity, must be able to manifest not only as spirit, but also as substance; substance, however, can be the expression only of an entity and cannot be one itself. We can understand spirit as entity, because we have encountered it as we encounter other persons. On the whole, we know who a person is, how he or she perceives, thinks, feels, wills, and acts. We can also discover from this person why that individual acts. Substance, or matter, can be seen through, but not comprehended. We know how it functions but not why. Thus, it is understandable why and how spirit becomes matter, but we will not be able to understand how matter becomes an entity of a personal nature, unless we assume that spirit itself is active within it. Moreover, we can also understand why and how matter is capable of revealing spirit, life, wholeness, meaning, and essence.

This is why it is possible with the first presupposition—primacy of spirit—to arrive at a fulfilled, meaningful knowledge of the world. The second presupposition, when dealt with as a primacy, leads to nothing but a meaningless, empty grasping of the outer aspect of the world.

In the Revelation of St. John, spiritual worlds and spiritual entities appear both in images of the sensory world and in images of the mineral realm. In what follows, I have attempted to engage in a discussion of these two sides of world manifestation.

Now the argument could be made that the images of the Apocalypse are intended in a purely symbolic way. If this is so, the mineral appears as a symbol for something of a soul-like and spiritual nature. The Apocalyptist, however, saw not symbols but realities; even a symbol can be genuine only if something of the reality for which it stands shines through. It must be inwardly identical, in a real way, with what it intends, with the essence from which it stems; thus it must arise from the same reality. Otherwise it contains no meaning. The images of the minerals in the Apocalypse are just as much reality as the minerals are on Earth. Neither is essential; both are simply manifestations of something essential. Hence, both are truly Apocalyptic—the mineral we hold in our hand and the image we hold in our mind. They reveal themselves mutually.

In this book, I juxtapose the objects of sensory appearance and natural-scientific research with the sayings of the Revelation of St. John to express the joint background of the appearances. One connected with the other can then lead to an encounter with the essence. Thus, we are dealing with "esoteric mineralogy." On its paths, we can strive to enable a renewed encounter between the human being and mineral being, from which essence and future can then shine forth.

Friedrich Benesch
Easter, 1981

Part 1
Apocalypse and Its Images

1. The Question

In the last book of the New Testament, the Revelation of St. John, the suprasensory image of a book appears at the beginning of the first chapter in the midst of a grand revelation. This book contains writing inside and outside (*esothen kai opisthen*), meaning that its content has an "esoteric" interior that exerts a hidden influence, and a manifest exterior on which the influence is exerted. At the same time, it is sealed with seven seals. From a "strong angel" the question goes out: "Who is worthy to open the book and loose its seals?"

> Then I saw in the right hand of him who sat on the throne a scroll with writing on both sides and sealed with seven seals. And I saw a mighty angel proclaiming in a loud voice, "Who is worthy to break the seals and open the scroll?" But no one in Heaven or on Earth or under the Earth could open the scroll or even look inside it. I wept and wept because no one was found who was worthy to open the scroll or look inside. Then one of the elders said to me, "Do not weep! See, the Lion of the tribe of Judah, the Root of David, has triumphed. He is able to open the scroll and its seven seals."
>
> Then I saw a Lamb, looking as if it had been slain, standing at the center of the throne, encircled by the four living creatures and the elders. The Lamb had seven horns and seven eyes, which are the seven spirits of God sent out into all the Earth. He went and took the scroll from the right hand of him who sat on the throne. And when he had taken it, the four living creatures and the twenty-four elders fell down before the Lamb. Each one had a harp and they were holding golden bowls full of incense, which are the prayers of God's people. And they sang a new song, saying, "You are worthy to take the scroll and to open its seals, because you

were slain, and with your blood you purchased for God persons from every tribe and language and people and nation. You have made them to be a kingdom and priests to serve our God, and they will reign on the Earth."

Then I looked and heard the voice of many angels, numbering thousands upon thousands, and ten thousand times ten thousand. They encircled the throne and the living creatures and the elders. In a loud voice they were saying, "Worthy is the Lamb, who was slain, to receive power and wealth and wisdom and strength and honor and glory and praise!"

Then I heard every creature in Heaven and on Earth and under the earth and on the sea, and all that is in them, saying, "To him who sits on the throne and to the Lamb be praise and honor and glory and power, for ever and ever!"

The four living creatures said, "Amen," and the elders fell down and worshiped. (Rev. 5:1–14)

Essentially, this motif holds for the entire Book of Revelation. Its content consists, from beginning to end, of suprasensory images and words—except for the two sentences (Rev. 1:9–10) in which John speaks of his earthly existence on Patmos on a Sunday (the Day of the Lord). True, these pictures derive their image substance and their wording from sensory aspects of the Earth, and so they have an "outside"; but their reality, the inside, belongs to a purely suprasensory etheric-soul-spiritual world. This is no image; rather, it is wielding reality within an image. The suprasensory worlds appear to the seer veiled in image elements of the sensory world. This has seduced many people to associate the Apocalypse directly with the sensory world, but to do so is methodologically false. Instead, a person has to seek out the essential soul-spiritual element of the appearances of the sensory world in its images, manifestations, gestures themselves, trace these appearances back to their suprasensory being, and in this way—through the suprasensory existence of the sensory world—break the seals of the Apocalypse's imaginations, inspirations, and intuitions. The enspirited sensory world breaks the seals of the image-pervaded spiritual world.

Even so, an undertaking of this kind will be dissatisfying. This is because in the Apocalypse deeds become visible that must be traced to entities of the spiritual world. And while these as well always do appear in the Apocalypse, it is only by means of suprasensory research and knowledge that they can be accessed or understood in their actual existence. So without Rudolf Steiner's research, we would not be in a position to read coherently in the images of the Revelation (cf. the exegeses in appendix 1 on the nature of Rudolf Steiner's Anthroposophy). On the other hand, it is necessary to acquaint oneself with the motifs and structural elements of the Revelation itself, in order to approach spiritual research in an insightful way. To a certain extent, the revelations are optical-painterly pictures; their interconnectedness is a musical, symphonic one that expresses itself in numeric mysteries. Spiritual spatiality reveals itself in the pictures, spiritual temporality in the numbers. Thus the Apocalypse is revelation of the past, action in the present, and vision of the future. Compositionally, the first number to appear in the images is seven, the number of movement, of development, of times and time-cycles. It always contains a beginning, an ascent or a descent to an evolutionary high point or low point, and then a descent or ascent to an involutionary conclusion. What lives in the letters to the seven churches in chapters 2 and 3 as an inner unfolding becomes openly manifest in the seven seals, the seven trumpets, and the seven vials of wrath as a world-creating, world-transforming, world-annihilating, and world-renewing drama.

CHAPTER 2: ITS FUNDAMENTAL STRUCTURE

The Four Streams of the Revelation

Upon contemplation of the images, it is striking that the account of the seer's earthly situation telling of Patmos on a Sunday is followed by transitions in his consciousness from the sensual to the suprasensory plane (I beheld—I saw—and so on). Suprasensory worlds and beings take action so that they can become perceptible (there appears—it was opened—the heavens opened up). These are two modes for the appearance of all of these entities and images of a spiritual-soul world. For one, they appear by the seer carrying elements of his earthly sense recollections into the spiritual world, which function as vessels of sorts for catching up the reality content of the suprasensory; for the other, they appear through the suprasensory world itself, assuming earthly image-form (it was like unto—it was as if), to reveal itself to a human being.

The main spiritual direction of flow of the processes presenting themselves as the Apocalypse goes from the suprasensory to the sensory world. What comes from the sensory world becomes suprasensorily visible; that is, it is the suprasensory aspect of the sense-perceptible, which the spirit world either receives or rejects, depending on how the spirit world is attuned to it. Everything is movement, wellspring, stream, flow, event, becoming and withering, estuary. In one single place after the opening of the seventh seal, there is a kind of standstill (8:1), a silence in Heaven, about the space of half-an-hour. The images differ as to the direction of their movement, of which there are three. The most striking images are those that depict the main streams of the Apocalyptic occurrence: the mighty currents issuing from the spiritual world, from the spiritual beings to the sensory world. These images' sources are always suprasensory; they are of uniform origin and pour forth in a sevenfold way.

The seven letters to the seven angels of the seven churches (Rev. 2–3) issue from the being and essence of the Son of Man. The streaming contents of the seven seals broken one after another by the Lamb (Rev. 5–8) pour forth from the sealed book. The contents of the seven trumpets stream forth from the seven angels standing before the altar (Rev. 8–14); and the seven streams debouching from the seven golden vials full of "the Wrath of God" come from the seven angels from the temple (ch. 15/16). This fourth stream pervades the second half of the

Revelation completely, whereby the seventh of these vials' streams is enwrought with events emerging from the totality of the Apocalyptic event as flow and current (Rev. 16–20). A "human being," a "book," an "altar," and a "temple" are the four output images of the four sevenfold streams.

In his book on The Apocalypse of St. John, Emil Bock shows the kinds of suprasensory perception that need to be taken into account in the depiction of the four streams. In addition, he refers to the emergence of these four streams from images possessing wellspring-character and at the same time also depicting grand cosmic imaginations. They appear in the fashion of the bordures or the tapping of the four springs of streams (cf. appendix 2).

Chapter 3: The Series of Source Images

The sources proper are entities (the One sitting on the throne, the Lamb, the angels, the Son of Man). But as with the Blautopf spring near Blaubeuren, Germany, or with the karst spring of the Brenz River near Heidenheim, Germany, or the karst springs of the Jordan near Banias and Dan in Palestine, where the water is surrounded by stone, these entities, too, are carried by reified and constructional image manifestations which themselves possess this very wellspring attribute (a throne, an altar, a temple, the Ark of the Covenant, a vessel for sacrificial frankincense, a lantern; but also the book, the seals, the trumpets, the vials). Likewise, geological, mineralogical, and meteorological elements occur (a mountain, a seashore, a river, a cloud, a rainbow, a precious stone, a precious metal; but also the Sun, the Moon, the stars, the heavens), and they do so in the individual aspects of the buildings (temple), objects (throne, altar), and implements (censer, book, trumpets, vials) and interwoven with cosmic structures. Thus it is necessary to distinguish between source images and stream images.

The inexhaustible abundance of the spiritually living allows the four streams to flow directly not only out of the four source images of the pictorial level mentioned above; this abundance also reveals itself in the sphere of the source images of the essential level, in manifestations of entities, who in turn undergo a sevenfold transformation in their fundamental nature. Three such different series of source images of a sevenfold transformation of essence/being are distinguishable in the Apocalypse. The first of these three series is marked by a particular being standing in the foreground, the actual "hero" of the entire drama, the Christ Being. Seven great manifestations and transformations of this being are worked into the Revelation.

Chapter 4: Seven Images of God the Son

In the first picture of this series, Jesus Christ appears, the Son of Man, in the midst of the seven golden lanterns and with the seven stars in his hand:

> I turned around to see the voice that was speaking to me. And when I turned I saw seven golden lampstands, and among the lampstands was someone like a son of man, dressed in a robe reaching down to his feet and with a golden sash around his chest. The hair on his head was white like wool, as white as snow, and his eyes were like blazing fire. His feet were like bronze glowing in a furnace, and his voice was like the sound of rushing waters. In his right hand he held seven stars, and coming out of his mouth was a sharp, double-edged sword. His face was like the Sun shining in all its brilliance. (Rev. 1:12–16)

This grand spirit image of the Son of Man, which shakes the Apocalyptist John to the point of a deathlike state, is something like the all-comprehending source image of the Apocalyptic vision. All the following things that Saint John experiences emerge from the encounter with this entity, hence the next six manifestations, in which this being reveals Himself in ever-new transformations. These transformations are no happenstance. In the first chapter's image of the Son of Man, the comprehensive divine being of God the Son shows the result of what Christ consummated on Earth in Jesus through the Mystery of Golgotha: "Do not be afraid. I am the First and the Last. I am the Living One; I was dead, and now look, I am alive for ever and ever! And I hold the keys of death and Hades" (Rev. 1:17–18).

The second manifestation of God the Son is found in the fifth chapter. He reveals Himself in an entirely changed shape. It is the image of the Lamb before or in the fourth chapter's throne-image. The Lamb has seven horn-like rays on its head, in its countenance seven eyes. It is the being who alone can open the book and its seven seals (Rev. 6–8). The sacrificial power and revelatory omnipotence of Jesus Christ appear in this second image:

> Then I saw a Lamb, looking as if it had been slain, standing at the center of the throne, encircled by the four living creatures and the elders. The Lamb had seven horns and seven eyes, which are the seven spirits of God sent out into all the Earth. He went and took the scroll from the right hand of him who sat on the throne. (Rev. 5:6–7)

The Lamb's revelatory might is then carried further. From the opening of the seventh seal there emerges the golden altar (8:3), to which the prayers of the saints stream upward from the Earth. It is at this altar that the "other" angel performs the ceremony of worship, which then flows to the Earth: There were voices, thundering, lightning, and an earthquake (8:5). Here the seven angels appear who inaugurate the stream of the seven trumpets, while the Lamb itself, though now remains invisible, as it were, in the background of the altar, behind all the revelations in chapters 8 to 14. His essential being in process of transformation shimmers through only slightly in the image of the little boy, the son to whom the woman clothed with the Sun gives birth. ("She gave birth to a son, a male child, who 'will rule all the nations with an iron scepter.' And her child was snatched up to God and to his throne" [Rev. 12:5].) More on this later. Early in chapter 14, the Son-God appears in His third shape, once more as a Lamb, but now on a mountain in the midst of the one-hundred-forty-four thousand. He is now the central entity of a redeemed humanity: "Then I looked, and there before me was the Lamb, standing on Mount Zion, and with him 144,000 who had his name and his Father's name written on their foreheads" (Rev. 14:1).

Immediately thereafter, this being shimmers in a completely hidden way as the everlasting gospel carried through all the heavens. The Son is a divine entity and has His own sphere of influence consisting of divine life forces, might of soul, and full spiritual omnipotence. He has a realm. This realm is charged throughout with His wielding might and borne up by angels. It is truly "the everlasting gospel": "Then I saw another angel flying in midair, and he had the eternal gospel to proclaim to those who live on the Earth—to every nation, tribe, language, and people. He said in a loud voice, 'Fear God and give him glory, because the hour of his judgment has come. Worship him who made the heavens, the earth, the sea, and the springs of water'" (Rev. 14:6–7).

The fourth manifestation of the Son-God is once more as the Son of Man, upon a white cloud and with a sharp sickle in His hand. In this image, the spiritual office of judgment of Jesus Christ is revealed. Yet another side of his nature:

> I looked, and there before me was a white cloud, and seated on the cloud was one like a son of man with a crown of gold on his head and a sharp sickle in his hand. Then another angel came out of the temple and called in a loud voice to him who was sitting on the cloud, "Take your sickle and reap, because the time to reap has come, for the harvest of the earth is ripe." So he who was seated on the cloud swung his sickle over the earth, and the earth was harvested. (Rev. 14:14–16)

The two images of the Son-God's manifestation in chapter 14 in turn initiate what is unveiled at the beginning of chapter 15 in the manifestation of the seven angels that unfold the seven trials of the fourth stream. The Son of Man with the sickle in His hand is the source image of the command, "Go, pour out the seven bowls of God's wrath on the Earth" (16:1). And as they flow forth, the divine being remains once more in the background.

But then the Apocalyptist experiences the fifth vision. In an entirely transformed shape, the "white rider" reappears. It is the Son-God as an "I"-being, the God of all "I"-beings, the Lord of human beings as kings and lords.

> I saw Heaven standing open and there before me was a white horse, whose rider is called Faithful and True. With justice he judges and wages war. His eyes are like blazing fire, and on his head are many crowns. He has a name written on him that no one knows but he himself. He is dressed in a robe dipped in blood, and his name is the Word of God. The armies of Heaven were following him, riding on white horses and dressed in fine linen, white and clean. Coming out of his mouth is a sharp sword with which to strike down the nations. "He will rule them with an iron scepter." He treads the winepress of the fury of the wrath of God Almighty. On his robe and on his thigh he has this name written: KING OF KINGS AND LORD OF LORDS. (Rev. 19:11–16)

The sixth vision shows the Son-entity on a great white "chair." Heaven and Earth flee and disappear before His countenance, and all the dead draw near. This sixth image has a cosmic dimension. The current cosmos begins to spiritualize, the Son-God becomes Him Who dissolves the old world and becomes the middle-point of a humankind that has passed through the old cosmos. He Himself now has the rank of One sitting on the throne. And unto Him all the destinies of all human beings are open in the "Book of Life"; in the course of the old world's dissolution, He is the Lord of Karma.

> Then I saw a great white throne and him who was seated on it. The Earth and the heavens fled from his presence, and there was no place for them. And I saw the dead, great, and small standing before the throne, and books were opened. Another book was

opened, which is the book of life. The dead were judged according to what they had done as recorded in the books. (Rev. 20:11–12)

At the conclusion of the Apocalypse, the Son-God is again fully present as "'I'-Jesus," as the bride's groom, the bride being the Heavenly Jerusalem; as the Morning Star, as the giver of the meal. The final, seventh source image in the series of the Son-God's manifestations is no longer actually an image; it has become entirely Word. Its sole imaginal aspect is the "Morning Star," but that too is a self-testimony. Over and over He now utters the Word concerning His own being. These are "words of the prophesy" (Rev. 22:10), such as in verses 12 and 13: "I am the Alpha and the Omega." And then verse 16: "I, Jesus, have sent my angel to give you this testimony for the churches. I am the Root and the Offspring of David, and the bright Morning Star."

Together, these revelations of the Son-God form the manifestations of the mid-point entity of the Apocalypse. Again and again new transformative impulses issue from Him, and within them this entity transforms Itself.

Chapter 5: Cosmic Source Images
The World of the Father-God

In the second series of source images in the Apocalypse, the cosmic-image elements have a strong part. This series of revelations as well has seven levels. The first, comprehensive image is the content of the entire fourth chapter:

> After this I looked, and there before me was a door standing open in Heaven. And the voice I had first heard speaking to me like a trumpet said, "Come up here, and I will show you what must take place after this." At once I was in the Spirit, and there before me was a throne in Heaven with someone sitting on it. And the one who sat there had the appearance of jasper and ruby. A rainbow that shone like an emerald encircled the throne. Surrounding the

throne were twenty-four other thrones, and seated on them were twenty-four elders. They were dressed in white and had crowns of gold on their heads. From the throne came flashes of lightning, rumblings, and peals of thunder. In front of the throne, seven lamps were blazing. These are the seven spirits of God. Also in front of the throne there was what looked like a sea of glass, clear as crystal.

In the center, around the throne, were four living creatures, and they were covered with eyes, in front and in back. The first living creature was like a lion, the second was like an ox, the third had a face like a man, the fourth was like a flying eagle. Each of the four living creatures had six wings and was covered with eyes all around, even under its wings. Day and night they never stop saying, "'Holy, holy, holy is the Lord God Almighty, who was, and is, and is to come."

Whenever the living creatures give glory, honor, and thanks to him who sits on the throne and who lives forever and ever, the twenty-four elders fall down before him who sits on the throne and worship him who lives for ever and ever. They lay their crowns before the throne and say. "You are worthy, our Lord and God, to receive glory and honor and power, for you created all things, and by your will they were created and have their being." (Rev. 4.1–11)

A throne becomes visible, a portal, a door that opens. A throne set in Heaven, on the throne a Being that cannot be compared with human, animal or plant images, but rather causes "mineralogy," "meteorology," "cosmology" to issue from Itself: throne, jasper, sard, rainbow, emerald, lightning, thunder, voices are the "earthly" imaginal elements of his manifestation. Round about the throne there shine 24 thrones, seven burning torches emanate their light from it, and in front of it is spread out the sea of glass like ice or rock crystal (the original Greek word means both). On the throne the Being with no name prevails, surrounded by the twenty-four Eldest on their thrones, the seven angels of God and the four living beasts (lion, steer, human being, eagle), and in the hand of the One on the throne lies the book. In the midst of these images and entities, the Lamb then reveals itself in the fifth chapter, which is standing, even though it has been sacrificed. Its seven eyes are the seven spirits of God sent out into all the world.

A comparison between the seer John's images and those of the great vision of the prophet Ezekiel in the Old Testament seems obvious. A whole series of imaginal motifs coincides. The essential difference is that, in Ezekiel (1:26), the One on the throne is of human form, while to Johannes He appears in the image of a precious stone. The latter motif is also found in Ezekiel, but only pertaining to the throne itself ("And above the firmament over their heads was the likeness of a throne, like the appearance of a sapphire stone"). John speaks only of the throne. One will hardly go astray if one makes use of the sapphire-imagination for the throne in the Apocalypse of St. John.

The second thing lacking in Ezekiel is the Apocalyptic Lamb. In Ezekiel, the Throning One is fire, inside and out, which emanates upward and downward from His loins and His lap. With John, it is jasper-light and carnelian-fire. Here as well, it is possible to conceive of the jasper-light as shining upward and the red carnelian-fire downward. If one beholds both pictures together, there appear in the source image of the Father God sapphire-blue, jasper-white, carnelian-red, and emerald-green, the latter in the rainbow surrounding the throne. The New Testament picture brings deeper mysteries of the Godhead to manifestation. The Throning One and His fatherly world, the profoundest and the most exalted of the entire cosmic nature and essence, the wellspring of all wellsprings, appearances, transformations, and decisions, manifest as "precious stone." The physical-mineral element has its origin in the sea of glass. Thus the world takes its course from the One on the throne, the throne, and the sea of glass as its starting point. This image as well runs through the Apocalypse in six further transformations. The seventh chapter speaks again of the throne, the Throning One, the twenty-four Eldest, and the four living beasts: "All the angels were standing around the throne and around the elders and the four living creatures. They fell down on their faces before the throne and worshiped God, saying, 'Amen! Praise and glory and wisdom and thanks and honor and power and strength be to our God forever and ever. Amen!'" (Rev. 7:11–12).

The second cosmic image deals with the true relationship between created beings and the Fatherly Ground of the world. It is a relationship of praising adoration and worship.

Through the interweaving of the divine Fatherly Being and His world with the worshipping creatures, the third source image is formed. The golden altar arises. The Father-world has become a site of sacrifice. Between the creatures and the Father, the Son is at work, albeit hidden, and this working becomes the source image of the seven trumpet streams of the Revelation. This second transformation occurs through the Lamb's participation. The Lamb opens the seventh seal. And what in this way ascends from human prayers and falls to Earth from the altar as fire, causes the world of God to become the "temple" round about the altar:

> When he [the Lamb] opened the seventh seal, there was silence in Heaven for about half an hour. And I saw the seven angels who stand before God, and seven trumpets were given to them. Another angel, who had a golden censer, came and stood at the altar. He was given much incense to offer, with the prayers of all God's people, on the golden altar in front of the throne. The smoke of the incense, together with the prayers of God's people, went up before God from the angel's hand. Then the angel took the censer, filled it with fire from the altar, and hurled it on the Earth; and there came peals of thunder, rumblings, flashes of lightning and an earthquake. (Rev. 8:1–5)

At the beginning of the eleventh chapter, the fourth transformation occurs: While the One upon the throne remains in the background and His presence is only hinted at, the events are concentrated on the altar and the temple surrounding it: "I was given a reed like a measuring rod and was told, 'Go and measure the temple of God and the altar, with its worshipers. But exclude the outer court; do not measure it, because it has been given to the Gentiles. They will trample on the holy city for forty-two months'" (Rev. 11:1–2).

At the end of the eleventh chapter, the innermost part of the temple opens; it is the Ark of the Covenant: "Then God's temple in Heaven was opened, and within his temple was seen the ark of his covenant. And there came flashes of lightning, rumblings, peals of thunder, an earthquake and a severe hailstorm" (Rev. 11:19). What is prepared in the third transformation becomes the content of the fourth. Emerging from the altar the temple appears, but then, in the innermost of the temple, the "Ark of the Covenant."

The Ark of the Covenant, belonging to the Israeli temple in Jerusalem, is fraught with profound mysteries. Its inauguration goes back to the installation of the ancient cult by Moses. For centuries, it was experienced as the magical site of the earthly seat of the Godhead, as the "Seat of Grace." It stood in the Salomonic temple's Holiest of Holies and was guarded by the wings of two Cherubim. The Ark's content was the secret of the initiates. Nowhere in the entire Old Testament is the mystery unveiled. Only in the New Testament's Letter to the Hebrews, chapter nine, do we learn the secret. There, it says:

> Behind the second curtain was a room called the Most Holy Place, which had the golden altar of incense and the gold-covered Ark of the Covenant. This ark contained the gold jar of manna, Aaron's staff that had budded, and the stone tablets of the Covenant. Above the Ark were the cherubim of the Glory, overshadowing the atonement cover. (Heb. 9:3–5)

What in the innermost temple were sensory–suprasensory symbols becomes spirit-image in the Revelation. Thus the three content images contain the archetype of the higher human being in the earthly human being, the substance, and essence yet at rest in the Godhead but which one day will come to unfolding within the human being. According to the terminology of ancient Indian esotericism and according to Rudolf

Steiner's spiritual research, this substance and essence are *manas* (spirit self), *buddhi* (life-spirit), and *atma* (spirit body).

In the fifth transformation of the cosmic source images, the sea of glass appears once more. It is no longer purely luminous in nature, though; rather, it is charged with fire. In the created world there now begins a mighty fire process, which takes hold of germinal zones of the mineral world. This process is wrought with the "Song of Moses":

> I saw in Heaven another great and marvelous sign: seven angels with the seven last plagues—last, because with them God's wrath is completed. And I saw what looked like a sea of glass glowing with fire and, standing beside the sea, those who had been victorious over the beast and its image and over the number of its name. They held harps given them by God and sang the song of God's servant Moses and of the Lamb:
>
> "Great and marvelous are your deeds, Lord God Almighty. Just and true are your ways, King of the nations. Who will not fear you, Lord, and bring glory to your name? For you alone are holy. All nations will come and worship before you, for your righteous acts have been revealed." (Rev. 15:1–4)

In this fifth cosmic source image of the sea of glass, an inner connection becomes apparent between the seven angels and the trials and the transformation of this sea itself. There is a mutuality between the final trials of human development and the transformations of the mineral world. On one hand: divine love in the golden vials—active for humankind as purifying wrath; on the other hand: the mineral world, which originally was the crystal sea, and is now pervaded with the human influences of the transformation.* Through human participation, the fifth cosmic source image passes over into the sixth. The world becomes once more a temple: but this time what was transformed in the sea of glass is enwoven into it. The "Song of Moses and of the Lamb"

---

* Part 3 of this book will deal with the profound alterations the mineral world will undergo at the hands of human beings.

renders a building out of the sea, which then becomes the well-ground of the fourth Apocalyptic stream, the pouring out of the vials of wrath:

> After this I looked, and I saw in Heaven the temple—that is, the tabernacle of the covenant law—and it was opened. Out of the temple came the seven angels with the seven plagues. They were dressed in clean, shining linen and wore golden sashes around their chests. Then one of the four living creatures gave to the seven angels seven golden bowls filled with the wrath of God, who lives forever and ever. And the temple was filled with smoke from the glory of God and from his power, and no one could enter the temple until the seven plagues of the seven angels were completed. (Rev. 15:5–8)

From the sixteenth chapter on, John describes how the seven vials of the divine will gush forth; the stream of the first one into the Earth, of the second into the sea, the third into the currents and springs of water, of the fourth into the Sun, the fifth onto the throne of the beast, the sixth onto the great "Euphrates," and the seventh into the air. The entire earthly and planetary cosmos is pervaded with the transformative fire of these seven streams. Its all-permeating power and influence is the final gushing forth out of the deepest interior of the first source image (Rev. 4). It is unveiled out of the seventh trumpet. The first image's Throning One makes His presence known in voice, thunder, and lightning; but He Himself keeps in the background: "The seventh angel poured out his bowl into the air, and out of the temple came a loud voice from the throne, saying, 'It is done!' Then there came flashes of lightning, rumblings, peals of thunder and a severe earthquake. No earthquake like it has ever occurred since humankind has been on Earth, so tremendous was the quake" (Rev. 16:17–18).

In the final, the seventh image of this series, the first one reemerges. But now Heaven is filled with hosts of angels and human beings uttering the great Amen and Halleluiah; the Throning One, the twenty-four eldest, and the four living beasts come as if out of their choirs:

> And again they shouted, "Hallelujah! The smoke from her goes up for ever and ever."
>
> The twenty-four elders and the four living creatures fell down and worshiped God, who was seated on the throne. And they cried, "Amen, Hallelujah!"
>
> Then a voice came from the throne, saying, "Praise our God, all you his servants, you who fear him, both great and small!" (Rev. 19:3–5)

This renewed pouring forth is no longer seals, trumpets and vials, but rather the grand communion, the wedding and the Last Supper of the Lamb:

> Then the angel said to me, "Write this: Blessed are those who are invited to the wedding supper of the Lamb!" And he added, "These are the true words of God."... And I saw an angel standing in the Sun, who cried in a loud voice to all the birds flying in midair, "Come, gather together for the great supper of God." (Rev. 19:9, 17)

Just as in the first great cosmic image of chapter 4 the series of cosmic images is penetrated with the series of revelations of the Son of Man, in the same manner the two series interweave in all seven cosmic images.

To summarize, we can say this: The first series of source images brings the manifestations of the Son. In revelations of the originary impulse, they contain the transformations, the deaths, and resurrections of the creating Logos.

The second series shows the source images of the substance of the Father-world, the archetypal ground, the deepest well of world events. In this series the mineral element becomes visible.

Chapter 6: Mediator Entities Transit Images
Bearers of the Good and Bearers of the Evil

In the third series of the source images, there appear entities that not only have the attributes of spring points and inaugurators, but also open up passageways; that is, trials, struggles of soul and spirit, victories and defeats, new creations. These beings act as conduits for the Apocalyptic event, a function that can run its course either in their consciously taking up and proclaiming, that is, revealing everything that comes from actual wellsprings of the higher spheres of the spirit, or in the higher powers passing over through this conduit into the active seven-times-four streams and they, the conduit beings, causing the trumpets to sound or the content of the vials to gush forth. A further possibility is that the cosmic-Apocalyptic event causes transformations within these beings themselves. The conduit beings are the entities that arise in this third series as mediators, carriers of the transit, as coworkers and joint formers. As early as in the comprehensive source image of chapters four and five, a being of this kind appears in the form of the "angel of great power," and calls out the question pertaining to the One capable of opening the seals (Rev. 5:2). The image of the Son of Man in the first chapter also contains this element, in the seven angels into which the seven stars He holds in His hand are transformed:

> In his right hand he held seven stars, and coming out of his mouth was a sharp, double-edged sword. His face was like the Sun shining in all its brilliance.... The mystery of the seven stars that you saw in my right hand and of the seven golden lampstands is this: The seven stars are the angels of the seven churches, and the seven lampstands are the seven churches. (Rev. 1:16, 20)

Thus this motif of transits and mediations also pervades as constituent parts the two series of source images we have observed up to now. However, the motif also arises on its own and in this way is depicted throughout the Apocalypse in seven manifestations. The first independent picture of this kind are the four angels at the start of chapter seven along with the fifth one, the one that mediates the sealing of the one-hundred-forty-four-thousand:

> After this I saw four angels standing at the four corners of the Earth, holding back the four winds of the Earth to prevent any wind from blowing on the land or on the sea or on any tree. Then I saw another angel coming up from the east, having the seal of the living God. He called out in a loud voice to the four angels who had been given power to harm the land and the sea: "Do not harm the land or the sea or the trees until we put a seal on the foreheads of the servants of our God." Then I heard the number of those who were sealed: 144,000 from all the tribes of Israel. (Rev. 7:1–4)

Through these beings space arises for humankind, the earthly space in which, in one direction, the occurrences open up to the well area, where the Throning One, the twenty-four Eldest, and the four living beasts appear. In the other direction, the occurrences open up to the sphere of the sealed twelve-thousand-times-twelve with the names of the twelve tribes. The event permeates entirely the spiritual-earthly theater held free by these five angels. They are coworkers with a purely mediating function.

The second picture in this series is provided by the tenth chapter. It is the "great angel," the genius of the whole of humankind. Around him he displays the rainbow, he is clothed with the cloud, and with fiery feet he stands upon the sea and the land. In his hand he holds the open book, which John the seer must devour:

> Then I saw another mighty angel coming down from Heaven. He was robed in a cloud, with a rainbow above his head; his face was like the Sun, and his legs were like fiery pillars. He was holding a little scroll, which lay open in his hand. He planted his right foot on the sea and his left foot on the land, and he gave a loud shout like the roar of a lion. When he shouted, the voices of the seven thunders spoke. And when the seven thunders spoke, I was about

to write; but I heard a voice from Heaven say, "Seal up what the seven thunders have said and do not write it down."

Then the angel I had seen standing on the sea and on the land raised his right hand to Heaven. And he swore by him who lives for ever and ever, who created the heavens and all that is in them, the Earth and all that is in it, and the sea and all that is in it, and said, "There will be no more delay! But in the days when the seventh angel is about to sound his trumpet, the mystery of God will be accomplished, just as he announced to his servants the prophets." (Rev. 10:1–11)

In the eleventh chapter, a third image of this series is added in the form of the two witnesses, also called two olive trees or two torches, who endure the human fates of slander, death and resurrection:

I was given a reed like a measuring rod and was told, "Go and measure the temple of God and the altar, with its worshipers. But exclude the outer court; do not measure it, because it has been given to the Gentiles. They will trample on the holy city for 42 months. And I will appoint my two witnesses, and they will prophesy for 1,260 days, clothed in sackcloth." They are "the two olive trees" and the two lampstands, and "they stand before the Lord of the Earth." If anyone tries to harm them, fire comes from their mouths and devours their enemies. This is how anyone who wants to harm them must die. They have power to shut up the heavens so that it will not rain during the time they are prophesying; and they have power to turn the waters into blood and to strike the Earth with every kind of plague as often as they want.

Now when they have finished their testimony, the beast that comes up from the Abyss will attack them, and overpower and kill them. Their bodies will lie in the public square of the great city—which is figuratively called Sodom and Egypt—where also their Lord was crucified. For three and a half days some from every people, tribe, language, and nation will gaze on their bodies and refuse them burial. The inhabitants of the Earth will gloat over them and will celebrate by sending each other gifts, because these two prophets had tormented those who live on the Earth.

But after the three and a half days the breath of life from God entered them, and they stood on their feet, and terror struck those who saw them. Then they heard a loud voice from Heaven saying to them, "Come up here." And they went up to Heaven in a cloud, while their enemies looked on. (Rev. 11.1–12)

This image has a particular mystery about it, since the seer John himself is taken up among the ranks of the mediator entities. Here, he is no mere beholder, proclaimer, as he is in large part in the Apocalypse; rather, he is also—the same as in chapters two and three, in which he receives the mission to write to the seven angels of the seven churches—fellow shaper of the Apocalyptic event, as it were, jointly with the two "witnesses." This ability of his is obviously the result of his having had to devour the Great Angel's book (Rev. 10:10–11). Hence he himself becomes a witness.

The series of the Apocalyptic appearances of the mediator entities has preparatory character, again and again. To begin with, the five angelic beings appear, and reserve a spiritual area on Earth for the enspiriting of humanity. Within this free space, from which all winds are held back, the angel becomes visible in the second transit image who is the inspiring genius of the entire earthly humankind. Through him, the Apocalyptist himself experiences the exhilarating and the "bitter" aspects of his initiation: he must "eat" the Book of Revelation. In the will sphere, which has endured the pain of the profoundest depths of his soul, he achieves the power of future revelations. The great angel of humankind, who has presented the book to him, represents in his head of clouds, his rainbow-breast, and his feet of fire the threefold nature of humanity. In his head of clouds lives the eastern, in his rainbow-breast the middle, and in his feet of fire western humankind.*

---

*   Emil Bock refers to this connection in his book *The Apocalypse of St. John*, Edinburgh: Floris Books, 1986.

In the two "witnesses," the Apocalyptist experiences a third thing, which is the archetype of the earthly destinies of all leaders of humankind, all initiates. Their destinies are always such that either they are sacrificed or else they sacrifice themselves for the true progress of human development.

Through their destinies, the witnesses prepare the central fourth image of this series. The core of chapter twelve fills the center of the entire Apocalypse: the woman clothed in the Sun, the child she births, the dragon that threatens him, the archangel Michael who leads the battle, and the Earth, which protects the woman:

> A great sign appeared in Heaven: a woman clothed with the Sun, with the Moon under her feet and a crown of twelve stars on her head. She was pregnant and cried out in pain as she was about to give birth. Then another sign appeared in Heaven: an enormous red dragon with seven heads and ten horns and seven crowns on its heads. Its tail swept a third of the stars out of the sky and flung them to the Earth. The dragon stood in front of the woman who was about to give birth, so that it might devour her child the moment he was born. She gave birth to a son, a male child, who "will rule all the nations with an iron scepter." And her child was snatched up to God and to his throne. The woman fled into the wilderness to a place prepared for her by God, where she might be taken care of for 1,260 days.
>
> Then war broke out in Heaven. Michael and his angels fought against the dragon, and the dragon and his angels fought back. But he was not strong enough, and they lost their place in Heaven. The great dragon was hurled down—that ancient serpent called the devil, or Satan, who leads the whole world astray. He was hurled to the earth, and his angels with him.
>
> Then I heard a loud voice in Heaven say, "Now have come the salvation and the power and the kingdom of our God, and the authority of his Messiah. For the accuser of our brothers and sisters, who accuses them before our God day and night, has been hurled down. They triumphed over him by the blood of the Lamb and by the word of their testimony; they did not love their lives so

much as to shrink from death. Therefore rejoice, you heavens and you who dwell in them! But woe to the earth and the sea, because the devil has gone down to you! He is filled with fury, because he knows that his time is short."

When the dragon saw that he had been hurled to the earth, he pursued the woman who had given birth to the male child. The woman was given the two wings of a great eagle, so that she might fly to the place prepared for her in the wilderness, where she would be taken care of for a time, times and half a time, out of the serpent's reach. Then from his mouth the serpent spewed water like a river, to overtake the woman and sweep her away with the torrent. But the earth helped the woman by opening its mouth and swallowing the river that the dragon had spewed out of his mouth. Then the dragon was enraged at the woman and went off to wage war against the rest of her offspring—those who keep God's commands and hold fast their testimony about Jesus. (Rev. 12:1–17)

We can call this image of chapter 12 the heart of the Apocalypse. The image-form of the woman clothed in the Sun is a manifestation of the soul of the whole of humankind. This image's mystery is that it receives something from the well-springs of the divine to which it can in turn give birth by transforming it within itself. The Son-God, born of the Father-God in the sacrificial form of the Lamb, is submerged into the human soul and born out of it as a childlike and masculine element. This birth is threatened by the adversary, protected by the archangel Michael, and guarded by the very Earth.

But the onslaught of the adversary has consequences for he himself, as well. He is forced to leave the heavenly worlds and thrown into a deeper dimension of the earthly world. This makes him unable to maintain the form of the dragon any longer, in which until then he would have been able to conceal his dual nature; in the end he must reveal himself within the earthly sphere.

And so it is only consistent that out of the image in the twelfth chapter the fifth image in the series of the beings of transit ensues in chapter thirteen. The as yet mixed dragon becomes the two beasts; the one arises out of the sea, the other out of the land (Rev. 13):*

> The dragon stood on the shore of the sea. And I saw a beast coming out of the sea. It had ten horns and seven heads, with ten crowns on its horns, and on each head a blasphemous name. The beast I saw resembled a leopard, but had feet like those of a bear and a mouth like that of a lion. The dragon gave the beast his power and his throne and great authority. One of the heads of the beast seemed to have had a fatal wound, but the fatal wound had been healed. The whole world was filled with wonder and followed the beast. People worshiped the dragon because he had given authority to the beast, and they also worshiped the beast and asked, "Who is like the beast? Who can wage war against it?"
>
> The beast was given a mouth to utter proud words and blasphemies and to exercise its authority for forty-two months. It opened its mouth to blaspheme God, and to slander his name and his dwelling place and those who live in Heaven. It was given power to wage war against God's holy people and to conquer them. And it was given authority over every tribe, people, language and nation. All inhabitants of the Earth will worship the beast—all whose names have not been written in the Lamb's book of life, the Lamb who was slain from the creation of the world.
>
> Whoever has ears, let them hear. "If anyone is to go into captivity, into captivity they will go. If anyone is to be killed with the sword, with the sword they will be killed."
>
> This calls for patient endurance and faithfulness on the part of God's people.
>
> Then I saw a second beast, coming out of the earth. It had two horns like a lamb, but it spoke like a dragon. It exercised all the authority of the first beast on its behalf, and made the Earth and its inhabitants worship the first beast, whose fatal wound had been healed. And it performed great signs, even causing fire to come down from Heaven to the Earth in full view of the people. Because of the signs it was given power to perform on behalf of the first beast, it deceived the inhabitants of the Earth. It ordered

---

* Cf. Emil Bock *The Apocalypse*.

them to set up an image in honor of the beast who was wounded by the sword and yet lived. The second beast was given power to give breath to the image of the first beast, so that the image could speak and cause all who refused to worship the image to be killed. It also forced all people, great and small, rich and poor, free, and slave, to receive a mark on their right hands or on their foreheads, so that they could not buy or sell unless they had the mark, which is the name of the beast or the number of its name.

This calls for wisdom. Let the person who has insight calculate the number of the beast, for it is the number of a man. That number is 666. (Rev. 13)

In answer to the full unveiling of evil in the fifth image, there follows a sort of threefold judgment of it by the spiritual world. It is the realm of the Son-God, the Eternal Gospel, which not only illuminates the verdicts resulting from the struggle with the Evil, but occasions them as well. Through the cosmic fact of the Gospel, through the Mystery of Golgotha, the decision has, in principle, fallen. The alternate soul is pre-formed which succumbs to the adversary, and which amounts to the counterimage of the soul of humanity that has in a way received the Gospel into itself. Before this soul of humankind filled with evil appears, the great warning goes out: If any man worship the beast and his image, and receive his mark in his forehead, or in his hand, the same shall drink of the wine of the wrath of God (Rev. 14:9–10).

The sixth image in this series speaks of three angels; the first with the everlasting gospel, the second as a harbinger of the defeats of evil, in which exaltation and demise begin to flow apart from each other, and the third as the great admonisher and herald of the resurrection of the dead:

Then I saw another angel flying in midair, and he had the eternal gospel to proclaim to those who live on the Earth—to every nation, tribe, language, and people. He said in a loud voice, "Fear God and give him glory, because the hour of his judgment has come. Worship him who made the heavens, the earth, the sea, and the springs of water."

> A second angel followed and said, "'Fallen! Fallen is Babylon the Great,' which made all the nations drink the maddening wine of her adulteries."
>
> A third angel followed them and said in a loud voice: "If anyone worships the beast and its image and receives its mark on their forehead or on their hand, they, too, will drink the wine of God's fury, which has been poured full strength into the cup of his wrath. They will be tormented with burning sulfur in the presence of the holy angels and of the Lamb. (Rev. 14:6–10)

The series of the mediator-entities concludes in the seventeenth chapter, in the appearance of the woman who is the soul of the city of Babylon, both the maternal and bride entity for evil. She, too, wears gold, precious stones, and pearls. In her, as well, human soul forces are refined and cultivated, but here lies a deep mystery of all true soul transformation. Within human soul life there is the difference between refinement and genuine transformation. A true transformation goes through sacrifice, through death and resurrection. Refinement, termed sublimation in psychological science, is preserved in the original nature of the psychic; it appears to be more cultivated. Thus the woman of the city of Babylon wears gold, jewels, and pearls:

> One of the seven angels who had the seven bowls came and said to me, "Come, I will show you the punishment of the great prostitute, who sits by many waters. With her the kings of the Earth committed adultery, and the inhabitants of the Earth were intoxicated with the wine of her adulteries."
>
> Then the angel carried me away in the Spirit into a wilderness. There I saw a woman sitting on a scarlet beast that was covered with blasphemous names and had seven heads and ten horns. The woman was dressed in purple and scarlet, and was glittering with gold, precious stones and pearls. She held a golden cup in her hand, filled with abominable things and the filth of her adulteries. The name written on her forehead was a mystery: BABYLON THE GREAT, THE MOTHER OF PROSTITUTES AND OF THE ABOMINATIONS OF THE EARTH. (Rev. 17:1–5)

The mediatory entities active in the third series pass through the demise described in the remarkable word texture of the seventeenth and eighteenth chapters. In the woman, her beasts, and their hosts and kings lay the roots of a mutual alienation or connection; they are chained together and yet hostile to one another; they promote or hamper each other mutually and drive themselves into destruction.

The images of the Apocalypse, then, bear various fundamental characters. For one, they arise from the four great streams of the overall spiritual occurrence (letters to the churches, seals, trumpets, and vials of wrath). In addition, there are the source images for the origin of these streams out of the cosmic-divine world of the Father-God (the Son of Man, the Lamb, the white rider). Then come the transit images for the deeds and sufferings, the struggle, the defeat and victory of spirit beings of the Good and of evil. These images are connected with the sources. The streams of the spiritual occurrence flow through them.

Then, however, the Apocalypse flows into the result of the great transformation, which is gradually taking on shape. On one hand, the groups of human beings appear in their transformed, exalted and transfigured shapes; on the other hand, they appear in the images of the final demise of the world of evil. Thus the estuary images stand opposite the source images and the transit images. But whereas the rows of the source and transit images are subject to the number seven, that is, the number of the circles or courses of time and levels of development, the estuary or mouth images belong to the number twelve. They form an entirely new world order, the spiritual order that is the precursor of space. To regard this row in its own right is also of fundamental importance.

Chapter 7: The Estuary (Mouth) Images

The first of the images becomes visible in the seven churches as the fundamental motif. As yet, times and places are still interwoven; good and evil are jointly active. But the separation of the spirits has already been announced, as chapter two and three report. The letters to the seven churches can be considered a first level at which, in addition to origins and transits, results—that is, estuaries—are also mentioned. What is being prepared here is finished in chapter 7, in the second image of this series, in the emergence from the seven churches of the first complete humankind of the future, the one-hundred-forty-four thousand "sealed ones":

> After this I saw four angels standing at the four corners of the Earth, holding back the four winds of the earth to prevent any wind from blowing on the land or on the sea or on any tree. Then I saw another angel coming up from the east, having the seal of the living God. He called out in a loud voice to the four angels who had been given power to harm the land and the sea: "Do not harm the land or the sea or the trees until we put a seal on the foreheads of the servants of our God." Then I heard the number of those who were sealed: 144,000 from all the tribes of Israel.
>
>> From the tribe of Judah 12,000 were sealed,
>> from the tribe of Reuben 12,000,
>> from the tribe of Gad 12,000,
>> from the tribe of Asher 12,000,
>> from the tribe of Naphtali 12,000,
>> from the tribe of Manasseh 12,000,
>> from the tribe of Simeon 12,000,
>> from the tribe of Levi 12,000,
>> from the tribe of Issachar 12,000,
>> from the tribe of Zebulun 12,000,
>> from the tribe of Joseph 12,000,
>> from the tribe of Benjamin 12,000.
>
> The Great Multitude in White Robes.
>
> After this I looked, and there before me was a great multitude that no one could count, from every nation, tribe, people and language, standing before the throne and before the Lamb. They were wearing white robes and were holding palm branches in their hands. And they cried out in a loud voice: "Salvation belongs to our God, who sits on the throne, and to the Lamb."

All the angels were standing around the throne and around the elders and the four living creatures. They fell down on their faces before the throne and worshiped God, saying: "Amen! Praise and glory and wisdom and thanks and honor and power and strength be to our God forever and ever. Amen!"

Then one of the elders asked me, "These in white robes—who are they, and where did they come from?"

I answered, "Sir, you know."

And he said, "These are they who have come out of the great tribulation; they have washed their robes and made them white in the blood of the Lamb. Therefore, they are before the throne of God and serve him day and night in his temple; and he who sits on the throne will shelter them with his presence. Never again will they hunger; never again will they thirst. The Sun will not beat down on them, nor any scorching heat. For the Lamb at the center of the throne will be their shepherd; he will lead them to springs of living water. And God will wipe away every tear from their eyes." (Rev. 7:1–17)

Emil Bock, in *The Apocalypse,* has worked out how the sealed ones bearing the names of the twelve tribes of Israel are no longer ordered according to places and times, the way that the members of the seven churches are, but rather according to the image of the consummation of humanity, that is, according to the nature of the Son of Man Himself.

Out of the seven congregations with their virtues and shortcomings, there arises the first image of a human race that, while distributed throughout all earthly sites and times, also appears in the spiritual world as a newly structured order of humanity, whose center point is the Christ-Being. His spiritual realm, His own world of divine strength, takes in all people who personally unite with Him, and forms the Kingdom of God, the Kingdom of Heaven on Earth.

It follows correctly then, that in the third in the series of estuary images (Rev. 9:1–12), the portion of humankind appears that hasn't joined the divine element yet. Their members as well are outwardly spread over every place and time on Earth. In spirit, they appear in the image of the "locusts." They are the first result of the contorting and counterfeiting of human nature through evil, which expresses itself above all in human beings losing their "I." The loss of "I"-being yields the image of the locusts.

Thus the one side of the effect of evil is humanity's divestment of its "I"; the other is the entanglement of the feeble human I in the nature of its base animalistic passions, in the soulless intelligence of practicality and in the belief in the exclusive reality of matter. In the second half of chapter nine's third estuary image, this humankind is depicted in the image of the Apocalyptic hosts of riders (nine):

> The fifth angel sounded his trumpet, and I saw a star that had fallen from the sky to the earth. The star was given the key to the shaft of the Abyss. When he opened the Abyss, smoke rose from it like the smoke from a gigantic furnace. The Sun and sky were darkened by the smoke from the Abyss. And out of the smoke locusts came down on the earth and were given power like that of scorpions of the earth. They were told not to harm the grass of the earth or any plant or tree, but only those people who did not have the seal of God on their foreheads. They were not allowed to kill them but only to torture them for five months. And the agony they suffered was like that of the sting of a scorpion when it strikes. During those days people will seek death but will not find it; they will long to die, but death will elude them.
>
> The locusts looked like horses prepared for battle. On their heads they wore something like crowns of gold, and their faces resembled human faces. Their hair was like women's hair, and their teeth were like lions' teeth. They had breastplates like breastplates of iron, and the sound of their wings was like the thundering of many horses and chariots rushing into battle. They had tails with stingers, like scorpions, and in their tails they had power to torment people for five months. They had as king over them the angel of the Abyss, whose name in Hebrew is Abaddon and in Greek is Apollyon (that is, Destroyer).
>
> The first woe is past; two other woes are yet to come.

> The sixth angel sounded his trumpet, and I heard a voice coming from the four horns of the golden altar that is before God. It said to the sixth angel who had the trumpet, "Release the four angels who are bound at the great river Euphrates.' And the four angels who had been kept ready for this very hour and day and month and year were released to kill a third of humankind. The number of the mounted troops was twice ten thousand times ten thousand. I heard their number.
>
> The horses and riders I saw in my vision looked like this: Their breastplates were fiery red, dark blue, and yellow as sulfur. The heads of the horses resembled the heads of lions, and out of their mouths came fire, smoke, and sulfur. A third of humankind was killed by the three plagues of fire, smoke and sulfur that came out of their mouths. The power of the horses was in their mouths and in their tails; for their tails were like snakes, having heads with which they inflict injury.
>
> The rest of humankind who were not killed by these plagues still did not repent of the work of their hands; they did not stop worshiping demons, and idols of gold, silver, bronze, stone, and wood—idols that cannot see or hear or walk. Nor did they repent of their murders, their magic arts, their sexual immorality or their thefts. (Rev. 9:1–21)

The fourth image of the estuary series deals with the enemies of the two witnesses. The initiate-destiny pertains not only to the witnesses themselves, but as well to individuals or groups of people who have brought it over them. In the face of their witness-ship they can awaken from evil to the Good, from error to the Truth. This is the substance that results from the fourth estuary image:

> For three and a half days some from every people, tribe, language, and nation will gaze on their bodies and refuse them burial. The inhabitants of the Earth will gloat over them and will celebrate by sending each other gifts, because these two prophets had tormented those who live on the Earth.
>
> But after the three and a half days the breath of life from God entered them, and they stood on their feet, and terror struck those

> who saw them. Then they heard a loud voice from Heaven saying to them, "Come up here." And they went up to Heaven in a cloud, while their enemies looked on.
>
> At that very hour there was a severe earthquake and a tenth of the city collapsed. Seven thousand people were killed in the earthquake, and the survivors were terrified and gave glory to the God of Heaven.
>
> The second woe has passed; the third woe is coming soon. (Rev. 11:9–14)

The actual path of the soul's erring into the hands of evil is couched in the human capacity for religion. For just as the divine good stands higher than the human being, so also does the godly evil. The adversaries are angels, too. The human being can behave religiously toward both hierarchical worlds: he can worship the godly good and the godly evil. The latter is the only thing capable of bringing him fully under the power of evil. In the fifth estuary image, this outcome is unveiled in the spiritual world. Thus it says:

> The whole world was filled with wonder and followed the beast. People worshiped the dragon because he had given authority to the beast, and they also worshiped the beast and asked, "Who is like the beast? Who can wage war against it?"
>
> The beast was given a mouth to utter proud words and blasphemies and to exercise its authority for forty-two months. It opened its mouth to blaspheme God, and to slander his name and his dwelling place and those who live in Heaven. It was given power to wage war against God's holy people and to conquer them. And it was given authority over every tribe, people, language, and nation. All inhabitants of the Earth will worship the beast—all whose names have not been written in the Lamb's book of life, the Lamb who was slain from the creation of the world.
>
> Whoever has ears, let them hear. "If anyone is to go into captivity, into captivity they will go. If anyone is to be killed with the sword, with the sword they will be killed." This calls for patient endurance and faithfulness on the part of God's people. (Rev. 13:3–10)

And further:

> Because of the signs it was given power to perform on behalf of the first beast, it deceived the inhabitants of the Earth. It ordered them to set up an image in honor of the beast who was wounded by the sword and yet lived. The second beast was given power to give breath to the image of the first beast, so that the image could speak and cause all who refused to worship the image to be killed. It also forced all people, great and small, rich and poor, free and slave, to receive a mark on their right hands or on their foreheads, so that they could not buy or sell unless they had the mark, which is the name of the beast or the number of its name. (Rev. 13:14–17)

Once the estuary images of evil have in this way reached their first level, the series of images turns to embracing the development of the Good. The-one-hundred-forty-four thousand assemble around the Lamb on Mount Zion. What before was sealed inside them now becomes manifest in their singing and harp playing in the sixth estuary image. This picture unites with the image of "the dead who have died in the Lord":

> And I heard a sound from Heaven like the roar of rushing waters and like a loud peal of thunder. The sound I heard was like that of harpists playing their harps. And they sang a new song before the throne and before the four living creatures and the elders. No one could learn the song except the 144,000 who had been redeemed from the Earth. These are those who did not defile themselves with women, for they remained virgins. They follow the Lamb wherever he goes. They were purchased from among humankind and offered as first fruits to God and the Lamb. No lie was found in their mouths; they are blameless....
>
> This calls for patient endurance on the part of the people of God who keep his commands and remain faithful to Jesus.
>
> Then I heard a voice from Heaven say, "Write this: Blessed are the dead who die in the Lord from now on."
>
> "Yes," says the Spirit, "they will rest from their labor, for their deeds will follow them." (Rev. 14:2–5, 12–13)

After this first flashing up of the future of the Good, the events pass through evil once more, as the hosts of the great whore Babylon stage their entrance. It is the seventh image in the estuary series:

> "This calls for a mind with wisdom. The seven heads are seven hills on which the woman sits. They are also seven kings. Five have fallen, one is, the other has not yet come; but when he does come, he must remain for only a little while. The beast who once was, and now is not, is an eighth king. He belongs to the seven and is going to his destruction.
>
> "The ten horns you saw are ten kings who have not yet received a kingdom, but who for one hour will receive authority as kings along with the beast. They have one purpose and will give their power and authority to the beast. They will wage war against the Lamb, but the Lamb will triumph over them because he is Lord of lords and King of kings—and with him will be his called, chosen, and faithful followers."
>
> Then the angel said to me, "The waters you saw, where the prostitute sits, are peoples, multitudes, nations and languages. The beast and the ten horns you saw will hate the prostitute. They will bring her to ruin and leave her naked; they will eat her flesh and burn her with fire. For God has put it into their hearts to accomplish his purpose by agreeing to hand over to the beast their royal authority, until God's words are fulfilled. The woman you saw is the great city that rules over the kings of the Earth." (Rev. 17:9–18)

The seventh image of the estuaries of the Revelation brings to full development the form of the soul nature of humankind astray. It is the spirit-form of a queen, a female called the Whore Babylon. All the powers that impulse, strengthen, and exalt this soul nature act, at the same time, in such a way that they cannot but contribute to the dissolution of this their own formation. The paradox of evil is shown here. In the eighth of the estuary images, a first doom of this illusory world descends:

> When the kings of the Earth who committed adultery with her and shared her luxury see the smoke of her burning, they will weep and mourn over her. Terrified at her torment, they will stand far off and cry: "Woe! Woe to you, great city, you mighty city of Babylon! In one hour your doom has come!" The merchants of the Earth will weep and mourn over her because no one buys their cargoes anymore—cargoes of gold, silver, precious stones, and pearls; fine linen, purple, silk, and scarlet cloth; every sort of citron wood, and articles of every kind made of ivory, costly wood, bronze, iron, and marble; cargoes of cinnamon and spice, of incense, myrrh, and frankincense, of wine and olive oil, of fine flour and wheat; cattle and sheep; horses and carriages; and human beings sold as slaves. They will say, "The fruit you longed for is gone from you. All your luxury and splendor have vanished, never to be recovered." The merchants who sold these things and gained their wealth from her will stand far off, terrified at her torment. They will weep and mourn 16 and cry out, "Woe! Woe to you, great city, dressed in fine linen, purple and scarlet, and glittering with gold, precious stones and pearls! In one hour such great wealth has been brought to ruin!" Every sea captain, and all who travel by ship, the sailors, and all who earn their living from the sea, will stand far off. When they see the smoke of her burning, they will exclaim, "Was there ever a city like this great city?" They will throw dust on their heads, and with weeping and mourning cry out, "Woe! Woe to you, great city, where all who had ships on the sea became rich through her wealth! In one hour she has been brought to ruin!"
>
> Rejoice over her, you heavens! Rejoice, you people of God! Rejoice, apostles and prophets! For God has judged her with the judgment she imposed on you. (Rev. 18:9–20)

In contrast to this first painful destruction, those hosts appear in the ninth image who, after the demise of great Babylon, intone the Amen and the Hallelujah:

> After this I heard what sounded like the roar of a great multitude in Heaven shouting, "Hallelujah! Salvation and glory and power belong to our God, for true and just are his judgments. He has

condemned the great prostitute who corrupted the Earth by her adulteries. He has avenged on her the blood of his servants."

And again they shouted, "Hallelujah! The smoke from her goes up for ever and ever."

The twenty-four elders and the four living creatures fell down and worshiped God, who was seated on the throne. And they cried, "Amen, Hallelujah!"

Then a voice came from the throne, saying, "Praise our God, all you his servants, you who fear him, both great and small!"

Then I heard what sounded like a great multitude, like the roar of rushing waters and like loud peals of thunder, shouting, "Hallelujah! For our Lord God Almighty reigns. Let us rejoice and be glad and give him glory! For the wedding of the Lamb has come, and his bride has made herself ready. Fine linen, bright and clean, was given her to wear." Then the angel said to me, "Write this: Blessed are those who are invited to the wedding supper of the Lamb!" And he added, "These are the true words of God."

At this I fell at his feet to worship him. But he said to me, "Don't do that! I am a fellow servant with you and with your brothers and sisters who hold to the testimony of Jesus. Worship God! For it is the Spirit of prophecy who bears testimony to Jesus." (Rev. 19:1–10)

This image's souls of Men, the souls of the great Song of Praise, are called to the wedding and to the Last Supper, the Holy Communion of the Lamb (Rev. 19:8–9, 19). It announces what in the final estuary image will be full reality. For the second doom is woven into this ascent of the humanity of the future, as the tenth estuary image (Rev. 19:17–21). The first doom is more an event of soul, the dissolution in soul of the illusory structures caused by the Evil. The second doom ensues from it as death within the human bodily element, which is brought on by a deep plunge of the powers of evil into a world-sphere no longer of the Earth, but rather belonging to a subearthly world:

And I saw an angel standing in the Sun, who cried in a loud voice to all the birds flying in midair, "Come, gather together for the great supper of God, so that you may eat the flesh of kings, generals, and

Part 1: *Apocalypse and Its Images* ∞ Chapter 7: *The Estuary (Mouth) Images*

the mighty, of horses and their riders, and the flesh of all people, free and slave, great and small."

Then I saw the beast and the kings of the Earth and their armies gathered together to wage war against the rider on the horse and his army. But the beast was captured, and with it the false prophet who had performed the signs on its behalf. With these signs he had deluded those who had received the mark of the beast and worshiped its image. The two of them were thrown alive into the fiery lake of burning sulfur. The rest were killed with the sword coming out of the mouth of the rider on the horse, and all the birds gorged themselves on their flesh. (Rev. 19:17–21)

Upon this demise follows the third and last one. It occurs in the eleventh of the estuary images in chapter 20 (Rev. 1–3, 7–10), not so much as the doom of evil and its human followers, but rather as a final divorce and decision, a separation of the two streams of development. The satanic power itself along with the diabolic power are fettered and pitched into an even deeper cosmic sphere, from which they can reemerge and be sure, but into which they must sink again. The evil humankind groups into smaller and greater "I"-less group souls (Gog and Magog), and so in this final image of doom, the Evil flows into a closed-off world of its own, one severed from the Good:

And I saw an angel coming down out of Heaven, having the key to the Abyss and holding in his hand a great chain. He seized the dragon, that ancient serpent, who is the devil, or Satan, and bound him for a thousand years. He threw him into the Abyss, and locked and sealed it over him, to keep him from deceiving the nations anymore until the thousand years were ended. After that, he must be set free for a short time....

When the thousand years are over, Satan will be released from his prison and will go out to deceive the nations in the four corners of the Earth—Gog and Magog—and to gather them for battle. In number they are like the sand on the seashore. They marched across the breadth of the Earth and surrounded the camp of God's people, the city he loves. But fire came down from Heaven and devoured them. And the devil, who deceived them, was thrown into the lake of burning sulfur, where the beast and the false prophet had been thrown. They will be tormented day and night forever and ever. (20:1–3, 7–10)

This sets the scene for the twelfth image, the appearance of the hosts of all of the dead:

Then I saw a great white throne and him who was seated on it. The earth and the heavens fled from his presence, and there was no place for them. And I saw the dead, great and small, standing before the throne, and books were opened. Another book was opened, which is the book of life. The dead were judged according to what they had done as recorded in the books. The sea gave up the dead that were in it, and death and Hades gave up the dead that were in them, and each person was judged according to what they had done. Then death and Hades were thrown into the lake of fire. The lake of fire is the second death. Anyone whose name was not found written in the book of life was thrown into the lake of fire. (Rev. 20:11–15)

Here is where the separation and the decision of the Apocalypse is consummated. In this twelfth image in the series, the becoming of the whole of humankind, and of each individual human soul, flows into a world of Good. The Evil, however, is plunged into yet a lower state of being than it had before.

Chapter 8: Final Image of the Revelation

The Future World

Through the world of evil's separation from humankind and its being cast into a lower cosmic level of existence on the one hand, and the formation of the redeemed humankind on the other, it might seem as if the Apocalyptic event had reached its goal. But this is not the case. For the old world, the cosmos, has not been separated from this humanity; it has much rather passed through and been transformed by all occurrences along with humanity and the Godhead. Thus, together with a new humanity there appears the great wonder of a new world of the future, of a new Heaven and a new Earth, only this time not in natural images, but rather in the picture of a city, a building. Nevertheless, what formerly was nature is now the substance of this construction, inasmuch as its transformed mineral world has provided this building with its image content. This mineral-human-divine future world is a miracle, a wonder. Its state of completion notwithstanding, it is nevertheless composed completely of developmental movement, descending as it does down from and out of Heaven, in keeping with its destiny as a wedding and a feast. The city is a bride. Its image elements reveal the mystical interpenetration of nature (the mineral realm and the plant realm), humanity and divinity to become a single entity of a kind that did not exist in this way in the fallen world. To be sure, in our present world this interpenetration of world, humanity, and divinity is in progress, but it is hidden. It is secretly at work on the future as unveiled in the final image of the Apocalypse. Gods and men have worked at it, have formed and structured themselves into it and transformed the former natural-mineral world substance, from the stones to the stars. This image is the content of chapters 21 and 22 (cf. also appendix 30):

> Then I saw "a new Heaven and a new Earth," for the first Heaven and the first Earth had passed away, and there was no longer any sea. I saw the Holy City, the new Jerusalem, coming down out of Heaven from God, prepared as a bride beautifully dressed for her husband. And I heard a loud voice from the throne saying, "Look! God's dwelling place is now among the people, and he will dwell with them. They will be his people, and God himself will be with them and be their God. 'He will wipe every tear from their eyes. There will be no more death' or mourning or crying or pain, for the old order of things has passed away."
>
> He who was seated on the throne said, "I am making everything new!" Then he said, "Write this down, for these words are trustworthy and true."

He said to me: "It is done. I am the Alpha and the Omega, the Beginning and the End. To the thirsty I will give water without cost from the spring of the water of life. Those who are victorious will inherit all this, and I will be their God and they will be my children. But the cowardly, the unbelieving, the vile, the murderers, the sexually immoral, those who practice magic arts, the idolaters, and all liars—they will be consigned to the fiery lake of burning sulfur. This is the second death." (Rev. 21:1–8)

The original substance of this new creation is of divine-mineral nature. It appeared as a divine aura in the source image of the fourth (verse 3) and fifth chapters, as jasper, carnelian and emerald: "And he carried me away in the Spirit to a mountain great and high, and showed me the Holy City, Jerusalem, coming down out of Heaven from God" (Rev. 21:10).

The second element is the light of this city, or its luminescence. It resembles the very noblest stone, crystallized jasper: "It shone with the glory of God, and its brilliance was like that of a very precious jewel, like jasper, clear as crystal" (Rev. 21:11). The following summarizes the building elements of the Heavenly City:

> Divine substance
> Divine revelation
> The city's own luminescent power
> The wall
> The gold of the whole city
> The gold of the city streets
> The twelve foundation stones
> The twelve precious stones
> The twelve gates of pearl
> The crystal stream of water
> The tree of life
> The leaves and the fruit of this tree

Three of these building elements are called *jasper:* the luminescent power, the wall, and the first of the twelve precious stones. If one adds the jasper of the Enthroned One in the fourth chapter, one comes upon one of the greatest enigmas contained in the Revelation. We will need to discuss this in depth later.

> And he carried me away in the Spirit to a mountain great and high, and showed me the Holy City, Jerusalem, coming down out of Heaven from God. It shone with the glory of God, and its brilliance was like that of a very precious jewel, like jasper, clear as crystal. It had a great, high wall with twelve gates, and with twelve angels at the gates. On the gates were written the names of the twelve tribes of Israel. There were three gates on the east, three on the north, three on the south, and three on the west. The wall of the city had twelve foundations, and on them were the names of the twelve apostles of the Lamb.
>
> The angel who talked with me had a measuring rod of gold to measure the city, its gates, and its walls. The city was laid out like a square, as long as it was wide. He measured the city with the rod and found it to be 12,000 stadia in length, and as wide and high as it is long. The angel measured the wall using human measurement, and it was 144 cubits thick. The wall was made of jasper, and the city of pure gold, as pure as glass. The foundations of the city walls were decorated with every kind of precious stone. And the twelve gates were twelve pearls; every several gate was of one pearl: and the street of the city was pure gold, as it were transparent glass.
>
> The first foundation was jasper, the second sapphire, the third agate, the fourth emerald, the fifth onyx, the sixth ruby, the seventh chrysolite, the eighth beryl, the ninth topaz, the tenth turquoise, the eleventh jacinth, and the twelfth amethyst. The twelve gates were twelve pearls, each gate made of a single pearl. The great street of the city was of gold, as pure as transparent glass.
>
> I did not see a temple in the city, because the Lord God Almighty and the Lamb are its temple. The city does not need the Sun or the Moon to shine on it, for the glory of God gives it light, and the Lamb is its lamp. The nations will walk by its light, and the kings of the Earth will bring their splendor into it. On no day will its gates ever be shut, for there will be no night there. The glory and honor

of the nations will be brought into it. Nothing impure will ever enter it, nor will anyone who does what is shameful or deceitful, but only those whose names are written in the Lamb's book of life.

Then the angel showed me the river of the water of life, as clear as crystal, flowing from the throne of God and of the Lamb down the middle of the great street of the city. On each side of the river stood the tree of life, bearing twelve crops of fruit, yielding its fruit every month. And the leaves of the tree are for the healing of the nations. No longer will there be any curse. The throne of God and of the Lamb will be in the city, and his servants will serve him. They will see his face, and his name will be on their foreheads. There will be no more night. They will not need the light of a lamp or the light of the Sun, for the Lord God will give them light. And they will reign for ever and ever. (Rev. 21:10–27, 22:1–5)

The remarkable thing about this description is its constant transitions from image elements of the mineral world to ones of life and of entities. The great source image of the fourth and fifth chapters has been transformed, and even humankind is completely and utterly enwoven with the building elements of the holy city. Out of shine and light, wall and measure, out of form and figure, out of gold, foundation stone, gemstone, pearl and crystal stream, life and living things constantly go forth, in a certain sense. This livingness issuing from the building elements is identical with the entities that carry this spirit substantiality within and around themselves: the One on the Throne, the Lamb, the tribes, the peoples and kings, and the apostles.

The Earth, the world-all and humanity interpenetrate in an entirely new state of being. The system of the zodiac has passed over into the twelvefoldness of the foundation stones, the gemstones and pearls; the Sun with its planets has turned into the gold; the sea of glass (Rev. 4:5, 15:2) has become the crystal stream on whose banks wood grows. The spiritual aspect of the gold, the astral-psychic aspect of the twelvefoldness, the crystal water of the etheric and the mineral images as such have been transformed into the germinal state of a new cosmos. Everything physical and sensory in our present world has been spiritualized; it has become spiritual-physical, radiance, light, color, measure, number, and form.

Twelvefoldness pervade the construction. These are the twelve building elements, the twelve foundation stones, the twelve gemstones, the twelve angels, the twelve apostles, the twelve tribes of humankind, the twelve pearly gates, and the twelvefold fruit. In addition, the city measures twelve thousand leagues and the dimensions of the wall are twelve cubits by twelve cubits. This numeric mystery is an articulation of the transition from the sevenfoldness of the streams of time into the twelvefoldness of the spiritual space of duration, the future world.

Only when one returns from this last sublime estuary image, to the twelve previous estuary images, does one notice that in the latter none of the mineral images occur yet. In these previous images, the spiritual and human beings stand in the foreground. In the seven churches, good and evil still interpenetrate; in the image of the one-hundred-forty-four thousand, there is a first yield of the Good; and in the ensuing images we find, in constant alternation, the unfolding, the maturing and the resolution of Good and evil. In the heavenly Jerusalem, all of these entities (human and spiritual) are completely transluminated and permeated by elements of the mineral sphere. The heavenly Jerusalem is not just a new world; rather, this new world is a new humanity, and the new humanity is the new world. The old humanity has become mineral, precious stone, pearl, gold, and crystal, and the peoples, apostles and kings are woven within this radiance. The great oneness appears as a "bride," that is, as a virginal state of being, one prepared for a wedding, for a higher conception and for a meal, a higher coming-together. The stars have become stones, the stones human, and human beings stones and stars.

In German literature, there is a correspondence for images of this kind of unity in the concept Novalis laid out for the completion of his novel *Henry of Ofterdingen*. Thanks to Ludwig Tieck, we have an account of Novalis's plans to continue the novel:

The Marriage of the Seasons

Absorbed in thought stood the new monarch.
He recalled now his dream of last night, and the stories as well,
When he first heard of the celestial flower, and stricken
Silent by the prophecy, first felt powerful love.
It was as if he still could hear the deeply working voice,
As if the guest had only now left the sociable round
And the Moon's scanty shimmering brightened the
    shuddering windows
And within the youth's breast the consuming fire still raged.
Edda, said the king, what is the loving heart's
Most intimate wish? What its unspeakable pain?
Tell it we want to help it; that it is within our power, and that
The times will become splendid now that you once more
    enrapture Heaven.
If the times were not so unsociable, the future
Would unite with the present and with the past,
Spring would join autumn, and summer join winter;
Youth and old age would be paired in playful earnest:
Then, my sweet spouse, the well of pain would dry up,
The wishes of all our sensing would be granted the heart.
Thus spoke the queen; her handsome beloved embraced her:
Truly, you have uttered a heavenly word,
Which long since has hovered on the lips of those who feel deeply;
But one that only now has been spoken, pure and wholesome,
    by yours.
Have the wagon pulled up, we will fetch them ourselves:
First the year's four seasons, then those of the human race.

For the continuation of this poetic fragment, Novalis noted the following: "First to the Sun, to pick up day, then to the night, then to the north, winter, to the south...to youth, to old age, to the past, the future."

The same Apocalyptic element lives in this rather fairytale-like sketch by Novalis that appears in the picture of the Heavenly Jerusalem. Novalis shows how the new monarch resolves to wed the "unsociable times" to a higher unity. The future, the present, and the past, day and night, the seasons, the ages of the human life, and the historical levels of human evolution are to be wed to a space of higher presence. What in Novalis's draft is still in the planning stages, a mere impulse: in The Apocalypse of St. John it has occurred. The same Apocalyptic experience is found in Wagner's Parsifal, when Parsifal enters the terrain of the Grail. This experience flows into the statement: "In this place, time becomes space."

In summary, one can say this: The images of the Revelation of St. John are events, through and through. In the seven appearances of the Son of Man, the pulsing, the release, or triggering, and the transformation are enacted. It is the world of the Son, of the Logos. However, everything He causes, through living and dying, through sacrifice and revelation, has its origin in the great cosmic source images. In these lives the Fatherly World, the One on the throne, the twenty-four Elders, the four living beasts, the sea of glass. Yet even this sphere undergoes transformation; even within the world of the Father there is transubstantiation (throne, altar, temple, Ark of the Covenant, seals, trumpets, and vials). Then these events continue in the series of the mediator beings, through them and within them proper, until in the estuary images they bring on the corresponding results, in both evil and good, both demise and ascent. It might strike one that, in this process, primal structures and primal substances of mineral nature occur repeatedly, precisely in the series of source images from chapters four to nineteen: the throne (sapphire), the One on the throne (jasper and sard), the rainbow with the emerald, the sea of glass with rock crystal, and ever and again gold and precious stones. The profoundest of springing points—those from which the image of the heavenly Jerusalem emerges—are enshrouded; this points to a sphere of the spiritual world shining through and resonating through in the figure of the One on the throne (chapters four and five), and in the cosmic music of the great *Amen* and the *Halleluiah* (Rev. 19). It seems significant that here the image content is of mineral nature. Rudolf Steiner hints at this sphere in his lecture course *Man in the Light of Esotericism, Theosophy, and Philosophy.* He speaks there of the unmanifest light, of the unspeakable word, and of consciousness without content. One day, the present cosmos, the entire sensory world, but also the spiritual revelations of the Apocalypse as light, word and consciousness, will all disappear into this innermost sphere of the divine Trinity. In his work *An Outline of Esoteric Science* (cf. Select Bibliography), Rudolf Steiner speaks of the *"pralaya* states" of world development, describing how the development of the cosmos oscillates in two states of being: in spiritual-divine being, the impulses and plans for a world-all find their origin; then the worlds and the beings stemming from them stream forth from the higher hierarchies.

When a cycle of this kind has run the course of its development and the powers of the creator-spirits are spent, a cosmos is dissolved and spiritualized back into the interior of these beings. This is the *prayala*. The result of the bygone state of the cosmos then forms within the heavenly entities in such manner that at the same time this result is the germinal state of the cosmic stage of development to come. The "Earth" state is the name Rudolf Steiner gives our current level in *An Outline of Esoteric Science*. The next level, foreseeable in the spiritual world, he calls the "Jupiter stage" of cosmic development. In the Revelation according to Saint John, this process of world-becoming is directly unveiled in imaginations, inspirations, and intuitions. And the "Heavenly Jerusalem" is the final state of the current cosmic development and at the same time the germinal state of a future one.

These grand developmental stages are unveiled in imaginations stemming from the mineral world. If the Apocalyptist is able to assimilate into his suprasensory beholding memory contents of what he has seen in the sensory world and designated in earthly terms; that is, if he is capable of putting them at the disposal of the spiritual world as soul substance and thinking consciousness; if in turn the spiritual world is capable of enveloping both itself and its entities in images of the sensory world for the sake of manifesting to the earthly consciousness of a human being—if this is the case, then between the earthly images and facts on the one hand, and the spiritual entities on the other hand, there must exist not just relationships of the nature of parable or simile or comparison, but also the deepest of intrinsic relatedness, even a kind of identity. For the images appearing in human figuration (the Son of Man, the angels, the eldest, the woman), this is more easily understandable. Gods clothe themselves in human images, for the human being is an image of the Godhead, even in the Old Testament. And all of Greek culture, too, depicted their gods in idealized human figuration. It is not quite so easy to understand with the animal forms (the three living beasts [eagle, lion, and steer], the dragon, Evil as beast, animals in the proper sense); but here as well, a kind of feeling comprehension is possible, since here it is a matter of heightened soul powers. It was self-understood for the ancient Egyptian culture, for example, to represent their gods in animal shapes. But how it is possible for a stone to depict the imagined sheath for the most exalted divinity and for the most all-encompassing cosmic image of the future of the Godhead, the cosmos, and humankind, is an enigma. It is, basically, the mystery of the mineral realm, of the Creation, of the sensibly—and materially—manifesting world.

Part 2
Spirit in the Mineral Realm

Chapter 1: Mineral and the Father-God

A Question

The content of the image in the fourth chapter of the Book of Revelation evokes a question: What is the prerequisite for the appearance of imaginal elements of the mineral realm, in particular the precious stones, in the Apocalyptic imaginations? Is it not possible also to find the justification in the very being of this realm of nature?

The Enthroned One appears in mineral images. This is not self-understood. The Christian artists, the painters especially, have always striven to depict the highest divine being, God the Father, in human form. There exist grandiose Father-pictures, such as Raphael's "Vision of Ezekiel," Michelangelo's paintings on the ceiling of the Sistine Chapel, or the one or other painting by William Blake. The traditional Creed of Christendom asserts this: "I believe in God the Father almighty, creator of Heaven and Earth." In the version of the Creed as it lives in the Christian Community, in addition to the concept of the Father, a further fundamental concept has been added: "An almighty divine being, spiritual-physical, is the ground of existence of the heavens and of the Earth, who goes before his creatures like a Father." The words "ground of existence" occur repeatedly in the cultic rituals of the Christian Community ("Father-ground," "divine ground of the world," "Fatherly ground of the world"). Thus being, substance and transit through all of existence are ascribed to the highest divine being, such that at the same time He is the resting primal ground of all becoming. Starting here, one begins to divine this entity not as appearing suprasensorily in fatherly human shape, but rather as One sitting on a throne (a being One, a throning One), and this entity being "the same as"—"to look upon like"—the stone jasper and sard; in addition: a rainbow round about the throne, in sight like an emerald. In Greek that is *homoios horazei*. We have a triplicity of precious stones here (jasper, sard, emerald), a center like jasper, a sheath like sard, a circumference like emerald. So the suprasensory appearance of the ground of existence is like precious stones. This is what the approximate rendering of the term *homoios horazei* should be. Thus, the Father God is not jasper, sard, and emerald; rather, he manifests suprasensorily, imaginatively, in the way that jasper, sard, and emerald appear sensorily. From this it can be concluded that the sense-perceptible manifestation of these precious stones bears something within them that is at least inwardly related, if not identical to, the spiritual appearance of the Godhead as primal entity.

Chapter 2: Minerals as Soul Experience

Outwardly, the mineral realm is with few exceptions (water, quicksilver, and air) solid corporeality, substance in crystal form. Chemical elements and chemical compounds are the substances, crystals the forms of this realm. On Earth, only about 2,500 to 3,000 individual minerals exist, a few dozen of which are called *precious stones,* a term resulting from certain feelings that take hold of the soul at the sight of those minerals. Amazement arises over how it is possible for a stone to be so clear, pure, and formed—thoroughly colored, luminescent, radiant—so splendidly beautiful. The amazement becomes reverence; reverence becomes enthusiasm; enthusiasm becomes the feeling for something valuable, rare, and precious (albeit not in monetary value). This experience awakens a need to know in the face of an entity that seems so utterly material, yet seems so enigmatic, mysterious, wondrous. The sight of the stone incites within the impartial beholder a profound divining, a higher inquiring which finds no answer through the means of conventional scientifically schooled consciousness. For neither knowledge of crystal forms, chemical composition, crystal lattice, geochemical origin, paragenesis, and occurrence, nor knowledge of the material value as an object of purchase can provide information about what fills the soul with wonderment.

To be sure, even any usual mineral—a piece of iron, any stone—displays essentially the same qualities: it is completely closed off within itself, static, without impulses, without desires; it is what it is or has become, chaste, pure, nothing but itself, yet not possible as something solid, liquid, or gaseous without the existence of the Earth, the planetary system, the cosmos as a whole. However, it is in the clearly formed, transparent, shining, shimmering, sparkling, hard, colored semiprecious, and precious stones that what a mineral is at all capable of revealing is revealed to its greatest extent, and that what must be hidden indeed remains hidden. Perhaps this revealing concealment is what makes for the entity that is "the precious stone."

What holds for the precious stones also pertains to the mineral sphere designated as the "precious metals." As diamond, ruby, and sapphire each work in their own way on the soul, so also do gold and silver: as mysterious, precious, genuine and dignified, unassailable. Both solid and as ore, the metals make up a special area in the mineral realm. They do crystallize, as do all minerals, but they stand out by virtue of a number of special qualities. Theirs is the ability to be forged—i.e., to change without breaking or forfeiting the nature of their substance. The precious stone stays hard, either as a crystal, or else it splinters. Gold flowingly yields to force, but indestructibly retains its noble character. Metal is a different side of the pure being of the mineral, which comes to meet us with particular clarity in precious metals.

Finally, there is yet a third group of substances of a mineral state, which are those of organic origin: limestone, coal (also as anthracite and graphite), certain silicones, amber, and petroleum oil. The infeed originates almost exclusively from the shell-forming and skeleton-forming activity of lower animals (protozoa, sponges, corals, shellfish, and snails). Even the most beautiful calcite crystals are not precious stones. But even this field of the organogenic minerals knows three entities that are deemed precious: the corals, the pearl, and amber. Just as one speaks of precious stones and precious metals, one can also speak of precious skeletons or precious shells. Here too it can be said that what the nonprecious representatives conceal, the precious ones display as a revelatory sign.

Chapter 3: Esoteric Tradition

In an effort to understand the nature of precious stones, many people take recourse to the tradition. It is ancient, and deals with the origin, character, soul-spiritual traits, qualities, powers, and effects attributed to precious stones. Modern scientific consciousness speaks in reference to this tradition of anthropomorphism (transfer of subjective human traits), superstition, delusion, and error. Many of its attributions, though, are precise and have been consequently upheld over centuries, even millennia. On the other hand, they can be complicated, often inexact, and contradictory, such that it seems impossible to penetrate them rationally.

The soul's direct experience of the phenomena, the materialistic and mechanistic approach of natural science, and the esoteric tradition all stand discretely next to each other or even in sharpest critical contradiction against each other.

The tradition sees in the precious stone a bearer of mystical virtues of spirit and soul. It has an invisible soul and magical powers that can be transferred to the bearer, whether it is a person, a garment, an instrument, a piece of jewelry. It has a spirit, an individuality, which is connected with the individual specimens; it is a mediator of protective, healing, but also of harming powers. It has a life also capable of being applied medicinally; it is an outer symbol or sign, and has mediating force. It is connected with one of the twelve signs of the zodiac or one of the seven planets, hence it has a cosmic affiliation and a cosmic origin that makes it a carrier of spiritual worlds and beings. Mystically—magically—mythologically—religiously—symbolically—representationally—cosmically—astrologically—amulet—talisman—medicament: a world of esoteric tradition surrounds the world of precious stones, even today.

In the religious documents of the Old and New Testaments, precious stones play an important role. Twelve of them are set in a central place, in the breastplate of the high priest Aaron, their arrangement and designation having been prescribed to Moses by way of direct divine inspiration from the Yahweh divinity (Ex. 28); thus they come from suprasensory experience. In the New Testament, twelve different precious stones appear to the author of the Apocalypse in the course of his suprasensory spirit vision of a new Heaven and a new Earth that exist once the present cosmos has fallen. He espies them in his imagination of a city, the "Heavenly Jerusalem." In them, the Sun, the stars, the Earth, and humanity have flowed together organically to form a shape and fabric of the future. The spiritual building components are the twelve "cornerstones," which are "adorned" with "precious stones" in soul colors and spirit powers of moral qualities, given names, and "inscribed" with the names of the tribes of the people of Israel. The Greek word for this is *keksomaemenoi,* "adorned"; the term that ought to be used is *cosmosed,* if such existed (Rev. 21:19–20). The twelve cornerstones adorned with these "images of precious stones" at the same time bear the inscription of the "twelve names of the twelve Apostles of the Lamb" (Rev. 21:14).

Chapter 4: Minerals and Natural Science

For the time being, let us stay strictly with the phenomena of the mineral world as accessible to modern natural science, irrespective of tradition, esotericism, and astrology. The interesting thing is that the analytic approach of this research leads ever further away from the phenomenon and toward a structure that is no longer sensual in nature. It ends with the ions of the chemical elements and the geometry of the crystal lattice. If we return to what appears to the senses, we find phenomena, substances with certain qualities and forms, polyhedric figures: the crystal. Is it possible to trace everything back to the mathematically expressed level of the quantum-mechanical laws of ions and elementary particles and to the point geometry of the crystal lattice, as if it were the sole reality, or is this not much rather a reduction—by means of method and research—to the only portion of reality within to the grasp of measurement and the calculative method? What does it mean when everything in the way of qualities, traits, or modes of behavior that encounter the human senses is extinguished or reduced to its atomic structure, which is interpreted as the sole, the comprehensive and objectively existing reality, while every other phenomenon present is explained or deduced as an effect of this objective element of the human senses—thus as "the subjective" emerging from "the objective"? Is the felt experience, the sense of the weight of a piece of gold, less objective than the gravitation involved? Is the red of a ruby less real than its corresponding electromagnetic waves? Is the crystal as a unified figure, as a continuum, less of a reality than the dis-continuum of the elementary crystal cell or the laws of crystal symmetry?

Here the fundamental cognitional question put in the foreword concerning the primacy of spirit, or of matter, arises with respect to interpreting the results of natural-scientific research, both in nature as a whole and in the mineral realm in particular: Is it enough for a truly critical consciousness to postulate scientifically, as the only legitimate way, a path away from the abundance of the sense-perceptible, away from direct human experience and into the element of the subsensory and atomistic, as the only way to apprehend reality, and to deduce everything sensory perceptible as an effect on the human being?

In his essay "Introducing and Verifying the Atom Hypothesis," J. Weninger begins with the question of how and when the concept of atoms should be introduced to schoolchildren. Pertaining to concepts arising along with the problem of the chemical elements and their compounds, he says:

> A hypothesis must...not only conform with the necessities of thinking, but it must also describe and explain adequately the

phenomena. In spite of this requirement, since the concept of the elements was introduced we have not gone beyond stating that the elements remain "unaltered" within the compounds. In contrast to today's methodological requirements on hypotheses, this assertion is quite simply false. Silver nitrate does not contain the unaltered substance of silver, despite the fact that something of it does indeed remain; silver can indeed be regained from silver nitrate in its original traits and quantity.

The fundamental idea that an element remains unaltered was grasped quite correctly by the natural philosophers of ancient Greece. Since the inability to recognize silver in silver nitrate is not due to an illusion of the senses, the element hypothesis needs to be replaced by adequate assumptions. For this purpose, it is not sufficient to say that it is not the simple substances that are maintained, but rather the smallest particles that make up the substances and are called atoms. According to naïve conception, the characteristics of the (elementary) substances result from the accumulation of invisible smallest particles to the point that their characteristics become visible. Hence an understanding of the atom hypothesis as cited above no longer emerges from the element hypothesis. For the question remains open as to why one "sees" the silver atoms (or their sense-perceptible traits, at any rate) in a piece of silver, but not in a piece of silver nitrate. The corollary to this question is the first decisive supplement to the statement to date: the smallest, invisible particles of a substance do not have the qualities of visible portions of substance. Atoms of silver do not have the silvery color of a piece of silver; atoms of sulfur are not yellow; atoms of mercury are not liquid. This sounds trivial, but is by no means clear to students from the outset.

With the assumption cited above, a further, fundamentally important question arises: Where do the substances get their sense qualities? Only one answer can be found to this question (and it will be found): The sense qualities of a substance must appear when the atoms unite to form a portion of the substance; thus they do not depend solely on the kind of atom, but are evidently also determined by their arrangement and mutual bonding.

Multiple research needs to be conducted to expressly determine that it is not permissible to draw conclusions regarding the traits of atoms from perceptible characteristics of a substance. *

Three hypotheses can be found for the world of material appearances.

The element hypothesis

There are substances that are chemical elements; they can bond with each other according to certain laws. The bond has completely different properties those of the elements; weight and atoms remain intact in the bond; the properties either disappear or else they appear in a completely new way.

The atom hypothesis

The atoms of a substance (what remains intact) have quite different, non-sensible properties from the manifest substance, in terms of both elements and compounds. Strictly speaking, the atom hypothesis leaves the question pertaining to the sense properties, of both the elements and the compounds, unanswered (an atom of silver has none of the properties of silver).

The arrangement and bonding hypothesis

The spatial arrangement of the atoms and the way they are chemically bonded by virtue of the atoms' properties and not according to sense-perceptible characteristics, are what cause these characteristics to manifest, once a sufficiently large number of atoms have joined to form a visible portion of matter. Based on their arrangement and bonding relative to one another, they take on a specific weight, hardness, crystal form, odor, taste, etc.

Confronted with the arrangement hypothesis, the questions asked previously pertaining to the origin of properties of the phenomena assert themselves more than ever. Thus, if the essential part of the atom

---

* In the teacher's periodical *Mathematisch-Naturwissenschaftlicher Unterricht* (Mathematics natural-science teaching), vol. 16, no. 8, pp. 369–370.

theory is to be seen in the arrangements of atoms and the types of their chemical bonds—which also emerge from the structural properties of the atoms themselves—and in their lack of identity with the phenomenal, sensorially manifesting qualities, then the bonding hypothesis as well actually merely shifts the explanation to a different part of this same field of subsensory structural facts. Thus the question remains in all its vividness: From where do substances get their properties?

However, it is possible to think quite differently. One can see what is manifest in the mineral, the precious stone, as the expression of something that only half-influences the senses from the structural, submicroscopic-atomistic side. From a different side, reality, in its qualitative and configurative/formative appearance, displays something that is inaccessible to any measuring analysis; indeed, such analysis eliminates it from the outset. Research in nuclear physics at the subsensory level has shown that the act of measuring itself alters the very reality to which it is applied.

In the spirit of a different approach, then, the question must be reformulated to read: Does what appears in the phenomenon arise as the mere effect of the atomistic, subsensory sphere, since this sphere demonstrates almost nothing of what makes up the phenomenon. Or is there another sphere, likewise non-sensible, from which just this phenomenon manifests? Does what becomes manifest to the senses come exclusively from the element of the subsensory, the element of mechanistic-atomistic structure? Or is there also something suprasensory, a soul or spiritual essence, which plays into the phenomena? If this were so, not even mineral materials would be mere "matter"; rather, they would be substances, which in the spirit of Platonic–Aristotelian philosophy means: material appearance with a part in spiritual essence. In such case, crystals are no longer mere abstract lattice structures, but rather ideas (i.e., thoughts) manifesting in space; their sense-perceptible appearance is not just an effect of subsensory structures; as well, it is the appearance of something of a suprasensorily, spiritually essential, ideal and thought nature

Every substance reveals itself in traits characteristic of it: on the one hand its specific weight, hardness, luminescence, transparency, fissibility; on the other hand its color, odor, and taste. Beyond this qualitative aspect, certain ways of behavior on the parts of substances become perceptible, as well—their respective relationships to warmth, electricity, and magnetism and the degree of their solubility, melting points, and boiling points all demonstrate the behavior of something like a spiritual entity having certain properties. Modes of behavior and properties are those aspects of a substance that are accessible to the human senses.

Chapter 5: Mineral as Entity

In years of effort over his theory of color, Goethe formulated this thesis: We actually undertake in vain to express the essence of an object. Effects are what we discern, and a complete history of these effects would likely comprehend the essence of said object. In vain we strive to depict the character of a person; let one's actions, or deeds, be compiled instead, and an image of that one's character will emerge. These words articulate a methodological principle of fundamental importance.

First, it refers the difference between essence and appearance; then it goes on to state how what an object, such as a mineral, reveals in its properties and modes of behavior is an entity that is of no material nature whatsoever. Therefore, our task is to understand the sense-perceptible qualities and behavioral modes of even the dead mineral world as indicating that in them something has come to a conclusion whose origin is of just as much a soul and spiritual nature as the sense-manifest expressions of life, soul, and spirit in plant, animal, and human, respectively. Weight, hardness, transparency, and chemical behavior demonstrate qualities of a volitional nature; color, smell and taste express qualities of a psychic, soul, or sentient nature. It is readily understandable that even the magnificent colors of precious stones alone are a display of resting, silently luminous soul moods.

The third aspect can be experienced, as well; the crystal form characteristic of the mineral. It is not really possible to speak of an open, living gestalt, as one can when referring to plant, animal, and human; the mineral is pure geometric figure, a polyhedral body ordered according to deeply founded symmetries that can only be apprehended mathematically and geometrically; that is, purely by way of the thinking mind. Materiality is where the mineral has its body; the modes of behavior of its substance and the processes of its origin are where it has its sedated life, which has broken into purely mineral being and existence; in its color and other traits the mineral shows its character—one could also say: its soul; but here as well in a state of perfection, insularity and rest. The name for perfection of soul, though, is virtue.

Finally, in the crystal something of the idea of the mineral, of its spirituality appears in bodily form as an individualized space, which in turn itself is an idea, once more in perfectly ordered, calmed, unpretentious, pure spiritual-embodied being and existence. At the conclusion of Goethe's Faust we find the sentence: "All that is transient is naught but a parable." The mineral as substance and crystal is the sensual parable of its own body, life, soul and spirit. Precisely this is what distinguishes it from the other three realms of nature. For in the plant realm life is active in the substance itself, manifests in an embodied state. In the animal realm, the soul is not simply material behavior; rather, it is itself embodied in the substance, ensouling the substance. In the human realm the "I," the spirit, completely inhabits the sensual-material, and in this way carries self-awareness and spirit-consciousness within the sensory sphere. The corporeality of the plant is enlivened substance, that of the animal is ensouled substance, that of the human being enspirited substance. The mineral has its body on the sensual-material plane of the world. It is pure substance and pure crystal form. Its life, however, its soul and its spirit, even if they are not themselves embodied in it, are nevertheless connected with it and present in the spheres of the suprasensory world, aurically surrounding every mineral.

According to the results of Rudolf Steiner's spiritual-scientific research, the life-forces of the mineral are found in the astral world of the cosmos. The soul-forces of the mineral live in the lower spirit world, and the individual spirit entities of the minerals can only be found suprasensorily in the higher spirit world. But in the crystal all of these forces are imprinted in the sensory world, in the visible body of the mineral. They are not active in the minerals' substance. This is why they appear in their final, remarkably consummate, insular, pure mode of existence. Chasteness, selflessness, rounded off and insular outer and inner orderliness, an unbendable firmness, and reliability are virtues experienced via the senses at the lowest level of the purely material, and at the same time contained in highest perfection in a picture. Thus someone like Angelus Silesius can say in his *Cherubinic Pilgrim:*

> Pure as the finest gold, unbending like a rock,
> Full genuine as crystal is how your soul should be.

The mineral becomes an image of the highest humanity.

So this is why the mineral is so mysterious. However, not only is it image and effigy; it is itself reality, as well. Existing at the lowest level of all natural forms of being, it displays and vouches for the reality of loftiest qualities, even highest ideals, as a silent imprint of suprasensory beings and their properties. It is absolutely possible, while experiencing the outer sight of precious stones, to uplift oneself to an inner view of the most exalted of human ideals. Ever anew, the question awakens within the human being: Are our ideals mere fantasies, sublimations, and hypostatization or is there a place where they are realities? Our human ideals form goals to realize, but in the spheres of the higher divine beings, the hierarchies in the divine-spiritual worlds, they already are realities. What for us human beings manifests as longing, striving, as goals, is moral reality for the godly beings. Here lies the abyss within the realms of nature. In human, animal, and plant, spirit, soul, and life are active in their visible permutations; the creator-entities are at work indirectly, through spirit, soul, and life of the created—and also along with them. Their influence in the mineral was direct; their releasing from out of themselves their purest expression was its appearance, in which they made the imprint of their essence. The nature, the entity of the minerals—especially the precious stones—is the most deeply descended accomplishment of the highest godly beings in its undistorted manifestation, because the minerals do not add anything of their own—which plants, animals, and human beings do. This is how the mineral comes to have something unapproachable, majestic, and lasting.

Hence, one begins to understand how mineral imaginations can be suprasensory pictures for the most exalted and profound—the fatherly divine being—and why it is that they occur in the Apocalyptic vision to depict the vision's teleological image of what belongs to the future. One also begins to understand the ideational side of the precious mineral. Its particular modes of appearance depict the possibilities of the human soul that are striving to become virtues. The corresponding images of precious stones in the Revelation of St. John are bearers of the imaginative-ideational content of what—through all struggles, defeats, victories, transformations, deaths, resurrections and spiritualization—will arise at the conclusion of the cosmic drama at the hands of the world-transforming sacrificial work of the Son of Man.

Chapter 6: Origin of the Mineral Realm

The question of the entity, of the essence of the mineral realm also involves the question of its origin. One will only be able to approach this question, as well, if one ceases to see in the minerals a mere material, geochemical process in the history of the Earth in which through sinking temperatures they were separated off as a crystallized final product of the phases of thermic cooling and hardening, and gaseous, and later magmatic, i.e., molten rock, and the gases and liquids dissolved in them. The large steps referred to here are said to have been preceded by a primeval state of the elements and of a few chemical compounds, before passing over into the "liquid magmatic," the "pegmatitic-pneumatolythic," and, finally, into the hydrothermic phases. Physical and chemical processes capable of being replicated in laboratories require high temperatures and pressure gradients of the magnitude postulated and extrapolated for the past. In completely lifeless material, the processes as conceived can only have occurred at very high temperatures and pressures, or at enormous expanses.

Anyone who sees how in the organisms of plants, animals, and human beings the most complicated chemical processes take place at normal mid-range pressures and temperatures feels called upon to bring into play an entirely different thought possibility for geochemistry and geophysics. One need only rethink the presupposition that originally everything was dead and life originated through complication processes, into the alternate one that originally everything was alive—that is, that in earlier stages of the Earth even what subsequently became the mineral earthly sphere was permeated with life forces, just as organisms are today. Instead of ionized gases and molten rock, one needs to see primeval states of a colloidal character, in which the most finely dispersed elements and compounds interacted livingly with each other in denser and thinner media. This colloidal state consists in the predominance within a proper gel of laws and principles in which, basically, the laws of the aggregate phases of matter cannot yet occur. The state in question is an incalculable material middle state that possesses a sensitive and instable capacity to oscillate between dissolution and solidification, between vitalization and devitalization, and which is susceptible to the influences both of subsensory forces (electricity, magnetism, nuclear forces) and of suprasensory forces (vitalization and organic configuration, ensoulment, and enspiriting).

A look at the colloidal state of matter leads to the question of the essence of the living as opposed to the dead, the organic as opposed to the inorganic. Even today it can be observed that life proceeds exclusively from life and that dead matter can only fall out of living matter. Nowhere can the observation be made that life originates from what is dead; it is observable, however, that dead matter can be taken up into what is alive and be enlivened. This takes place, though, only through what itself is alive. These are only seemingly truisms; in actual fact, we stand here before primal truths—truths in which the primacy of life over death is expressed.

What is life, actually? Experience and research have a plethora of life phenomena at their immediate disposal. Research in the biological sciences—from behaviorism to biochemistry—endeavors to solve the secret of life by means of physical methods. But physics is exclusively the science of the inorganic, the nonliving. If we approach the phenomena of the living using methods suited only to the nonliving, the mechanical: and if we regard even the behavior of the soul and the phenomena of life (growth, reproduction, etc.) as mechanisms founded on structures, we must make clear to ourselves that here, in a purely methodological sense, one is performing an abstraction that eliminates life from the very approach of the research process. Thus all these paths must lead from what is alive to what is dead.

Life can be experienced and investigated only by life itself. To grasp life, as such, methods and organs are required that are themselves life. These methods need to be schooled accordingly, just as the methods for the nonliving, mechanical-atomistic do. Approaches to such a science of the living have been developed in the past already.

Goethe is, according to Steiner's formulation in his introductions to Goethe's natural-scientific writings,* the Copernicus and Kepler of the organic sciences. Taking Goethe as his point of departure, Rudolf Steiner expanded the science of life on the basis of suprasensory research. What for Goethe is the creative idea of the type becomes for Steiner a comprehensive world sphere of life, an etheric world within the cosmos, and this world has its own suprasensory substances, forces, processes, and laws. Students of Steiner endeavor to further research

---

*   Steiner, *Nature's Open Secret*.

and practice in the science of the etheric in such fields as medicine, education, art, agriculture, etc.*

For mineralogy, geology, and cosmology, there is likewise a science of the living. If one makes the fundamental presupposition that the mineral world was originally permeated by life forces when it moved in its state of colloidal sensitivity, it is no longer necessary to extrapolate high temperatures and extreme states of pressure back into the past. What today is generally understood as having been a primeval gaseous state could be conceived of as a chaos, albeit ensouled and creative; and what today is thought of as a "liquid-magmatic" and "pegmatitic-pneumatolytic" phase could just as well be understood as having been early colloidal states, plantlike and living, and cloud-like, such that progressing development went on not simply through a purely physical process of cooling off, but chiefly by a progressive devitalization of matter, similarly to the way that even today calcareous shells, exoskeletons, skeletons, calluses and corns are solidified in organisms through a progressive devitalization. Even the recent volcanism of the Earth could be regarded from such points of view, provided there is willingness to conceive of warmth influences in matter at least partly as vital processes of life** (see appendix 27).

The precious stones and with them the entire mineral world have a different origin than interpretations extrapolated by natural science into the past would have one believe. Spiritual Science's fundamental

---

*   For example, Wachsmuth, *Etheric Formative Forces in Cosmos, Earth, and Man: A Path of Investigation into the World of the Living*, vol. 1.

** It is possible today to build bridges between research of natural phenomena aiming at mathematical structure definitions on the one hand, and spiritual research that includes nature, on the other. This also holds for mineralogy. To date, the best endeavor in this way of treading the path of Goetheanistic, spiritual-scientific views and methods are the two books by Walther Cloos: *Kleine Edelsteinkunde. Im Hinblick auf die Geschichte der Erde* (A brief gemology in the light of Earth's history); and *The Living Earth: The Organic Origin of Rocks and Minerals*. Behind these endeavors stand the spiritual-scientific research results achieved by Steiner, which brought ordering, corrective, and deepening light into the abundance of the tradition.

idea yields a common suprasensory origin of the macrocosmic universe and the microcosm human being.* All members of the cosmos arose simultaneously and in common with all the members of the human being out of the same spiritual sources, and have diverged in the course of their development throughout the spiritual, soul, and etheric, living levels and down to the level of physical matter in a way that their correspondences can be found yet today. Such correspondences can be only briefly outlined here.

The Sun in the cosmos corresponds in its enlivening influence to the heart and the human "I," which experiences itself in the heart. The Earth in its total formation of the realms of nature corresponds to the human head and the consciousness living therein. The planets in their characteristic constellations and movements correspond to the human being's inner organs. The stars, and in particular the zodiac, correspond to the individual members of the human gestalt as a whole. And the animal kingdom carries within itself—in specialized form—the totality of the human soul life, as the plant kingdom does the totality of the human life forces in its outspread diversity.

Even the mineral realm has correspondences in the human being, which were exactly known to the ancient tradition. Such correspondences were the ones between certain metals and the inner organs. Why is gold a medicine for the heart, even though not a physical or chemical trace of it is to be found there?

All these correspondences serve to draw attention to the fact that there are originary relationships at play between the entities of nature and the human being. Everything in the macrocosm has its correspondence in the microcosm human being. Thus certain minerals and certain human organs or organizations came to be at the same time and out of a common spiritual source. The human organs developed on the microcosmic evolutionary track, while on the other side the beings of nature developed on the tracks of macrocosmic evolution.

---

* Cf. Steiner, *An Outline of Esoteric Science.*

This inner primal relationship of mineral, plant and animal to the human being is the true reason why certain natural beings can have a curative effect on certain ailments in human beings. Here we have the cosmic rationale for an expanded production of medicine and therapeutic practices.

Everything in the world has a material body, has life, soul, and an individual spiritual element. Thus, on these paths of research one reaches a world of suprasensory individual spirit beings. It is clear that enormous difficulties lie here for modern science, seeing as it is so firmly attuned to structures and interaction between mechanisms.

Chapter 7: Future of the Mineral Realm

The fundamental notion of the relatedness between the world and the human being also has a bearing on the future of world development. Here as well, it is not only a matter of the material world mechanism of natural science with its law of entropy, but rather of lasting intervention on the part of spiritual entities, human beings included, in the development of the world. Through perpetual reformation of the world at hand—including the material world—by spirit beings, the most mighty and potent of whom is the Christ entity, evolution will guide the world's descent through the material state into a future state of renewed spiritualization and marriage of the cosmic entities. It is from this perspective alone that the imagination of the heavenly Jerusalem—where John beholds this betrothal in the image of the twelve cornerstones and the precious stones with the twelve names of the Apostles—can be understood. Vastly separate elements, such as the precious stones, the human being. and the world of the fixed stars appear to the beholder in common, suprasensory-future reality. But this would not be possible if this future were not even now able to have an effect.

Chapter 8: Minerals and the Fixed Stars

Just as there are correspondences between the human being and natural entities, there are also correspondences among the natural entities themselves. We know about correspondences between metals and planets. In ancient traditions and mysteries, these correlations are fully identical. A certain metal originates along with or out of the planet associated with it.

The association of the precious stones to the signs of the zodiac, and the months of the Sun's course through the zodiac, is much more complicated. Here, one is confronted by the astrological tradition, but also by a medical one. Ever and again, the irresolvable contradiction is emphasized between the traditional astrological assignment of the annual positions of the Sun and its months, and the factual position of the Sun in the zodiac. Through a shift in the spring equinox in the platonic year, the astronomical and the astrological assignments of the solar positions have come to diverge. Astrologically, the Sun "stands in the sign of Aries" from March 21 to April 20. Astronomically and factually, though, the Sun stands before the sign of Pisces from March 21 to April 18, not reaching Aries until April 19. Moreover, the partitioning of the signs of the zodiac is, as seen by astronomy, pure scientific convention, which designates certain spherically and geometrically, polygonally separated areas in the vicinity of the ecliptic by their old mythological names, without ascribing even the slightest bit of reality to these lines and borders. In astronomical and astrophysical terms, the zodiac is no reality whatsoever, except that the ecliptic is outlined in it, which for its own part is a mere optic projection of what seems to be the Sun's orbit on the background of the sky of fixed stars. The stars making up a "constellation" can even belong to different galaxies and not have the slightest thing to do with each other, save that they seem to stand next to one another as seen from the Earth. All the more senseless must the assignment of some "influences" to these groupings seem to the astronomer.

And the interpretation of the astrologer seems utterly absurd that, in March and April the Sun "stands" in the sign of Aries—while in actual fact it is crossing over in front of Pisces.

This "nonsense" is only resolved if the twelve spatial directions in the zodiac are not comprehended in the sense of their materialistic extrapolation and as being the only possible way to think them. Seen from the viewpoint of Spiritual Science, the zodiacal constellations are script-like, readable signs of suprasensory realms, out of which the influences of spiritual beings stream forth. The positioning of their component stars next to each other yields a kind of pictograph of these beings.* There was a time when astronomy's zodiacal constellation and the astrology's sign of the zodiac converged with regard to the position of the Sun. At that time, the spring equinox moved in front of Aries. During this time, Jesus Christ walked the Earth and the Mystery of Golgotha took place. Along with Christ's descent to the Earth, the influence of the Cherubim was divided. One part of their activity remained cosmic, which is expressed in the progression of the vernal equinox always bringing on new epochs of time (Age of Aries, Age of Pisces, etc.). The Sun's position in front of Pisces from March 21 to April 20 is attributable to this influence. Another portion of the Cherubim's activity united with the life of the Earth and humanity, once and for all, under the guidance of the Christ-being, creating a kind of "birth horoscope" for the Christ impulse, which since then has been binding for human destinies on Earth. It is owing to this influence, whose aim is the permeation of the Earth's future with spirit and with Christ, that

---

* They appear in Steiner's Spiritual Science as the twelve "world initiators" (*Man in the Light of Esotericism, Theosophy, and Philosophy*). They are the actual reality of the zodiac. In this cosmic sphere, the imaginations of the first hierarchy, the Seraphim, Cherubim, and Thrones appear to suprasensory vision. Above all, it is the Cherubim (Spirits of Harmony) who show themselves to suprasensory vision as animal-like figures. The present-day beholding of the spiritual scientist corroborates the dogmatically formulated tradition of the Christian worldview as it stands in both the New and the Old Testaments; but also the writings of Dionysius and the medieval Scholastics.

the Sun always "stands" in the "sign" of Aries from March 21 to April 20. Astronomy and astrology can mutually supplement each other.

It is within these spiritual contexts that the Apocalyptic images of precious stone can be assigned to the months of the year and to the signs of the zodiac.

In the Apocalypse according to Saint John, the list of the precious stones begins with jasper. The twelve precious stones' relationships and correspondences are retrograde, beginning with jasper for Pisces, on to Aquarius, Capricorn, and so on, until Aries. This sequence corresponds not to the course of the Sun, but to that of the spring equinox in the platonic year. The configuration of the forces of the equinox, which has the strongest spiritual influence, moves in the direction opposite the configuration of forces of the annual course of the year, which has the strongest physical influence.

The descriptions of the individual mineral entities occurring in the Revelation of St. John will each include a brief report on relevant natural-scientific research.* An understanding of the precious stones' respective connections with the months, the signs of the zodiac, and the festivals of the year, is only possible if the correspondences are regarded not just as pertaining to the object, but to the spiritual background—i.e., their origin and goal. The ancient mysteries knew these connections. The Spiritual Science of Rudolf Steiner opens new, furthering insights unto the consciousness of today. The common ground for precious stones, the human being, and the world of the stars is the spiritual influence of the Cherubim (Spirits of Harmony), whose creational impulses manifest as a differentiated material cosmos by way of subordinate spirit beings. According to Rudolf Steiner, in the course of their creating they differentiate the twelve primary figures of the animal and the plant realms. Within the human organization,

---

* They are dealt with extensively in every book on minerals—e.g., Felix Machatschki, *Spezielle Mineralogie* (Vienna, 1953); or Klockmann, et al, *Lehrbuch der Mineralogie* (Stuttgart, 1978). The deeper treatment of the natural-scientific approach in the Goetheanistic and spiritual-scientific sense is in the books cited by Walther Cloos.

they form the parts of the body, the twelve senses and the twelve constitutional types of human character. This twelvefold is represented in the disciples Jesus Christ gathered around him. The most profound essence of such twelvefoldness, though, only manifests if and once one has ascended to the soul and spiritual virtues and fundamental powers of the spirit entities themselves. In the form of "verdict words," Rudolf Steiner developed the twelve "moods"; in lectures on eurythmy, he developed the totality of the modes of behavior of the entire human being in the form of eurythmic gestures; and through the guidance he gave in esoteric training and self-education, he developed the "twelve virtues."* In these areas, one is closest to the spiritual entities themselves, because, in truth, they shine within us human beings as our highest ideals. But the minerals manifest as the final creations of these cosmic entities, and within the mineral realm the precious stones manifest as those among these final creations that depict the creator-beings the most purely, and in which at the same time they are "minerally incarnated." The problems that the tradition has, concerning the correspondence between certain precious stones and the zodiac, stems from there being not just one twelvefold of precious stones. Each of the twelve zodiacal influences is modified by each of the seven planets and their spiritual influences; thus, one is justified in assuming the existence of seven twelvefoldness of precious stones. This does not mean that individual precious stones, owing to the diversity of their properties, are excluded from occurring in more than a single twelvefold. A stone's occurrence in multiple twelvefoldness would simply indicate that this entity emerged from the convergence of the influences of more than one creator force. But this question cannot be dealt with here.

The twelvefold named by the Apocalypse is the picture of a vision of the future. It can be assumed that, in this twelvefold, influences from the future are the actual formative element. Thus this twelvefold

---

*   See, for example, *Guidance in Esoteric Training*.

can be placed over against the aforementioned seven twelvefoldness as an eighth one, as "the Apocalyptic twelvefold of the precious stones." However, that likewise does not exclude these stones from occurring in other twelvefoldness. These are the stones that, along with the properties they bring out of the past, also unite with those of the future in a germinal way. The striking thing here is that half of these Apocalyptic stones belong to the quartz group, and that precious stones like ruby, diamond, garnet, tourmaline—but also rock crystal—are absent from the "eighth twelvefold."

The twelve spirit beings of the zodiac manifest to the beholder of the suprasensory in animal-like imaginations. This is also the case in the Apocalypse with regard to the four noblest spirit beings (Rev. 4:6–8). In the future imaginations of the Holy City, however, the zodiacal entities can be beheld as twelve cornerstones and twelve precious stones, which moreover are inscribed with the names of the twelve tribes of the people of the future and of the twelve Apostles. In this fact a collaborative influence of hierarchic beings, the mineral cosmos, groups of human beings, and individual human beings is revealed to suprasensory vision. This is the aspect of the future. In the same way as the twelve precious stones of the Heavenly City are assigned to the twelve signs of the zodiac, the remaining mineral image elements are likewise assigned to other spheres of the cosmos: water corresponds to the etheric, rock crystal to the cosmic being of the light, gold to the Sun entity.

How are we now to think of the human being's connection with all this? The initial mutual bond between the human being and precious stones is, of course, their sheer sensory nature. Twelve senses connect the human being with the world, each making a definite and specific sphere of existence accessible to him. The human will, streaming in, out, and within a certain sense organization, is permeated with a certain area of the world-constituting "cosmic will"—this is what actually constitutes sensory perception.* In the senses' perceiving of the minerals, especially the precious stones, the human being encounters the revelations of the pure, "rippling," "trickling" cosmic will of the Thrones. The cosmic will of the first hierarchy, that of the Thrones (Spirits of Will), the Cherubim (Spirits of Harmony), and the Seraphim (Spirits of Love), exerts its influence in the spiritual zodiac consisting of the four leading Cherubim as Bull, Lion, Eagle, and Water bearer. Each of these four is accompanied by its two neighboring entities. These beings are the actual reality, the creating deities of the spheres of the zodiac. As on the one hand the human being finds his spiritual and soul connection with these beings from within, by unfolding certain ideals and virtues, he can on the other hand attain to the revelation of the same beings in the mineral world, by way of sense beholding. This shows that the creator activity of the spirit beings has an either entirely outward aim, with its revelation in mineral, plant and animal, or else an entirely inward one, where the human being can ultimately achieve this influence as morality. In mineral substance, what is accessible to the human being is the conclusion of the creator activity of the Cherubim; in the virtues, it is its beginning (cf. appendix 25).

Walther Cloos depicts the emergence of the precious stones out of a living primeval Earth and its precursors. Both the precious stones and the other minerals are no mere result of the cooling off of magmatic masses; rather, and above all, they are the result of a comprehensive devitalization of former plant-minerals, the outcome of which was the minerals, for one, and also the plants and lower animals. Cloos also shows how individual precious stones stand out—for instance, rock crystal by virtue of its omnipresence and its ten combinatory laws of crystal formation; the diamond through the extremes it displays of certain properties, such as hardness; tourmaline by virtue of its extreme plantlike quality; and garnet—because

---

* Steiner points to the essence of sense qualities in *A Psychology of Body, Soul, and Spirit*.

of its manifold basic forms, which despite its various chemical compositions—always occurs in the exact same crystal form and almost always in precious stone quality.

An understanding of the spiritual essence of the minerals is prerequisite to an understanding of the mineral images of the Book of Revelation. How will the present mineral cosmos turn into the great final image of the Apocalypse?

Part 3
Heavenly Jerusalem and Minerals

Hymn

Few understand
The mystery of Love,
Know insatiableness,
And thirst eternal.
Of the Last Supper
The divine meaning
Is to the earthly senses a riddle;
But he that ever
From warm, beloved lips,
Drew breath of life;
In whom the holy glow
Ever melted the heart in trembling waves;
Whose eye ever opened so
As to fathom
The bottomless deeps of Heaven—
Will eat of his body
And drink of his blood
Everlastingly.
Who of the earthly body
Has divined the lofty sense?
Who can say
That he understands the blood?
One day all is body,
One body:
In heavenly blood
Swims the blissful two.

Oh that the ocean
Were even now flushing!
And in odorous flesh
The rock were upswelling!
Never endeth the sweet repast;
Never doth Love satisfy itself;
Never close enough, never enough its own,
Can it have the beloved!
By ever tenderer lips
Transformed, the Partaken
Goes deeper, grows nearer.
Pleasure more ardent
Thrills through the soul;
Thirstier and hungrier
Becomes the heart;
And so endureth Love's delight
From everlasting to everlasting.
Had the refraining
Tasted but once,
All had they left
To set themselves down with us
To the table of longing
Which will never be bare;
Then had they known Love's
Infinite fullness,
And commended the sustenance
Of body and blood.
—NOVALIS, *Spiritual Songs,* VII

"Earth, is it not this that you want: to rise invisibly in us?"
—RILKE, *Ninth Duino Elegy*

"Give me the sight of your being, oh world."
—CHRISTIAN MORGENSTERN

Chapter 1: Forming the Question

In what has preceded, a schematic attempt was undertaken to consider the nature, the essence, and the being of the mineral realm according to the following points of view:

1. The mineral as a sense perceptible-material-figural crystal manifestation of a total entity that, outside its body, is a life of its own, a soul being and a spiritual being.
2. The mineral as a result of Earth's development, having emerged from previous states of existence in which it was still connected and permeated with life, soul, and spirit being, but had not yet descended to crystallinity. The more this occurred, the more the mineral realm relinquished its vitality.
3. The connections the mineral has with the hierarchies living in the starry worlds, connections given by just these higher aspects of its being.
4. The mineral's connection with humanity in the sense of a mutual origin out of those spiritual worlds, hence also in the sense of a correspondence between certain organs of the human body and certain minerals.
5. The character of the mineral world's perfection, especially that of the precious stones and precious metals.
6. The possibility this totality yields, especially with the precious minerals, of revealing on the one hand the highest divine being, and on the other hand the final aim of human and earthly cosmic development; indeed, of the entire cosmos, in spiritual-suprasensory imaginations.

A final question remains open: To what extent is the whole spiritual development of the world not only a cosmological one, a divine-spiritual

Christological one, and an anthroposophic one, but also a mineral one as well? When one looks at the spiritual nature of the minerals in connection with the Revelation of St. John, one can say: through an understanding of the mineral world, it becomes possible to comprehend why the minerals are suited as image elements and media of the revelation of the spiritual world. The mineral world is no mere picture for the spiritual revelation; rather, it is itself a component of world development. Through the Christ influence, this is why something of this mineral world, by passing through the human being, must itself in some way be able to be the origin, building material, and goal of a new world. Even more: there would have to be something of the very human being interwoven with the mineral world that makes it capable of this future, and something of this same mineral world would even have to be woven into human beings that helps them toward their cosmic future.

How it is possible for something as inward as the spiritual, soul, and moral life of a human being, and something as outward as the substances and characteristics of minerals, to work together? How can interaction become mutual transformation in such a way that this transformation leads to germination, penetration, betrothal, even identification and communion with a future cosmic existence? Once more we can see that without Rudolf Steiner's exploration of the spiritual world and the spiritual side of nature and humankind, such questions would necessarily remain questions. Through his research, the possibility opens up for the future development of the world—a development going on even now, albeit hidden from general sight—to be revealed and become understandable. This future development is being prepared on the one hand within the inner and outer human being on Earth; on the other hand, on the interior and the exterior of the mineral; and, finally, on the interior and the exterior of humans that arises when one has passed through death.

The Revelation of St. John is quite impartial toward these three points of view. It speaks of a real cosmic occurrence, using images that embrace the areas of the origin and the estuary. Developments are consummated from jasper, sard, emerald, crystal, and gold to jasper, precious stone, gold, crystal, and pearl; the Son of Man gives the impulses and causes the transformations, which in turn pass through humanity. Even with identity, the moral and the natural world orders enter into closest relationship with each other.

Chapter 2: Minerals and Humanity

Working on the Earth

The realms of nature, including the mineral realm, were initially a gift of the creator gods. They were given to humanity as an enveloping environment in which to live. Moreover, human sense perception, breathing, and nourishment come from them. Primal humanity experienced nature as the earthly ground, as sensual perception, as nourishing substance, and as a blessing, starry heavens. Above all, he experiences her inner side, her life, her soul, her spirit.

Irrespective of how we see the primal stages of earthly human development—as Darwin theorized, ascending from animal ancestors or, as shown by spiritual-scientific research, descending into matter from suprasensory ancestors,* at some point a step was taken to something entirely new: the mineral world became implements and materials for performing work. Wood, horn and bone, but above all the cherts (flint, obsidian, nephrite, hornfels, jasper, etc.) provided the first tools for human beings. At the same time, the mineral also became the material for works of art and, finally, for religious worship. Clay and fiber were added in the Young Stone Age and, ultimately, metal in the Stone-Copper age. Simultaneously with the advent of agriculture and cattle-breeding cultures, that is, of planters and peasantry, minerals became the object of architecture, sculpture, and painting. This occurrence was prepared in the paintings and sculptures of the Paleolithic Age (cave paintings), in which specially fashioned pieces of the mineral

---

*   Cf. Steiner, *An Outline of Esoteric Science.*

world were assimilated into the artistic process. The first great inclusion of the mineral world into art and religion occurred on a worldwide scale in the "monumental" structures of the megalithic cultures. Since then, both stone and wood have been components of the artistic process. Minerals were processed, and this processing always served a specific purpose, developing in step with the growing rationality of humankind. Once more, it is unimportant whether one explains this development in Darwinist terms or as a result of cultural impulses stemming from the initiates, and emerging from humanity's most ancient mystery sites.

According to the results of Spiritual Science, the human race of the past was originally not fully aware of the entire mineral world. Human beings lived on and with it, to be sure, but they did not yet perceive it as "mineral" (i.e., with the senses*), because they had no individual "I"-awareness. The polarity of "I" and object had not yet developed in human consciousness. Human beings lived with the life of nature in a childlike and clairvoyant way; the nonliving, or purely mineral, remained in the subconscious.

The more humankind developed an individual self-consciousness, the more it set itself apart from the world; one could also say that the more human beings distanced themselves from the world and the more the world became an object, the more self-consciousness arose. And it is now that the object, the objective, the nonliving, the mineral emerges for humankind. In the very earliest mysteries, the human being had to be educated in sense perception. The Paleolithic cave paintings were such means of education in the perception of the sense-perceptible and of the animal world. Perceiving animals, hunting them, and ultimately producing stone tools constituted the means of education for a total apprehension of the mineral world (cf. appendix 3).

Thus, through education, human beings had to be brought to the point where they could perceive the mineral realm with the senses. The mineral manifested as the environment only to the degree that

---

* Steiner describes this condition in the lecture cycle entitled *The Cycle of the Year as a Breathing Process of the Earth*.

the old clairvoyance was sacrificed to sensory perception. This process only fully unfolded in the most recent epochs of human history; but it also became one-sided, beginning approximately with the Greek Philosophy of Nature. With its mode of knowledge, all of modern natural science penetrates the mineral realm down into the subsensory spheres of quantum physics and physical chemistry and into the investigation of the biochemical processes in the corporeality of plant, animal, and human.

The human being today understands the mineral realm through and through—not in its integral spiritual nature, but rationally and according to natural law—all the way into its subsensory depths. This leaves the mineral realm open to the intervention of human intentionality. The knowledge and know-how prerequisite to an atomic bomb, a nuclear reactor, a laser beam, a computer, a space vehicle; the technological reality of a particle accelerator, a modern factory, a flying machine, a weapons system—all that is mineral substance and physical systems of force permeated, formed and structured by human intelligence. This development has not reached its conclusion. Humanity will go on and on increasing its knowledge and command of the world of mineral substances and forces.*

According to Rudolf Steiner, it is the present mission of human destiny to enter the mineral epoch (cf. appendix 4). Through human intelligence, every mineral, every artifice, every machine component, every chemical substance is wrenched from nature, rationally processed, and changed. Therefore, it is that through this work matter will be penetrated by and permeated with the outflow of human intelligence and human will. This causes the mineral world to receive a stamp; and to become something different—down to the very last atom—from what it was in its pure natural state. Millennium by millennium, mineral nature will be minted again aurically in tools, machines, buildings, and works of art of every kind. It is torn away from its natural

---

* Steiner in a lecture in Berlin, March 30, 1905, "The Future of the Human Being," in *Ursprung und Ziel des Menschen* (CW 53).

habitat and, in a way, destroyed; but also—precisely through this partial destruction—rendered receptive for the influence of human forces (intelligence and work) left to it. Mineral nature is receiving the esoteric impulse of future spiritualization. It stems from the creation—that is, the yield of its past. It is processed by humankind and will meet its outer demise, or transit. It is inwardly permeated with a substance of human influence—that is, its future (cf. appendix 4).

The "royal art"—to use a concept from Freemasonry—extends today not only to tools, architecture, works of art and crafts, but above all to machines. The sheer quantitative magnitude of substances and forces mobilized by people today has already reached that of a geological formation. Not just in the mineral, plant, and animal spheres is human intelligence at work on a global scale, but also in the sphere of human social fabrics capable of being organized. Superpowers (the United States, China, and Russia) and international world organizations (the world economy, world transportation, news media) are permeations of the sensual-material-mineral spheres.

In a lecture of December 23, 1904, on the task of secret societies in the world, Rudolf Steiner also speaks of these states of affairs:

> We are living now in the epoch of evolution that may be called the mineral epoch; and our task is to permeate this mineral world through and through with our own spirit. Grasp exactly what this means. You are building a house. You fetch the stones from some quarry. You hew them into the shapes needed for the house and so on. With what are you joining this raw material obtained from the mineral kingdom? You are joining raw material with human spirit. When you make a machine, you have introduced your spirit into that machine. The actual machine does, of course, perish and become dust; it will be broken up. Not a trace of it will survive. But what it has done does not vanish without a trace, but passes into the very atoms. Every atom bears a trace of your spirit and will carry this trace with it. It is not a matter of indifference whether or not an atom has at some time been in a machine. The atom itself has undergone change as a result of having once been in a

machine, and this change that you have wrought in the atom will never again be lost to it. *

Chapter 3: Inner Life and Future Earth

The transformation of the mineral through intelligence and work is of meaning not only for the mineral, but for the human being as well. Thus Rudolf Steiner continues: "Moreover, through your having changed the atom, through your having united your spirit with the mineral world, a permanent stamp has been made upon the general consciousness. Just so much will be taken from us into the other world."**

This touches on a motif Steiner always returns to—for example in Dornach, October 21, 1921.*** In one part of this lecture he discusses what is inward for human earthly consciousness, and what is outward. The thoughts that we think ourselves, our mental pictures and recollections, and our feelings, emotions, and moods all appear as our inner soul world. At the outer border of this inwardness we have our sense perceptions, which touch both our inwardness and our outwardness equally. But their contents, already, are outside of us. What is entirely external to the human being is the life of his willing. To be sure, the life of the will is impulsed from the unconscious depths of a person's own being and set in motion with the help of mental pictures and motives, but it only becomes conscious as the perception of actions one has actually implemented. Within, the origin is unconscious, and the implementation is every bit as external as any other perception. A person must visually follow the movement of his hand if he wishes to have an experience of this movement. This is also the reason why the very slightest thing we do intentionally alters both the substances of our own body and the substances and forces of the world outside us (cf. appendix 3).

---

*   Steiner, *The Temple Legend,* pp. 110–111.
** Ibid., p. 119.
*** Steiner, *Cosmosophy,* vol. 2.

Part 3: Heavenly Jerusalem and Minerals ∞ Chapter 3: Inner Life and Future Earth

In the second part of this lecture, Rudolf Steiner goes on to speak of the sphere of life after death inaccessible to normal consciousness. The aspect of it that pertains here is the human inner side of what on the outside is work on the mineral realm. Firstly, through human intelligence and volition, the mineral is inculcated with something that changes it in its deepest being and thereby makes it capable of future existence. On the other hand, for the sake of the same future, something happens with the will, something that manifests in activity and work and which, notwithstanding the fact that this soul initiates it, for human consciousness is external to the soul. Thirdly, it is a matter of fact that not even thoughts and feelings always stay with a person as his inner world. But this can only be understood by beholding suprasensorily how a person lives on after death. A person's soul and spirit are altered after death; the formerly external life of the will now become the content of the soul. The person is now himself all of his impulses, deeds, and actions. The true inner qualities of all willing become conscious, and thus inward. By contrast, everything thought and felt on Earth, everything experienced and suffered, the inner life, disengages from the individual after death and becomes one's outer environment. This occurrence has a definite relationship to the Earth. Through death, human beings endure an inversion of the circumstances of their soul. One constantly looks toward the Earth and experiences how the earthly inner life envelops the Earth in contents and forces that appear in cloudlike and starlike spiritual formations. The dead enrich the aura of the Earth with these contents and forces. "What is external becomes internal, what is internal becomes external," says Rudolf Steiner (cf. appendices 4 and 5). This substance, relinquished to the earthly world by the dead, supplements what by means of intelligence and work the human being added to the mineral world on Earth. The two interact to form a further prerequisite for the future of the Earth (cf. appendix 5). The following example makes especially clear how concrete these events are—how all contents and forces that humanity releases today into the world will in the future be "geology":

You know, in the way that, by means of geology, we dig into the lower level of the earth and sometimes excavate this or that level that was formed long, long ago; in the same way, one day in the future—during the Jupiter-epoch—people will be able to examine the individual levels that will have been formed by then. And so then one will also find all kinds of layers built up out of human feelings and thoughts. For example, geologists on Jupiter will excavate layer after layer, and in the same way as today earth geologists say "this is the Rotliegend [a sequence of rock strata], this the Tertiary," geologists on Jupiter will be able to observe: "Ah yes, this is a layer that points us back to a time that on Earth they called the twentieth century, the early twentieth century. This layer was deposited by all those wanglers who unfolded their feelings and thoughts over nearly the entire Earth." The way we now speak of the Silurian, in the future people will be able to speak of "wangler layers." Obviously, there will also be other layers to talk about. But these are definite realities.*

Thus our gaze rests on a connection between Anthroposophy and cosmology, which is the only thing capable of making the "basic idea" of the Apocalypse understandable to us, and which consists in the fact that the current cosmos will dissolve and the seed of a new cosmos "of mineral nature" will arise, among other things out of what happens to the mineral world at the hands of humankind (cf. appendix 6A). Finally, how deeply founded the connection is between the human spirit and matter, is demonstrated in the connection between electricity and human thinking (cf. appendix 6B). The more this connection is understood, the more understandable will become how in the future humans will be able to influence the atom ever more deeply. The bridge can be seen even today in the fact that atomic events can only be grasped by purely mathematical means—even more: that atoms actually are mathematics.

---

* Steiner, *Die Gestaltung des Menschen als Ergebnis kosmischer Wirkungen* (English ed. *Cosmosophy,* vol. 2).

CHAPTER 4: MINERALS AND THE HUMAN BODY

The third point of view results when one's gaze falls on the study of humanity developed by Rudolf Steiner quite early on. His book *Theosophy* shows that human corporeality is no mere mineral, material manifestation, but that these substances are much rather kept alive by a second, the etheric corporeality, which was referred to in the second part of this book during the discussion of the origin of the mineral realm. This human etheric body in turn is permeated with the organism of the soul forces, the instincts, urges, desires, emotions and natural sensations and feelings, which in their entirety Rudolf Steiner calls the astral body. It is only in the interpenetration of these three bodily sheaths that the actual individual human being lives as a spiritual person, "I"-awareness. This "I" appears inwardly within thinking consciousness. It lives outwardly in the mineral world in volitional movement and action, constantly carrying itself into this world and taking in its manifestations through the senses.

For a basic understanding of how the human being is embedded in the world, it is important to know that this "external aspect" already begins where the "I" enters its own etheric and physical body when it incarnates. The human "I" works its way as a spiritual being into the sheaths so that it can manifest in the mineral body as it does so. Thus the work of human beings on the mineral world begins within their own corporeality; our earthly existence itself is the "humanization" of its mineral substances. This creates a preliminary stage for further transformations.

From the perspective of the "I" this deeply concealed and yet very real process of world events proceeds from the inside outward. In it, the human spirit takes hold of the mineral world from within and impresses its work outward onto this world. Once it has passed through human intelligence and human work, this process then crosses over into the extra-human mineral world, changing it down to the last atom. However, human beings take hold of the mineral world much more intimately within their own corporeality than by means of their work. This corporeality is structured according to seven fundamental systems,* on the one hand the sense organs, the glandular organs, the digestive system with its glands (liver, kidneys), and on the other hand the nerves, the muscles, and the bones. In the middle between these two trinities is the circulatory system, consisting of the blood and the lymph.

By perceiving, digesting, and secreting, on the one hand, human beings live in the physiology of constantly changing, transitory processes. This is where the exchange of body substances predominates. In the nervous system, on the other hand—which is shot through by the light of thinking, mental pictures, memory images and the feelings of soul life—human beings have a bodily foundation that remains static for as long as we live.

The muscle system is charged with the will's movement impulses, which permeate it with the "resonance" of its tonicity. In the bone system, the most highly mineralized area of the physical body, which guarantees uprightness, the human I finds a solid earthly hold. As the human being acts and works on the latter three organ systems, they are transformed through and through by human spirituality. This is significant for life on Earth first. Nerves, muscles, bones, even the skin are marked with ever-greater individuality. Faces of the elderly document a their intervention in the mineral realm. Even the phosphorous calcium of the skeletal system, which consists mainly of mineral substances, has become entirely "human" here.

These phenomena give us a first inkling of the predisposition for a future world in transit through the human body, of which the mineral is a part. The mineral substances of these three organ systems have not only endured spiritualization at the hands of human beings, as has the outer mineral world through work, but they have also received human figuration. As we think, we gain concepts and ideas through intuition, which are reflected off the nervous system and become conscious. As

---

*   Steiner, *The World of the Senses and the World of the Spirit*.

human beings move, we impulse our musculature with decisions of the will, which shoot into the will forces as inspirations. When human beings hold themselves up on their skeletal system, they do so with the help of the congealed image of a real imagination. When a human corpse decomposes or is cremated, the mineral materiality that has gone through humanization—along with a new spiritualization—leaves the sphere of earthly existence and passes into the spiritual world of the sphere after death.

We want once more to take as our point of departure the issue of the entire chapter, that is, the paths the mineral aspect takes through the creation to the cosmic future of the Heavenly Jerusalem. This will enable us in our spiritual research to grasp the beginnings of the construction of the future world from yet a different angle, namely that of the human body.

The first part of this book describes how the mineral realm manifests for the Apocalyptist in suprasensory perceptions. Experiences, things lived through, sufferings and achievements, abilities and virtues are the form and substance of a future world that takes on the form of gemstones. The beginning of this consummated future lies even today in what humans assimilate into their physical body from the mineral realm and give back over to the world after death. In *The World of the Senses and World of the Spirit*, Steiner describes what the trained clairvoyant perceives when he sees the living earthly body, and the corpse after death; in earthly life, the skeletal system is an imagination become material, the muscle system an inspiration become material, the nervous system an intuition become material. After death, these three organ systems emanate the mineral components they have taken in and transformed, into the Earth's aura in the form of spiritual substances. This in turn causes a portion of the material processes of the Earth to be transferred, in the form of a future force and substance influence, to the earthly cosmos and "salvaged over to Jupiter existence" (cf. appendix 7).

This is an exact characterization of the extent to which the mineral portion of our body becomes a building stone of the future. It can become a "precious stone" if what the human being takes along from the three organ systems in the way of imagination, inspiration, and intuition is suited for the future, that is, if it is morally in order, if it has taken on gemstone character. According to Steiner, the cosmos receives only what is true, good, and beautiful, and rejects anything else (cf. appendix 8).

Thus we can say that only what is gemstone-like is suitable for building the future, is all that becomes the Heavenly Jerusalem.

In addition, everything that innumerable individual people contribute to the construction of the future over very long periods of time will ultimately become One and an entirety. Rudolf Steiner referred to this as well. In *Cosmosophy*, vol. 1, he speaks of the convergence in action of what is individual, to become something universally human (cf. appendix 9).

To summarize, then, we can say that the future of the cosmos is in part founded in the mineral world in two ways. For one, it is founded on mineral substance that will have passed through human corporeality and into the substance and figuration of the future; for the other, this future is founded on what passes over into the mineral world through human work at it, which can make it a component of the future.

In another lecture course, Steiner associates this latter fact with the interaction between development of the human soul and that of the interior Earth, the mineral world. In the first part of this cycle's last lecture,* he addresses the topic of self-knowledge, self-development, and training for all future times. In the second part, he reveals the zones of the interior Earth and their respective influences, and delineates the mutual activity between human virtues and vices on one hand, and the inner layers of the Earth, all the way to its core. It becomes particularly clear how deep the connection is between humanity and

---

*   Steiner, *Founding a Science of the Spirit*, Sept. 9, 1906.

the mineral world. He states (p. 143): "It is still true that a bundling of evil passions and powers causes earthquakes and volcanic eruptions." He goes on to conclude:

> Thus the human will is connected with what occurs on Earth. Along with itself, humankind transforms its domicile at the same time. By spiritualizing oneself, the human being spiritualizes the Earth. One day on a planet to come, we will have refined the Earth with our own productive power. In every moment that we think and feel, we are working on the great edifice of the Earth. The leaders of humanity have insight into such matters and seek to provide humankind with the forces at work on behalf of human and earthly development (cf. appendix 10).

Chapter 5: Cultic Action

As we have seen, the transformation, humanization, and spiritualization of the mineral world takes place to begin with in two ways: first, in the minerals' transit through the human body, through human corporeality, human soul life and spiritual life. Second, in human work on the mineral world in the way of all manner of treatment, both through human intelligence and through human willing as labor power. This is the area known in Masonic lore as "building." All technology in handcrafting, industry, and artistry belongs here. A third way consists in the preparation of the human interior as a building stone of the future. But there is yet a completely different transformational path of the mineral into the future: the path of religion, in particular through cultic actions. This is the sphere of magic, of intervention into the mineral world by means of the God-given cultic word. Since primeval times, humankind has performed rituals in which mineral substances are significant. This includes all "ritual consecration." This area, of course, lies quite outside of technical-materialistic-natural-scientific research, but it can be suprasensorily investigated quite precisely. The implements, garments, and substances both of mineral origin (gold, water, salt, ash) and of plant origin (frankincense, oil, bread, wine) are transformed by means of the active cultic word such that, along with them and through them, spiritual and soul forces and suprasensory realities of the gods—and ultimately those of the very highest divinity Himself—unite, to begin outside the human being, and become incorporated into the processes of forming the future world. In his book *Man or Matter,* Ernst Lehrs strips the notion of "magic" of its burdened, obscured contents and reinterprets it into a scientifically useful concept (cf. appendix 11).*

In spiritually justified cultic occurrence, there is an area in which the influence of the future world becomes active. Wherever there is genuine ritual and religious worship, the Heavenly Jerusalem already belongs to the present. Within the worshipping congregation, the future Earth and the future Heaven are both factually and virtually an auric presence. Here, those seeds of a future world are planted that not only people can directly unite with, but the godhead as well. In the spirit of the fundamental tenets of Christianity, this divine entity is Jesus Christ, who has lived in the mineral world of the Earth since the Mystery of Golgotha. When during the Christian worship mineral substances are connected with the Christ impulse and the Christ power, what even now generates the seed formations of the future world arises within these substances. They are described in the Heavenly Jerusalem by the Apocalyptist as a new world depicting "the tabernacle of God among human beings."

CHAPTER 6: FOUR QUESTIONS FROM ONE

From what has gone before, it has become increasingly clear what is actually revealed in the pictures of the Revelation of St. John, and what can cause the realities in the world events of the cosmos, Earth, and the human being to manifest.

---

*   Ernst Lehrs, *Man or Matter.*

The whole world of the materially appearing mineral kingdom will in the course of world development be permeated by human inwardness streaming outward. Sensual perception—scientific penetration in cognition—practical technological work and processing—corporeal-soul-and-spiritual permeation in the physiology of the human body—religious-cultic action: this entire materially manifesting world of the mineral realm will be lifted over into future processes. On the other hand, an aspect of the mineral realm will enter human interiority and will become one's own content, being, and essence. The mineral will become human, the human will become world, even mineral. This is why this real occurrence appears in the seven great source images of the Apocalypse and in the final, all-encompassing estuary image. Thus what reveals itself in these pictures are not symbols of visionary fantasy, but rather substantial realities.

And so a continuation of the comprehensive question pertaining to the transformation of humanity and mineral results in four questions:

1. What will have happened with humankind that leads to the creation of the cosmos, the human being, and the city depicted in the final image? This is the question pertaining to humanity.
2. What will have become of the member of nature that today is the mineral, which provides the body of Earth, plant, animal, and human, and causes the city to manifest in a mineral state? This is the question pertaining to the mineral realm of the Earth.
3. What will have become of the member of the world that today manifests to humankind as the mineral corporeality of the world of the stars? This is the question pertaining to the macrocosm.
4. What will have become of evil, the adversarial powers, which in the imagination of St. John's Revelation appear as an integral part of the whole process? This is the question pertaining to the meaning of evil.

Chapter 7: The Human Being

The first of these four questions calls for an answer taken from an expanded knowledge of humanity. For the human being, as a being of nature, is a creature; i.e., the human has become what it now is, as a part of the body of the powers of the creator. In a spiritual world and surrounded by spiritual entities, the human spirit seed, the "I" and its sheaths of soul, all lived in the creator ground of the world or, to use the language of the Apocalypse, in the bosom of the One sitting on the throne. He is enfolded in and woven of jasper light (snow-white, divine interiority); carnelian red (glowing, divine-creative love); and emerald-green life. He is enveloped in sevenfold divine creative force. In the lecture of December 23, 1904 (mentioned previously), Rudolf Steiner formulates this:

> You all have a soul and you all have a spirit. This soul and spirit are called upon to reach one day the highest stages of perfection. But you were already there before your first physical incarnation. You were first physically incarnated in the preceding races after the time of the Hyperborean and Polarian epochs. Before, you were purely beings of soul. But, as beings of soul, you were a part of the world soul, and as spirit you were part of the general world spirit. The world soul and the world spirit were spread around you as nature is spread around you today. Just as the mineral world, the plant world, and the animal world are around you today, so were the worlds of soul and spirit spread around you then. And what was once outside you is now your soul; you have made inward what to begin with was outside. This has now become your soul. The spirit, too, was once spread around you.*

Humanity as a creation has a part in its own origin, it receives itself out of the living, ensouled, and spiritual gaze of the Godhead; but in this process the human being is a subject who actively takes in, imitates, and learns. Thus, Rudolf Steiner says:

---

*   Steiner, *The Temple Legend*, pp. 112–113.

> You understand that this must be so. Take a child who is just learning to read and write. To begin with, all the equipment is around the child. Today, the child begins to learn to read. Nothing is yet in the child yet, but the teacher, the primers, and so forth are there. So it continues until what was outside the child has now been instilled within, and the child acquires the capacity to read.*

The world arises together with and at the same time as human beings—with the wealth of the human soul, the animal realm, the soul of the plant realm, the soul of the minerals. The life of the animals, plants, and minerals—including of the forces of growth and reproduction—arises with human life. The materiality of the mineral world arises with his bodily organs. Thus, for example, along with the human sense organs, the precious stones come about.

After this, human beings enter the nature that has densified to become sensuality. Step by step, the creator powers release humankind from paradise and into nature. Earthly incarnations of individual human souls begin. Increasingly, the mineral world becomes the human environment between birth and death, just as the spiritual world does between death and new birth. From each of their incarnations, human beings take transformations of mineral substances and forces along with them, incorporating them into the spiritual world and connecting them with what other human beings likewise bring along. Steiner discusses this at length in his lecture of October 21, 1921. In a lecture of 1904, he states:

> And what is now spread around you will become your inner life. You will take into yourself what is now the mineral kingdom, and it will become your inner part. The plant kingdom will become your inner part. What surrounds you in nature will become your inner being.**

---

*   Ibid., p. 113.
** Ibid., p. 114.

Thus, Steiner states that we human beings become what is spread out around us in nature.

> And so it is with nature, too. In times to come, we shall have within us what is now spread around us. We are souls; we spring from the world soul, and we drew it in when it was spread around us. The spirit was likewise drawn in, and nature, too, will be drawn in by us in order to stay within us as an active ability.*

The thoughts mentioned here from the lecture of 1904 display a further, fifth aspect of what will pass over into the future of a new world by way of the development of human beings on Earth—our experience of the mineral world through sense perception. This mineral earthly world surrounds human beings as the creation. In perceiving it, we draw something of it in from the stars and the crystals within us; perception becomes sensation, experience, recollection—it becomes our inner world and "active capacity." The transitory image that we permeate with thinking becomes permanent thought.

If I apprehend the nature of a rock crystal with my perception and knowing, in a sense that nature knows itself within me, and I know myself within it. Doing so, I apprehend my relatedness with that entity. The act of knowing the entities of nature is a real-world process within human beings. Through perception and knowledge, the world arises anew in us. Within human beings, this world—mainly the mineral world surrounding us, which we process, assimilate, and make a part of us—becomes human. This explains why the gemstones bear human names in the Apocalypse (the names of the twelve tribes and the twelve Apostles). This is the result of an *involution*—incorporation of the world into human beings. Later, it will become *evolution*—emanation of the newly formed as "active capacity" (cf. appendix 9). At the current level of future development, therefore, the mineral realm becomes world within human beings, which we draw in and work over. This transformation has to do with everything of mineral and

---

*   Ibid.

bodily nature. As we penetrate nature with our knowing, we gain power over it. Knowledge becomes power. Power becomes technology. Nevertheless, knowledge and power can be implemented in both a good and an evil sense. Both good and evil are consummated within humanity out of necessity and freedom. Both good and evil are shown in the twelve estuary images of the Apocalypse.

We can see in the estuary images how development and heightening occur, step-by-step, in the direction of goodness and in the direction of evil. This development and heightening ultimately lead to the fall of evil in the Book of Revelation, chapters 19 and 20, and at the end of chapter 20 to the resurrection of all the dead. Heavenly Jerusalem emerges from all of this. Whereas the mineral world is missing in the twelve estuary images—i.e., at the foundation of the human being—in the final image, or Heavenly Jerusalem, it is back, fully present, and visible. Even in the mineral world, something in the way of morality must lie hidden. To be sure, this element of morality does unfold the possibility of evil to the full extent, but it can also be overcome. Rudolf Steiner addresses this motif as well in the lecture of 1904:

> It is impossible to conceive what might happen in such circumstances if humankind has not by then reached selflessness. Only through the attainment of selflessness will it be possible to preserve humankind from the brink of destruction. The downfall of post-Atlantean culture will be caused by the lack of morality. The Lemurian race was destroyed by fire, the Atlantean by water; ours will be destroyed by the War of All against All, evil, and the struggle of one against another. Humanity will destroy itself in mutual strife. And the despairing thing—more desperately tragic than other catastrophes—will be that the blame will lie with human beings themselves.*

These few latter sentences touch on the absolutely decisive issue: human behavior. In the Creed spoken by The Christian Community,

---

*   Ibid., p. 115.

it goes like this: "He will in time unite for the advancement of the world with those whom, through their bearing, he can wrest from the death of matter."

"He" is Jesus Christ, Son of Man, the Lamb, the Bridegroom. He bears the reality of development within himself. He gives people the all-decisive impulse, the impulse of selflessness. Selflessness is, in fact, the highest human ideal. One can ponder on its nature and will find that selflessness is not possible without a self—that is, without an element that posits itself, wills, asserts, and realizes itself. Only a being that has become a self can also become selfless. An "I"-less entity is not selfless, because it does not determine its own selflessness. However, where is selflessness realized in humanity? Nowhere, actually, because the initial prerequisite for selflessness is self-assertion. How is a person to know and practice something for which there is no full reality? It is possible only if strength and virtue work and live all the same.

In the figure of Jesus Christ, selflessness is the fullest, deepest, highest, and most comprehensive reality. This is why the question of the human being can be answered only by the gaze upon Christ. It is through him alone that people, humankind and humanity, receive the impulse and the strength to lead into the future of the world. Through him alone are soul and spirit developed in the human body, such that they can take on gemstone character. Christ is, in the sense of the New Testament, the foundation stone and the cornerstone of the future construct of human individuality, community, and the entire cosmos. His selflessness guarantees the gemstone character of the human future and that of the world. Nevertheless, all this is conceivable only if not just human beings, but also the substance of the cosmos, are capable of spiritualization. It is not entropy that ultimately awaits world development, but rather spiritualization. Very early on (in 1909), the principle of the spiritualization was described by Rudolf Steiner (the reader is referred to appendix 12).

Chapter 8: Minerals

The gaze upon true selflessness in Christ also sheds light on the question of the mineral realm, since there is selflessness in the mineral, too. The stone, the crystal, the gemstone, and precious metal all bring selflessness to appearance in a pure form. They are selfless in their substance and essence, because they do not want to be anything but what they are. Moreover, as they are, they are completely and utterly at our disposal. When we view them in a pure way, they call to the human being: Become intentional in the enactment of your being—selfless, as we are when we enact our being.

In the stream of all streaming—that is, in water; in the crystal of all crystals, rock crystal; in the metal of all metals, gold; in the virtue of all virtues, the twelve precious stones; in the gemstone of all gemstones, jasper and its soul-spiritual corollaries of diamond, garnet, tourmaline, and opal—selflessness is in all of these, manifested in the gemstones and more or less hidden in all other minerals. Even loam is selfless, not just granite, basalt, and shale.

This selflessness allows the mineral realm to carry over, transformed, into the Heavenly City. It also allows it to be transformed within human beings to participate as a germinating force, making this future possible. This selflessness connects the question of the human being in relation to that of the precious stone. Through selflessness, the individual soul forces become virtue. All ideals become soul reality. Instincts, desires, and passions are transformed by selflessness into moral forces. Through selflessness, the various classifications of mineral entities become precious stones. Quartz becomes amethyst, chalcedony, chrysoprase, heliotrope, sard, and sardonyx.

Through selflessness, all human life forces become sensitivity for the life of nature beings and the gods, and thereby cooperation of human life force with the life and reproductive forces of, say, plants. In some striking manifestations of the interaction between human and plant, today humankind is starting to discover the very first germinal levels of things that even now are leading life with the minerals beyond the mineral epoch. Through selflessness, again, even the life of the senses is altered. The Gospel of Matthew contains the following important words of Christ:

> The eye is the lamp of the body. If your eyes are healthy, your whole body will be full of light. But if your eyes are unhealthy, your whole body will be full of darkness. If then the light within you is darkness, how great is that darkness! (Matt. 6:22–23)

Selflessness in sensory perception leads to transformed perception in the twelve senses of inner and outer.

Through selflessness, finally, even the material, mineral element of the human body is transformed. This occurred in a unique way through the Christ-being dwelling within the man Jesus of Nazareth. He was crucified and went through death and consummated the Resurrection in form and substance, in the figure, body, and blood of the person Jesus. This mystery is concealed in the selflessness of the mineral world. Jasper becomes diamond; this is unthinkable in mineral terms, but absolutely conceivable in spiritual terms. The diamond-born, pure form of the human body becomes a lantern. Thus, however, even bodily flesh becomes, in a sense, mineralized in the exact measure that it is spiritualized; the same holds true of human blood. Images for this transformation exist even today in the minerals tourmaline and garnet. Thus, in the future a mineral scale, or measure, will arise in the walls and the foundation stones of the Heavenly City, and this measure will at the same time be that of the human being; in the twelve gates of pearl, a mineral element will arise that is open both inwardly and outwardly. In this connection, we are reminded of a thought written by the medieval mystic Meister Eckhart: "A stone also has noble love, and the stone's noble love seeks the foundation." These words are capable of expression the whole future configuration of the human being, humankind, and the world in the Apocalypse.

What enables the stone's substance to accomplish these transformations—that is, to be this foundation and ideal? In the mineral, as it occurs in nature all material processes have reached an end. They have sunk below the reach of life, soul, and spirit. The power and striving to be purely material substance has been fulfilled in them. This is an expression of perfection and consummation, but at the same time a comprehensive sacrifice, since the life, soul, and spirit of the mineral exist separately from it. We can find them only as symbols in it. This is especially the case with gemstones and precious metals. They are the purest, noblest material image of themselves; the same holds for the crystalline shape as the most perfect form of pure spatial being. In no other sphere of nature is space—as space, as figuration on the one hand, and as a point-matrix framework on the other—as consummate as in the symmetries of the crystal. Thus the crystal is not merely an image and a mirror of its own special spatiality, but also the image and mirror of space overall—an image of the very idea of space. Both the polyhedral crystal figure and the point structure of the matrix are utterly complete and hence transparent to thought. The diagram of every X-ray analysis yields a perfect reproduction of this beauty.

The mineral as gemstone and precious metal is pure, selfless, noble, untainted, genuine, in a word: perfect. It is in no way sentimental to see in the grandeur of its mode of being something majestic, awe-inspiring, and sublime. Consequently, the highest Godhead can appear in mineral images. In the mineral as a sense-perceptible object, the sensory world is something of the very loftiest nature and is at the same time transparent to rational thinking. What has manifested in this way through the creation is transformed by human beings through knowing, technology, and work. The mineral world is taken into the human being and is reunited within with its original inwardness. In this process, however, something is added to it that it did not possess originally. In the previously quoted lecture of 1904, Rudolf Steiner says:

You will understand now how this is connected with the first example given: you build a church for others, not for yourself. You can take into [yourself] a world full of majesty, beauty, and splendor in you make the world majestic, beautiful, and splendid. To do something for the higher self is not selfish, because it is not done only for the self. This higher self will be united with all other higher selves, so that it is for all at the same time.

It is this that the Freemasons knew. The Freemason knew when he helped build the spiritualized mineral world that this would one day become the content of his soul—and to build means nothing but to spiritualize the mineral world. That is the significant thing. God once gave us the nature that surrounds us as mineral, plant, and animal nature. We take this [into ourselves]. It is not because of us that it is there; all we can do is to appropriate it for ourselves. But, what we ourselves create in the world, that is what will, through us, constitute our future being.*

Thus the mineral world can be spiritualized. Future human beings and humankind in general will not only have transformed themselves into building stones; they will also have transformed the mineral world into the stones of a building whose cornerstone is the Christ. The New Testament speaks of this.

In view of the pictures of the Revelation and the mineral world, one might be tempted to construe only the precious stones, precious metals, and, at best, water as capable of a future. However, in reality this world process has a bearing on the entire mineral realm. Not even precious stones themselves are conceived outside the mineral realm as a whole. They emerge from it as products of refinement, as the highest intensification, as blossoms blooming from the life stem of the mineral whole. They are as flames congealed from the fire of the Earth's becoming.** From the granite-pegmatite-shale process arise beryl, topaz, corundum, spinel (balas ruby), zircon, garnet, chrysolite, and tourma-

---

* Steiner, *The Temple Legend*, p. 113.
** Walther Cloos describes this comprehensively in *Kleine Edelsteinkunde* (Handbook of precious stones).

line—but also solid gold, silver, and copper. From the diabase (dolerite) process arise nephrite, jadeite, diopside, epidote, vesuvian. From the feldspar process arise sun-stone, moonstone, amazonite, and labradorite. From the ore process arise hematite, malachite, lazurite, chrysocolla, dioptase, and rhodonite, as well as gold, silver, and copper. From the quartz process arise rock crystal, amethyst, smokey quartz, citrine, and rose quartz. From the nodule formations of the melaphyree arise agates, chalcedony, carnelian, sard, onyx, and amethyst. From the volcanic processes arise diamond, as well as jasper, chalcedony, opal, and chrysolite. From contact and regional metamorphoses arise minerals such as emerald. Thus, we can proceed from the great variety of groups in the mineral world that are formed by specific processes to arrive at the precious stones; or we can proceed from the precious stones to the mothers from which they stem. Thus we can conceive of the gemstone substance in the Heavenly Jerusalem as depicting not only the respective gemstone itself, but also all the minerals from which it is derived. In the beryl, topaz, sapphire, and so on of the Heavenly City, the entire granite family from which they originate has also been transformed. The same holds true of all the previously mentioned motherly processes.

Chapter 9: Earth and Macrocosm

Our gaze on the totality of the mineral realm leads from the human influence on and into it back to its very own nature. At the same time, it is important to notice how manifested nature, in its attribute of the selflessness of its pure earthly material existence, is not the only future-directed nature of the mineral realm; rather, there is yet another, concealed aspect of its selflessness, which can be found through spiritual research.

Toward the end of his earthly life, from his sickbed Rudolf Steiner wrote leading (or guiding) thoughts and essays in letters to the members of the Anthroposophical Society. Among these writings we find

the brief essay "What is the Earth in Reality within the Macrocosm?"*
He speaks first of the significance of the earthly, which endows humanity with self-awareness. Then he raises the question of the Earth's significance for the macrocosm. Although measured according to spatial size, the Earth seems no more than a speck of dust; in reality, however, it is a seed of enormous germinating force, comparable to the acorn, which bears within itself germinating force for a huge tree.

The Earth with minerals, plants, animals, and humans lives in an outwardly visible way within the synthesizing and degrading processes of the year (spring, autumn). For example, in all that is synthesizing (growth and sprouting) in the plant world, there is always a surplus of germinating power. It is never possible for all the seeds of a single season to be used for the actual growth of the following season. Innumerable plant seeds that have formed wither externally without becoming plants. Suprasensory consciousness perceives that this surplus of germinal force flows out from the Earth's plant world to the starry cosmos. From these germinal forces comes "a newly arising macrocosm." The plants work at the formation of the cosmos of the future, the Heavenly Jerusalem, in a way that prepares its images (cf. appendix 13).

Such germinal forces proceed not only from the plant world, but also from the mineral realm. The mineral realm consumes nearly no life forces in earthly existence. To be sure, it was formed from these life forces in earlier stages of development, but then they withdrew, and as the mineral realm gradually begins to deteriorate today (natural radioactivity is an outer aspect of these processes), germinal force flows out from the mineral realm into the starry cosmos.

The suprasensory germinal forces emanating from the mineral realm determine the stream of the plant realm's germinal forces. In the previously mentioned essay [in *Anthroposophical Leading Thoughts*], Rudolf Steiner touches on the profound mystery hidden in the Saint John's Revelation image of the Heavenly City, which appears only in the

---

*   Steiner, *Anthroposophical Leading Thoughts*, pp. 167ff.

place that mentions the wood (the Tree of Life) that bears fruit twelve times each year without blossoming (Rev. 22:2), and whose leaves are "for the healing of the nations." This image shows that, basically, all mineral substances and structures are mineralized germinal forces, or growth forces. Wood, after all, is a plant with mineral character.

The gemstones, the water, the gold of the Eternal City are "plant-minerals"; they are soul-spiritual virtues of mineral structure, which have proceeded from etheric plant-mineral substance. This is likely the deepest mystery of this gigantic image. In the plant's germinal forces of a future world, the creator and growth force of the Godhead also lives in a mineral image. Through this, the plant-mineral contains in its spirit-substantiality the possibility, through a conception out of the being and essence of the Father and the Son, thus through a wedding and a meal, ultimately to provide the seed state for the future cosmos designated the "Jupiter Stage" of world development.*

The future world will be not only a new Earth, but also a new Heaven. In essence, "the heavens" are certainly the spiritual hierarchies, which manifest as light—with light being the highest of mineral manifestations. It emanates from the Sun and the fixed stars and is reflected by planets and moons. In a lecture of October 21, 1921, Steiner spoke of how earthly human experiences of the outer light of the Sun and starry world become inwardly available to human experience after death as the mutual consciousness among the hierarchies (cf. appendix 5).

Chapter 10: Evil and Minerals

Based on Steiner's Spiritual Science, we have tried to understand the construction of the Heavenly Jerusalem as carried by the Christ impulse in the earthly mineral realm, in the world of the stars, and in the human world of working and living. In pictures of the Revelation, evil unfolds

---

*   Cf. Steiner, *An Outline of Esoteric Science*.

parallel and simultaneously with goodness. The two streams flow into images of cities. Before the Heavenly Jerusalem appears the Infernal Babylon, and the mineral realm is woven into both streams of development. The images of unfolding evil display a fundamental difference from those of the unfolding of goodness. Evil has no source images; it appears gradually in the series of stream images until, in the series of transit images, the mediating figures increasingly reveal themselves. It sneaks, as it were, into the course of evolution.

In the letters to the seven churches, the influence and process of evil is still delineated as errors on the part of human communities. Only with the opening of the seven seals does evil itself gradually begin to emerge. The fourth chapter of his book *The Apocalypse of St. John,* Emil Bock discusses the archetypes, symbols and mirror images, and the revelatory substance of the first four seals. There he shows how God's thoughts pass into human thoughts. In the image of the white horse, the thoughts are still God's own within the human being; in that of the red horse, they are thoughts immersed in the emotional, egoistic sphere of the human soul; and in the image of the black horse, thought has arrived in the realm of materialistic practicality and self-interest. Evil itself then appears through these pictures. The lord of the thoughts that appears in the pictures of the red and the black horses is no longer the human being but rather subjective and objective evil, the luciferic and ahrimanic powers in the anthroposophic sense. However, those powers do not show themselves directly yet, but only as a reflection in human knowledge.

In addition, with the picture of the fourth, pale horse, Death appears as its rider Hades, the "rootless intellectuality" detached from humanity and lived out in the mechanical world as an emancipated intelligence become objective. This is the result of the thought world's descent from the Godhead, through the human being, and down to the adversarial powers (cf. Rev. 6:1–8).

Bock then goes on to refer to the further unfolding of the motifs of intelligence from the machine world to the world of horse-like demons that come forth during the blasts of the fifth and sixth trumpets in chapter 11. In the sense of the primal Greek text: These locusts are as horses; the horses and the riders appeared to me in seeing consciousness as fire-red, hyacinth-colored, and sulfur-yellow armor (Rev. 9:7). Even here, however, the actual working of evil are shrouded—from human to mechanical intelligence to a demonic host of specters. Moreover, evil itself does not yet appear fully, even in the revelations of the sixth trumpet, although it has had a world-forming effect. It is proclaimed in advance as "beast that comes up from the Abyss" (Rev. 11:7) and appears in a "city figuratively called Sodom and Egypt." Thus, the emergence of evil becomes definite first in the human soul life of thought; it is displayed in the pure intelligence of human consciousness, then in the sphere of the machine and the world of demons, and ultimately in the construction of a city. From the sphere of the soul, thinking, and the world of work, another sphere is formed through collaboration with evil, which evil appropriates from the mineral world. This happens as human beings take hold of the mineral world and unite with it. Pertaining to this, Bock says:

> Of course, it is not the purpose of the Apocalypse to dissuade people from employing technology. It would be foolish not to use of the machines that our intelligence has constructed. But when we learn to see our mechanized civilization as a reflected image of our own human condition, we will be have to acknowledge that we cannot use technology and at the same time continue to live as true human beings unless we also add to this outer culture a strengthening and cultivation of our spirit that provides a balance to increased such mechanization—unless we can reunite the intelligence that is slipping away from us with the reinforced spiritual core of our being.*

At the sounding of the seventh trumpet, evil must reveal itself as an entity. This self-revelation also occurs in three steps—in the image of chapter 12 of the dragon as a kind of preposterous whole, consisting

---

* Bock, *The Apocalypse of St. John*, p. 60.

of irreconcilable opposites (reptile and bird), and in chapter 13, in which evil appears in its ultimate true form as two different beasts: one ascending from the sea, the other from land.*

The question of evil's past in the transformation of the mineral world poses a problem that belongs to an area concealed deeply from our modern human consciousness, including scientific consciousness. The chapter on the spiritual essence of the mineral realm attempted to explain the kind of mental pictures that can be formed if one bases this realm on the primacy of spirit, life, and the soul. Knowledge derived from the world surrounding the human being must not be inquired after in one sole direction, as modern physics does by means of investigative methods and concepts capable of finding only measurable effects of a nature it observes indirectly. True, its regularities can be precisely expressed mathematically, but its very structures are reliant on the construction of hypothetical models. This holds for thermal energy, electricity, magnetism, and nuclear power.

Measured against a comprehensive knowledge of nature, atomic theory, quantum theory, and the theory of relativity lead only to subsensory nature, which in Rudolf Steiner's sense one can also call *subnature*. Its research methods seem at first to follow the primacy of physical substance, of matter, but in the course of examination its objects of investigation display less and less material character, and ultimately dissolve into energetic processes, whose effects are indeed half-material, but in their essence and regularities are purely spiritual and mathematic. Thus, we end up at the primacy of the spirit, although our point of departure was the primacy of physical matter. Nonetheless, those who approach nature intending to inquire after the spirit are led not to electricity, magnetism, and atomic energy, but to life, soul, and spirit. Those who isolate subnature from nature are involved more with forces and entities that are either waste products of nature or even antagonistic toward life—or even more, are absolutely destructive and

---

*   Cf. Alfred Schütze, *The Enigma of Evil*.

represent powers over which humanity no longer has any control. This is the direction in which human technological history has developed.

To begin with, any tool is an extension or specialization of the human limbs. When the elements (fire, air, water) are drawn into human technology, a tool begins to free itself from humanity, and as forces of nature are applied or implemented in machines, the energy source is also freed from humankind and animal (steam engine, windmill, water wheel); but when electricity was discovered and applied, subnature became the source of energy (such as the electric motor). Thus an energetically autonomous area arose—external to human beings and below the world of nature—that was derived from nature but, in this configuration, was merely added to it. The moment we turned utterly toward subnature by drawing on fusion technology, we gained machines withdrawn from human control that are not only isolated from natural occurrence, but also confront it (the mineral realm included) in a destructive, hostile way.

This shows clearly that this subnature can exist only in connection with another area of "nature." This other area immediately enters our field of vision when, within the sensory world, we look not for the subsensory but for the suprasensory. In this way, we move from the mineral realm into the plant, animal, and human realms, where laws different from those in subnature hold. This is how life, soul, and spirit can be found. Goethe took these paths consistently, and Steiner, building on Goethe's work, expanded them. If we join the two spheres of "subnature" and "supranature," real "nature" is the result. We reach something spiritual on either path of investigation, but one leads to destructive forces, the other to constructive, healing ones (cf. appendix 31).

When kinetic heat, electricity, magnetism, and nuclear forces manifested as subsensory powers, it became clear that they are associated with evil. For modern natural-scientific and technological consciousness, the notion is doubtlessly absurd that powers of this kind are also components of the whole world constitution. Nevertheless, they have their rightful place in the constitution of nature, because they are compensated there by the powers of goodness. However, when human beings on the downward paths of intelligence regard these powers as the only ones that exert any influence, and when we isolate them from nature in order to operate with them, we fail to notice that in doing so we have stumbled into the realm of the luciferic and ahrimanic powers, since we think of these subsensory forces as neutral and as dangerous only when misused or intentionally abused. They are not neutral, however; rather, they are one-sided forces of atomization. Their inner aspect manifests as the spirit of resistance, pertinacity, isolation, and destruction. So long as the subsensory forces are active as the basis of all nature, they are bridled and serve to solidify the manifestation of the suprasensory. When they are unleashed, they become the demise of the world, including the mineral realm. Before this, they are at least subservient, if not neutral; afterward, they are evil.

This thought seems less absurd once we realize that the four subsensory power influences have their respective counterparts in the suprasensory. They are merely the matrix—the substrate or buttress—needed by the suprasensory for it to be lived out sense-perceptibly as spirit, soul, and life. Without the service of the adversarial forces, the Good is not fully capable of assuming bodily shape. To be sure, plant, animal, and humanity also have a part in the buttress that is subnature, inasmuch as they bear mineral corporeality; but since the elements of their suprasensory constitution (life, soul, and spirit) are also active in their mineral components, they are able to maintain a position above the existential boundary between nature and subnature. The plant's hold is life; the animal's hold is life and soul; the human being's hold is life, soul, and spirit.

Here, the nature of the selflessness that manifests in the mineral realm as an entity becomes understandable. The mineral has entrusted itself to the buttressing powers of subnature. This is why it seems at first glance—precisely to natural-scientific research—to be no more than what we can get from it, depending on how we treat it—subnature, matter as conceived in atomic theory, quantum theory, the theory of relativity, and so on; it seems to be no more than electricity, magnetism, and nuclear power.

However, in its crystalline form, in color, luster, and other attributes, the mineral displays elements lost in the descent into its subnature. This leads research to the conviction that subnature is the full reality of the mineral realm, while its qualitative attributes are mere influences on the human senses. An unmediated phenomenological observation contradicts this conception. Subnature is not the mineral's essence; rather, it is a regularity of conditions and possibilities that enable the mineral to fetch its supranature into the sphere of its corporeality. What it brings to qualitative manifestation is selflessly reliant on the help of subnature. The mineral is so selfless (i.e., good) that it can surrender to the conditions of evil without becoming evil itself; it can, precisely in this way, manifest in all its purity Thus, the deepest essence of the mineral world reveals itself: it is the world of the Good come to rest as its purest qualitative manifestation in the realm of evil. It is the image of life in the sphere of death, the image of soul in the sphere of the soulless, the image of spirit in the sphere of the anti-spirit.

Thus the powers and beings of evil have a share in the mineral realm. But this share involves, first, carrying, serving, and mediating. The selfless nature of the mineral element forces these powers and beings to be selfless. But if human beings begin to intervene in the mineral world so that its corporeality bursts, processing it in a way that its qualitative attributes disappear and all that can be comprehended and used of it by humanity is its share in the subsensory, then evil ascends from matter, works back on the life, soul, and spirit of nature and humankind, and confuses, darkens, and seduces them. It is only now that the power of evil becomes actively evil. By virtue of its own nature, this might has the power to hinder both the human transit through the mineral world to a future world, and the mineral world's transit through the human being to a future world. The power of evil tries to insinuate itself to replace nature and to fetter human beings to this "spurious" or "partial nature," which we have brought on ourselves, and thus to hinder the mineral from attaining its intended purpose of becoming the seed for a new cosmos. The mineral can be disintegrated by the subnature it contains; the mineral world can be delivered up to heat death, can become slag and dust. Modern nuclear physics is aware of such prospects (cf. appendix 31).

The Revelation of St. John is aware of them, too. After evil has been revealed in chapters 12 and 13 as a might of soul and spirit in twofold primal form, the image activity of the "city of Sodom and of Egypt" passes into the second "city," the Great Babylon. Evil has built a city. With human assistance, it has torn the subsensory, sub-natural powers away from the mineral world that normally inhere in it, united with them the human soul and spiritual forces that have become evil, and in this way created a geological layer that means something quite new in contrast to nature. "The great city split into three parts, and the cities of the nations collapsed. God remembered Babylon the Great and gave her the cup filled with the wine of the fury of his wrath" (Rev. 16:19). The edifice of the city comes about, but it deteriorates from the very beginning of its own accord into three parts. The might of subnature has also taken hold of human beings. They have become evil in soul and spirit and are included in the edifice of evil. In the technological, mechanistic, and material world, human beings live with bodily existence, work, will, and consciousness, as well as with the noblest ideals. Humankind has been seized by the most reckless of pragmatic thinking, the most materialistic kind of mechanistic thinking, the shrewdest, most sophisticated technology, as well as socialism and self-centeredness directed wholly toward outer existence. The ideals have become a rhetorical embellishment and illusionary superficiality. Mass media, power politics, economic egoism, and sentimentality are the reality of consciousness. The consequence is the socialization of art, science, religion, the state, and the economy. They sparkle like gems on the raiment and crown of the great mother of whores, Babylon, and her kings:

> Then the angel carried me away in the Spirit into a wilderness. There I saw a woman sitting on a scarlet beast that was covered with blasphemous names and had seven heads and ten horns. The woman was dressed in purple and scarlet, and was glittering with gold, precious stones and pearls. She held a golden cup in her hand. (Rev. 17:3–5)

Then, in Revelation 17:15, it says, "The waters you saw, where the prostitute sits, are peoples, multitudes, nations and languages." Water, gold, gemstones, pearls, colors—it is the mineral world "word for word," the same as in the Heavenly Jerusalem.

In what way are the two cities different? In *The Apocalypse of St. John*, Emil Bock tells us that, whereas the mineral world is a city in the Heavenly Jerusalem, here in the city of Babylon it is a mountain.* "The seven heads are seven hills on which the woman sits…(Rev. 17:9)." Emil Bock discusses this motif extensively (cf. appendix 15).

Thus the mineral world can take two courses in the world process. One leads from its nature to its subnature; it becomes "appearance" inside the human soul, a false gemstone. And in work, in all mechanical science and technology, it becomes "mountain"; it becomes the bearer of atheism and materialism, precisely through the subnature inherent in it.

The other course it can run leads from nature into the future. Through work, by passing through the human being by cultic action, the mineral-material world is taken to a point where the rigidified morality within it is transformed as it transits, carried into a spiritual form of the future. In the subnature of the mineral world, evil is good. It is the buttress for the manifestation of the supranature of the mineral world; as such, it becomes a member of the Earth. Through its supranature, the mineral is a member of the hierarchies, the world of the stars, the plant spirits, and beings of the fixed stars. Subnature (thermal technology, electricity, magnetism, nuclear power) serves the manifestation of supranature (the life, soul, and spirit of the mineral can appear in

---

* Bock, *The Apocalypse of St. John*, p. 148.

sense-perceptible form). Supranature uses subnature to reveal life, soul, and spirit in corporeal existence.

The future depends on human beings and on whether we follow the impulse of evil, which becomes truly evil only when unleashed from nature, or whether we follow the impulses of Christ by seeking and finding the good, the virtuous, the divine as mineral manifestation and by developing our own moral nature in all that we do in and with the mineral world. So doing, we unite the germinal force for a future cosmos ever-more strongly with the supranature of the mineral realm, from the stones to the stars. Knowledge of and differentiation between the true being of subnature and supranature are the necessary prerequisites for such a development.

The essays Rudolf Steiner wrote on his sickbed with *Anthroposophical Leading Thoughts* for the members of the Anthroposophical Society (mentioned previously in connection with the germinal power of the mineral realm), include the final essay he wrote in March 1925, shortly before his death. It is titled "From Nature to Subnature" and describes the demand placed on modern human consciousness. It includes this comment: "We must understand subnature for what it really is. This we can do only if we rise, in spiritual knowledge, at least as far into extra-earthly supranature as we have descended, in technical sciences, into subnature."* Natural science calls for Spiritual Science; Spiritual Science calls for natural science (cf. appendices 14 and 16).

CHAPTER 11: SUMMARY

What is meant by "construction of the Heavenly Jerusalem through the mineral realm"? This:

1. Along with human beings, the mineral arises as a gift of the gods.
2. The mineral emerges from the sphere of the gods of origin, the "suprasensory," and descends into the subsensory sphere of

---

*   Steiner, *Anthroposophical Leading Thoughts*, p. 218.

the counter-gods. This causes it to become sense-perceptible. Human being consummate the same descent with respect to bodily nature, causing our consciousness, also, to be annexed to the mineral world through the body. However, the mineral world also bears within itself the possibility of becoming spiritualized. (cf. appendix 18).

3. Human beings take spirit, soul, and life with them into sense-perceptible, earthly, mineral existence. We inhabit the mineral world with all the members of our being. The mineral renounces this, leaving its life, soul, and spiritual nature behind in the suprasensory, cosmic element by disconnecting from it and entering in a purely physical way into the sense-perceptible earthly world. The mineral is existentially selfless.

4. Having become sense-perceptible Earth, the mineral gives human beings their earthly impulse and the impulse of self-awareness of the "I." It is the confrontation with the mineral that endows human beings with the experience that they are an "I." Human beings no longer perceive the spiritual aspect of the mineral.

5. Human beings, by allowing the mineral to pass through them (with their body, their work, their experiencing and knowing) themselves pass through the mineral with their consciousness and experiencing, their body, their work and activity, and their knowledge (cf. appendix 19).

6. Through this occurrence, the possibility for two different paths begins. On one path, the mineral world and human beings go through a state that can become the seed condition for a future world. The other possibility is that human beings are exposed to the danger of considering the subnatural influence of the adversarial powers to be all that exists. However, this influence is good only for rendering suprasensory–supranature sense-perceptible. It becomes evil when human beings permit themselves to be drawn down by it from the sense-perceptible to the subsensory sphere, thus caught in chains by it. The mineral realm then

becomes an opportunity to believe in matter and the possibility of materialism, with all its consequences, while the material realm is itself drawn into the power spheres of the adversarial powers of evil (cf. appendix 20).

7. If human beings avoid this danger in all that is sense-perceptible through knowledge of the suprasensory—knowledge of the being and essence of subnature—and by distinguishing among supranature, nature, and subnature, we gain a connection with the Christ being. In this way, we can guide the mineral in its transit through us and through our work in technology, culture, and ritual action into a future that is carried by the seed force of the plant realm and imbued with the cosmic future impulse of the Christ being. This causes the seed of the future cosmos, which will proceed from the demise of the present one, to be planted (cf. appendix 21).

8. This seed appears to the seeing consciousness of the Apocalyptist in magnificent imaginations, which manifest as veiled in images of the mineral realm. Their springing forth, formation, and consummation is the mineral process of the Apocalypse (cf. appendix 31).

Part 4 of this treatise will address the possibilities provided by the individual building stones. The overall principle at stake can be reexamined in each individual component.

PART 4
BUILDING ELEMENTS
OF HEAVENLY JERUSALEM

In Part Four, the individual building elements are not listed in the sequence in which they occur in the description given by the Apocalypse. Rather, the point of departure is the elements of water and crystal, which pervade and illuminate the whole, and in so doing set the common context for what manifests in the other building elements. It is according to these points of view that the following discussion of the building elements is structured. The sequence is as follows:

1. WATER
   Selflessness in Sensing and Bearing Life
2. CRYSTAL
   Selflessness in World Mediation
3. JASPER
   Mineral Names in Light of the Apocalypse
4. JASPER EXPERIENCE
   In Diamond, Tourmaline, Garnet, and Opal
5. THE TWELVE PRECIOUS STONES
   *Cosmic Jewelry in the Foundation Stones
   of the Heavenly Jerusalem*
6. GOLD
   Sevenfold Unity in the "I"
7. THE PEARL
   Purified Pain—Sense Organ for the World Essence
8. WOOD
   Death from Life—Life from Death

Muhammad's Song

See the rock-born stream!
As the gleam
Of a star so bright
Kindly spirits
High above the clouds
Nourished him while youthful
In the copse between the cliffs.

Young and fresh
From the clouds he dances
Down upon the marble rocks;
Then towered Heaven
Leaps exulting.

Through the mountain passes
He chases the colored pebbles,
And, advancing like a chief,
Tears his brother streamlets with him
In his course.

In the valley down below
'Neath his footsteps spring the flowers,
And the meadow
In his breath finds life.
Yet no shady vale can stay him,
Nor can flowers,
Round his knees all-softly twining
With their loving eyes detain him;
To the plain his course he takes,
Serpent winding,

Social streamlets
Join his waters. And now moves he
Over the plain in silvery glory,
And the plain in him exults,
And the rivers from the plain,
And the streamlets from the mountain,
Shout with joy, exclaiming: "Brother,
Brother, take your brethren with you,
With you to your aged father,
To the everlasting ocean,
Who, with arms outstretching far,
Awaits us;
Ah, in vain those arms lie open
To embrace his yearning children;
For the thirsty sand consumes us
In the desert waste; the sunbeams
Drink our life blood; hills around us
Into lakes would dam us! Brother,
Take your brethren of the plain,
Take your brethren of the mountain
With you, to your father's arms!"

Let all come, then!—
And now swells he
Lordlier still; yes, even a people
Bears his regal flood on high!
And in triumph onward rolling,
Names to countries he gives—cities
Spring to light beneath his foot.

Ever, ever, on he rushes,
Leaves the towers' flame-tipped summits,
Marble palaces, the offspring
Of his fullness, far behind.

Cedar houses bear the Atlas
On his giant shoulders; fluttering
In the breeze far, far above him
Thousand flags are gaily floating,
Bearing witness to his might.

And so bears he his brethren,
All his treasures, all his children,
Wildly shouting, to the bosom
Of his long-expectant sire.
—Johann Wolfgang von Goethe (1772)

Chapter 1: Water

Selflessness in Sensing and Bearing Life

Images of Water in the Old and New Testaments

In the Apocalyptic descriptions of the Heavenly Jerusalem, the opening sentences of chapter 22, water appears, having been preceded by the images of solid minerals, precious stones, gold, and pearls. Water flows forth from the chair of God and the Lamb and flows through the city.

In the Old Testament, the book of the prophet Ezekiel contains a description of spiritual worlds and beings that is most intimately related to the Revelation of St. John. Ezekiel's vision is defined by two great images. In the first chapter a kind of source image is developed. The One sitting on the throne occurs here too, shown in humanlike form, bright as light and radiant from His loins upward and downward. He too is shown round about by a rainbow. The images of the four Cherubim with the fourfold countenance—human, lion, bull, eagle—have preceded. "Below" the Cherubim and together with them, the four wheels are at work, above their sphere there hovers the crystal Heaven. Then, starting at chapter 40 in Ezekiel, there appears the great estuary image, the mighty temple with its countless vestibules, gates, doors, halls and passageways, and with the Holiest of Holies.

> The man brought me back to the entrance to the temple, and I saw water coming out from under the threshold of the temple toward the east (for the temple faced east). The water was coming down from under the south side of the temple, south of the altar. He then brought me out through the north gate and led me around the outside to the outer gate facing east, and the water was trickling from the south side.

As the man went eastward with a measuring line in his hand, he measured off a thousand cubits and then led me through water that was ankle-deep. He measured off another thousand cubits and led me through water that was knee-deep. He measured off another thousand and led me through water that was up to the waist. He measured off another thousand, but now it was a river that I could not cross, because the water had risen and was deep enough to swim in—a river that no one could cross. He asked me, "Son of man, do you see this?"

Then he led me back to the bank of the river. When I arrived there, I saw a great number of trees on each side of the river. He said to me, "This water flows toward the eastern region and goes down into the Arabah, where it enters the Dead Sea. When it empties into the sea, the salty water there becomes fresh. Swarms of living creatures will live wherever the river flows. There will be large numbers of fish, because this water flows there and makes the salt water fresh; so where the river flows everything will live. Fishermen will stand along the shore; from En Gedi to En Eglaim there will be places for spreading nets. The fish will be of many kinds—like the fish of the Mediterranean Sea. But the swamps and marshes will not become fresh; they will be left for salt. Fruit trees of all kinds will grow on both banks of the river. Their leaves will not wither, nor will their fruit fail. Every month they will bear fruit, because the water from the sanctuary flows to them. Their fruit will serve for food and their leaves for healing." (Ez. 47:1–12)

In the vision of Ezekiel, the water streams from the temple. In the Revelation of John, by contrast, it flows directly from the throne of the fatherly divinity; this water-entity appears in the Apocalypse in images of both streaming and the fountain or well:

The hair on his head was white like wool, as white as snow, and his eyes were like blazing fire. His feet were like bronze glowing in a furnace, and his voice was like the sound of rushing waters. (Rev. 1:14–15)

In his right hand he held seven stars, and coming out of his mouth was a sharp, double-edged sword. His face was like the Sun shining in all its brilliance. When I saw him, I fell at his feet as though dead. Then he placed his right hand on me and said: "Do not be afraid. I am the First and the Last." (Rev. 7:16–17)

The third angel sounded his trumpet, and a great star, blazing like a torch, fell from the sky on a third of the rivers and on the springs of water—the name of the star is Wormwood. A third of the waters turned bitter, and many people died from the waters that had become bitter. (Rev. 8:10–11)

Then from his mouth the serpent spewed water like a river to overtake the woman and sweep her away with the torrent. But the earth helped the woman by opening its mouth and swallowing the river that the dragon had spewed from his mouth. (Rev. 12:15–16)

Then I looked and there before me was the Lamb, standing on Mount Zion, and with him 144,000 who had his name and his Father's name written on their foreheads. And I heard a sound from Heaven like the roar of rushing waters and like a loud peal of thunder. The sound I heard was like that of harpists playing their harps. (Rev. 14:1–2)

Then I saw another angel flying in midair, and he had the eternal gospel to proclaim to those who live on the Earth—to every nation, tribe, language, and people. He said in a loud voice, "Fear God and give him glory, because the hour of his judgment has come. Worship him who made the heavens, the earth, the sea, and the springs of water." (Rev. 14:6–7)

The third angel poured out his bowl on the rivers and springs of water, and they became blood. (Rev. 16:4)

One of the seven angels who had the seven bowls came and said to me, "Come, I will show you the punishment of the great prostitute, who sits by many waters. With her the kings of the Earth committed adultery, and the inhabitants of the Earth were intoxicated with the wine of her adulteries." (Rev. 17:1–2)

He who was seated on the throne said, "I am making everything new!" Then he said, "Write this down, for these words are trustworthy and true." He said to me, "It is done. I am the Alpha and the Omega, the Beginning and the End. To the thirsty I will give water without cost from the spring of the water of life." (Rev. 21:5–6)

In connection with this single motif, we can trace a kind of development and transformation throughout the entire Book of Revelation and see how the water issuing from the primal font of existence—the throne—and pervading the future city becomes an all-encompassing streaming of life.

The Name Water

The English word for water has been formed by two Indo-Germanic influences.* The one leads back to the streaming of the consonants *S* and *T*: Old High German *wazzar,* Gothic *wato,* German *Wasser,* Old Friesian *wetir,* Old Nordic *vatu,* Swedish *vatten,* and Hethitic *watar.* The other leads more to the sounds of *U* and *D*: Old Indian *udan* and *udakam,* Old Bulgarian *woda,* Latin *unda.* Only ancient Greek aspirates this form: *hydor.* This is why the word *water* is traced etymologically back to two roots; first to *WED* and *UD,* which means "gush" "billow," "soak," or "moisten." Moreover, the other root is *UGWE,* also *WEG* and *UG,* which means "to be moist" (in Sanskrit *ugschade,* in Latin *uvidus*). Thus, one sees that the primal Indo-European root sounds frame the image in the one case more as the swelling, wetting, gushing activity of water, and in the other case more as water's own state of being wet and watery. We are hardly in a position today to trace with our feeling the way the primal languages expressed this. The easiest way to approach the profound mystery of the essence of water is via the pure vocalic and consonantal aspects of language.

---

* Translator's note: Obviously, in the original German text the author speaks of the history of the German word for water. It seems equally clear that the history of the English word *water* be dealt with in this translation, since it is for speakers of English. As German and English have a common origin, all that needed to be done was to switch the German word *Wasser* and English *water* in this passage.

Water in the Mineral Realm

In the entire mineral world, there are only two entities that appear on the Earth's surface in a liquid state at normal temperatures. One is found in the form of minute droplets in the erosion zones of cinnabar deposits: cinnabarite (sulfide, HgS), oar of the metal quicksilver, or mercury. The other covers the Earth in gigantic masses, fills the air in the densest and most delicate way, and flows as precipitation down to the Earth and into her, and back out of her into the oceans: water. We might say that water holds a unique position in the mineral realm. It has a primal relationship with the warmth states occurring on Earth; its melting point lies within the normal temperature range of the air. In addition, it evaporates at all normal temperature ranges, and so it is always able to pass through any of the three aggregate states—solid, liquid, and gaseous. In this way, water never comes to rest. On one hand, it is exposed to the air and its movements; on the other, to gravity and the movements it causes. If we allow for sufficiently long periods of time, we can say that even the Earth's glaciers are involved in this unceasing circulatory movement.

The average depth of the oceans, which cover three-quarters of the Earth's surface, is approximately three or four miles. If all the Earth's water were evenly distributed, the surface of the Earth would be submerged more than one-and-a-half miles below the water's surface. This continuous movement of water has an inner balance; it equalizes itself in such a way that there is always a nearly constant amount of water in the oceans, air, and fresh water, and ice.

Although the solid minerals at rest make up the Earth's organs, the gaseous minerals circulate within themselves, the fluid mineral, water, moves back and forth between the aggregate states, all the while maintaining the equilibrium mentioned above. Water has a balance sheet, an economics. H. Pleiss and E. Schenk* have worked out and published the figures of this balance sheet, based on the following questions:

---

* Pleiss, *Der Kreislauf des Wassers in der Natur* (The circulation of water in nature), and E. Schenk, "Wasser und das Gesicht der Erde" (Water and the Face of the Earth), in Schröder (ed.), *Wasser*.

Where "is" water?
- 7.8% in the air
- 27.1% on the Earth's surface (rivers, lakes, ground water)
- 8.6% in the shallow sea at depths up to one mile
- 52.4% in the deep sea (1.25–3.75 miles)
- 4.1% in the ocean trenches (3.75–6.25 miles)

How does water "flow" between the land and the sea?
- Each year, a 3.5-foot-thick layer evaporates from the oceans' total surfaces, which makes 91,887 cubic miles.
- Of this layer, 32 inches fall back into the ocean, and the remaining 10 inches, or 8,877 cubic miles, onto the land.
- One-third of this enters the rivers and thus ultimately the ocean. The other two-thirds enter the air by evaporating from the land, and slightly less than half of this falls into the ocean, the other half returns to the land.

How does water flow at all?
- One can see the entirety by looking at the rivers. The total of the Earth's rivers contain 408 cubic miles in a flowing state.
- The Earth's lakes contain much greater water masses; 12 cubic miles in Lake Constance (Bodensee) alone.
- The quantity of water on the continents (ice masses, lakes, rivers, ground water) amounts to 8,013 cubic miles.
- There are 3,120 cubic miles circulating constantly in the air as water vapor, clouds, and precipitation, an enormous amount compared with the rivers at 4,080 cubic miles; eight times the amount of the water in the rivers is constantly hovering in the air.

Considerably more water is found in living beings, particularly plants—approximately thirty times more than in all the rivers. These facts show that the main mass of water not found in the oceans flows not in the rivers, but rather in the lakes, air, and plant world. The oceans, too, are entirely integrated into this whole; the main mass of water within them is in constant exchange (328,680,479 cubic miles).

Each ocean within itself, its currents, and all the oceans together are interwoven through extraordinarily complicated circulation. The most important warm and cold currents are shown in any good atlas. The Gulf Stream alone conducts 20 to 22 cubic miles of water into the Atlantic Ocean each second, almost a hundred times the amount poured into the oceans by all the rivers of the Earth.

This brief overview shows how, in all of water as a mineral, a meaningful whole is at work. This whole is set at a level higher than that of the physical processes of circulation, and it constantly maintains the proper relationship among them, between the atmosphere and the Earth, and among all entities in the entire sphere of the living.

The Physical and Chemical Properties of Water

Water is odorless, tasteless, transparent, colorless, and, in larger quantities, a delicate blue. The blueness of lakes and seas is the reflection of the sky's blue on the water, not its own color. Nevertheless, water in nature is never pure—not anywhere. It always contains dissolved or swollen components. Cloud-water in the air always contains gases that are dissolved in it. On the Earth, it takes in salts and dust particles of dead and living matter; then it becomes cloudy and colored. The more calcium and magnesium salts it dissolves, the "harder" it becomes. Likewise, all freshwater contains dissolved and gaseous minerals; even precipitation water (rain, snow, and hail) is never entirely pure. Anyone who wants pure water must clean it artificially through filtration or distillation.

An especially interesting characteristic of the water in the world's oceans is its remarkable self-will relating to what it dissolves and carries within itself. First, the range within which the salt content of seawater varies is very narrow. In the open ocean, it never drops below 32 thousandths and never exceeds 38 thousandths—an average of 35 thousandths. This ratio changes only in extreme areas, such as the Red Sea. There it reaches 40 thousandths. Near melting glaciers, the ratio is close to zero thousandths. The normal range, however, is always reestablished in the open oceans.

Second, there is always a remarkably constant quantitative ratio among the various salts of seawater solution for each ton of water: NaCl, 62 pounds; MgCl, 8.4 pounds; $MgSO_4$, 3.8 pounds; $CaSO_4$, 2.8 pounds; K_2SO_4, 1.8 pounds; $CaCO_3$, 0.27 pounds; KBr, 0.22 pounds; $SrSO_4$, 0.62 pounds; H_3BO_3, 0.06 pounds. The constancy of these proportions is a mystery.

At least as important is the third fact: the salts previously mentioned are all properly dissolved—that is, ionized—and in such way that the *cations* (bases) are always stronger than the *anions* (acids). This is why seawater is never acidic but weakly alkaline. In addition to the main components of this stable equilibrium of the approximately twelve elements (Cl, Na, Mg, S, Ca, K, Br, Sr, B, O, H, N), the last three of these also occur as air dissolved in the water as gases: Si, F, and Li are found in traces.*

In its circulation, water not only passes through the lithosphere, atmosphere, and biosphere, but, as mentioned, also constantly passes through the three aggregate states of ice, water, and vapor. The way it does this shows its relationship to warmth, on one hand, and to pressure, on the other, to which it is exposed in the air in its vapor state. Under the normal pressure of one atmosphere, water boils at 100° C (212° F) and freezes at 0° C (32° F). At any given temperature and pressure, water itself has a specific vapor pressure—the degree to which it escapes a fluid or solid state into a gaseous state. A sort of equilibrium exists among solid, liquid, and gaseous states at 0.0099° C (32.018° F), or just above the freezing point. At this temperature, it has a vapor pressure of 4.58 mm, and the relationship among its vapor, heat, and

---

* Cf. F. Rosenkrans, *Das Meer in seiner Nutzung, Studienbücher Geographie für Lehrer* (The sea and its use, study books in geography for teachers), vol. 14, p. 42, which states, "In addition to the substances mentioned up to now, it is probable that seawater also contains all the other elements" (in grams per ton, P, 0.02; J, 0.05; Zn, 0.01; Cu, 0.01; Mn, 0.005; Ag, 0.0002; Au [gold], 0.00001.)

ice states does not change; a kind of rigidifying occurs among these aggregate states. By increasing the pressure, the freezing point can be reduced by 0.0007° C (32.001° F) per atmosphere, so that at 2,000 atmospheres ice melts at -20° C (-4° F) and can, by contrast, also be cooled to this same temperature without congealing. In sealed kettles at high pressure, the boiling point can be raised to above 100° C. The critical temperature is 374.1° C (705.38° F) at 218.3 atmospheres of pressure. In this state, water has a specific weight of 0.32 g (0.0113 oz.). Higher than this temperature, it cannot be made liquid no matter how much pressure is applied.

Water's relationship to its so-called specific warmth is a peculiar one. The specific warmth of a substance is the amount of heat it takes to increase the temperature of a gram of this substance by one degree. Even the heat of fusion for ice is considerably higher than for any other liquid. The same holds true of the heat of vaporization when it vaporizes and boils, where the specific warmth of water behaves quite abnormally. Up to 35° C, it takes less heat per degree, while from 35° C upward it takes more and more per degree, until the boiling point (100° C) is reached and vaporization begins.

Moreover, water's inner mobility (its thickness and viscosity) in relation to pressure and temperature is extremely peculiar. Contrary to all other liquids, water at first becomes increasingly mobile under increasing pressure and up to 35° C (95° F). Actually, it ought to become thicker and thicker, the greater the pressure applied to it. But the opposite is the case. It only does become thicker and thicker at temperatures above 35° C. Apparently, then, water carries within itself a kind of inner pressure and warmth marker—in addition to its melting point of 0° C and its boiling point of 100° C as inner markers, 35° C (a temperature similar to that of warm-blooded animals and human beings) is also a kind of boundary marker.

Frequently, many of a certain kind of chemical compounds display similar behavior in connection with the position of their elements in the periodic table. Thus hydrogen compounds, for example, possess increasing melting and boiling points as their atomic weight increases. H_2S melts at -85° C (-121° F); H_2Se at -66° C (-86.8° F); H2Te at -49° C (-56.2° F); and water at 0° C (32° F). Moreover, H_2S, H_2Se, and H_2Te boil at -60° C (-76° F), -41° C (-41.8° F), and -2° C (28.4° F), respectively, whereas water only boils at 100° C. If it behaved in a way that is consistent with the compounds related to it (that is, if one bears in mind the sequence O, S, Se, and T), water would have to boil at -100° C (-148° F) and freeze at -150° C (-238° F). Thus, it freezes and boils at temperatures much too high. This means it has ascended to a higher warmth sector than its chemical nature (H_2O) would seem to permit.

Yet another anomaly of water exists; it is capable of descending more deeply in weight than should be possible according to its cosmic nature. So there are small amounts of "heavy water" that occur in nature. While at 20° C (68° F), normal water has a density of 0.9982, the density of heavy water is 1.1059. Heavy water does not melt until it reaches 3° C (37.4° F); nor does it boil until 101.42° C (214.56° F). In nature, for every 100,000 molecules of normal water there are 30 to 200 molecules of heavy water.

There are also a number of special chemical features of water in addition to its extraordinary physical properties:

- Water is the universal solvent for all polar substances, especially salts. In principle, we can even go so far as to say that nearly all minerals are soluble in the mineral water, if only in the most minute traces.
- Chemically, water is extraordinarily amenable to chemical reactions. It dissolves easily into positive H and negative OH ions, whereby the concentration of H-ions—the positive molecular particles—becomes the gauge for the acidity of a solutions.
- Water is unsurpassed not only in its ability to absorb other substances and to mediate reactions among them, but also in the way it can give itself over to other substances. It has the greatest capacity to wet (adhere to) other substances without losing its cohesion, or connection with itself. It remains in connection with

itself in the thinnest of films and capillary filaments. In places where it has free surfaces, it forms an extremely thin skin in its surface tension, upon which small insects (waterbugs, or *Heteroptera*) can walk without sinking.

- Water is the suspension medium par excellence. It carries smallest portions of solid, fluid, or gaseous substances, hovering equidistant from one another, allowing the saturation of suspensions (such as clouded water through particles of matter) and colloids.

The Molecular Structure of Water

How does the nature of water reveal itself in physical and chemical terms? In its solid state, as ice, water is lighter than as a liquid (the density of ice at 0° C is 0.9991 g; at 4° C is 1.000 g). This is nearly unique, since in almost any other case matter becomes heavier when cooled and lighter when warmed, with a respective density jump at the melting and boiling points. This makes ice approximately one-tenth lighter than water; just under a tenth of it protrudes when it floats in water, since between 0° and 4° C, water molecules cohere in partially, albeit loosely, crystalline groups; thus, we can say that between 0° and 4° C water is a kind of fluid partial crystal. How can this be explained?

When fully crystallized, ice is hexagonal. It forms six-sided panels and six-sided prisms in a needle shape. Thus it tends to be both scaly and a radial crystal. In midair and in a thin breath onto solid objects, it forms "skeletal" crystals that are the basis of snow crystals, rime (hoar frost), and frost patterns. When standing water freezes, the main axis of the ice crystals' figures always forms perpendicular to the water surface. Along the surface of the crystals' bases, the crystal portions of the ice can be shifted slightly toward each other in lamellar fashion. They can slide over each other without separating, and this means that ice possesses the ability to flow. Ice breaks as a shell does, and splitters like quartz and glass do. Ice shines like glass and has no color, but appears greenish or bluish in thick layers. It can

Hoar frost, or soft rime, on a cold winter day in Lower Saxony

also assume a solid, crystalline state, and then it becomes grainy like hailstones, firn,* and icicles.

Water is not chemically an element but a liquid compound comprised of two gases, hydrogen and oxygen. Above a certain temperature, the gases disappear, accompanied by the release of enormous heat energy, and water appears in the form of steam. It is clearly a chemical compound whose formula is H_2O, but this says nothing about its unique properties, behavior, and place within the mineral realm. How does its subsensory structure manifest in the atomic and subatomic sphere? In other words, what subsensory substrate provides the basis for manifesting the suprasensory properties of water?

X-ray and neutron-beam analyses have shown that a crystal matrix in ice is similar to that of tridymite quartz, in which the quartz molecules form the tetrahedral matrix units from oxygen to oxygen. Silicon sits in the middle of the tetrahedron. In ice, the hydrogen ion sits at

---

* Firn is granular snow that has been lying for at least a year but has not yet consolidated into glacier ice.

Tridymite crystals

the corners of the tetrahedron, with oxygen in the center. Only in ice are the hydrogen ions shifted toward the oxygen points; this causes a kind of asymmetry. Then, the tetrahedra are packed together to form hexagonal and cubic complexes. Thus, the quartz in the tridymite is pseudo-hexagonal (actually, there are two trigonal crystals), and ice is dihexagonal (two hexagonal crystals).

Here a profound relatedness shows between two natures as materially distinct as water and quartz. The Greeks must have had an inkling of this. They considered rock crystal to be ice that in high mountains and at either very low or (as some paradoxically assumed) very high temperatures had frozen so solidly that it would no longer thaw. This is why the Greeks' name for ice was also the name for rock crystal. The word *krystallos* (ice, rock crystal, and glass) came from the word *kryos* (frost or extreme cold).* When water evaporates in a vacuum at -120° C (-184° F), a modification of ice is created that crystallizes in cubic form—yet another parallel with quartz in its modification as cristobalite. Again, this mysterious relationship appears between water and rock crystal. Modern research in

---

* Glass, even lead "crystal" glass, is actually an amorphous (noncrystalline) solid material.

physics attempts to attribute the anomalies of water to its molecular structure by finding a covalent bond between the "molecules" within themselves, and a hydrogen bridge bond between the "molecules" (cf. appendix 22).

However, the observation of crystal forms and molecular bonds does no more than touch on the subsensory substrate that helps the entity, the nature of water, live out its properties in space, perceptible to the senses.

Water and Life

"Water is life." The following sentences are found in the 1981 edition of the *Brockhaus Enzyklopädie* (a German-language encyclopedia):

> For life to exist and an organic exchange of substance to take place in any organism, water is of the utmost importance (hydrologic balance). It is the means of transport (blood, urine, sweat) and the solvent for nearly all substances in the cells. Plants consist of up to 90 percent water, and the higher animals and the human body consist of 60 to 70 percent. The higher a living organism's stage of development is, the less variable its water content is. Water mediates the chemical and physical processes within and outside of the cells—the flow, and diffusion of the liquids of the tissue and of nourishment—and the development of the colloidal state of the body's components (osmosis). Furthermore, it regulates the body's temperature, from which it takes warmth by means of surface evaporation (perspiration). Its vaporization warmth is very high. Also noteworthy is the dipole nature of water molecules, such as water bonded with proteins and non-bonded water. The quantity of water a person takes in and secretes each day is approximately 2.5 to 4 liters.

In a groundbreaking essay in *Sternkalendar 1952* (p. 66), Friedrich Kipp reformulates the relationship between "water and life" in a completely new way. He shows living materials (protein, carbon compounds) in their opposition to inorganic substances and points to the fact that this opposition does not exist for the relationship between living substances and water. He states, "The assimilation of it by living organizations without opposition and the crucial role it plays in them are possible only because this substance has a primal relationship with life."

In his remarks, Kipp juxtaposes the natural-scientific concept, according to which the inorganic existed first and life evolved from it in one way or the other, with spiritual-scientific knowledge of the primacy of everything living (all nonliving matter was at one time alive; lifeless substances arose from the living through *devitalization*). For this reason, then, dying always has to be prevented by what is alive. The living realms of nature, self-enlivened as they are, maintain themselves in their confrontation with and by dead substances. However, this is possible only inasmuch as even dead substances stem from life and, hence, are endowed with substance attributes that, even in the dead state, are able to preserve the stamp of their life-derived origin. This holds to varying degrees from substance to substance. It is just these substances (the elements carbon, nitrogen, oxygen, sulfur, and phosphorus, but, above all, water) that play the most important role in life, displaying through their extraordinary (anomalous) behavior toward their relatives this originary connection with life.

Water's first anomaly is that it is liquid at all. By far, the most mineral of substances are solid, fewer are gases. The fluid state of water is not only the great exception (along with mercury), but also "breaks the rules" compared to analogous substances (as previously mentioned in the section on the physical-chemical properties of water); the significance of this fact cannot be overestimated. It means that ice and water conform with the warmth conditions of the Earth surface. This makes for a kind of "pre-stabilized harmony" (in Leibniz's sense) between circumstances of the Earth's warmth and the nature of water; there would be no water circulation otherwise. This is the only way it is possible for water to serve life. Hence water must also stem from life. The second great anomaly is a further relationship between water and warmth (also previously mentioned). The specific warmth of water is extremely high. Stones warm up and cool off quickly; water does both very slowly. If we set a specific warmth of 1 for water, the values of all other known solids and fluids are below this (glycerin, 0.57; alcohol, 0.57; clay, 0.22; limestone, 0.17; iron, 0.11; mercury, 0.03). These examples demonstrate how, on the average, organic substances have a higher specific warmth than mineral substances. This would make water the most organic substance there is. Without water, life would have no warmth protection.

The third anomaly of water pertains to its behavior with regard to its density. All liquids become heavier when cooled, including water—but only down to 4° C (39.2° F). Water at 10° C (50° F) is heavier than water at 20° C (68° F), water at 1° C is lighter than water at 4° C. Which also means that cold water carries ice along its surface. It protects itself against rigidification in its depths; it remains fluid and living.

The fourth anomaly is biochemical. The hydrogen compounds analogous to water spoken of above are all strong poisons (H_2S, H_2Se, H_2Te, HCl, NH_3, PH_3); water alone is completely nontoxic.

The fifth anomaly: of all the compounds, each of which is either acid or base, water is completely neutral chemically. It holds the exact middle between the acids and bases, which is precisely what makes it the indispensable solvent for acids, bases, and salts.

The sixth thing that is special about water is again crucial. Water is the solvent for colloids. In cloud-form, water is itself a colloid (aerosol). Here, too, there is no substance to equal it. Silica substances perhaps come closest, which, again, bear witness to a mysterious relationship between water and quartz.

The seventh anomaly is the strong cohesive force of water as a liquid. This enables, in a unique way, the processes of its capillary activity. Even the thinnest thread of water does not break in a capillary. This is crucial for conducting water in vascular plants. As Kipp points out, "Thus, we gain the insight that water's very nature must be characterized by life; life is its actual home. At the same time, however, it acts as a border crosser by virtue of its activity in the inorganic sphere, where it establishes the external preconditions for life" (p. 71).

⊙

The previous chapter on the nature of the mineral kingdom referred to the fact that real life is a realm of its own in the cosmos. It is the sphere of the substances and forces suprasensorily active as cosmic ether, the spiritual-scientifically ascertained kingdom of the four ether types incarnated in plants, animals, and human beings. Just as the subsensory fields and forces originate in quantum mechanical laws of probability amplitudes, likewise the suprasensory fields of life originate in the sphere of etheric laws. Only the earthly regularities of the "central forces" and the cosmic-etheric regularities of the "universal forces" together (R. Steiner) form the fabric of the sensory world and its perceptibility to human senses. In the mineral world, water is the only substance that, even as a mineral, reveals the lawfulness of life—doing so on the broadest scale—while also having the ability to mediate that lawfulness with ease. It is precisely the anomalies it displays in the physical-chemical sector that provide the preconditions for its capacity for life. It owes the capacity for life, however, to its openness to both the laws of the central forces and the laws of the cosmic forces. Theodore Schwenk points to this side of the nature of water: "We search in vain for a place on Earth that water calls its home."* Mineral bodies have certain earthly sites; water never rests. Water envelops and eternally sojourns the planet Earth itself as a whole. This affiliation with the Earth as a whole is its primary planetary and cosmic characteristic.

The second thing—flowing water never moves in a straight line. It swings in zigzag rhythmic areas in brooks, rivers, and streams, rotating around itself in their beds in a spiral course.

---

*   In *Sternkalendar*, 1952, pp. 65ff.

The third thing—it rinses, washes, and dissolves all solid objects and, through its buoying force, neutralizes their weight, entirely or in part.

Fourth—resisting gravity, it draws itself upward in capillaries in the ground, in rock, and in the veins of plants.

Fifth—in currents, it dissolves itself into countless layered lamellae, in the process forming gigantic inner surfaces; and as the lamellae flow over each other at different velocities, vortices are created. The circumference speeds and the revolving motions increase with the inward turning of the vortex, always in inverse proportion to the distance from the center. Schwenk writes:

> At the vortex's center the velocity ought to reach the value infinity. The spatial connection breaks off, though, because infinite speeds are not possible. This causes compressive forces to pass over into negative thrust....
>
> A minute particle marked with an arrow and floating on the water would always point to the same place in space, in spite of the circular motion....
>
> Actually a vortex represents a miniature planetary system, inasmuch as its rotational velocities are arranged above the radius according to Kepler's second law of planetary movement...
>
> Thus vortices of water are oriented toward the heavens in a threefold way (leaving aspects of viscosity out of account):
> 1. Arrangement of circumference speeds according to planetary motion.
> 2. Forces of suction dominate the center.
> 3. Orientation according to stellar space as an entirety.
> 4. Even water flowing through a pipe neutralizes the pressure on the pipe's walls.
>
> Ultimately, suction forces concentrate in the vortex, and in this field what until then was invisibly active in the water emerges as an observable structure: the planetary system as a vortex (water vortex) with a center that strives toward infinite dynamic motion, and this center spirals into the depths as a suction-exerting hollow

funnel. The spiraling form appears once again; it is part and parcel of water's open secret.*

Observations made on water at motion reveal its place between the cosmos and the Earth in all forms of its manifestation. It situates itself as a mediator between the air and the ground, it joins the two, without itself uniting with them entirely. Thus Schwenk concludes: "In water, a comprehensive planetary entity comes toward us, one that belongs to the entire Earth with everything it performs and endures, but also one that points out to the cosmos."

The Soul of Water

Theodor Schwenk explains the task and nature of water more at length in two later works.** Movement appears to be the proper state of water—rest emerging from movement. The primal structure of water is the drop, a sphere. Even the totality of the oceans is spherically shaped as they envelop the Earth. From this primal form there emerge two movements:

1. evaporation, caused by warmth
2. flow caused by gravity

Between warmth as expansion and gravity as contraction, the drop, the sphere forms the balance of the middle. This is its shape, its gestalt. Inwardly, water in motion disintegrates into surfaces. The water surface maintains the balance of the middle between vapor and water. Inner and outer surfaces show the motion aspect of water; as the surface lamellae run over each other, the water unites itself to form waves, vortices, Kármán vortex streets, and vortex rings. Drops form as mist droplets, cloud droplets, raindrops, and dewdrops. All formation is movement.

The second fundamental character trait of water is its sensitivity, its receptivity. It is related with surface-forming activity; the innumerable inner and outer membranes respond like the receptive surfaces

---

*   Schwenk, *Sensitive Chaos*, p. 68 (German edition).

**   Ibid.; *Bewegungsformen des Wassers* (Forms of water in motion).

Swelling surf wave
(Damming up – flowing out – swelling – layering –
dripping – spraying – aerating – illuminating – evaporating)

Rainbow: Dynamic image of the Sun veil of drops;
1. Sunlit interior: light gray. 2. Etheric, physical interior edge of the Sun: inner rainbow, violet interior, red exterior. 3. Sunlit physical edge: dark gray between the two rainbows. 4. Outer edge of the Sun: outer Rainbow, purple outside, red inside. 5. Wider circle around the Sun (corona): lighter gray outside of the second arch.

Land reflected in the still waters

*The lower half mirrors the sky (brighter), the upper the Earth (left);
Mirror image of a dandelion (right)*

of sense organs to the slightest of influences from the environment. Water is the most impressionable medium that exists. Schwenk demonstrates for example how by watering plants with potentized water it is possible experimentally to prove constellation changes. Also, his drop-picture method shows this kind of connection with the cosmos on a broad scale.

The third characteristic is the way water set in motion behaves toward the Earth. Its power to dissolve minerals, as well as its power to transport, alter, and redeposit them, and to shape the Earth through its erosive activity, reveals this character. Therefore, we have water's relationship to itself: movement. Then there is its relationship to the planetary cosmos: sensitivity. Finally, its relationship to the Earth: activity.

It is from this threesome that Schwenk deduces water's modes of activity:

1. Activity within substance as substance (metabolism, warmth exchange)
2. As a polar opposite to this activity—active sensitivity as an organ of sensing
3. In between these two—rhythmizing through movement

This makes water the carrier of the three life spheres: the metabolism, the functioning of the nerves and senses, and the rhythmic functions. Schwenk shows how—in the intestines, for example—the ear and the heart organic forms occur that are also found in the respective types of water movement.

Through water's occurrence between the cosmos and the Earth as mediator and bearer of life itself and of the vital functions, its relatedness with life as a whole becomes evident. According to spiritual-scientific research, this relatedness is revealed in etheric substances and forces at work in the cosmos. Thus Schwenk says, "The laws of the etheric world are reflected in the world of water; they are engaged in a form-creating dialog."*

---

* Schwenk, *Sensitive Chaos*, p. 93.

Exact observation of the attributes of water reveals its relatedness with the four ether types.* It behaves in a motherly receptive and holding, embracing way toward the warmth ether. It takes warmth into itself slowly and in large quantities and likewise gives it off slowly and in large quantities.

It is, in turn, reflective toward the light ether in a motherly way. Being colorless, it nevertheless reflects and thus enables light to reveal its own nature and content.

Water shows itself to be the most closely related with the chemical ether: water allows itself to be imbued with this ether to such extent that it is virtually identical with it and thus can become a bearer of countless chemical transformations.

Water is highly sensitive toward the life ether and its influences. It places itself in the service and at the disposal of whatever life requires of it.

These characterizations also bring us into the area of water's inner nature, its soul. As it takes on the laws of the world of life, it also takes in wisdom, and it takes in the very wisdom that a person can grasp pertaining to the world: "In water's flowing, the wisdom of the world-all flows along."**

The properties of the water entity can be shown schematically:

1. Water is the bearer of life. Where there is water, there is life; where there is no water, there is death.
2. It strives for compensation, for balance.
3. It is the mediator of opposites.

---

* The question of the etheric and the four ether types was elevated by Steiner to the rank of a "science of the etheric." The results of what he stimulated were taken up and expanded by many of his students. Research results show that the etheric forces of life and formation manifest in four different elementarily active forms of force. These are: 1. the all-permeating warmth ether; 2. the light ether, which endows every living thing with form; 3. the chemical or sound ether, which transforms all chemical processes into living organic chemistry; and 4. the life ether, which impulses all that is living, which causes the incarnation and excarnation of life.

** Ibid., p. 95.

4. It wants nothing for itself, gives itself over to everything, then steps back again and practices renunciation everywhere.
5. Since it is itself pure, untainted, transparent, it can purify, refresh, heal and strengthen everything.
6. It is open for light, warmth, air.
7. It is open for harmonies and orderings of the star world and in this way maintains the middle between the Earth and the cosmos of the stars.

What, then, is the first soul virtue of water? Hegel states in part 2 of his *Philosophy of Nature:* "Water is the element of selfless opposition, passive being—for the other.... Hence water's existence is for the other.... And this is why early on it was called the 'mother of all that wields.'"* Selflessness as the stream of life—the stream of life as selflessness: in this, water reveals the highest human virtue.

We can now go a bit beyond this point and consider water's relationship to light. The perfectly still surface of water at rest becomes a mirror of the light-born images of the world. Anyone who has stood at the foot of a Norwegian fjord and observed in the still, clear air of an autumn day how the eye is unable to distinguish between the landscape—mountain, glacier, rock, and tree—and its equally distinct and nearly equally bright reflection in the water, experiences water as the carrier of a selfless consciousness for the surrounding world. It reflects pictures as pictures in a pure and undistorted form—the way human consciousness does thoughts and images. Anyone who observes the Sun or Moon rising or setting over the sea is in a position to perceive a unified picture of the forces emanating from the Sun or Moon as a single track of light—despite the fact that this picture is broken by every individual wave. Water's image consciousness passes into a consciousness of forces. Anyone who views a double rainbow while standing facing a dark wall of rainclouds can see what occurs on the Sun when its suprasensory interior reaches the periphery and assumes physical substantiality in the photosphere, chromosphere, and corona, exerting its dynamism outward; one sees in the rainbow

---

* By "early on" Hegel means the ancient Greek philosophy of nature.

Part 4: Building Elements of Heavenly Jerusalem ◊ Chapter 1: Water

Sun dogs in Fargo, North Dakota

an effigy of the Sun's activity. Inside, the inner arch the Sun's image is dark; between the inner and the outer arch, it is bright; outside the outer arch, it is dark again. The raincloud's various shades of gray show this quite clearly. These five zones belong together and are a genuine force-image of the Sun's being in the veil of droplets that is the rain cloud. It depicts in its millions of droplets the play of forces in the Sun's cosmic activity. Water's force-consciousness passes into its Sun-consciousness. Finally, anyone who perceives a halo and a parhelion (sun dog) in cirrus cloud ice crystals sees as an image the Sun's own spirit being, which in turn escorts consciousness of life through the water in crystal form and over into the consciousness of actual essence. The halo reveals not only an image of the Sun's life, because the Sun is not reflected in the halo as it is in the rainbow; rather, in the halo, the Sun is the phenomenon's center. As a light and color generating entity, the crystallized water reveals the

Sun itself. (The halo and gloria are intermediate steps in the mist of fog and clouds.) At each level of these reflections, water proves itself the carrier of a cosmic consciousness.

This series of revealing images of the nature of water comes together, as it were, to form the very simplest picture, one that water makes of itself: the dewdrop. When a dewdrop comes to terms with itself and with the light as it sparkles in the light of the rising Sun, it becomes the simplest likeness of the entire cosmos.

The Spirituality of the Water Entity

Water itself is a spiritual being beyond life, soul, and consciousness. By virtue of its power to pervade all substances, as it dissolves them to make them able to accommodate life it can, immersing itself into life, itself conduct life into substance. All-pervading power is its proper spiritual existence. It selflessly receives both the enlivened and the material, but it also carries life and matter through their own transformations, and once it has received and carried them through, it relinquishes them to themselves anew. It gives birth out of itself in a motherly way, is a birth-giver of worlds.

Endowed with these capacities, it is also able to reunite entities alienated from their origin and perhaps heading toward destruction with the creating ground of the life of the world. It possesses the faculty to lead them back to their origin in spiritual existence. In this way, however, it succeeds in reverting as a mineral back to its spiritual-physical primal foundation. It can integrate its own closest relatives in particular, such as silicon—that is, quartz—into this process.

It is the intent of the next chapter to work out the fundamental, primal nature of quartz, of silicon. It will become clear that there as well a profound selflessness predominates, but one that bears more the character of a primal mediating function for all processes of perception. Silicon is the primal sense for everything that is light, or perception; whereas water, in its selflessness, is the entity of perception for all of life. Thus it becomes clear that, in the stream of the Heavenly

Jerusalem, a future formed by water arises in which water itself is life, crystal, and stream. The Book of Revelation (22:1) says, "Then the angel showed me the river of the water of life, as clear as crystal flowing from the throne of God and of the Lamb." (*Crystal* here in the sense of mountain, ice, or rock crystal.)

This river of the life of the world always issues out of the Father; however, in the river flowing through the Heavenly City the accompanying influence of the Son is also included. For He, the Son, the Lamb, receives the river from the Father and fills it on his own with the light. What is contained in the water stream of the Heavenly Jerusalem is threefold: The primal substance of the Father (the crystal-silicon process becomes a stream); the primal livingness of the Son (the water process become purest, most selfless devotion); and the healing nature of the Spirit (the consciousness process of water as a mirror of life). The future stream of the water of life no longer flows in a merely unconscious way, as does the "I." Compare with this Christ's words: Whoever believes in me, as Scripture has said, rivers of living water will flow from within them (John 7:38). Water is the one component of this stream; the other is silicon, or quartz.

Spirit Song over the Waters

The human soul
Resembles water:
From Heaven it comes,
To Heaven it soars.
And then again
To Earth descends,
Changing ever.

Down from the lofty
Rocky wall
Streams the bright flood,
Then spreads gently
In cloudy billows

Over the smooth rock,
And welcomed kindly,
Veiling, on it roams,
Soft murmuring,
Toward the abyss.

Cliffs projecting
Oppose its progress—
Angrily it foams
Down to the bottom,
Step by step.

Now, in flat channel,
Through the meadowland steals it,
And in the polished lake
Each constellation
Joyously peeps.

Wind is the loving
Wooer of waters;
Wind blends together
Billows all-foaming.

Human spirit,
You are like unto water!
Human fortune,
You are like unto wind!

—Goethe

Chapter 2: Crystal

Selflessness in World Mediation

The Name

The names given to the whole range of minerals with pure silicic acid anhydride (SiO_2) as their material basis all seem in some way to hover; the German name *Kiesel*,* for one. This word is traceable to the Indo-Germanic stem *Gis* and *Geis*. A sound shift in the evolution of the language yielded *Keis*, which in Middle High German became *Kis*, and in New High German *Kies*. The original meaning refers to approximately the same thing as the word "stone," in the sense of an individual, more or less smoothly worn piece. Later it also came to mean stones, coarse sand, gravel, or crushed stone (of the kind strewn as ballast between railroad tracks), thus the current meaning of the German word *Kies*. There is a "diminutive" form of this word stem: Old High German *Kisili*, also *Kisilink*. This word passed over into *Kieserling* and *Kaiserling*. It means "little stone," belonging to *Kiesel*; but it also means "hail," "hailstone," or "graupel stone" (snow pellets).

The experiential association between *hailstone* and *gravel stone* is obvious; the Germanic tribe had an experience of the connection between ice and pebbles, similar to that of the Greeks. Today's use of the word *Kiesel* is ambiguous; it designates a particular mineral of the silicic acid group as coarse *Kieselstein* [silicic rock] and *Kieselsinter* (siliceous sinter); on the other hand, in the chemical and pharmaceutical industry and also in agricultural contexts one speaks simply of *Kiesel* (*Silicum*) when referring to the chemical substance and its effects.

---

* The German word *Kiesel* is pronounced "keezl." According to most current German dictionaries, it can mean pebble, gravel, or flint. According to the context, the author generally uses *Kiesel* to mean "silicon" in the broad, chemical sense. In this translation, *silicon*, the element number 14 of the periodic table, will be designated *Silicium*.

The second name that seems to hover is *quartz*. There are diverging opinions as to this word's origin. According to one opinion, it comes from the Old German stem *Urios*, which also means "gravel." Other authors opine that it comes from Bohemian mining in the fourteenth century and arose from the West Slavic word *Kwardy*, meaning "hard." However, it can stem from a term used in mining in the Hartz Mountains between the twelfth and sixteenth centuries to designate the ore content of a lateral or cross-vein: *Quererz*.* Moreover, it might also come from *Quiad* (ice), derived from the Middle High German word *Quad*—evil, disgusting, hence "bad ore," ore not containing silver. Yet another term it is said to derive from is the Old High German word *Quarz*, which means "kobold" or "dwarf." Thus quartz is seen as an elemental being of the earth. Today it is used, albeit imprecisely, for a group of minerals containing silicic acid.

The third "hovering" name is rock crystal; the word *crystal* is of Greek origin. *Kyros* means "frost," great coldness; and *Krystallos* means "what is frozen." The ancient Greeks used it to designate ice at first, but then just as directly as the name for rock crystal, because they had the same experience toward it, and interpreted it so: rock crystal is nothing other than ice that has congealed at great height and over long periods of time, and so strongly that it can no longer thaw. The conception also exists among the ancient authors that it froze out of great fire. The meaning of the word *crystal* then passed over to mean the body found in the mineral realm in its geometrically determined spatial structure and figure, which was ultimately dealt with in a mathematical manner. Even today the word *crystal* exists both for rock crystal in particular and for the forms of the mineral realm overall.

The Substance

Chemically, silicon—quartz—rock crystal is the anhydride of an acid, of silicic acid; in other words, it is the oxide of a semimetallic

---

* *Quererz: quer*, meaning "lateral" or "sideways"; *erz* meaning "ore."

element, the metalloid silicon, or *Silicium*. The oxide's chemical formula is SiO_2. The metalloid *Silicium* (number 14 in the periodic table) has an atomic weight of 28.086, a melting point (according to Hollemann) of 1,410° C (2,570° F), a boiling point of 2,630° C (4,766° F), and a density of 2.32. It crystallizes cubically, albeit not like rock salt, but rather like diamond, which means its ions sit at the eight corners of the cube, as well as in the centers of the six surfaces, whereby two such surface-centered cubic lattices are shifted against each other by a quarter of their edges' length, and in this way form unit cells. Its crystals are dark gray, with a metallic shine. They are soluble neither in water nor in organic acids. Only fluoric acid corrodes it.

Silicium unites with hydrogen to form silenes (SiH_4, Si_2H_6), with oxygen to yield SiO (monoxide) and SiO_2 (dioxide). A quarter of what surrounds us on the Earth is *Silicium* (25.8% by weight, according to Holleman). We walk around on it, are surrounded by it. It constitutes the mineral earth up to thousands of kilometers deep, but we never set eyes on it. Even though if, spiritually seen, this substance is will, at the same time we see that if in quartz and feldspar, in mica and hornblende, in garnet and beryl and topaz, in granite, gneiss, basalt, slate, loam, clay, and farming soil—if in all these one-quarter of the substance is *Silicium*, then it is obvious that it does not want to appear. We have to use force to remove the sheaths of *Silicium*, and then it appears, a semimetal, hued in deep blackish, bluish gray, harder than most metals, almost as hard as corundum, repellent to oxygen and nearly all acids; but at the same time lighter than most metals, open toward bases and quick to unite with the metals with the help of oxygen to form thousands of mineral substances, the silicates, into which it vanishes in an instant. Fractured with a hammer, it sprays, crackling, apart. It screeches when being ground. Johann Killian states:

> Silicium is hard, but not raw. Although it is reclusive and repellant... it is anything but coarse. It is stern and unrelenting

in its demeanor, but sensitive and delicate in its being.... No wonder it hides its interior.... However, it dreams in its depths and is active in concealment. It is the strictest will in a thousand crystals, the font of their existence, the donor and guardian of their strength.*

Together with oxygen and hydrogen, *Silicium* forms acids, but it is not stable in acid form, either. It is always on the way to becoming a salt, a crystal. The acids have to be produced, their lives maintained artificially. As stable as its salts are, just as delicate and frail are its acids. But its ashes, oxides, and alkali salts** are also stable. By means of force, the acids, polymers can be produced (ortho and oligo polysilicon acids). The acids readily form colloids and coagulate to firm gel. In nature, such substances as siliceous sinter, flint, and opal emerge from such processes. With multivalent metals, the delicate ortho-silicic acid passes over into the above-mentioned lasting silicates, or it "ashes" to become quartz. Hard, stern *Silicium* makes the crystals of the mineral world hard, stringent, brittle, and firm. They are distinguished by a consolidated will and well-ordered spiritual structure.

The other substance is oxygen. Oxygen is the substance of which half the Earth consists, and not just the atmospheric portion, but the solid Earth as well. Oxygen makes up a mere quarter of the air, comparable to *Silicium* in the solid-mineral realm; here, though, the share of oxygen is nearly half, or 49.8 percent by weight (per Holleman). Thus oxygen and *Silicium* combined make up 60 percent of all solid minerals, 85 percent of all water, and 23 percent of the air by weight.

Oxygen is a nonmetal. It is number 8 on the periodic table, it melts at minus 218.4° C and boils at minus 183.0° C. Liquid and solid oxygen are bright blue. Ozone is a modification of it. Along with fluorine and chlorine, it is one of the most powerfully electronegative elements, and is extraordinarily fond of reacting. It stands

---

* Killian, *Das Du im Stein. Die Sprache des Anorganischen* (The you in stone: The language of the inorganic), pp. 82–83.

** Also known as basic salts.

in a kind of opposition to *Silicium*, and so, accompanied by the production of light and warmth, it as well unites with countless elements and compounds, either quietly, tenaciously, and steadily (e.g., rusting iron) or else violently, dramatically (with explosions). This makes it the universal unifier that transports life into matter and enlivenment into life (breathing). It is also oxygen, by way of silicic acid, which helps *Silicium* bond with metals.

What does each of these two substances, *Silicium* and oxygen, give up when they withdraw, withhold themselves for the sake of allowing the substance of *Silicium* to appear? Silicium sacrifices its somber isolation, permits itself to be brightened up, and becomes gregarious and open. Oxygen sacrifices its levity and becomes sensitive for what it chases out of the materials it bonds with, for light and warmth. As a gas in the air, it lets these two pass through it completely. But as oxygen and *Silicium* sacrifice their own material existence, what comes about in the subsensory substrate of silicic acid's crystalline state is not some closed molecular structure, but rather a kind of tissue of forces, which in endless self-repetition and through layering and uniting with itself furnishes the matrix for the incarnation of the entity of quartz.

Silicic acid forms the material netting for its own and the incarnation of most of the other elements, especially the metals and their compounds. This happens by the *Silicium* ion surrounding itself with four oxygen ions so that the little *Silicium* ion forms the midpoint of a tiny tetrahedron at the four corners of which the four oxygen ions sit, which themselves are in turn part of the next tetrahedron. In this way, silicic acid accomplishes the same thing in the inorganic field as carbon in the organic world. It forms islands, chains, bands, leaves, rings, and scaffolds of SiO_4 tetrahedrons in the quantum mechanical fabric of the subsensory, which provide the basis for the suprasensory substance entities to incarnate and bring their qualities to sense-perceptible appearance. Practically speaking, the silicates are the mineral realm and *Silicium* is their base frame.

The Crystal

The crystal figure unites with the subsensory tissue of the SiO_4 tetrahedron. It takes hold of this scaffolding, which itself is of the cubic spatial order, and brings it into the trigonal order. In this way, a unified, cohesive, three-sided column arises as a crystal that ends at the top and the bottom in three-sided pyramids. But it never stays with this fundamental form. A hexagonal construction principle always usurps this trigonal figure by twelve such figures interpenetrating in such manner that they exactly develop a six-sided column with two three-sided rhombohedrons at each end. A high degree of symmetry arises. Each of the two crystals has its own fine material lamellae inside the other, which interpenetrate freely and perfectly. One gets a similar picture if one throws two stones into the water at the same time and observes how the two trains of waves freely interpenetrate at the places where they meet and after passing through each other continue on in their original order. Thus a laminar parallel adhesion of two crystals occurs. Here, too, the deep relatedness between water and quartz is displayed: quartz crystallizes in lamellar fashion, water moves in lamellar fashion.

This is how the habits of rock crystal occur. The most frequent ones:

1. The six-sided prism with the indices (10 −10).*
2. Two three-sided pyramids, the main rhombohedron, with the indices (10 −11) and the secondary rhombohedron, as represented with the somewhat smaller surfaces (01 −11).
3. Two trigonal bipyramids, which, however, always occur alone and join up with the one or the other of the two trigonal crystals. This causes an outer asymmetry because the surfaces unite either to the

---

* The conventional designation of negative numbers in the Miller index is to place a bar above the negative number; this is how the author designates them, as well. In this text—the translation—negative numbers, which by indexing convention would normally have a bar above them, are designated with a minus sign (−) to the left.

left with the indices (2 −1 −11) or to the right with the indices (11 −21). This is how left quartz and right quartz arise.
4. Finally, two trigonal trapezohedrons usually occur (51 −61) right and (6 −1 −51) left. (See appendix 23 for a better understanding of this information.)

These lamellar parallel adhesions, which are fundamental constructions, occur within the concrete context of manifold crystal twinning, which is very frequent. There are three fundamental laws:

- Common Dauphiné Law: either two right quartzes or two left quartzes interpenetrate, whereby one crystal is turned 180° toward the other along the main axis. One could say that this is now the complete quartz crystal, fully symmetric, made up of four individual crystals, ordered according to hexagonal symmetry, and permeated by a kind of staggered spiral tendency. This means that the original singular crystal form is covered over multiple times.
- Brazil Law: a right quartz and a left quartz interpenetrate in lamellar way, so that the imaginary turning movement is balanced out. The completed quartz becomes consummate quartz.
- Japan Law: two crystals lean against each other in such way that their lower parts interpenetrate, and so that they stand nearly perpendicular, one above the other, separated from each other by an adhesion seam.

All three of these laws occur worldwide. Frequently seen as a fourth law, the appearance of twisted quartzes, is not crystal twinning, but rather a kind of mutual overrunning of the lamellae of several individuals, similar to the way the hosts of lamellae overrun each other in the formation of whirls and vortices in water. Here, too, the profound relatedness manifests between water and rock crystal. Thus slanted, completely and regularly layered aggregates occur that wind to the left or to the right, depending on the right quartz or the left quartz they are made up of. Quartz has a total of 18 twinning laws. However, the crystal forms of the quartzes are not just characterized by adhesions in the lamellar construction; another influencing factor here is the temperature milieu in which the quartz lives. SiO_4 tetrahedrons shift at different temperatures without departing from the fundamental ordering of the lamellae. Thus, SiO_2 displays not only the previously mentioned basic lower-temperature forms (low quartz, trigonal), but also six different main appearances, each pair of which can be inverted into each other, depending on the temperature scale.

At temperatures above 573° C (1,063° F), trigonal low quartz passes over into hexagonal high quartz, which is stable up to 870° C (1,598° F), and melts at 1,600° C (2,912° F). What at lower temperatures is a mere covering-over now becomes actual structure. If the temperature falls back down to below 573° C, the hexagonal crystal deteriorates, as it were, back into the two trigonal crystals.

Next to the trigonal low quartz, rhombically crystallizing low tridymite also occurs naturally; this mineral as well passes over into hexagonal high tridymite, and that at a mere 120° C. It melts at 1,670° C (3,038° F), and likewise returns to the trigonal rhombic state upon cooling.

The third crystal form that occurs naturally, albeit only seldom, is cristobalite. It is tetragonally crystallized, and passes over into cubic high cristobalite at 200° C (392° F), following the same crystal law as cooking salt, diamond, and six forms of ice. It melts at 1,710° C (3,110° F), thus with the greatest difficulty. Above 1,710° C, all three forms pass over into a watery molten state.

In addition there are: keatite (at 1,000 atmospheres), coesite (at 20,000 atm.), and stishovite (at 150,000 atm.), as well as melanophlogite and "fibrous SiO_2," none of which, though, is found in nature, but is produced synthetically in experiments.

This liveliness and sensitivity of rock crystal's crystallinity toward warmth, the lamellar constitution of its interpenetrating crystals, and its transition at higher temperatures into hexagonal form, which is the

Snow crystals: table crystals and skeleton crystals of increasing intricacy

Quartz crystal: crystal in crystal, crystal on crystal; completely free orientation

Red-zoned, coarse jasper (Africa)

Nephrite; fibrous structures (New Zealand)

form of ice and snow at lower temperatures, demonstrate a commonality between water and quartz that, of course, is impossible to justify in chemical terms.

The Spectrum of Appearances

Just as mobile and fluid as the silicate minerals' crystallinity are the forms in which they manifest. There are essentially four fundamentally different ways in which the entity of quartz manifests:

1. phanero quartz or macrocrystalline quartzes
2. microcrystalline quartzes as filament quartz and grain quartz
3. colloidal quartzes
4. solid quartzes

The substance of quartz constitutes 18 percent of the mineral realm by weight.

1. It is generally distributed in geodes and crevice spaces in the form of crystals as heavy as hundreds of kg., or else in solid, crevice-filling form.
2. Quartz is part of the composition of rock masses themselves, more or less coarse-grained, in solid form as common quartz. In broken rock it is discernible by its oily shininess.
3. Larger veins are filled pneumatolytically and hydrothermically with solid vein quartz, where it is oftentimes very pure.
4. Finally, it is found in sedimentary rock as sand grains and as a bonding medium of sandstone, and as metamorphosed sandstone, as quartzite.

The first group, the purely macrocrystalline quartzes, is rock crystal. Clear as water, sometimes clouded by enclosures, it is the definitive crystal. If the enclosures run along the lamellae of its crystal formation, phantom quartz comes about. The "angels' tears" in Carrara marble and the "marmorosch diamonds" from Siebenbürgen/Romania are smaller crystals formed on both sides that shine as vividly as precious stones. These pure [macrocrystalline] rock crystals display variations in five different directions. Through one-sided and/or flawed growth (different rates of growth in the directions of certain surfaces or edges), window quartz and frame quartz, skeleton quartz, scepter quartz, and Babylon quartz* occur. This is the first variation.

Second, cracks and enclosures of air or residual solutions expelled by the crystal cause cloudiness to occur. Third, there occur enclosures of a solid matter, which the crystal has grown around. These can come from colloids, hovering substances (clay, ferrous oxide, and hydroxide), which take away the quartz's transparency. Or there are enclosures that are crystals of other minerals; these can range from finest, even microscopic, filaments to visible, needle-shaped crystals: rutile, tourmaline, actinolite, scapolite, anhydrite, epidote, byssolite; and, on the other hand, leaflike enclosures: ilmenite, hematite, brookite, mica, chlorite, and others.

Depending on distribution, type, and size of mineral, these enclosures then yield the varieties of the following quartzes:

Milky quartz (gas and fluid enclosures and cracks): iron quartz (ferrous oxide); sapphire quartz and blue quartz (riebeckite and tourmaline); aventurine quartz (mica); emerald or green quartz, or prasem (green caused by actinolite); rose quartz (rutile, titanium ions, manganese ions); hawk's eye (asbestos filaments); tiger's eye (asbestos and limonite filaments). Fourth, the influence of radiation can cause changes to take place after the crystal's formation, and the rock crystal becomes tinted: citrine (yellow), smokey quartz (blackish brown);

---

*   *Window quartz:* sometimes the incomplete surfaces of frame quartz grow over, so that thin panes of quartz form over the surface hollow (www .mineralienatlas.de/lexikon/index.php/MineralData?mineral=Hornstein). *Frame quartz:* the formation of its edges is overhasty; its surfaces are not filled in fully with lamellae. *Skeleton quartz:* in over-saturated solutions, crystal growth is rapid, growth occurs especially along the crystal edges and corners (www.chemie.de/lexikon/Quarz.html). *Babylon quartz, or cathedral quartz:* a central large crystal is surrounded by smaller ones grown in parallel and tightly attached to the central crystal. It may resemble a cathedral tower. "Cathedral," "babel," or "Babylon" quartzes resemble quartzes that show split growth, but in cathedral quartzes all crystals, and accordingly all rhombohedra faces at the crystal's tips, are in parallel, and light reflections appear almost simultaneously on faces of the same type (www.quartzpage .de/gro_text.html#cathedral).

morion (completely dark); amethyst (purple); however, these changes can also be influenced by additional metal ions. Heating to temperatures above 300°C (572° F) usually causes the coloration to be lost. The foreign ions in the crystal lattice are, instead of *Silicium*: lithium, natrium, and hydrogen. It has been calculated that a mere trace of aluminum ions (as few as 10 to 150 per million *Silicium* ions) causes the color alterations. In citrine, traces of ferrous hydroxide have been proved, in amethysts traces of manganese.

The fifth variety of macrocrystalline quartz consists in the formation of SiO_4 tetrahedrons, but ones with the ability to cling perfectly to the outer crystal of other minerals or to the cell structure of organic materials, the substance of which the *Silicium* then crowds away. This process is called *pseudomorphosis*. Its most extreme forms are petrifications of wood, bones, and calcite shells. The quartz substa actinolite nce assumes the exact structure of the cells.

The second large group of quartzes is the microcrystalline varieties. They look "rough" but are not. The one variety consists of delicate, microscopic filament crystals, the direction of which runs perpendicular to the main axis of the columnar form of the crystal. There are as many as 800 filaments to a single millimeter in the lamellae. That is nearly one one-thousandth of a millimeter; but the filaments are even smaller than that, as there are just as many delicate strips of opal quartzes in colloidal form running between them. This creates a meticulously detailed fabric. It is the chalcedony group. Sometimes, the filimentation runs parallel to the main axes of the crystals, and then the chalcedony is called quartzine. The filaments of some kinds of chalcedony contain the cristobalite lattice: lussatite. All forms of chalcedony with their colored variants are transparent (less frequently), translucent (as a rule), or opaque. They are clustery, crusty, layered, or nodular. Foreign enclosures cause them to be vividly colorful: carnelian (red, translucent), chrysoprase (green due to nickel), moss agate (transparent with green dendrites of hornblende), and the layered varieties of chalcedony found in the agates: onyx, (dark, smokey brown, black-and-white striped), sard, often given the same name as carnelian (red, brownish red to white-striped), the enhydro agate (chalcedon druse with fluid enclosures) and, finally, jasper (reddish brown, brown, opaque). (Cf. appendix 26 concerning the origin of agates.)

The other variety of microcrystalline quartzes contains not only fibrous, but also grainy microcrystals. To this variety belong the different kinds of genuine jasper, such as plasma (green, opaque); heliotrope (green, transparent with red specks of ferrous oxide); many yellow, brown, red and white jasper varieties, and the nodular and plated flint and hornfels. Among these are the jasper orbs, which have especially beautiful colors.

The third major group of quartzes is the manifestations of quartzite and vein quartz.

The fourth group is, strictly speaking, not quartz at all, but rather solidified, amorphous, aqueous silicic acid, with a clustery surface, sometimes nodular, sometimes layered and sometimes, as previously mentioned, as petrification mineral for fossils. This is the group of the opals (precious opal, fire opal, milk opal, hyalite), and the wood opal. (More on this in the chapter on opal.)

❧

I. Origin and context: It is necessary to have an overview of the full abundance of the research results pertaining to the silicic minerals if we wish to apprehend the living essence of quartz.* Quartz enters into remarkable proximity to water in the process, with regard to the following aspects:

1. Quartz and ice are subject to the same crystal lattice structure in the subsensory sphere. This structural similarity manifests experimentally as the SiO_4-tetrahedron in quartz, the OH_4 tetrahedron in water. While ice crystallizes hexagonally from the outset, quartz always strives to achieve this spiritual gesture, actually attaining it

---

* Cloos, p. 17.

only at high temperatures. The buildup that manifests both in the movement structure of water and in the crystal structure of quartz is always lamellar.

2. Water is in highest degree sensitive to all life. It proves to be the very mediator of life overall, the sense organ of the Earth that enables life to access the world of dead matter. Silicon is sensitive to light; this is discernable in quartz only indirectly. But the moment silicon can exert its influence in living organisms, its sensitivity for everything pertaining to perception becomes manifest. In his course on agriculture, Rudolf Steiner calls it the Earth's light-sensing organ for the cosmos. As water is the sense for life, quartz is the sense for light and form. This is evident from the spiritual-scientific study of past states of the Earth. In the lecture cycle on mystery centers,* Rudolf Steiner describes the origin of the substance of silicic acid. It stems from the Sun: on the trails of light and warmth, primal plant entities came to Earth as etheric beings after the Sun had separated from the Earth, bringing along with them as they came the etheric archetypal silicon as bearer and mediator of the light, for the purpose of implementing within the protein of the primeval Earth the archetypal, leaf- and algae-like form of the plant. In this fully alive mediator—which continually incarnated in colloid form out of the Sun-ether (only to reetherize) and carried the plants (living in the light) to the protein atmosphere—the living origin of the substance of quartz can be found in this mediator. Separating from the plant structures and mineralizing, silicon then became the chief material component of the Earth, through which the Earth itself can remain open for cosmic influences. Thus, seen from the aspect of life, silicon is the bearer of the processes of sense perception and of the perception of living structures and forms.

3. Silicon, like water, is profoundly selfless; as water provides life with its material foundation, silicon provides the material foundation

---

* Steiner, *Mystery Knowledge and Mystery Centres*.

for the mineral world. It becomes quartz; it becomes silicate. Even as substance, though, it remains light and form.

4. In this context, it is significant that these early cosmic states are visible in the images of the mineral realm as they appear in the Revelation of St. John. In the third section of his previously mentioned book on the Apocalypse, entitled "The Creation of the World and the Sacrifice of the Lamb," Emil Bock engages in a thoroughgoing discussion of the contents of the great source image in Revelation 4 (pp. 61–66). Through the heavenly image of the opened door (Rev. 4:1) and the voice of the trumpet sounding ("Come up here"), the consciousness of the beholder attains to contact by touch, and to an encounter (*egenomehn en pneumati*: "I caused myself, becoming, to occur in spirit"). The throne appears (according to the spirit vision of the Old Testament, the throne is a sapphire—which in the Apocalypse is not named explicitly). On this topic, Emil Bock tells us:

> The solemn picture that now appears before the soul of the seer consists of several symmetrical figures, arranged in concentric circles. The center is formed by a throne and one that sits on it. But while we are tempted to picture the one who sits on the throne in human form, the seer deters us from doing so: "He that sat was to look upon like a jasper and a sardine stone." He is a starry center of light, from which two diversely colored rays proceed. Jasper is a greenish shimmering jewel; but in the past, the type of jasper that was almost white was considered the most valuable; it shone like a diamond, its pure white light gleaming green only from a distance. The sardine stone is, like the carnelian, a blood-red gem. From the throne, which forms the central point of the heavenly sphere, red and white beams of light issue in harmonious accord; these are the revelation of the very Godhead. Here, in the realm of prototypes, we meet the polarity of white and red, familiar everywhere in fairy tales, legends, and the symbols of historical life. Whether it is the charming story of Snow White and Rose Red or the legend of Flos and Blanchefleur, the Red Rose and the White Lily or the polarity of the Red and White Roses in English history, the duality of white and red always expresses the consonance between spirit

and soul. The spiritual element shines in the clear white light; the soul element glows in the color of red blood. He who sits on the throne is the radiant source of the original light differentiated according to spirit and soul, as in light and heat, revealing the eternal consonance of soul and spirit.*

Bock goes on to describe the concentric circles surrounding the throne: the rainbow, the 24 elders, the seven flames. Then he says:

Around all this, in an enigmatic picture, appears a sphere. To the circles and symmetrical polygons, an all-embracing globular form is added: "Before the throne there was a sea of glass like unto crystal" A spherical sea in the process of crystallizing surrounds the throne and its circles. (Ibid., p. 42)

In the image from the Revelation, the throne is surrounded by the original zodiac heavens: the Four Beasts. Emil Bock has dealt extensively with the appearance of the sea of glass (cf. appendix 17). He mentions the Book of Genesis as prophesy of retrospect, and places opposite it the Apocalypse as prophesy of prediction. However, before the Apocalypse comes to the nature of its own future, one also finds elements of the prophetic retrospect in it as well. The cosmological source image in chapter four contains one such element in the image of the "sea of glass." In this image, the mineral world appears in its original spiritual state. In the Apocalypse, virginal material essence, emanating from the spirit as *"prima materia,"* reveals the origin of the mineral world. It is the moment of birth of the material world out of the surging sea of the spirit. Along with it arises the first predisposition within the human being to be able to stand opposite oneself. This predisposition is given in the very first seed of human thought. Along with the germinating crystal world, the germinal state of the total subsequent world of matter, there also germinates the human being's own inner nature: the beginnings of his self-awareness and life of thought. In this connection, Bock recalls Novalis's fairytale in

---

* Bock, *The Apocalypse of St. John*, p. 41 (tr. revised).

the fragmentary novel *Heinrich von Ofterdingen,* which begins with the crystal realm of Arctur (cf. appendix 24).

When making an observation of this kind, three elements in the image of the Apocalypse, chapters 4 and 5, can converge—the Apocalyptic image in its own character: a Novalis-style fairytale image and the results of Steiner's spiritual investigation. All three refer to the origin of the mineral world in the light. In the quartz-silicon processes and their mineral variations, we can to this day discern in the mineral world itself the purest likeness of this origin: light and form (crystal) in the image of the quartz entity.

II. Soul virtue: At the base of any particular sense perception, and of all sense organization, lies a hidden foundation. It is the general ability to weave between world and entity, between object and subject in such way that this weaving occurs in a completely selfless, mediating way. This ability is what constitutes the sense nature, the "sensibility" of the senses. In his *Outline of Esoteric Science,* Steiner describes how through the Spirits of Love (Seraphim) working together with the Archangels, the "light-archetypes" of the sense were created for the primeval human being, as an archetypal blueprint of all the senses. In the interplay between the receiving Archangels and the power and substance of the mediating Seraphim, the foundation for the human senses was laid, as well as the foundation of the precious stones (this will be dealt with in depth later). Since most precious stones are based on silicon processes, one may also say this: The same power that formed the precious stones must also have formed the fundamental sensory power of the senses. A kind of love force and love materiality is the basis of all senses—a force of love that no longer goes from entity to entity, but has separated from the spirits and is still placed at the free disposal of the universe. Thus, it becomes interwoven with all sensory processes. It is love as light and light as love, both entirely selfless sensibilities. Quartz rock crystal originates ultimately from the all-encompassing sphere of the Seraphim above the twelvefold of the Cherubim. This spiritual archetypal silicon substance lives in all the twelve human senses, in all the Earth, in plants and animals. It is sacrifice, love, and the senses, all at once. In the Apocalypse, this area is called "the sea of glass like crystal" (Rev. 4:6).

III. Spiritual future. The human being would not be able to see, hear, and otherwise perceive with the twelve senses if the ability of the "I"-being to attend to the respective sensory content had not been made possible through the Seraphim's love substance.* After all, anyone who truly perceives is an "I"-being. In the "I" a uniform central sense is at work that actually perceives through all of the senses. Not only can a human being distribute this central sense over the twelve senses, but one can also concentrate it to the point where one disengages it from the senses and, through an inner awakening, direct it spiritually toward the Christ who came to Earth. This causes the head's perception awareness to connect with the heart's feeling perception; thus, human beings can perceive the Christ with a single sense in which the innermost of the twelve senses—awareness of the head, feeling of the heart, and will of the "I"—melt together as a unity. When this happens, we realize how deeply we are perceived by the Christ. This knowing and finding is a "Christmas experience." Consequently, rock crystal can be displayed before the cradle in the Christmas nativity scene as an image of the "Christ sense."

Inasmuch as "crystal," in all its manifestations in the mineral, plant and animal realms and as an active foundation of all perceptions in the human being and the world, is the central sense for the perception of Christ and can become the spiritualized bearer of the human soul's sense of the light of Christ, it is also capable of being built into the Heavenly Jerusalem.

Characteristically enough, it does not appear independently there, but rather as properties of other building components. The image of jasper as the most precious of all the stones contains it (21:11: *hos*

---

* See Steiner, *The Foundations of Human Experience*, lect. 8.

litho jaspidi kristallizonti), as does *phostér,* the heavenly light of the whole city; it permeates the imagination of the luminous shine emanating from the city. It occurs the second time, in the jasper substance of the city wall (Rev. 21:8). The third time, it lives in the six precious stones belonging to the quartz minerals: jasper, chalcedony, sardonyx, sard, chrysoprase, and amethyst (Rev. 21:19–20). Fourth, it illumines the river of the water of life *(lampron hos kristallon,* Rev. 22:1). All these picture elements—light, material substance, virtue, and life—are always connected and permeated with the sense of the Christ, the sense of life, the deepest of the senses. It is the Heavenly Jerusalem's sense of itself, the purest deep contemplation—the Christ sense. Adapting Goethe's words from the "Marienbad Elegy," we can say:

> The heart rests there, and nothing can disturb
> The deepest sense: the sense *one's own* to be.

Chapter 3: Jasper

Mineral Names in Light of the Apocalypse

Likely the most enigmatic things concerning the mineral image-process in the Revelation of St. John are four motifs. The first one is the imagination of the fatherly divinity in chapter four, which manifests in the image of jasper, sard, and emerald. The second is in chapter 21, verses 10 and 11:

> And he carried me away in the Spirit to a mountain great and high, and showed me the Holy City, Jerusalem, coming down out of Heaven from God. It shone with the glory of God, and its brilliance was like that of a very precious jewel, like a jasper, clear as crystal. (Rev. 21:10–11)

The third thing is in chapter 21, verse 18: "The wall was made of jasper." The fourth thing, finally, is in chapter 21, verse 19, the first of the twelve precious stones, which again is called jasper.

The stone jasper appears four times, but when one looks closer, it appears each time in fully different contexts, and with different characteristics. The innermost aspect of the Father entity is jasper; the luminous shine of God issuing from Him as the heavenly light of the city, the shine the descending city brings with it as doxa, is jasper; the walls of the city consist of jasper, and the first of the stone embellishing the foundation stones is again called jasper. Owing to the great diversity of appearances, it certainly cannot always be the same thing, even though it has the same name each time.

What we have here is basically the ancient and Middle Ages "jasper problem" of precious stone designations, a problem passed down to today. It is most acute when one considers the name of the carbuncle stone. This name comes from the Latin *Carbunculus*, meaning "small, glowing coal." In Greek, the same thing is called *anthrax*, also meaning glowing coal, and is again the name of a precious stone. Attempts to discover exactly which mineral is meant encounter difficulties, because the term *carbuncle stone* during the Middle Ages designated blood-red stones, whether rubies, red garnet, red spinel (balas ruby), perhaps rubellite, or whatever other blood-red stone one might have found. The important thing was that the stone should be transparent or have a red glow. One sees immediately how the name is not purely objective but an expression of past experience, whereby the color is most important.

This is even more the case with the name *jasper* in the Apocalypse. We can attempt to find which respective mineral this name designates and encounter considerable obstacles, since the name *jasper* was used to designate a whole series of precious stones. In his *Natural History,* book 37, Pliny the Elder (AD 23–79) distinguishes the varieties of jasper according to color, pattern, and habitat. In principle, for him jasper is green, transparent, and, to be sure, surpassed by many other precious stones, but maintains its "fame of old" as the very highest:

1. One of them comes from India, similar to emerald.
2. One comes from Cyprus, hard, fatty, gray.
3. One is from Persia, similar to the air, called *Aerizusa,* or "air jasper," sky-blue.
4. One is from the Caspian Sea, bluish.
5. A scarlet colored one from the river Thermodon.
6. From Phrygia and Cappadocia, a bluish-scarlet one, but dark and with no luminescence.
7. One similar to emerald from Amisos.
8. A cloudy, dark one from Chalcedony.

Pliny then distinguishes different qualities. The highest quality has something scarlet about it; the second best has something of the rose; the third something from emerald; the fourth is also called boria ("northerly," or air jasper); the fifth is a red stone similar to jasper. There are also another twelve added to the eight:

9. One imitates the violet and is called *Cyanos.*
10. One is similar to rock crystal, only bluish.
11. One similar to the jujube, or red date.*
12. One similar to the terebinth, or terpentine tree (*Terebinth i zusa*). All of these are bluish and have a short shimmer that neither extends far nor goes inward.
13. One similar to emerald and often surrounded by a whitish shimmer; this one is called *Monogrammatos,* and…
14. When it has several white stripes, is called *Polygrammatos.*
15. Jasponyx, related to onyx.
16. One that encloses a cloud.
17. One that imitates snow.
18. A starred one with red specks.
19. One similar to Megarian salt.
20. One tinted by smoke, called *Capurias.*

Three hundred years later, around AD 400, the Syrian Christian bishop Epiphanius published his book *Lapidarium.* According to him, jasper is a stone like the emerald. One is green, similar to

---

* Rienecker and Rogers, *Linguistic Key to the Greek New Testament.*

copper oxide. Another is redder than water and darker than blood. Yet another one is red like blood. One is like mother of pearl, another one wine red like amethyst, one like the flame, whiter, and more luminescent than white smoke. One is not as luminescent, but green with small red specks. One is, like opal, similar to the snow and the white foam of the ocean wave, as if one had mixed milk with blood, the way the Massageteans drink it.

According to Dioskurides' *Lapidarium,* "One like emerald, one like rock crystal, which helps against phlegma; one like air called kapnios and, finally, one similar to terebinth." Authors of the Middle Ages speak later in their registers of seventeen types of jasper. This categorization is often divided into ten and seven (according to Isidore of Seville, Beda Venerabilis, Hrabanus Maurus, Arnoldus Saxo, Bartholomeus Anglicus, Marbod of Rennes). For all of them, the best jasper is green, transparent or translucent like emerald, and ought to be mounted in silver. Albrecht von Scharfenberg, for example, in his epic poem *Jüngerer Titurel:* "Ten and seven colors doth jasper bear."

From around the time of Thomas of Canterbury onward, one finds this identification more and more clearly: jasper is green with red specks, according to Heinrich von Kroll, Albertus Magnus (*Rubeas habet venas*) and in the Saint Florian Book of Stones. All the old authors also mention the soul virtues, spiritual powers, and medicinal effects of jasper. Beda says: "Jasper awakens, promotes and strengthens faith." He associates it with the Apostle Peter.

The constantly repeated emphasis in ancient times that the best jasper is green quite clearly displays a logic of designation that has no correspondence whatsoever with today's nomenclature. For the basic definition of jasper today is the following: opaque chalcedony. And so researchers as early as Abel-Rémusat felt an incentive to resolve this problem. On page 17 of his book *The History of the City of Khotau,* he performs his investigation of the substance of the mineral the Chinese call *ju,* and of the ancients' *jasper.* He derives the name *jasper* not from the Hebrew, as is normally done, but rather from Chinese.*

Abel-Rémusat ascertains that all these designations refer not to jasper, but rather to nephrite, which in turn is related to jade, and whose toughness and hardness is the actual characteristic for the name given. But what plays an even greater role is the rarity of the stone's occurrence, for the only place it could be found in the entire Near and Far East was the Kün-Lün mountain range. This was the stone being referred to when the name "jasper" arose from all these words of Asiatic languages and passed over into the Hebrew and Greek language spheres; this is the actual pure, green, transparent, or translucent jasper from which, in the conception of the ancients, the other types of jasper stem. Only the Arabian authors of the Middle Ages acknowledged this and dissociated nephrite from jasper in their registers.

Even a short survey like this shows the difficulties involved in identifying the mineral and the name definitively. What mineral should we associate the name jasper with if we want to understand the language of the Apocalypse? The matter becomes all the more complicated with one considers that not even in modern systematic mineralogy can the designation for jasper be clearly defined. To begin with, it is called simply *opaque chalcedony.* However, within the groups of different SiO_2 minerals one distinguishes between macro-crystalline and micro-crystalline series. The latter group of quartzes, which all appear to have a solid crystalline structure, actually consist of ultrafine crystals that are fibrous and form densely interconnected aggregates. But they are constructed in such manner that crystallized chalcedony substance and amorphous opal substance interpenetrate in finest lamellae. This is how the chalcedony variety of silicic acid is composed. It becomes transparent to translucent, and then is formed, by metal impurities, as carnelian, chrysoprase, moss agate, and other agates, such as sard, sardonyx and onyx. All of them are translucent.

---

*   Chinese *ju,* or *ju-chi;* Manchurian *gou;* Mongolian and Turkish *gas* and *khasch;* Persian *yeschm* and *yesmp;* Arabic *jeschet.*

When chalcedony becomes opaque and, in addition becomes predominantly tinted with iron, it is called *jasper*. Yellow, brownish-red to red, green, blue to black, also multicolored, refracting in a shell-like manner, as plasma green throughout, as heliotrope with bivalent iron-green, with trivalent iron oxide, and with iron hydroxide containing red specks. All these transitions, though, are seamless; when is chalcedony still chalcedony, at what point does it become jasper? Even in analytical terms this means that in plasma and heliotrope a portion of the substance is no longer fibrous, but rather rigidifies as finely grained microcrystals, which leads to jasper containing a substantial and structural trinity in flowing transition: crystal fiber, crystal grain, and amorphous colloidal opal. This is the origin of the exceedingly large variety of the jasper group, which of course is associated with the formational circumstances under which it is created. Along with this threefold structure, there are another four types of impurities: clayey-earthy, metallic in ions, and metallic-oxidic. They cause the rich color diversity. The grainier jasper becomes, the more it passes over into chert (flint and hornstone). So the spectrum ranges from plasma and heliotrope, which can still be termed chalcedony, to chert; from fibrous to amorphous opal-like structure. And in chert we have the fourth type of the above-mentioned impurities, the organic type (burnt flint becomes snow-white, because its organic components combust). Thus to summarize his discussion of jasper, Cloos states, "The diversity of jasper formations is extraordinary."*

The dubbing of jasper has an effect on opal, as well. Certain varieties of opal are called *jaspopal*, often even jasper, though they are pure opal. Among these are the fabled milk opal in the front plate of the emperor's crown of the Holy Roman Empire, which will be discussed at a later time. Is heliotrope a chalcedony then, or is it jasper? Is chert flint or jasper? Is milk opal actually opal or jasper? In any case, there are seven components that interact in order to compose the substance

---

*   Cloos, *Kleine Edelsteinkunde*, p. 42.

of jasper: three forms of crystallization (fibrous, grainy, colloidal) and the four interweaving types of impurities (clayey, metallic-ionic, metallic in compounds, and organic). Between chalcedony and opal there hovers the jasper manifestation of the SiO_2 minerals. Even in the sphere of scientific precision the naming has something imprecise about it.

> As mentioned, one encounters the same imprecision in the spiritual sector of the Apocalypse. Only there the span of the spectral arch is even greater. It ranges from the jasper-light of the One on the throne both by way of jasper crystal luminescence of the hovering city and by way of the jasper substance of the walls, to the precious stones of the twelve foundation stones. This provides an outline for the jasper problem from two angles: from the mineral outside and from the purely spiritual and imaginative inner side. Moreover, there is a further problem, which stems from the Old Testament. There we find the twelvefold of the precious stones of the high priest's breastplate, with 4-times-3 precious stones (Ex. 28:15–21; 39:8–14). In Hebrew, these stones are named as follows: *odem, pitedah, barequed, nopek, sepper, jahalom, leshem, schbo, ahlamah, tarschisch, schohan,* and *jaschpe;* in both places this sequence is identical. Luther and most Bible translators render these names as follows: sard, topaz, emerald, ruby, sapphire, diamond, lyncurian, agate, amethyst, turquoise, onyx, jasper. Not so the translators of the Old Testament into ancient Greek (this Greek Old Testament is called the *Septuagint*). They translate: *sard, topaz,* and *emerald,* the same as Luther; but then: anthrax (rather than ruby), sapphire, then jasper (rather than diamond), ligurian, agate, amethyst (same as Luther), then chrysolite (rather than turquoise), beryl (rather than onyx), and onyx (rather than jasper). The ancient translators developed the most painstaking learnedness. As Hellenistically illuminated Jews, they were at home in both Greek and Hebrew. What in the Middle Ages is understandable as ruby and anthrax is actually unintelligible as *jahalom.* Luther says *diamond,* the ancients *jasper.* And in the place where in Hebrew it says *jaschpe,* the actual name from which the word *jasper* is derived, the ancients name the stone *onyx.**

---

* Cf. Bock, *The Apocalypse of St. John* (tr. from German edition).

Overall, one needs to try to feel one's way into the connection between the word or name, the concept, and the appearance or object that existed for ancient prescientific humanity. For in those times—and this is what matters—people used the name to designate not so much the object as the experience of soul that a person associates with the object. Now this experience is no less subjective or objective than pure sense perception. In truth, it means much rather that ancient humanity was considerably more capable of experiencing the essential, the auric, the soul-and-spiritual of the things, than their purely sense-perceptible objective outer side. The name *carbuncle* is a good example for this. The same thing, caused by the glowing red color, was experienced in the ruby, as well as in the garnet and the balas ruby—something to do with the experience of the human soul's inner mystery of the blood (which is where the soul lives). This is the experiential background for the Latin *Carbunculus* and the Greek *anthrax*. They had the same experience with glowing coal: this is what coal, ruby, garnet, spinel, maybe red tourmaline, too, is like. Similarly, ice is also rock crystal and "glass," frozen light essence (*crystallos*).

What did the Apocalyptist's jasper experience consist of that caused him to use the same word to designate the Father God, divine light, heavenly luminescence, the cubic form of the city walls, their substance, and the first stone used to embellish them? This situates the discrepancy not between the Septuagint and the Masoretic (Hebrew) text, but rather between Luther (and/or us) and the ancient names. This makes it impossible to identify directly, and in an outer sense, the ancient designation with one, and only one, certain mineral, as it is done today. Thus, one will have to try to find the "jasper experience" of the ancients, then, to see where it manifests throughout the mineral realm. Hence jasper, in the Apocalyptic sense, means much more than jasper in mineralogical terms, much as it does mean there.

What one needs to do is to find which mineral can unite the greatest phenomenological force of expression with the respective spiritual image experience designated by the term *jasper;* in the process, minerals may need to be included that today have no connection with the name *jasper*.

Mineral Names as Expressions of Ancient Human Mineral Experience

The ancient names for minerals have five different origins. The first is given according to geographic place of origin (agate after the river Achates in Sicily; sard after the city of Sardes in Asia Minor). The second is its outer appearance. Thus, even today for natives of Sri Lanka, tourmaline = *turmali*, meaning "yellow precious stone"; there are a whole series of precious stones that bear this name; also, *chrysoprase* and *chrysolite*, meaning "gold-yellow-green stone." Mining practice led later to the third source of mineral names (such as *feldspar*, yellow copper ore). The fourth type of designation origin contains the soul experience a person has with the stone (anthrax and carbunculux, blood-red glowing coal, related by blood; *lynchius* = strongly luminous stone in lamp light: this is the tourmaline experience). From here the fifth origin of stones' names developed from their magical and/or medicinal effect (*amethystos* = literally: keeping from intoxication).

Thus, to solve the jasper problem it will be necessary to find the experience of it. As a start, one can leave the Indian, Persian, Mesopotamian, and Egyptian names out of the picture and take the names of the twelve stones of the high priest's breastplate in the Old Testament. But we will have to base our inquiry on ancient identifications used in the Septuagint; then one finds the following nine of the twelve Apocalyptic stones: *odem* = sard; *pidetah* = topaz; *barequed* = emerald; *sepper* = sapphire; *jahalom* = jasper; *lesham* = ligurian, hyacinth; *ahlamah* = amethyst; *tarschisch* = chrysolite; *schohan* = beryl. It is a characteristic of the Hebrew language that its entire vocabulary can be traced to a number of root words possessing a remarkable structure. They are all bisyllabic words, with three consonants of any sort and two vowels between them, usually the vowel "a." They are verbs that express activities. Even when they designate properties, as adjectives do, they do so as verbs do. The classic example is the second word in Genesis: *BRH*, pronounced "barah"—i.e., to create. The derivations of the nine names of the stones in the high priest's breastplate are the following:

1. *odem* = sard, carnelian
   a) *ADEM* = to be red; related to *DAM* = blood, rosiness of the cheeks, scarlet color of the blood.
   b) *ADAM* = to be a living, rosy human being
   c) *ADAMAH* = fertile red earth, yellow earth.
2. *pitedah* = topaz. This word is borrowed from Sanskrit: *pita* = yellow stone. Golden yellow is the experience of topaz.
3. *baraqued* = emerald
   a) *BARAQ* = lightning (Greek: *margus* = fool, crazed one, debaucher, insane person; in Sanskrit: *marahata*). The emerald experience has something do to with ecstasy and flashing inspiration. One need only bear in mind the rainbow-like emerald around the One sitting on the throne in chapter four of the Apocalypse, the One shone round about by lightning flashes.
4. *sepper* = sapphire
   SAPPAR = to scrape, to clean, to sweep clean, to smooth or polish. But also: to count, order, harmonize. It was applied subsequently to the smoothing and polishing of paper and leather in the manufacture of writing-scrolls and, ultimately, to writing itself. The *sepper* is a scribe or a captain who brings his army in order. The ancients' sapphire experience has something calming, carrying, ordering, and spiritualizing.
5. *jahalom* = jasper
   HALAM = to make something solid or condense something, make it constant, lasting, by means of hitting (with the foot or the hammer) or stamping (using the feet). This is the mood of the primal jasper experience: something that has been densified or made constant. This understanding led Luther to translate the word *jahalom* as diamond, the hardest and most precious mineral, while the Septuagint says jasper. Something shimmers through here that helps to connect the jasper experience with the one a person can have of the diamond.
6. *leshem* = ligurian, hyacinth

LASHAM = using one's feet to destroy something; but also: to spiritualize something by physically destroying it. *LASHAM* contains this connotation. For the ancients, this was the experience of hyacinth.

7. *ahlamah* = amethyst
CHALAM = mild, soft, fleshy, to be healthy, to be dreaming, also: to have dreams. Chaldean for "dream"; Helenic and Hebrew: *achalah* = "God willed this, let God prevail." For the ancients the experience of causing someone to dream means to have prophetic dreams, i.e., to experience the spiritual world. Amethyst makes a person clairvoyant; this is the amethyst experience.

8. *tarschisch* = chrysolite
It is hard to say whether this name traces to the city of Tarnish (Tartessos in Spain); if it were, a chrysolite would be a "tartesian." The corresponding Hebrew root would be: *TERESCH* = to be stern, dark, veiled. In this case, the Saturn-like strictness and this attribute of veiling would be a highly noteworthy experience of the nature of chrysolite.

9. *schohan* = beryl.
SCHOHAM = to be thin, pale, darkened. Here as well one might encounter a remarkable contradiction between the mineral manifestation and its experience. But in this place, in which the Septuagint says *beryl,* Luther says *onyx.* This is completely in keeping with the experience. What did the translators of the Septuagint have in mind when they rendered *schohan* as beryl? After all, it is clearly the onyx experience that is meant.

This mystery becomes even more complicated by the name *jasper* occurring at the end in the Hebrew version. It is the word that for the most part the Greek jasper was derived from, and the Septuagint renders it as *onyx.* Has there been a mix-up here, a corruption of the texts? In the Old Testament's description of the institution of the high priest's breastplate, the shoulder parts are also described (Ex. 28.9–12). And Luther translates this passage as follows: "You shall take two onyx stones." In Hebrew it says: *EBENI–SCHOHAM. Eben* means precious stone, and here as well Luther translates *onyx*. The Septuagint uses *emerald* to translate this word. Thus for the shoulder stones it uses emerald to translate *schohan*, and for the breastplate it uses *onyx*; it never uses *onyx* both times, as Luther does. Now emerald is a variety of beryl, to be sure; but the experiential content of the word root points clearly to *onyx*. The word *jaschpe*, which the Septuagint translates as *onyx*, has the following roots in Hebrew:

a) SCHAPPAH = to rub, to scrape, to clean, to sweep clean, to smooth or polish; but also: to purify, strain with a sieve, to filter.
b) SCHAPPAH = to place, set, lay, bring to rest.
c) JISCHPAH = to denude, make bare, strip (e.g., to strip the bones of a skeleton of flesh).
d) SCHAPPAH and SCHEPPAH = figuratively: white, cheese-colored, curdled (sour) milk.

This last meaning in a way comprehends all of the preceding: the purifying straining, settling (the soured portion of milk that settles), a being or existence stripped of whey. In such a profane, everyday image of an organic process, the experience of what is meant by the Hebrew word *jaschpe* becomes clear. But if this experience is brought to bear on a mineral, one can associate it with milk opal, for instance, which is also called *jaspopal*. So here one has a complicated experiential process that is tied together in the simple image of milk. But if jasper is connected with the *jahalom* experience, this leads one to the highest, most luminous, hardest mineral, to diamond. In this case, then, the jasper experience is based on the image of diamond. If on the other hand one connects the jasper experience with *jaschpe*, this leads one to the image of the milk opal. But then jasper as an experience means not only an association with all types of jasper in the modern sense, but rather, additionally, with diamond on one hand and milk opal on the other hand, in the same way as the word *carbuncle* as an experience refers figuratively to ruby (clay), garnet (an iron-magnesium silicate), and the balas ruby, or red spinel. Except that with jasper the associations are founded much more deeply and with no such evident "logic" as the carbuncle.

Hence the jasper problem is not one of designation, but rather one of experience. And this jasper experience, if one be permitted to call it that, has a number of different components. The experience of utmost light-filled hardness and clarity leads to diamond (*jahalom*); the shine, shimmer, the cloud-likeness, the mutual devotedness leads to milk opal (*jaschpe*); the interweaving of the experiential components of consolidation, purification, settling, unveiling is replicated in the substance tissue (filament, grain, colloid, clouding, and tinting), in what we call jasper today. And, finally, this experience ends in a kind differentiation in heliotrope and in the inflamed, multicolored varieties. Diamond, milk opal, jasper, and heliotrope are the outer mineral images for the totality of the jasper experience, when this experience appears to beholding consciousness in spiritual images. And that is the case in the Apocalypse. If one adds the thoughts of Abel-Rémusat, one can even include nephrite as an image of the jasper experience. The emerald-sapphire character with its lightning element then becomes settled, precisely in heliotrope. One comes from the jasper of the Far East via the jasper of the Old Testament to the jasper of the Apocalypse.

But there is also one final element that must not be overseen. The considerations up to now have already drawn attention to the depths to which the Apocalyptist's experience of jasper extends. There is nothing more profound, nor exalted, more comprehensive nor originary than the Father God. For the Apocalyptist, this is "jasper" enveloped by sard and emerald. The Father entity shines forth out of the depths of the world, just as what can be called jasper does, in a certain segment of its appearances. This is the diamond experience. The revelations of the Father God proceed from Him in the Son, who is the Logos. This is Johannine experience through and through. It flows into the stone that is the first of the twelve, the heliotrope. This side of the jasper experience displays itself red like the blood of sacrifice and green like the selfless life-corporeality of the plant. In the Son, what emanates in the light of the diamond-jasper streams forth spiritual love out of the Father, and becomes the imagination of jaspopal. As the Son receives a body in the human being Jesus, body and the blood become an experience whose mineral image can be found in heliotrope.

But this raises the question as to whether perhaps both experiences—the ones that are cosmic reality in the body and blood of the resurrected Jesus Christ—are contained in the Apocalyptist's jasper experience. In the Middle Ages, it was self-understood that precisely this was the content of the image of the carbuncle stone—garnet, ruby and balas ruby. Thus even the garnet experience can be included in the total jasper experience of the Apocalyptist. Now the figure of Jesus Christ has been associated with the zodiac sign of Pisces (as it has, from a different point of view, with Aries, the lamb, or from yet another one, with the lion Leo) of the tribe of David.

In the image of heliotrope as the first foundation stone, what is called jasper is consolidated for suprasensory vision into a portion of this twelvefold. Through just this consolidation, the jasper so designated becomes a bridge to the much more comprehensive jasper experience pervading the whole Apocalypse as the life and death, the sacrificing and transforming, as the Resurrection of the Son of Man, who is the Alpha and the Omega. Through His Resurrection, He transformed the body and blood of the man Jesus of Nazareth into a hovering figure of form and light, a body shot through with spirit and transformed into an ensouled blood. Thus something of the deepest primal ground of the Resurrection corporeality must have become active in the twelve foundation stones, the twelve pylons (Rev. 21:12) with their twelve angels and the names of the twelve tribes of the people. For the Resurrection body of Jesus Christ forms the foundation stone—the foundation stones—of the germinal construction which is the Heavenly Jerusalem.

The Apocalyptist's jasper experience must contain this cosmic mystery as well. The twelve foundation stones, the twelve angels, the names of the twelve tribes, the twelve precious stones, the names of the twelve apostles, and the twelve pearls belong together. They are the germinal power of the Resurrection body that has become the resurrecting world. One feels called upon to expand the mineral images of diamond, milk opal, jasper, heliotrope, and nephrite to include the images of those precious stones that depict the body and blood of the Resurrection. In the Middle Ages, these precious stones were garnet accompanied by ruby and spinel for the blood. In the present day, it will become possible to find the image for the Resurrection body in tourmaline, and in diamond the image for the purest, most consummate formative power of this body and this blood.

The Apocalyptist's Jasper Experience

For the Apocalyptist, "jasper" is initially the entity of the Father God as the source of light, love and life. Diamond, sard, and emerald are the images of this: in the Father, jasper is diamond. Furthermore, it is the Father's love of the Son in the Spirit. Milk opal is the image of this. In the Spirit, jasper is milk opal. Thirdly, it is the love of the Son toward the Father. In the Son, the Word has become human; in Jesus of Nazareth it has become flesh and blood. Diamond, tourmaline, and garnet are the image of this. In the Son, jasper is diamond, tourmaline, and garnet. Moreover, finally, the Son is the nature and essence of the human being pervaded with Christ. The Logos is individualized, the potential for Resurrection implanted in every human being. Heliotrope is the image of this. In Christ and in the human being, jasper is heliotrope. To be sure: an endeavor to bring together such diverse minerals as diamond, sard, emerald, milk opal, hydrophane, tourmaline, garnet, heliotrope, and nephrite not with the mineral jasper, but rather with the jasper experience as one's point of departure—such an attempt is no longer scientific or systematic in any chemical or crystallographical sense. The content of the jasper experience is connected with a higher unity, as opposed to the multiplicity of its individual appearances. It can no longer be apprehended in a purely phenomenological way. But it can be apprehended as something that is a process, even an essence, on which the diverse phenomena are based. This understanding leads to a higher essentiality on which an equivalent experience is founded, an essentiality that inheres in all the phenomena as its various metamorphoses. What can be the common essence of these manifold precious stones? What is it that makes them what the Apocalyptist calls "the most exalted, most precious of all precious stones"? This, after all, is the characteristic aspect of the jasper entity in the Apocalypse. The jasper experience of the Apocalyptist is the experience of the deepest unity of the triune Divinity within Itself, within the hierarchies, within the world and within the human being. It is for this reason that for him "jasper" is the very most precious of the precious stones, the godly epitome of all power of the Father, all virtue of the Son, all creative forces of development, consciousness, and the light forces of consciousness. So what is its image in its manifold qualities? The very power of spiritual enlightenment itself, the power of Apocalyptic vision. John is a jasper-initiate. This means his Apocalyptic experience is based on a "jasper entity," which is Apocalyptic because it enables the seer to behold and to know the Godhead in imagination, inspiration, and intuition, just as in turn the Godhead beholds the seer.

Moreover, the process of cosmic development as such is the foundation of the jasper experience. The former is the descent from divine spiritual origins to an end-point in the mineral manifestation of the world. And it is the transit through this final mineral state, where the reascent to a new spiritual existence of the future germinates. An essential aspect of this process is that what is the most exalted descends the most deeply, what is the lightest becomes the hardest, what is the brightest becomes the darkest, what is primally unified takes on the greatest manifoldness. The mystery of the Logos is revealed here, the mystery of the Godhead in the Son, in the Christ. Saint Paul formulated this in his letter to the Ephesians: But to each one of us grace has been given as Christ apportioned it. This is why it says, "When he ascended on high, he took many captives and gave gifts to his people" (Eph. 4:7–10). What does "he ascended" mean except that he also descended to the lower, earthly regions? He who descended is the very one who ascended higher than all the heavens, in order to fill the whole universe.

This mystery of descent and ascent is ultimately the jasper experience; and in the above-mentioned precious stones belonging in the spiritual sense to the jasper group, something can be experienced that is uttered in the spirit-word of Saint Paul.

The Middle Ages were aware of these mysteries. This awareness emerges in two places, one in an esoteric sense, in the saga of the Grail. The Grail image as a chalice is an imagination of comprehensive significance. Attempts by linguists to interpret the term *lapis exillis* in Eschenbach's *Parzival* move among *lapis ex coelis, lapis ex soelis,* and *jasper ex coelis*. Nevertheless, there are contradictions to these interpretations. For one, the Grail chalice is jasper, white, or milky moon-blue; for another, it is a carbuncle stone from the crown of Lucifer, glowing red, ruby, and garnet; in a third case, it is glass-clear transparent diamond or rock crystal. In truth, the Grail chalice is "lapis jasper," but it is this in the deepest and most all-encompassing sense, the one in which ultimately even the very vision of the Apocalyptist forms a Grail chalice. The luminous head of this chalice is diamond-like; its loving heart garnet-like; and its devoted will jasper-like.

In an exoteric sense, this mystery is proclaimed in the emperor's crown of the Middle Ages. It was fashioned in 933 in a goldsmith's shop in Mainz or Regensburg, under the rule of Rudolf of Burgundy. In the year 1032, it was passed on to the emperor of the Salian dynasty, Konrad II, along with the Burgundian inheritance. After his coronation on Easter Sunday, 1037, Konrad gave his own crown as a gift to Saint Odilo, the abbot of Cluny, for his monastery. He then had the royal crown of Burgundy refashioned into a combination diadem and helmet crown, to make it the imperial crown. It was made of pure solid gold. The diadem is surrounded by eight semicircular plates. The front plate bears the forehead cross. Below this, the legendary and wonderful stone called "the Orphan," Orphanus, was mounted. In his book on stones, Albertus Magnus says of this stone that "it was never seen anywhere else, for which reason it was called *Orphanus,* 'the Orphan,' which gives off its light even at nighttime." Walther von der Vogelweide also sang of this stone. According to research conducted on the subject, the stone was a milk opal that found its way from the Orient to the goldsmith atelier. The stone has been missing since the fourteenth century and was replaced by a sapphire (Schmidt, p. 93).

According to legend, the "Orphan" was a gift form the one Duke Ernst. In the literary work of an anonymous Franconian author around 1180, a description is given of how Duke Ernst rebelled against the emperor and was exiled. He ended up in the Orient and spent his life there as a poor exile in the midst of the affluence of a legendary kingdom called Grippia, which was overflowing with gold, silver, and precious stones. He strove to serve the king of Grippia but was not recognized in his efforts and instead was prosecuted and pursued by the might of the griffins, which according to legend collect gold and precious stones. Pursued by them, Ernst fled on a raft that ultimately carried him on a river into a dark mountain that was illuminated by stones embedded in its cliffs. There, he suddenly found the "Orphan" in the rock walls. The legend gives an account of how Duke Ernst broke the stone out of the rock and how the stone gave him the strength to escape the griffins with his faithful followers; he gained untold riches, returned to his homeland, and gave the stone to the emperor for his crown. "The Orphan" is just as unique by its own nature. It is virginal and is called *jasper.* According to a different interpretation, the name "the Orphan" refers to the circumstances under which Duke Ernst broke the stone out of the rock wall. For he was in a state of absolute abandonment, in the very direst situation, himself an orphan. "The Orphan" comes to a person's aid in this human situation, even if the person has caused it through his own sinful behavior. Thus the view of the Middle Ages; its name is jasper.

This shows not only how the jasper experience still echoes in the Middle Ages, even into the outer world circumstance of the sanctification of secular might, but also how the inner side of the jasper experience shimmers through, even into the verbal designation of the Grail chalice. So anyone wanting to do justice to the Apocalypse needs to strive to visualize the diamond—its designation as jasper notwithstanding—wherever in the presence of the Father God and the doxa of the heavenly Jerusalem the Apocalyptist speaks of "jasper." Even modern commentators do this. Thus, it says in Rienecker's linguistic key to the New Testament* that the doxa emanates radiance as that of the brightness of the most precious stone, the crystal clear jasper, which means that it likely is identical to the experience of diamond. Where Saint John speaks of the "jasper light of the City," one can think of the "Orphan," milk opal. Where John uses the word *jasper* in speaking of the wall in its cubic shape and its measurements, one can in turn think of diamond or rock crystal, but now not as luminous shine, but rather as perfect crystal in cubic shape. Where John speaks of the substance of the wall and once again says *jasper,* one can think of the substance of jasper in the modern sense, with all its mineral manifestations. Where John speaks of pylons, of the foundations stones, one can picture the images of the Resurrection corporeality in diamond, tourmaline, and garnet. Finally, where he calls the first of the twelve precious stones "jasper, shining forth from the zodiac sign of Pisces," one can call to mind heliotrope as a specific manifestation.

The innermost jasper experience of the Apocalyptist is the foundation of all these images. Diamond, opal, jasper, tourmaline, garnet, and heliotrope have all become "jasper." The prophetic awareness of the Apocalyptist lives in their virtues of soul and spiritual forces of the future as the power of imagination, inspiration, and intuition—as vision of the Godhead, to which Christ is the guide. Thus Saint John says in his Gospel: "No one has ever seen God, but the one and only Son, who is himself God and is in closest relationship with the Father, has made him known" (John 1:18). Thus, in a spiritual sense, we can speak of a "jasper group," just as, in a mineralogical sense, we speak, for example, of a garnet family. Spiritually, this means the experience

---

*   Hadorn, *Die Offenbarung des Johannes* (The Revelation of St. John).

in soul gained from a group of minerals connected by a joint mystery. This jasper experience arises from quite specific mineral experiences, through development of the ability to experience the following: These minerals are connected with the highest divine activity, and through the spiritual manifestation of this activity they have descended the most deeply and nevertheless have remained virginally "precious." This causes them to assume a germinal power that enables them once more to ascend to the very highest. The mystery of descent and ascent is the true content of the Apocalyptist's jasper experience.

In the following short poem, in which Christian Morgenstern speaks of human beings in regard to the jasper experience, in thought we might replace the words *human beings* with "God in the image of the precious stone."

> I have beheld *human beings* in their deepest form;
> I know the world down to its foundational content.
>
> I know that love is its profoundest meaning,
> and that to love ever more and more I am here.
>
> I spread my arms out wide, as He did;
> I wish I could, as He, embrace the whole world.
> —CHRISTIAN MORGENSTERN

CHAPTER 4: JASPER EXPERIENCE

In Diamond, Tourmaline, Garnet, and Opal

Bodily Resurrection: Portrayals of the Resurrection

Christian painters have depicted the Resurrected One time and again. The impetus to do so comes directly from the Gospels. In the plainest of scenes and the naïvely spiritual language of the Evangelists, accounts are given of the resurrected Jesus Christ in the presence of women and the disciples. A perfect human figure in form, face, hands, and feet—filled with a spiritual-physical substance, a hovering corporeality whose center of gravity is found within itself—charged with the brightest luminescence and the pulse of the inexhaustible life stream of a blood that has been ensouled and embodied. For the earthly human being bound to the material existence of the sensory world, to the abstractness of the thought world and to the subjectivity of the emotions, the very act of thinking this at all it is tremendously difficult.

Of all the painting attempts one calls to mind, including even Rafael's *Transfiguration,* the Isenheim Altarpiece by Matthias Grünewald is the one to which we always return. In doing so, it is important always to hold the two paintings together: the *One on the Cross* and the *Resurrected One*—bearing in mind equally, however, that the former image goes together with the depiction of the Crucifixion on exhibit at the art gallery in Karlsruhe.

The drastic nature of a naked, tortured, destroyed materiality that one experiences in each of the Crucifixion paintings is unsurpassed. On the other hand, in the picture of the Resurrected One a pure process dominates—a self-generating dynamic of manifestation, even Apocalyptic. The colors of this painting can also be expressed in terms of minerals; ruby shines from the eyes and mouth. The aura is gold; the auric rainbow is emerald. Diamond incorruptibility displays itself in the whitish shimmer of the countenance, chest, hands, and feet. The blood from the five wounds is garnet; tourmaline is in the colors yellow, red, purple, blue, and white of the flowing, exposing-yet-covering burial cloth. It is this cloth that maintains the connection to the granite block of the tomb and the marble hulks of the grave with its ashen content. Only the green has detached itself and surrounds the aura—the creative font of the body's formation, as it were—which is shone through and woven round with stars and connected with the aura's gold in a way different from the colors of the cloth.

Finally, the guards, who have fallen in four different directions (the fourth, near the granite rock in the right background, is hard to see) become contorted images of fragmented elements and temperaments in human form. In addition, at the lower right in the very foreground, the tree stump, the Earth is grown old. Is it perhaps even now the bearer of the hidden buds of a future greening?

Resurrection of the Body

The materials the painter uses are of physical-mineral nature. The images they portray express active, creative life—glowing soul—luminous spirit. Is it not the case that what we see is both manifestations of the suprasensory and sense-perceptible manifestation—ruby, gold, emerald, diamond, garnet, tourmaline, pearl, and wood?

What makes the body a body? Is it also possible to bring the human body to expression in mineral terms? We have the pure form that makes the human body an upright structure. In his lectures *From Jesus to Christ* (lecture 6), Rudolf Steiner calls this form the phantom; the Rosicrucians saw it in the "philosopher's stone," the carbon process. In mineral terms, the pure carbon process manifests as diamond. Something diamond-like shimmers from the bodily forms in Grünewald's painting.

We have the bodily substance—the flesh and bones. By virtue of the stars' formation, they are a tool and a dwelling for the human soul. This tool is structured according to the number twelve; the dwelling is twelve-chambered. This earthly human body is a life of its own according to natural law and is only partially at the command of the human being. In the Resurrection body, this life of its own becomes a process of development and formation. It produces its own substantiality—each time anew according to the given momentary state—and spiritualizes it back again as it forms corporeality, forming the bodily state as it spiritualizes. There is no other mineral that manifests the overflowing abundance of substantiality, color, and formation as the tourmaline entity does.

Grünewald's artistic genius symbolizes this in the wafting, falling, and ascending burial cloth.

Matthias Grünewald (c. 1470–1528): image of the risen Christ from the Isenheim altarpiece in Colmar; the microcosmic Resurrection

Albrecht Altdorfer (c. 1480–1538): the macrocosmic Resurrection

We have the blood, which mediates between body and soul, just as its warmth bridges and mediates between spirit and matter. In the mineral realm, ruby and garnet replicate to perfection what Grünewald casts as a physical image in the eyes, the mouth, and the wounds.

As the fourth thing, we have the state in which all bodily substance abides, the colloidal state of all enlivened, ensouled, and spirit-filled matter. The primal substance of this state is living protein, with its macromolecules. In the white feet of the Grünewald painting, it shimmers like opal; in fact, the opal variety of silicic acid is nearly the only mineral that does not crystallize as a solid, but hardens into a solid gel.

The material human body contains substances in a living state. They are found in all living beings as the basis of all living corporeality The substances form a kind of center between the substances of the mineral world on the one hand (which remain fully lifeless in their crystalline state) and the substances that in completely spiritualized form make up the Resurrection body of Jesus Christ. The Risen One within the substances of His Resurrection body appears to the disciples. The Christ spirit created this Resurrection body anew out of the Father-God, through the Jesus soul and out of the Jesus body during the three years of its indwelling, and then through crucifixion, entombment, and Resurrection.

The Risen One is also the Resurrection—an active and creative transformation of all that is dead into life, all that is evil into good, all that is weak into strength, all that is diseased into health, and all that is demise into exaltation. This primal power of transformation proceeds not just from the Christ "I" but from the entire Resurrection body of Christ. In the course of cosmic events, it is transferred to those who unite with Christ, and through Christ and humanity it is transferred to Earth, including the mineral realm.

At the same time that Grünewald painted his picture, Albrecht Altdorfer created the Resurrection painting that hangs in Munich today. The colors that Grünewald gives the aura, the bodily figure, and the burial cloth, Altdorfer applies to the banner and to nature, especially the clouds—the color-borne effects of the Resurrection pass over to the cosmos. Grünewald depicts the microcosmic aspect of the Resurrection, Altdorfer the macrocosmic aspect. Altdorfer leads to the germinating force of the Resurrection of the Earth along with its mineral realm. What the Risen One bears as form, body, and blood becomes form, body, and blood of a future world—the germinating force of the future Jupiter existence.

Resurrection as Creative, Active Power

The primal force of transformation is the jasper experience proper of the Apocalyptist. What manifests in the mystery of descent and ascent is the obverse aspect of the jasper experience—Resurrection from the dominion of the Risen One. For the Apocalyptist, all those minerals in whose physical appearance and suprasensory spirit images this power resonates—resonates such that a jasper experience of this kind can come about—bear the name *jasper*. This is why the image elements of the Apocalypse contain the four minerals that function as conveyers of the jasper experience wherever the name *jasper* occurs. In chapter 4, "white jasper of the One on the throne," it is diamond, the image of utmost hardness and highest luster; it is likewise hidden in the "jasper of the city walls," but even the "cubic form" of the city contains something of diamond's nature. This shows in the gold that makes up the city, which, after all, is transparent like crystal, so that gold's purity and soundness is pervaded with the purity, luster, and clarity of diamond.

The wealth of the twelve precious stone colors contains a further overarching common mystery: heliotrope (dark green with blood-red specks); sapphire (deep dark blue); chalcedony (sky-blue); emerald (deep green); sardonyx (red-white-black); sard (red shot through with a white shimmer); chrysolite (gold-green); beryl (transparent and bright); topaz (gold-yellow); chrysoprase (apple-green); hyacinth (yellow permeated with red and red permeated with yellow); amethyst (purple-red passing through blue and blue passing through red). This spectrum of colors throughout the twelvefold receives something higher, something that all the individual images have in common. The first of these twelve stones is not called *heliotrope,* but rather *jasper.* It betrays something that points to a deeper experience within the totality of the twelve stones—to tourmaline. Such a mind-boggling wealth of colors is one of the several unique aspects of this mineral. Thus, we can see that the twelve stones are shone round about by an experience of tourmaline, which gathers them into a higher unity. That unity is in fact a jasper experience of the power of the Resurrection. The most mystery-laden spot in the description of the Heavenly Jerusalem is the sentence pertaining to the power of its luminosity: "It shone with the glory of God, and its brilliance was like that of a very precious jewel, like a jasper, clear as crystal" (Rev. 21:11).

We could also translate this as "like a jasper in its act of crystallizing." Clearly, when we hear the word *luminosity,* we think not of color but first of *light.* Light becomes stronger precisely when it assumes a golden, rose-colored, or delicate-blue shimmer. In this instance, it appears more spiritual (gold); in the second, more soul-like (rose-colored, light red); and in the third, more etheric and physical. It is only such a soul-like luminosity of the spirit, however, that is the foundation of the power of the Resurrection, and hence also the foundation of the jasper experienced by the Apocalyptist in the luminosity of the Heavenly City. This delicate mystery of soul and spirit is, actually, the nature, or essence, of the "most precious and noblest of precious stones."

In the Middle Ages, the diamond as well as the so-called carbuncle were the most precious stones. Those such as the ruby and garnet were given this name when their luminescence was experienced as resembling the blood's fire; the aspect of the human body that comes closest to that luminescence is the blood. What the Apocalyptist designates as jasper here is actually the *jasper experience in the blood.* In the blood, life, soul, and spirit are the most perfectly incarnated and interconnected. The blood experience triggered by ruby and garnet is the mineralogical aspect of what constitutes the blood-borne aspect arising in the Resurrection forces. In garnet, this "blood likeness" can be experienced even more strongly than in ruby. However, blood also has a bluish nuance. The etheric-material aspect joins spirit, soul, and life.

All objects and entities in the world manifest in three different ways. One is what they are for themselves in contrast to other objects and entities. We need to proceed *analytically* to apprehend individual aspects and the final elements of the composite. The second way manifests in what an object or entity has in common with others of the same kind. We need to *arrange and classify* to see what they have in common. The third is that objects and entities can transform. To apprehend this, we need to be able to see and think in terms of *metamorphosis*. The greatest, most profound, and comprehensive transformational event in the world is the Resurrection of Jesus Christ. It is based on the all-encompassing cosmic force of transformation itself. Its carrier is the Christ entity. This power pervades the entire Apocalypse. Because St. John receives this power, the jasper experience arises within him; after all, it contains the source of power on which the experience of descent and ascent is based. There can be no single precious stone that provides an experiential image for this force.

Spiritual jasper must contain at least as many individual images as there are spheres in which this power of transformation is at work. The first sphere of this transformational power, the creation and maintenance of form, becomes the Resurrection experience in the diamond. The second sphere is the transubstantiation of matter, which becomes the Resurrection experience in tourmaline. The third sphere is the Resurrection as life force. It is active in the blood and leads to the garnet-experience. What they have in common is the very experience of transformation and the power on which it is founded. This power can cause consolidation but it never becomes solid itself. It can cause dissolution, but in itself always remains constant. It can conduct one thing over into another and back again, but it hovers within and above all transition in a state of weaving and wielding. The image-bearing carrier of these forces in the mineral world is the opal. Opals as minerals are solid but are the only minerals that are not crystalline; rather, they "opalize"—that is, they go from one color to the other, hovering, weaving, and shimmering, even in a glowing, fiery way. Light and darkness, brightness and obscurity pass over in them from one state into the other. In boundless devotion to all weaving of color and light, opals reveal the primal transformational force in mineral being. Something of this is also the basis of the jasper experience in the image of God the Father in chapter 4; thus, there is an interpenetration of the most completely crystallized stone—the diamond—and the noncrystallized one—the opal. For the Apocalyptist, a jasper experience weaves within the interplay of the twelvefold in the Heavenly Jerusalem; its image bearer is the essential nature of opal.

Mineral Images of the Resurrection Forces

The Spiritual Jasper Group

I. Name: The Greek term *damao* means "to fracture." *Adamanthinos* means "unbreakable, indestructible, and firm," as well as "invincible, unshakeable, and unalterable." The Greeks also used this word for steel. From this, the word *adamas* arose, and from it the word *diamond*.

II. Research: In the material sense, there is no simpler precious stone than diamond. It consists of plain, pure carbon; we could also say this of coal. It crystallizes in cubic, holohedral* form—mostly in octohedra—and is always fully crystallized and fully developed; in other words, it has always assumed crystalline form before its habitat did. The surfaces of its crystals are always strongly rounded, nearly spherical; the planar nature of its crystal form is marked by a spherical principle.

The hot mother liquor, still partially molten, has cauterized the crystal afterward, and carbonic substances such as hematite or ilmenite, but also quartz and rutile, occur as enclosures. This means these substances solidified previous to the diamond's crystallization. It has

---

*   *Bort* (or *boart*) refers to non-gem-quality diamond shards.

a hardness of 10 out of 10 on the Mohs scale. In fact, however, it is 140 times harder than corundum (ruby, sapphire, which are 9 on that scale), and corundum is 8 times harder than rock crystal (a hardness of 7). Only here can we gauge the extreme hardness of this precious stone. Its density is 3.52. It is fully cleavable.

Diamonds occur almost exclusively in a bedrock called *kimberlite,* which is greenish or brownish peridotic vulcanite that is strongly loosened and tuff-like, containing phenochrysts of olivine, serpentine, pyrope, biotite, augite, spinel, zircon, titanium iron, chromite, and of course diamond. Kimberlite volcanic vents have two different geological age levels. The older ones are Precambrian–Proterozoic, but most ascended later, during the Cretaceous period. In addition to these primary deposits in kimberlite, diamonds are also found mostly in erosion deposits in placers and river sand. In only infrequent but recurring instances, diamonds are also found in meteorites. On Earth, they were created at very great depths and under very high pressure, after which, inside the kimberlite of their bedrock, they ascended relatively swiftly.

The Diamond's shine is a characteristic possessed by no other substance. The diamond is transparent, "of purest water"; however, it can just as well be cloudy or opaque and colorless. But it also occurs in all colors: delicate yellowish, bluish, reddish, brownish, greenish-gray, or blackish; all in varying degrees of saturation. Moreover, there also exist diamonds of saturated red—like rubies—or blue—like sapphires. Stones of this kind fetch unreal prices. A further characteristic of the diamond is its supremely strong light refraction (in red, 2.465). The diamond also has the highest electromagnetic wave-dispersion level. These phenomena are the reasons for its high luster; even when light enters at such slight angles as 24.5 degrees to the surfaces, there is total reflection from both within and without.

The diamond is also a very good conductor of heat. It conducts heat about one to three times as well as copper. Thus, it allows the warmth of the Sun to pass through it while capturing its light all the more strongly. When exposed to ultraviolet light, the diamond is vividly luminescent in blue, green, and yellow—i.e., it retroactively renders visible the invisible range of the sunlight (the chemically active portion).

Precise examinations have shown that the diamond matrix—its subsensory atomic structure—is cubic. All of the cube's corner points and surface-center points are occupied by an atom (thus eight and six points of force, respectively). Five atoms each form a tetrahedron with one another; four with the corners and one at the center of the cube. This means that each atom belongs to two tetrahedra. Microanalyses have shown that, as a rule, every thousandth carbon atom is replaced by a nitrogen atom. Thus, one one-thousandth of the carbon is nitrogen; even aluminum and silicon atoms occur.

The size of diamond crystals ranges from microscopically small to weighing about 600 grams, the giants among diamonds. It is within this range that the different varieties occur. First, the diamond proper, fully crystallized; second, bort,* which occurs in fibrous form and in dense masses. Third is the carbonado,** which is porous and resembles coke or coal slag in its appearance. It is more the result of cooling than of crystallization. (Regarding the origin of diamonds from the natural-scientific point of view, see appendix 28.)

III. Origin and habitat: According to indications from Rudolf Steiner, carbon (C) is the basic substance for the scaffolding, the endowment with form that enables invisible life to be applied toward visible form and figuration in plants, animals, and human beings (see Cloos, p. 117). From black coal to the brightest diamonds, the element carbon unites light and darkness within itself. Diamonds are the most highly transparent and hardest of material—the substance born of light. At the levels in which it is found inside the Earth—as diamond, graphite, bituminous coal, and brown coal—it repeats the developmental levels of the Earth from the Precambrian via the Carboniferous through the Tertiary, each time falling out of a living entity or state. In kimberlite,

---

* *Carbonado*, or "black diamond," the toughest natural diamond.
** Cf. Cloos *Kleine Edelsteinkunde*, p. 119.

the oldest of bedrock, we in turn have the sun-level of the greenstones, at which level carbon crystallize out as diamond.

IV. Soul virtue: The actual revelation of diamond is what it does with light. It condenses light within itself by reducing its front velocity of 300,000 km/sec by half. Through this condensation, tensions arise in the light, which in turn cause the colors to appear. This is how the diamond shows its sparkling fire, which refracts into the eye so suddenly and sparkles instantaneously from one color into the other. If, in the spiritual sense, we construe *light as consciousness* and *color as soul,* we experience the soul life of the diamond. Condensed light becomes color; consciousness condensed in an orderly way becomes soul. In a sense, in the fire of diamond we watch with our own eyes the birth of soul from spirit, or the spirit's internalization into soul. Soul is spirit that, in the face of resistance, has condensed and become internalized. Hölderlin expresses this: "The heart's waves would not foam so splendidly or rise so high as soaring spirit were it not that destiny, the mute old rock, obstructs their course" (*Hyperion*). In the diamond, what represents this "dark rock" is diamond's enormous hardness.

V. Spiritual future: If spirit is to be internalized into soul, and if soul is to be lightened through into spirit, the spirit-soul element has to have bodily form. In the pure spiritual forming force of the body, the inner and outer aspects of the cosmos assume order in the universe and in the human being. When Steiner speaks about how the human material body is based on a purely spiritual-physical form he calls the *phantom,* and about how this basis arose at the same time as the diamond, we come to understand the inner connection between the formation of diamond and the primal human being.

Through the Fall and the burdening of the human phantom with the substance of the material body, the human being of Paradise, who was originally conceived of as suprasensory, descended into matter and now causes the vessel of the body's pure form to be filled with matter.

Matter burdens and damages the phantom. Through Christ's Resurrection, he made matter subordinate to the phantom. If in the context of tourmaline, matter is the image of the human being's restoration; in the context of the diamond, we can say the same of form. Through Christ's Resurrection, the broken (refracted), darkened form of Jesus' human body became luminous; the darkened state was transformed into light, and this gives it the ability to live in the light, guiltlessly and weightlessly, as the bearer of the Resurrected One.

Placing a diamond in the sunlight of a midsummer day and allowing it to sparkle can add special radiance to the celebration of the Christian St. Johnstide festival.

Tourmaline: Blossoming Soul Wealth as Matter

I. Name: *turmali*, "unknown yellow stone," from the language of the Sinhalese in Sri Lanka.

II. Research: tourmaline crystallizes ditrigonally and pyramidally. Its hardness is 7 to 7.5, its density 3 to 3.5. The tourmaline is polychromatic, meaning that the same crystal can have several colors. This can occur either concentrically within each other or, as if in different stories, one above or below the other or, finally, pyramidally in triangles inside and above one another. It is pyroelectric and piezoelectric, meaning that it assumes a polar electrical charge when warmed or cooled, or when under pressure. Parallel to the main axis, it is always darker or opaque; perpendicular to the main axis it is brighter, more transparent.

Tourmalines occur in all possible colors and color nuances; from pure colorless to black; from the most delicate hint of color to the deepest of saturation; from clear transparency of color to cloudy, translucent, opaque formations—they come in all varieties. The tourmaline is by far the most richly colored mineral on Earth. It is found in granite pegmatites, granites, and their gneisses, in argillaceous shales, limestones, ore-deposit sites, and ore veins, and as new formations in sediments. It can also occur as a rock formation of its own—as tourmaline rock. It is also partially rock forming in luxullianite. The most important varieties are achroite, colorless, iron-poor; rubellite, rose-red, ruby red, brownish red, containing lithium and manganese; indigolite, blue, greenish-blue, deep blue to blackish-blue, containing iron; verdelite, greenish, emerald-green, bluish-green, yellowish-green, apple-green and moss-green on account of bivalent iron; dravite, brown, often opaque, rich in magnesium, poor in iron; schorl, black, opaque, with a lot of bivalent and trivalent iron.

Tourmaline is spread over the entire Earth. Scientific mineralogy speaks not of "the tourmaline," but rather of the tourmaline complex, the tourmaline group or the tourmaline series. This is owing to the fact that, in chemical terms, the tourmaline is something absolutely unique: it contains many elements, as compared to other minerals, whose chemical makeup is clearly fixed. Thus one has become accustomed to thinking in terms of "ideals," as it were, of not actually occurring final members; of models that form the real series of the tourmalines by intermixing. It is important to note, though, that not all pure final members can mix with all others. There are seven main chemical members that have been set up. They are the following (ideal formulas):

elbaite (a natrium-lithium tourmaline)
$Na(Li,Al)_3Al_6[(OH)_4/(BO_3)_3/Si_6O_{18}]$
dravite (a natrium-magnesium tourmaline)
$NaMg_3AL_6[(OH)_4/(BO_3)_3/Si_6)_{18}]$
schorl, the iron tourmaline
$NaFe^{2+}_3(Al,Fe^{3+})_6[(OH)_4/(BO)_3/Si_6O_{18}]$
buergerite, likewise an iron tourmaline
$NaFe^{2+}_3Al_6[F/O_3/(BO_3)_3/Si_6O_{18}]$
tsilaisite, the natrium/manganese tourmaline
$NaMn_3Al_6[(OH)_4/(BO_3)_3/Si_6)_{18}]$
uvite, a calcium-magnesium tourmaline
$CaMg_3(Al_5Mg)[(OH)_4/(BO_3)_3/Si_6O_{18}]$
liddicoatite, the calcium-lithium tourmaline
$Ca(Li2Al)_3Al_6[(OH)_4(BO_3)3/Si_6O_{18}]$

These chemical formulae say the following: there is a basic atomic framework common to all: the tourmaline complex. It consists of the following components:

- a six membered ring of SiO_2 tetrahedra (Si_6O_{18})
- a triangle of three boric acid radicals $(BO_3)_3$
- a garland of six aluminum atoms, which is assigned octahedrically to the six membered ring of the silicic acid and the boric acid triangle
- a tip upon which the natrium ion sits, surrounded by four OH ions

This union of ions is related to the kaolin minerals. Each such total union is enmeshed with twelve other such complexes, via aluminum and oxygen. Thus we see how the light foundations of the silicic acids and boric acids are connected with each other through more earthy foundations, but that natrium, which of course is the carrier of the salt-aspect, also plays in. Thus the ion framework tells us in a way that in the tourmaline something lightlike, something earthy, and something saltlike are all interwoven. Within this total complex, certain ground points and ion forces are interchangeable. This allows elements like lithium, magnesium, bivalent and trivalent iron, manganese, calcium, fluorine, and additional aluminum to come into play. Hence one can say: the basic framework contains the constitutive elements *Silicium*, oxygen, boron, hydrogen, and aluminum. To these five constitutive elements, lithium, magnesium, ferrum, manganese, calcium, and florine are added as secondary constituents. Since iron appears in two valences, there are a total of twelve elements whose subsensory substrates are woven into the construction of the tourmaline framework. Now add to these twelve elements another thirty (which occur with greater or lesser frequency, or only in traces) to achieve the abundance of all the tourmaline phenomena, and one sees that about one-half the total 92 natural elements occur in tourmaline. No other mineral or even organic substance possesses this frequency.

III. Origin and habitats:[*] The enormous wealth of the tourmaline's coloration points to blossom-likeness. It is a revelation of the interplay between the blossom-likeness of minerals (precious stones) and that of the plants, but also of the animals, in the sense of the butterflies. The tourmalines are the most organic of the precious stones. In its pneumatolytic environment, the growing crystal was obviously played round by butterfly-like alternating clouds of the metals' colors as it deposited substance. In the case of multicolored tourmalines, the coloration alternates rhythmically and is dispersed throughout the crystal in frequent, repeating changes, like the year's seasons (in dark, autumnal-to-wintry and bright, springlike-to-summery ones). In their prismatic parts, the crystals seldom have strict crystalline shape. The prisms hardly ever have exactly triangular or hexagonal cross sections; their surfaces are much rather rounded by countless stem-like and rippled elevations that run parallel to each other, which originate through the parallel formation of similar crystal surfaces. It is obvious that the tourmaline's plant-forming tendency easily overcomes its mineral aspect, which endows the tourmaline with its stemlike character. In the plants' stem and blossom formation, the Sun is at work. Tourmaline is reminiscent of this. It stems from an epoch in which the Sun was still connected with the Earth and was at work from within it.

IV. Soul virtue: What expresses itself in the wealth of the tourmaline's colors is, in reality, blossoming wealth of soul. The tourmaline is far superior to all other minerals in this. However, this sensual material expression of soul wealth as abundance of color would not be possible without the above-mentioned wealth of elemental substances. This material abundance is the proper mystery of tourmaline's nature. Precisely because it has not become so deeply or exclusively mineral, but rather has maintained much that is plantlike, it is possible for it, through the abundance of its wealth of substance, to bring to manifestation the whole of the soul wealth in the whole that is its wealth of

---

[*]   Cf. Cloos, *Kleine Edelsteinkunde*, p. 122

color. And in the very way in which rock crystal bears within itself the mystery of the sensuality of all life, tourmaline also bears the mystery of soulfulness in material form. It is a gatherer and bringer-in-order of substance for the sake of revealing soul in matter through color.

V. Spiritual future: An ensouled and enspirited human body carries within the matter making up its corporeality the wealth of the organic substances of all its bodily members, into which the totality of both the unconscious and the conscious soul are incorporated. The human soul becomes flesh when it incarnates. Only a portion of the soul remains soul when a person incarnates; a different portion is transformed into flesh.

The great mystery of the Resurrection of Christ remains fully incomprehensible as long as one does not grasp the notion of what the incarnation of a human being is. The word of the gospel according to St. John is never taken in its full reality "And the Word became flesh." In terms of feeling, one always has the sense that we have the body (matter), on the one hand, and soul and spirit on the other. But it is actually absurd to think that a part of what is contained in a human being's physical-mineral body could stem solely from the mineral world. To be sure, it is unusual to conceive of something in a human body as directly incarnating, materializing out of spirit. This is only thinkable as long as one has not yet begun to think the transition of an etheric, suprasensory element into a material, sensory one, and vice versa. It is possible today actually to enact the path from the material to the suprasensory etheric; this happens every time one potentizes something, which consists in the physical matter being thinned by means of diluting and agitating it to the point where it can no longer be detected by physical means, but is nonetheless clearly present in the watery solution in etheric terms, since it displays specific effects in experiments and in practical application. The inverse path is equally thinkable. One need only take as one's point of departure the fact that every time a human being incarnates, not only the soul-spiritual aspect of the human being immerses into already existing substance, unites with it and permeates it (enlivened substance, ensouled substance, enspirited substance), but that even part of the soul-spiritual aspect itself becomes flesh, that is, material substance, with every incarnation. So when it becomes possible to think materialization and dematerialization, it likewise becomes possible to think the Resurrection of the body of Jesus Christ.

What holds for substance as material also holds for the material's appearance, for its quality. The materialization of something non-material and suprasensory expresses itself precisely in the appearance of certain properties and modes of behavior in matter. Here is where we find the connection between tourmaline and Resurrection. With the help of its wealth of substance, the tourmaline renders sensual such things as the totality of its color-wealth. But since all sense phenomena of color are manifestations of soul moods and soul states, the formation of tourmaline is based on the principle of full authority to manifest as color everything of a soul nature. The tourmaline entity consummates this by means of a relatively rigid ion framework, which at the same time is exceptionally loose, so that the most diverse ion forces can stream in and out when tourmaline is being formed. Herein lies the Christ principle of "the Word": "To me is granted full authority over all flesh."

When the human being incarnates, it always means a loss of some of this human being's soul and spirit, as these have become flesh. As well, this means that the person's full authority over the flesh is weakened. But one time a soul became flesh in which the Word of Worlds, the Logos, was incarnated. The Gospel of St. John also says this. And this being overcame the darkening of the flesh, spiritualized the flesh in the Resurrection, and exerted full authority over the flesh as soul and spirit. This is the mystery of the Resurrection of Christ. In the wealth of tourmaline's color and substance become precious stone, but in wealth of its form as well, something of this future also reveals itself out of the past, as if in a mineral imprint. And this is why the tourmaline can lie on the table next to blossoms and lights at Easter.

Garnet: The Heart's Love-Bearing Blood as Color

I. Name: from Latin *granum,* meaning "grain." *Granatum* therefore means "the grainy precious stone," or "grain."

II. Research: The garnet group of minerals is composed by the alternation of manganese, iron, calcium, and aluminum. The garnet varieties arise in compounds with other elements and silicic acid. There are seven of these:

> Magnesium-clay garnet: pyrope, blood red to deep dark red, almost black. $Mg_3Al_2[SiO_4]_3$. Occurs in olivine rock, in kimberlite along with diamonds, eclogites, and serpentinites.
> Iron-clay garnet: almandine, plain garnet, red to blackish-red, bluish-red to purple. $Fe_3Al_2[SiO_4]_3$. Occurs in crystalline states, granites and gneisses.
> Manganese-clay garnets: spessartine, yellow to reddish-brown, yellowish, brown to dark red. Occurs in pegmatites. $Mn_3Al_2[SiO_4]_3$.
> Limestone-clay garnet: glossular garnet, colorless, whitish, green, grayish brown, reddish $Ca_3Al_2[SiO_4]_3$. Occurs in contact limestone rock.
> Limestone-iron garnet: andradite, brown, red, green, black; topazolite, yellowish-green. $Ca_3Fe_2[SiO_4]_3$. Occurs as a contact mineral in skarns; demantoid: emerald-green.
> Limestone-chrome garnet: uvarovite, deep emerald-green. $Ca_3Cr_2[SiO_4]_3$. Occurs in skarns.
> Calcium-vanadium garnet: goldmanite. $Ca_3V^{3+}{}_2[SiO_4)_3$. In all colors.

It is noteworthy that in these chemically widely diverging compounds the crystal compound is unified, chiefly cubic-rhombo-dodecahedral; hence a crystallized drop or a crystallized grain. The grain size ranges from microscopically small to centimeters large. The remarkable thing is that in slates garnet, like emerald, is fully crystalline, i.e., it crystallized before the shale surrounding it solidified. Garnet is widely distributed and often forms rock.

III. Origin and habitats: Garnet's color harmony shows itself in the grown rock of gray and green slate like ripe fruits. In the grayish-green, green to deep green, emerald-green slates it appears red, brownish, and yellow. In the reddish-yellowish serpentines, green garnet appears.* Red garnet is at its most beautiful in eclogites, accompanied by a green pyroxene, the omphacite. This provides a picture "for the cheerful harmony of the mineral plant life of the Sun epoch of the Earth," and reminds one of a green apple tree with its red fruit. In the red and reddish-brown garnets, iron is trivalent, even bloodlike; in the green garnets it is bivalent, more plantlike. Thus in combinations of green and red minerality, this displays a higher principle, a kind of goal that unites the two. Cloos says:

> Red garnet belongs to those remarkable stones designated in ancient times and in the Middle Ages as carbuncle; what was meant by this—independently of the stone's substance—was a particular color approaching that of the blood. In stones of this kind, one saw the purified, chaste and passionless counterpart of the human blood.**

IV. Soul virtue: The above sentences by Cloos actually utter the mystery of the garnet. Novalis describes it more vividly in his *Heinrich von Ofterdingen:*

> There is a sign mysterious in the stone,
> Deeply engraved within its glowing blood.
> To a heart it can be compared,
> Wherein the image of the unknown one rests.
> The stone is coursed about by myriad sparks,
> The image surged about by flowing light.
> Within the former lies the shine of light,
> The latter: will it nest the heart of hearts?

---

*   Cloos, *Kleine Edelsteinkunde.*
** Steiner, *Das Miterleben des Jahreslaufs in Vier kosmischen Imaginationen* (The co-experience of the year in four cosmic imaginations).

A Diamond on kimberlite, octahedron crystal-formation layer

Diamond crystallized as a cube

If we wish to speak of the blood, we can, besides its material components, also look at this organ system's vital functions: The blood is active as

> the bearer of life
> the stream of substances
> the organ of the "I"
> a generator of warmth
> a mediator between body and soul
> the receiver of karma
> the mediator between the breath and sense perception

The deeper background of this sevenfold functioning then shows in the actual being of the blood: It is the creator, the mediator and the destroyer of itself. It bears its own previous developmental stages, as well as, in seed form, its future ones; this is because it is capable in a subtle manner of spiritualizing itself within the living human organism. "Blood is a very special fluid" (Goethe's *Faust*). As matter, it is what has become soul and spirit to the greatest extent; conversely, as soul and spirit it is what is material to the greatest extent. In the peculiar sevenfoldness of the garnet group one finds, in the mineral state already, an expression of the totality of what we have in the blood.

V. Spiritual future: The greatest disease of the blood is its alienation. It is the noncorrespondence of the human being with its own self, the loss of one's own spirituality. The expression of this disease occurs in the blood when its living flow and pulse stops and manifests as fear. Any kind of fear is actually the disease of the blood. By the human spirit turning its thinking and willing in freedom to the world spirit, the human being partakes of freeing the blood from fear, a process of which Rudolf Steiner speaks in connection with the autumnal iron process of the Michael mysteries. In the image of the dodecahedral garnet crystals and the color of the blood that manifests in them, the pure future image of a blood is displayed that no longer knows fear, but rather causes courage for the spirit to ray forth out of the spirit. *

This is why on the morning of the festival of St. Michael garnet can be placed on the table, sheathed in green.

> Christ is risen
> From the womb of decay.
> Wrench yourself joyously
> Free from your bonds!
> Actively praising him,
> Love demonstrating him,
> Traveling preaching him,
> Promising bliss of him,
> To you the Master is near,
> To you He is here!
> —GOETHE, *Faust*, I

Opal: Boundless Devotion as Surging Transformation

I. Name: In Greek, the word is *opallios*, in Latin *opalus*. It stems from ancient Sanskrit, *upala*, which means "precious stone." It goes back to the root *PALA*, meaning rock or cliff. It is also related to the German word *fels* (rock or cliff), and the prefixed "u" lends it the meaning "primal cliff," "ur-cliff," "primal rock," "ur-rock," precious stone, bedrock.

II. Research:

1. Opal's chemical formula is SiO_2 + x water.
2. The substance in all opals is colloidal in gel state. There are three kinds of opal:
    a) the entirely amorphous opal: opal-A (A = amorphous);
    b) the finely crystalline, disordered, that is, felty-chaotic crystallized opal: opal-CT (C = cristobalite, T = tridymite). These two quartz varieties make the tiny crystals.
    c) The finest crystalline, ordered opal: opal-C (C = cristoballite).

---

* Cloos, *Kleine Edelsteinkunde*, p. 48ff.

These minute structures (the colloidal gel, the chaotic, and the ordered crystal formation) are the cause of opalescence. In 1963, this fine structure was able to be photographed for the first time. At magnifications of up to 30,000 times, small spherulites appear in densest spheric packing of silicic acid; these are minute roundish spheres that have solidified out of a colloid. They are the actual cause of the phenomenon of the opalescent play of colors. In opals formed from volcanoes, these spherulites consists of opal-CT and opal-C, in precious opals of opal-A.

3. In some opals there are traces of quartz, tridymite, and cristobalite in cryptocrystalline form.
4. Thus the opal is aged colloidal silicic acid containing 1 to 20% water. Sometimes the water content can be as high as 35%.
5. Compact opal masses have a hardness of 6, and their density and light refraction is dependent on their water content.
6. Opal fractures in shelllike manner, forming bowls.
7. The opals' skin ranges from glassy to waxy, transparent, translucent to opaque.
8. Their coloration varies widely, colorless, milky-white = milk opal; grayish brown, reddish brown, dark brown to black = common opal.
9. Origin: opals are created from hydrothermally disintegrated silicates, above all in volcanic processes. The opal precipitates from hot solutions, geysers, thermal waters, and hot springs. This is its watery origin. On the other hand, it makes up the filling of crevices and druses in rhyolites, trachytes, andesites. In these cases it is of volcanic origin.

    Opal originates from relatively warm circulating water, in sandstone—e.g., in the desert, or oftentimes in chalky deposits in the form of bulbs, flint, and chert, with all transitions to jasper. Most opals of precious-stone quality stem from sedimentary formations.
10. Opal's silicic acid is also created by the protoplasm of plants and animals for the formation of crystal skeletons.

11. Opal can silicify organic deposits of shells and bones of animals, and wood from plants, particle by particle, through pseudomorphosis. The opal assumes the exact form of the organic substances it replaces. In these cases it is called *wood opal*.
12. The varieties:
    a) Precious opal: white to bluish gray, with enormous play of colors over the entire spectrum, called forth by finest lamellar structure between air spaces and opal substance. It is assumed that these air spaces are caused by other mineral substances having been deposited out of the opal and their spaces filled with air. It occurs in andesites and sandstones and is, basically, a solid aerosol.
    b) Glass opal: colorless, clustery, in crusts on basaltic rock. There are a number of different sorts: hydrophane, hyalite, and cacholong, which contains chalcedony.
    c) Milk opal: white to delicate bluish, translucent with strongest play of colors.
    d) Fire opal: orange-red to fire-red like carnelian, almost transparent, so that the strong fire also glows out from inside the opal.
    e) Common opal: as wax opal-yellow to yellowish-brown, as prasopal-green on account of nickel, as jaspopal in many colors, and opaque like jasper, as menalite in bulbs and as forcherite-yellow owing to sulfur.
    f) Geyserite, which precipitates out of hot springs and geysers.
    g) Diatomite: loose stone deposited by diatoms.
    h) Hydrophane: cloudy on account of dehydration.

III. Origin and habitats: Walter Cloos deals extensively with opal in his book. He sees it in polarity with rose quartz as one of the more recent formations of the mineral realm, but in which it is precisely the primal states of the colloidal form of matter that emerge. He goes on to show how opal is related to the lung in the water and air tissue of stones*; in particular, he describes the hydrophanes, which are hardly translu-

---

* Killian, *Crystals: Secrets of the Inorganic*, p. 62 (German edition).

cent until one places them in water, and which in water become nearly perfectly transparent and display a beautiful play of colors. They are also called *world eye, Lapis mutabilis,* or *chameleon stone*. One also often finds hydrophane in a soft jelly-like state. Cloos shows how opal also still has its relationships to light, air, and water—that is, to the life-elements; and this becomes even clearer if one considers that the opals originate out of vulcanism, which means that heat has a part. According to him, one might speak of a kind of hot porridge pervaded with forces (warmth, light, air, and water), which affect it from without and move it, so that it flows and streams into fissures and crevices of the solid earth. Cloos points to the significant difference between the magma on the interior of volcanoes, which has lower temperatures (900°–1,000° C; 1,650°–1,830° F) than when it reaches the atmosphere, reaching 1,100°–1,200° C (2,000°–2,200° F). Since the melting point of silicic acid is 1,800° C (3,275° F), that of other minerals 1,500° C (2,735° F), it becomes clear that the water contained in magma lowers the melting point. This means that in the magma inside the volcano the elements intermix, but that they separate when the magma reaches the surface. Then everything deteriorates into gases, steam, and molten substances, and the heat is released. These are processes out of which opal emerges. In the final hydrothermal phase of vulcanism, it preserves and/or first assumes the state that is the primal condition of the mineral world overall; it becomes a colloid.

IV. Soul virtue: The circumstances described above lead to a fundamental question about the cause of opal's extraordinary state. The solid aggregate state and the crystalline form are typical for the entire mineral world. Liquids and gases are unusual: of the 92 elements, 11 are gases (the 6 earthly gases and oxygen, nitrogen, hydrogen, fluorine and chlorine), 2 are liquids (quicksilver and bromine), and the remaining 79 elements are solid at normal temperatures. The same is true of minerals in chemical compounds. They are solid, with a single proper exception: water (if one disregards the gases and quicksilver).

The second characteristic, the crystalline state, is again the rule for the mineral world. Now, precisely the substance that normally forms the most beautiful crystals, that is, *Silicium*, forms colloids with the opal. The only minerals that metals can occur as colloidal additions in crystals are metals.

But what are exceptions in the natural world? Are they nothing more than what does not adhere to the rules, or do they point to something latently present as a possibility in the "normal" phenomena? There is something precisely in the exceptions that betrays aspects of earlier stages of "the norm." This is how Goethe always regarded the exception in nature. In the extraordinary, something always appears that has otherwise hidden or enshrouded itself or has withdrawn into the usual.

Seen in this way, the colloid on one hand and the crystal on the other become entities. A crystal is a point space structured strictly according to straight planes and lines; a colloid, by contrast, is an interpenetration (rather than a differentiation) of the three aggregate states, consisting of simultaneous flowing transitions of the one into the other with no calculable structure at all.

There are always two or three phases that are interwoven, particles regularly distributed within their medium. These particles can be spherical, or they can be long like sausages. Their dimensions lie just below the visibility range of a light microscope. In the ultramicroscope they appear as luminous refracting lenses in unceasing and lively Brownian motion, a fully accidental trembling back and forth. Their size ranges between one-one-hundred-thousandth and one-millionth of a millimeter. One distinguishes between the loose or dispersed phase of the particles and the dispersion medium ion in which these particles are atremble. All three aggregate states can occur within each other. Hence:

        liquid in gas   e.g., fog
        solid in gas   e.g., smoke

gas in liquid	e.g., foam
liquid in liquid	e.g., emulsion
solid in fluid	e.g., suspension
gas in solid	solid foam, e.g., opal
fluid in solid	solid foam, e.g., hydrophane
solid in solid	solid sol

One sees that the only combination lacking is gas in gas, for gases interpenetrate entirely. In sol, the particles are still freely mobile even though it is solid. When they are interconnected in netlike fashion and no longer freely mobile, the sol becomes a gel. Thus one can characterize the colloid in the following way: In the colloid, the laws that hold for the aggregate states of matter are, for all intents and purposes, virtually suspended. Even smallest droplets of gas enclosed as remainder colloids within fluids of the crystal continue to tremble for thousands of years—above all, however, in all living beings, in which most of the organic substances are colloids, especially the living protein. Thus, this trembling motion is constantly present in every living thing.

The colloid cannot be comprehended spatially; the particles do not follow any mathematical structure and their size and arrangement is in constant fluid transition. The colloid is not; rather, it occurs. "It does not exist; rather it goes on."*

The colloid has no power points, as does the crystal matrix, which determine its structure; rather, it has surfaces. However, that means it is determined not from point to point by central forces, but rather through cosmic forces of surface-to-surface; if it does belong in the point space, then it belongs to a plane space.

The colloid causes colors to appear out of the light. In terms of physics: it disperses electromagnetics. Spiritually in Goethe's terms: it weds light and darkness in the same way as the colloid itself is wed in gas, fluid, and solidity, in a way that enables the color to manifest. Colloids are the color mediators even of the mineral world. Therefore,

---

* For an alternate translation of these verses, see the chapter on topaz.

ions released from the crystal matrices or substitute ions distributed irregularly in the matrix can be designated as ultra-colloids in the proper sense (this designation is no longer used today). These processes make for the coloration conditions of the manifestations of color in all colorless-transparent crystals (such as beryl in the form of aquamarine or emerald; rock crystal as citrine; amethyst, smokey quartz, rose quartz; tourmaline as achroite, rubellite, vercelite, indigolite). Colloid-like metallic when embedded in crystalline, reveals color.

V. Spiritual future: This is the way mineral substances will be able to be once again in the future. This very future appears to the Apocalyptist in the image of the Heavenly Jerusalem when he speaks of the "light," the *phostér,* as the very noblest of precious stones, the crystal-clear jasper (Rev. 21:11). The jasper experience of the doxa emanating from the Godhead passes over into the jasper experience of the *phostér* of the city. The word *phostér* means heavenly light, starlight, light's shine, and stars in general. This word does not exist in the literature of classical Greece, but only in the New Testament.

Therefore, it is in the jasper that is the most precious that the very noblest aspect of the soul and spirit of the human being is revealed: the capacity for boundless devotion to something higher. Just this spiritual future existed once in the figure of Jesus of Nazareth. It provided the possibility for the Christ Logos to become active in earthly humanity. From Him it passes over onto humanity, from humanity to the kingdoms of nature, to the mineral realm. And precisely in one of its most recent formations, in opal, there appears on one hand the memory of its origin, but on the other hand the luminescence of the future. In milk opal (future) and fire opal (past), this becomes visible; and in the Apocalypse it is the force and the substance of the most precious of all precious stones, the jasper that is an "opal." The doxa of the diamond becomes the milk and fire opal of the *phostér* and illuminates the Heavenly Jerusalem. The Alpha (the beginning) and the Omega (the end) are reunited.

Verdelite; green tourmaline (Africa)

Rubellite; red tourmaline (Mozambique)

Tourmaline cross section; pyramidal polychromy, in the center three-rayed twin; large crystal, sliced perpendicular along longitudinal axis (Madagascar)

Red Garnet; Pyrope, fragments of a crystal (East Africa)

Green Garnet; uvarovite, double crystal (Finland)

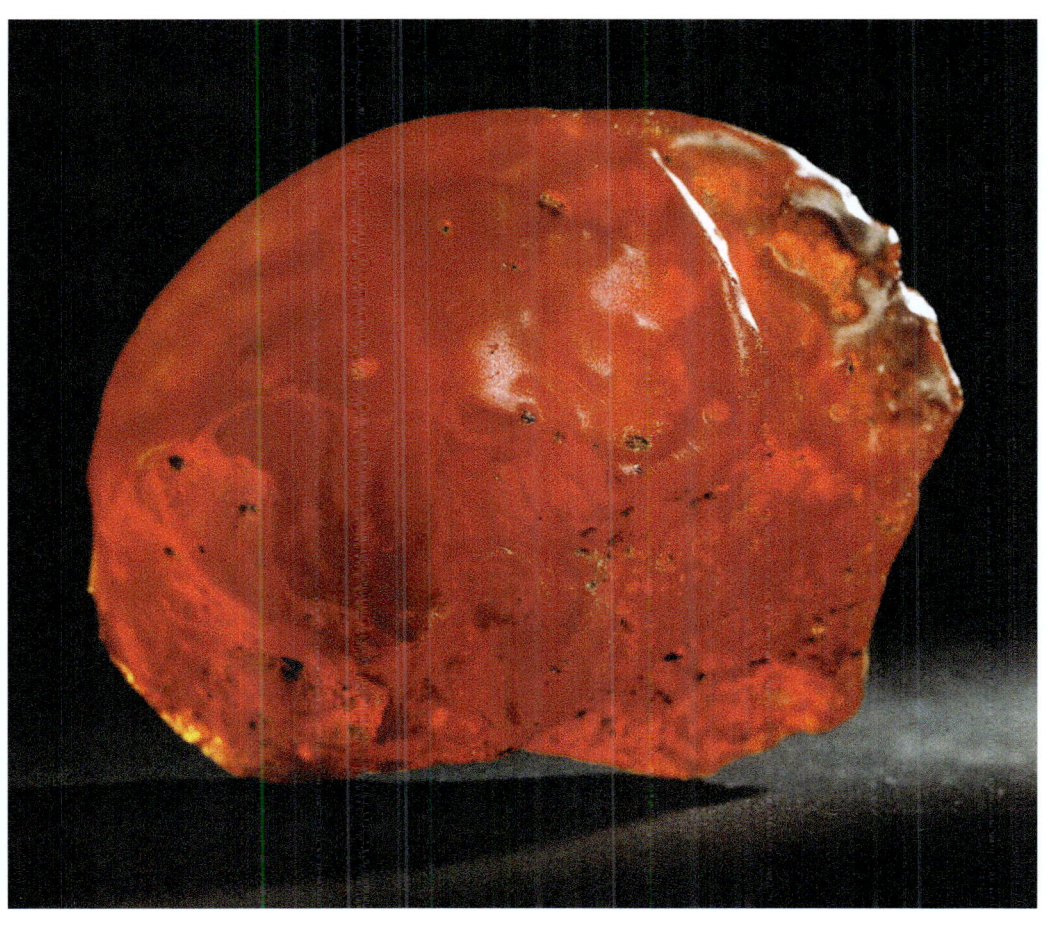

Fire opal, natural condition (Mexico)

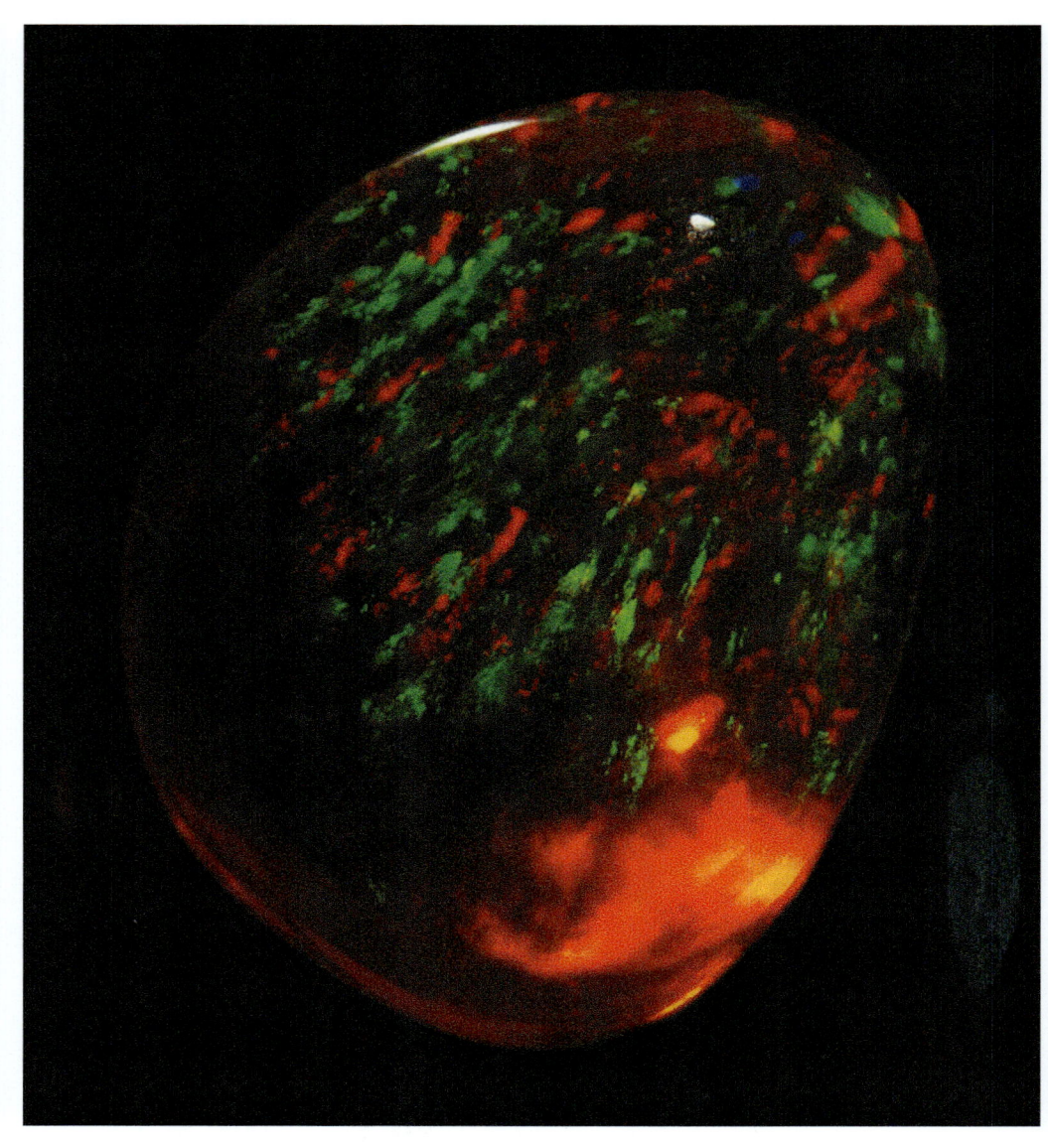

Fire opal, cut as a cabochon (Mexico)

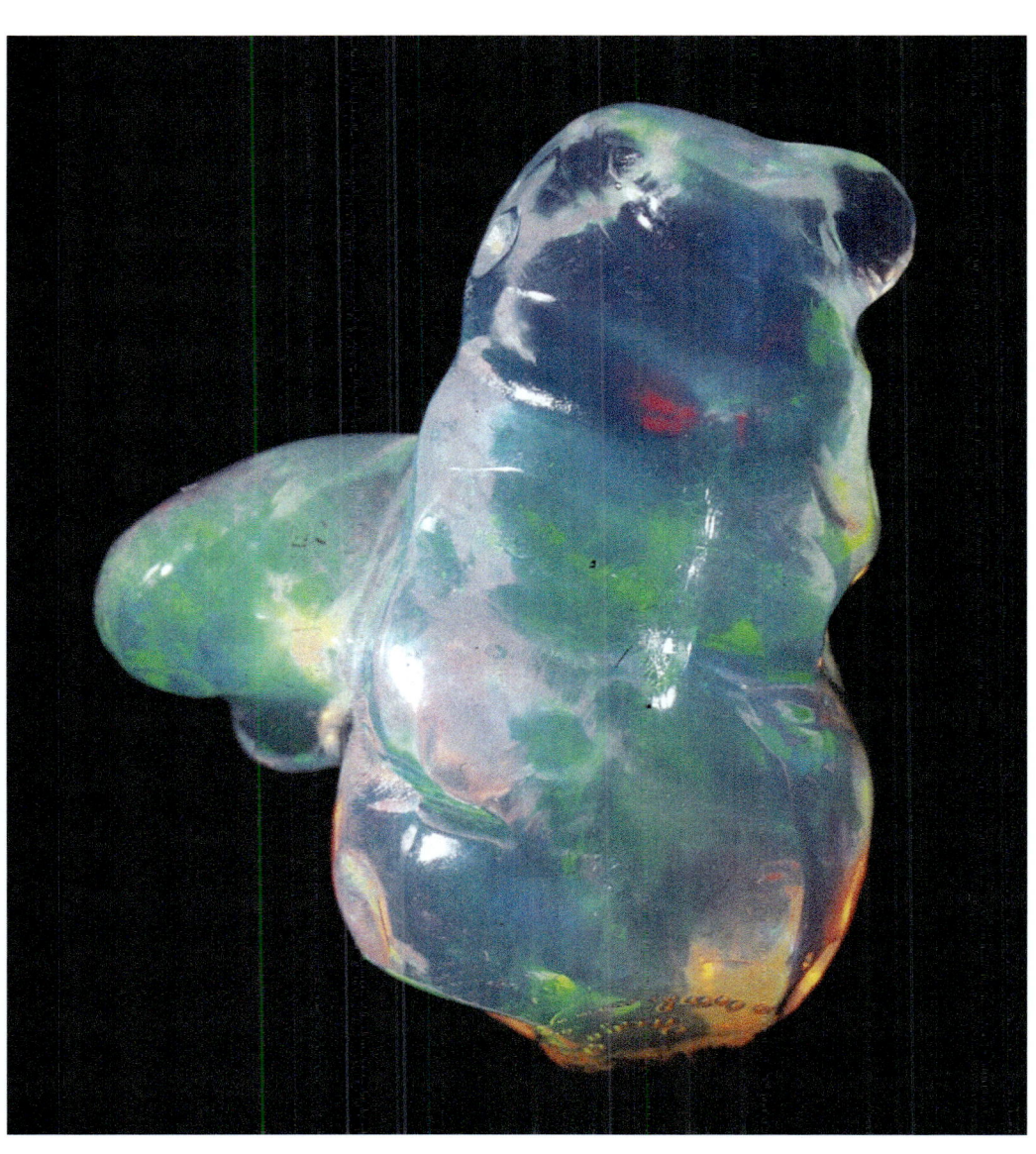

Milk opal, unpolished (Mexico)

In the "luminescent power" of the city, boundless devotion is revealed that originates inwardly as virtue. Outwardly, this power becomes radiant through the primal transformative force—that of the awakening of life after death, or light out of the darkness, of liberation from all chains and fetters.

One of the most mysterious of the Greek gods is Proteus. At the conclusion of the "Classical Walpurgis Night" scene in his *Faust* drama, Goethe has this god of all transformation appear. Proteus "opalizes," curiously enough, from one form into another. In *Faust,* he is the transformative power of all natural processes, the bearer of Goethe's idea of metamorphosis. In the Apocalypse, transformation lives as the jasper experience of the essential nature of opal: the transformation of the entire old cosmos of Earth development into the new Earth, the new Heaven, the humanity of the future, the future Godhead, the future city. Everything within the Apocalypse is opal, the glory of a transformation, which is radiant in boundless devotion.

Chapter 5: Twelve Precious Stones

Cosmic Jewelry in the Foundation Stones of the Heavenly Jerusalem

> In pureness of our breast a striving surges,
> Ourselves to a higher, purer unknown thing
> To dedicate in gratitude and freely,
> Unriddling thus the eternal, nameless One;
> We call it "being pious."*

We can say that, of all the image components belonging to the Heavenly Jerusalem, it is in the names of the twelve precious stones that the imaginative power devoted to these images is guided the most clearly to a concrete experience. If, in a state of complete contemplative silence,

---

* Cloos, *Kleine Edelsteinkunde.*

one permits these twelve names to pass through one's soul, concrete memory images will appear, images of everything one has perceived over the course of one's life in the way of raw stones and gemstones connected with these names; if one goes on to add their cosmic association with the twelve signs of the zodiac, the images and moods that emerge before one's inner vision in the process of pondering on or sensing everything connected with the names of these heavenly constellations become ever more definite. This is why the names of these twelve precious stones have also played a large role in the history of Christendom. This is why it is methodologically justified first to examine these names as such, and to look into aspects of their respective origins and meanings; then, to contemplate everything known to natural-scientific research and analysis about these mineral entities. This will make one all the more able to ascend from the pure phenomenon and its subsensory foundations to an examination of what shimmers throughout the suprasensory-intrinsic aspect of these twelve precious stones in their sense-perceptible existence.

This brings us first to the area in which these substances are processes, and herein lies the great accomplishment of Walther Cloos, who in his book on precious stones pursues this process element, guided as he is by indications given by Rudolf Steiner, which help him trace the stones back to aspects that are not purely material in nature, but that also have a bearing on the origins and habitats of these entities. This totality of material-sensual and living-etheric behavior reveals these entities' soul being, which epitomizes perfection, beauty, purity, and mature substantiality in the mineral world. Compared to the human soul, the soul of the mineral epitomizes virtue; one could also say the ideal. It was mentioned previously that there are probably seven twelvefold qualities of precious stones, and that what appears in the Apocalypse as the eighth twelvefold leads a step further, out beyond the soul of the crystal and into its spiritually creative primal being; moreover that this primal being contains in seed-form what—in the form of soul forces created through development of virtue and through inner exercise—unites within it the germ and the consummation of the purification and harmonization of the future human being and the future world. Thus, the following will be an attempt to observe each of the precious stones from five points of view: its name, natural-scientific research relevant to it, its habitats, its soul character, and its spiritual essence. Thanks to the indications given by Rudolf Steiner pertaining to the connections between the virtues and the months, it is also possible to further this endeavor by establishing the stones' connections with the signs of the zodiac.

In a lecture not yet published (Berlin, Oct. 9, 1906), Rudolf Steiner pointed to the connection between the entities of the zodiac and the twelve gemstone images in the Apocalypse and determined their affiliation in the sequence of the shift in the vernal equinox of the Sun, beginning with the image of heliotrope in the sign of Pisces and proceeding backward through Aquarius, Capricorn, and so on (cf. appendix 25). This enables us to contribute to a spiritual understanding of the twelve Apocalyptic gemstone images by giving a synopsis of a whole series of mineral, human, and cosmic twelvefold qualities. Their joint origin must be sought in the realm of the spirit and is initially expressed in the two great visions in the Bible. The four Beasts appear to both Ezekiel and John: the steer, the lion, the eagle, and the angelic human being. These images proceed from the four corners of the spiritual zodiac: the steer, the lion, the scorpion, and the water bearer.

At the same time, these four spirit beings are the inspirers of the four Evangelists Luke, Mark, John, and Matthew. They are the creative forces of the human organism—the metabolic-will forces, the heart-breathing-rhythmic forces of feeling, the sense-nerve-thought forces, and the unity of these three in the entire human being. The suprasensory manifestation of these entities is written by both Ezekiel and John in a momentous, living way.

> I looked, and I saw a windstorm coming out of the north—an immense cloud with flashing lightning and surrounded by brilliant

light. The center of the fire looked like glowing metal, and in the fire was what looked like four living creatures. In appearance their form was human, but each of them had four faces and four wings. Their legs were straight; their feet were like those of a calf and gleamed like burnished bronze. Under their wings on their four sides they had human hands. All four of them had faces and wings, and the wings of one touched the wings of another. Each one went straight ahead; they did not turn as they moved.

Their faces looked like this: Each of the four had the face of a human being, and on the right side each had the face of a lion, and on the left the face of an ox; each also had the face of an eagle. Such were their faces. They each had two wings spreading out upward, each wing touching that of the creature on either side; and each had two other wings covering its body. Each one went straight ahead. Wherever the spirit would go, they would go, without turning as they went. The appearance of the living creatures was like burning coals of fire or like torches. Fire moved back and forth among the creatures; it was bright, and lightning flashed out of it. The creatures sped back and forth like flashes of lightning.

As I looked at the living creatures, I saw a wheel on the ground beside each creature with its four faces. This was the appearance and structure of the wheels: They sparkled like topaz, and all four looked alike. Each appeared to be made like a wheel intersecting a wheel. As they moved, they would go in any one of the four directions the creatures faced; the wheels did not change direction as the creatures went. (Ez. 1:4–17)

The depth to which this vision can move the soul can also be experienced in the paintings of Rafael. St. John says:

Also in front of the throne there was what looked like a sea of glass, clear as crystal.

In the center, around the throne, were four living creatures, and they were covered with eyes, in front and in back. The first living creature was like a lion, the second was like an ox, the third had a face like a man, the fourth was like a flying eagle. Each of the four living creatures had six wings and was covered with eyes all around, even under its wings. Day and night they never stop saying, "Holy, holy, holy is the Lord God Almighty" who was, and is, and is to come. (Rev. 4:6–8)

The prophet of the Old Testament and the Apocalyptist of the New Testament behold the essence of the zodiac in the imaginations of these four spirit beings belonging to the hierarchy of the Cherubim. What here remains enshrouded to normal consciousness, or at best reveals itself in a pure picture, becomes perceptible for spirit investigation in such a way that each of these four Cherubim is accompanied by two other spirit beings, the beings of the zodiac signs that emanate their power from the right and the left of the respective entity. In this manner, spiritual research arrives at the spiritual beings Rudolf Steiner calls the twelve "World Initiators," and about which he spoke in various contexts (cf. appendix 25). Suprasensory vision experiences these spiritual beings in the cosmic areas that today outwardly appear to the human being as the signs of the zodiac. In the spirit of Christian esotericism, these beings belong to the first hierarchy of the Seraphim, Cherubim, and Thrones. These beings reveal their divine-creative lives to spirit vision. Beholding their revelations, the spirit-researcher finds the sources of their past deeds. He experiences what they shaped in their creational activity. He finds it once more in the orderings of nature, in the twelve precious stones of the mineral realm, in the twelve large classes of the plant and animal realm, respectively, but as well in the twelve areas of the human physical body and the twelve areas of his sense organs.

The second thing the spirit researcher learns from these entities is their present living and weaving. This activity of theirs is still active today in human beings, as long as they live on Earth. They are the motivators of the soul, they inspire the nuances of our worldviews, and after death they assume the task of transforming past fate into future earthly lives.

The third thing that appears to the beholder is the future being of these spirits. They themselves consist of a soul-spirit-moral reality that makes up the moral substance of the very highest of ideals and virtues. To grasp this future working, a fundamental change in the way one sees things is necessary. For the sequence of the Apocalyptic stones does not follow the course of the Sun through the year as it progresses through the zodiac from Aries to Pisces; rather, it follows the course of the vernal equinox through the zodiac in the course of a platonic year (from Pisces backward to Aries). Thus the following contemplation begins with jasper in connection with Pisces and runs "retrograde" via sapphire-Aquarius, chalcedony-Capricorn, emerald-Sagittarius, sardonyx-Scorpio, sard-Libra, chrysolite-Virgo, beryl-Leo, topaz-Cancer, chrysoprase-Gemini, and hyacinth-Taurus, to amethyst-Aries. It is possible to feel how, in the progressing time stream of the spatial-earthly world in its eternal repetition from Aries to Pisces, the spiritual current of creation moves in a twelve-times-larger, rhythmically ever-new creation from Pisces to Aries.

We must also endeavor to experience the individual images, zodiac signs, and contents in a kind of transition from the one to the other, in order not to move as it were from spring through summer and autumn to winter, but rather from winter through autumn and summer to the spring. This helps one also to enter into a mood of or a sense for the total interconnection, and then to trace in one's thoughts and feelings the course of the images of the Apocalypse as they appeared to the Apocalyptist himself. Thus the experience of jasper beneath the starry heavens of Pisces transitions back into the sapphire experience beneath the starry heavens of Aquarius, and so on. This enables the experience of a totality of being, in which the twelve foundation stones, the twelve precious stones, and the twelve pearls are gathered together as the inner unity of the Heavenly Jerusalem. One finds access to the living and weaving of the whole that eternally leads out of the primal font, which is the Father, through the eternally sacrificial creating of the Son and back into the light of the Spirit's consciousness. But we also learn that this world-becoming can consummate itself by way of the human being. To be sure, for us human beings today that belongs to the future; however, as was explained in the chapter on the construction of the Heavenly Jerusalem, this future is also always and already the present.

To provide an overview, some of the twelvefold qualities found in nature and humanity as an effect of the creator spirits are cited in appendix 25, along with their associations to their respective zodiac signs, and thus to the twelve Cherubinic world initiators. Initially, of course, this yields nothing more than an abstract chart. But as one beholds it and gains knowledge, one fills this chart with life over and over, provided one devotes oneself to it with the proper intensity.

The Twelve Individual Stones

Jasper as Heliotrope

I. Name: The question of jasper's name was dealt with extensively in the chapter on the jasper problem. There the endeavor was also made to attribute the first of the twelve Apocalyptic stones, the one called jasper, to the particular jasper experience visible in the heliotrope. The name heliotrope stems from the Greek language and is a composite of the two words *Helios* ("Sun") and *tropeo* ("striving toward" or "belonging to"). Thus the stone's name means "Belonging to the Sun."

II. Scientific Research: Heliotrope is light to dark green, fully opaque, and its green fundamental mass is interspersed with red enclosures of larger or smaller, variously shaped granules of iron oxide. The green crystalline basic mass is plasma; one could also say leek-green chalcedony in the broader sense.* Machatschki distinguishes chalcedony from the jasper minerals by observing that the microcrystalline quartz variety of chalcedony consists of fiber crystals, whereas the jaspers contain more or less microscopic granules of crystal and are rendered opaque by metallic and/or earthen "impurities."

Thus if one examines heliotrope according to its material components, one finds: crystalline tissue, chalcedony structure, jasper

---

*   Cloos, *Kleine Edelsteinkunde*, p. 42

structure, colloidal opal structure, bivalent or trivalent iron, and an "earthen" aspect (aluminum compounds). These are its seven constituent components.

Heliotrope is found in volcanic rock and layered rock as crevice-filling material, in layers, deposits, clumps and spheres.

III. Origin and habitats: The substance of jasper stems from a formational period of the Earth in which the materiality of silicon had fallen out of the Earth's life processes to a much greater extent than during the formational period of the agates and chalcedony.* It is for this reason that, while it still contains the color distribution of the metals, it largely lacks any fibrous structure: the silicon is no longer formed through by the forces of the plants. Earlier, it was also more readily water-soluble than today. Through its descent it takes on an "earthen" darkness.

IV. Soul virtue: In this first of the twelve gemstones, the being, the virtue of jasper manifests as the image of heliotrope. If, now, we do not take the mineral as our point of departure, but rather the virtue assigned to the month of March, and endeavor to grasp what magnanimity truly is, we actually need to touch our way to the very highest. C. F. Meyer speaks along these lines in his poem "Everyone": "Far above their heads He invited the Earth / With an all-embracing gesture." These words speak of a magnanimity that is all-encompassing.

The ancient authors are evidently right when they presume heliotrope to be the jasper of the Apocalypse, which with its saturated, earthly dark green containing the red sprinklings of iron is an image for the working of Christ, who sacrificed his blood for the earth and planted seeds for the future. What must take place in the human soul so that it can develop the capacity not to succumb to petty moralizing or dogmatic sectarianism, and not to reject everything different from itself, but instead magnanimously to learn to sense and acknowledge what must be at work in another entity in the way of necessary errors,

---

* Ibid., p. 108

transgressions, and weakness, even if it means taking in the sacrificial fragrance created by the loss of one's own worth and given off from the depths by fallen entities who are a sacrifice unto themselves? A loss of being can lead to a becoming, and true renewal will always turn loss into gain and the greatest of misfortune into good fortune. This is what Goethe says in his *Fairytale of the Green Snake and the Beautiful Lily*.

In the emergence of heliotrope's green from the power of the darkness of its substance lives the image of the magnanimity that comprehends all earthly facts, even the darkest ones, because this magnanimity feels: there is nothing that appears to be senseless in which hidden sense cannot be found. One need only be magnanimous enough to find it.

V. Spiritual future: In the bottom-most members of the human shape, the hands and feet, there are forces at work that actually enable the human being to take hold of the earth and to set foot on it. In threefold walking (lifting, carrying, placing, lifting…), a mystery inheres. It is the process of uniting with the earth and releasing oneself from the earth. The same holds for every grip we do with our hands. In these modest processes lies the image for the most all-encompassing human dare, for with every incarnation the human being takes hold of and sets foot on the earth and with every death we release ourselves from her. The same thing is consummated in reduced form in waking and sleeping, as well. However, the human being can unite with the earth in such a way that, working with our hands, striding with our feet, assimilating the earth, assimilating ourselves into the earth, we can also engage the spirit of our origin. And when we then release ourselves from the earth, we take the fruit of this earthly life into our spiritual hands; the yield of this comprehensive, magnanimous activity of destiny wrests from the earth her proper purpose and sense: love. In the heliotrope image, jasper flashes up to the Apocalyptist as the very first picture—in the green, the purpose of the Earth's destiny; and in the red spots, the love he has already perceived once in the garment of the white horseman, about whom it says, "He is dressed in a robe dipped in blood, and his name is the Word of God" (Rev. 19:13). However, this is possible only if the essence of the human heart and that of the heart of Christ touch. This touch is *perfusion*. The green of the trusting heart permeates itself with the red drops of blood of the loving Godhead. Already, the first gemstone picture of the Apocalypse emanates from this interpenetration.

Sapphire

I. Name: Greek: *sappheiros*, a word borrowed from the Hebrew *sappir* or *sepper*, from the verb *SAPPAR*—to clean, set in order, or harmonize.

II. Scientific Research: Sapphire is pure corundum (Al_2O_3, also called *alumina*), and belongs to the corundum group. Its crystals are ditrigonal-scalenohedral, often occurring as twins. Degree of hardness: 9, density: 4.0. In truth, sapphire is nine times harder than rock crystal. The opaque corundums are intense red, gray, or brown; the transparent ones are red, blue, purple, in a few cases green.

> Brown corundums: mixture with iron oxide (Fe_2O_3)
> Red ones: ruby, 1–2% chrome instead of aluminum
> Blue ones: sapphire, mixture containing iron or titanium instead of aluminum
> Green ones: oriental emerald = green sapphire
> Yellow ones: oriental topaz = yellow sapphire
> Purple ones: oriental amethyst = purple sapphire
> In addition, there are colorless varieties

The opaque brown corundums and the yellow and green gemstone sapphires come about through a mixture of alumina with bivalent iron (iron oxide). The proper blue sapphire contains a mixture of trivalent iron, sometimes along with titanium, instead of aluminum. The purple color is caused by traces of vanadium.

Corundums occur in syenites, granite, pegmatite, peridot, in contact with alumina sediments; in schist rock drawn into the contact process, they become sedimentary components especially of river pebbles. They occur mainly in East Asia: Sri Lanka, Burma, Thailand, Cambodia, Cashmere; then in Australia, Eastern Africa, and in Montana in the American West.

III. Origin and habitats: The corundums belong to those minerals that blossom from the interaction of the contact processes between the pegmatites developing out of plutonic rock, the schist surrounding it, and the crystalline limestone and dolomite folded in among the schist.* In pegmatite, the blossom-like quality of stems—e.g., of granite, lives in crystal hollows. In schist there lies what originally were leaf processes but have now become woody, rigidified. What has been preserved in limestone and dolomite is what was deposited out of the activity of plantlike animals. Thus these three elements interact etherically and in a material chemical manner, since within them a series of minerals arise that assume the lightest characteristics of precious stones, among which are the corundums. The three components of the plantlike blossom nature, the plantlike stem and blossom nature and the plantlike animal and soul nature are capable of uplifting so strongly earthbound a substance as aluminum to the highest forms of manifestation. The harmony of an all-encompassing trinity, a harmony that is so fully permeated by and identical with itself, is heightened in these precious stones to a unity. Here I quote verbatim what Cloos has to say on this subject:

> When the substance of corundum is separated out from its intimate connection with the ancient mineral plants, cosmic forces come to expression whose uniqueness is surpassed only by those on which the formation of diamond is based. One must bear in mind that here a material universally present in massive quantities, in any farming soil, is singled out and purified to a nearly unparalleled extent in other earthly substance. We do not presume to plumb

---

*   Cloos, *Kleine Edelsteinkunde*.

the depths of these cosmic forces' mysteries, whose origin Rudolf Steiner himself said lies beyond the zodiac.*

IV. Soul virtue: In the pure, saturated, and deep colors of ruby and sapphire, the above-mentioned harmony finds its full expression. And whenever, through his willing, the human being harmonizes the nature of thought, feeling, and will in the depths of the soul, ruby red shines forth out of the heart. A balance of the very greatest depth arises, one that both creates and perceives itself. Here we find the spiritual foundation of our life sense. It is here that human beings are first truly human, where they themselves encompass their bodily and physiological nature, their biological and biographical nature, the nature of their rejoicing, suffering, experiencing soul, and the nature of their waking spirit, in this way comprehending the totality of their human life, and themselves perceiving this life.

Within this encompassing, this comprehending and perceiving, the trinity of the eagle, the lion, and the bull are angelically united. If human beings turn this harmonization to the other, inner side, where in silence we tend and nurture within ourselves both what goes on inside us and what pertains to the intimacies of the lives of others, this is when the blue of sapphire will shimmer in our soul. Discretion, or reticence, is the virtue that has become sense perceptible in sapphire-blue. It is the silence kept before all speaking.

V. Spiritual future: In the forces of the lower arms and lower legs, there lives a carrying power that causes movement in the action of bearing up, and that in the process of this moving has holding power; something that, in the state of becoming, is, and that in the state of being, becomes. This force, located near the bottom end of the human shape in the limbs, is the basis for the grasp and the step able then to come to life in the hands and feet. The inner taking-hold and setting foot capable of unfolding in soul silence and discretion is capable of

---

*   *Smaragd* is also the German word for the English *emerald*.

realizing both a person's own higher being and that of others, both out of boundless, infinite possibilities and out of painful limitations as well, in order to grasp this being. In guidance given for meditative life, attention is always drawn to the necessity of silencing everything in the soul that is rambling and restless. The ability to observe silence is the most important prerequisite to all meditation. In the power of meditation as highest devotion, and in the power of concentration as highest attention, an entity shines forth out of the Heavenly Jerusalem whose entire existence has become meditation, even when this entity is in action. Sapphire-blue is also this spiritual future.

At this point I would like to draw the reader's attention to the fact that, in the vision of Ezekiel, the throne of the divine Being appears in the image of sapphire. It is probably permissible to make the same claim for the throne in the Apocalypse. What in the Heavenly City flashes up blue in the sapphire out of the entity of Aquarius, as out of one of the twelve Apocalyptic precious stones, is likely the foundation of the images of chapters four and five of the Apocalypse. The great creative observance of silence on the part of the most exalted deity—as the founding ground of this very deity itself—is the basis for all creative speaking. It is the primal, archetypal meditation of the Father God on Himself, His eternal being, the throne on which He, observing silence, rests within Himself, the "ground of existence of the heavens and of the earth" (from the Creed of the Christian Community). This is the originary oneness and all-ness of the Father, before any and all beginning. Those who can observe silence can meditate; those who can meditate live in the primal ground of the world.

Chalcedony
I. Name: After an ancient city on the Bosporus.

II. Scientific Research: In the chapter on rock crystal, the varieties of quartz were discussed. Chalcedony belongs to the microcrystalline filament quartz mineral group. As mentioned, it consists of an ultrafine fabric of alternating crystal fibers and amorphous opal lamellae. Thus it holds the middle ground among the quartz-silicon processes, between the large crystals and the amorphous colloids. Moreover, within its own group, that of chalcedony in the broader sense, genuine chalcedony forms the basic substance, which is the basic substance of a whole series of manifestations. It is the common center of its colored relatives: *carnelian* = flesh-red and translucent; *chalcedony-jasper* = brownish-red to red; *sard* = yellowish-red; *heliotrope* = opaque green with red specks of iron oxide; *chrysoprase* = apple-green, leek-green, owing to additives of nickel compounds. As a fine, alternating interpenetration of chalcedony fiber layers and hydrous opal layers (500–700 per millimeter), chalcedony is also the basis for all agates (onyx, sardonyx, sard, carnelian, and chalcedony derived from agates). Pure chalcedony is transparent to translucent, sometimes nearly opaque (ranging from milky-white to whitish gray, to whitish gray-blue, whitish-blue, grayish-blue to a lovely bright sky-blue like the clear blue near the horizon. It occurs in two different forms: in clumps in porphyry and basalt-like vulcanite; otherwise in the agate geodes or nodules of melaphyre.

III. Origin and habitats: In chalcedony, the substance has become mineral that, according to Rudolf Steiner, entered from the Sun into the protein atmosphere of the Earth during the Lemurian epoch of Earth's development, as upward and downward surging plant life, and in the form of etheric silicon substance (Cloos, p. 36). In the maternal "gel" state, this etheric substance constituted the form and frame-providing element, and subsequently precipitated the material silicon process out of itself. Its filament structure is a crystallization of the tendencies in plant growth (cell growth, annual rings); its coloration is a crystallization of the metal additives of the plants' tendency to blossom. Chalcedony represents to the highest degree—both structurally and substantially—the maternal state of the primeval world of plant-minerals. It leads in the one direction to rock crystal, in the other to opal.

IV. Soul virtue: In contrast to its baser, tinted relatives, the sky-blue coloration of gemstone-quality chalcedony is not substance-bound. This blue arises the same way as the blue of shadows cast on the white of the snow, and the same way as the blue of the sky is created in the interaction between light and dark within the motherly womb of cloudiness. Chalcedony's blue is situated in the middle between the colors of the gemstones that are more substance-bound and traceable to metals, and a few others, which opalize owing to formation of ultrafine leaflets. In chalcedony's selfless, motherly substance, light brings itself to expression in its most intensive activity, and this activity is a repetition of the forceful light-born movements that chalcedony underwent as a living substance in primeval plant formations.

As a soul quality, the sky-blue of chalcedony is something quite different from the deep dark blue of sapphire. In the latter there inheres the direction toward the internalization, the observing of silence, the darkness that meditates. If the blue goes in the direction of light or bright blue, the soul-aspect moves toward the permeation of the dark with brightness, toward the overcoming of dark through light. In dark blue, true courage arises in the observance of silence, courage that gathers its strength in restraint or reticence. It becomes strong, free, filled with selfhood. Only in this way does it stream outward, from the darkness and into brightness, from what is past and into what is to come. "I"-being must first ground itself before it can act courageously. If the "I" is present, courage is also present. If it is only partly or hardly at all incorporated in its soul and bodily sheaths, a vacuum arises between the "I" and soul, the experience of which always amounts to fear. Fear means: one is not fully present. Hence, courage means being fully present, going from dark blue to light or bright blue.

V. Spiritual future: The human knee, similar to the elbow, is a remarkable center of force. In these two joints, the forces of the musculature of the upper and lower arm, the thigh, and the lower leg converge when one is standing, walking, climbing, jumping, when one spreads out, crosses, stretches or bends one's arms. In performing these actions, the respective joint is entirely selfless, courageously directing as it does the whole human being's forces of movement toward gait and grip, while at the same time perceiving and controlling these movements. The creative spiritual power that is at the foundation of these processes and that, via the sense of self-movement, demands of human beings, with every action, that they confront the world with thinking, this power can stimulate the courage to do something that has never been done before. In grasping and taking a leap beyond one's own shadow, the virtue of courage becomes an act whereby something that did not exist before can be worked through, found, taken up, and surmounted. It is the spiritual power of redemption. In the grayish sky-blue of the Apocalyptist's chalcedony imagination, the power of redemption shimmers in the future Capricorn-sphere of the Heavenly City. It enables us to make everything from the past able to bear up under whatever future load is in store, and it enables us to incorporate what comes from the future into the past. The sense of movement itself becomes movement—development from seed to blossom, from blossom to fruit and to new seed. Redemption is liberation for growth.

Emerald

I. Name: A word transformed from the Hebrew word *barequed.* Its root is the Hebrew *BARAQU* = lightning. This name probably stems from Assyrian-Babylonian *barraquito, barraqtu,* or *barraq* = to shine or flare up. It is called *smaragd* in Phoenician, in Syrian *barqa,* in Egyptian *smer* or *asmer.*

II. Scientific Research: chemically and mineralogically, the emerald belongs to the precious beryls, and is related to beryl, aquamarine, and morganite. It is, however, different from these with regard to the circumstances of its formation, since it occurs only very seldom in pegmatite, which is otherwise characteristic for beryl minerals; emerald is found almost exclusively in pneumatically or hydrothermally permeated types of schist and grainy limestone. Its deep green saturated color is due to its being tinted with aluminum oxide, chrome oxide, or vanadium oxide. Occurrence: Colombia, Brazil, the Ural Mountains, India, East and South Africa, and Austria's Habach Valley.

III. Origin and habitats: The emerald is formed in the leafy schist-like or limey plant and animal metamorphic and sedimentary surroundings of pegmatite (Cloos, p. 97). This causes it to become a carrier of the light-permeating processes at work in schist overall, similarly to granite. According to an indication given by Rudolf Steiner, it originated at the same time as the solar plexus in the sympathetic nervous system, which regulates the unconscious movements of the human life forces and raises them to a dull consciousness. The emerald is one of the very few minerals that has preserved the soft state within schist that schist itself once had. This is another thing that distinguishes it from granite. When it is mined from schist, it is sometimes so soft that it is often destroyed. It can only be extracted as a beautiful crystal if it is permitted slowly to "dry." Then, however, it becomes quite hard. In human hands it "flashes," lightning-like, from the material-soft state over into the crystalline "hard" state.

IV. Soul virtue: The deep, saturated emerald-green carries within it a remarkable spiritual force. From a lecture in Helsinki on April 3, 1912, Rudolf Steiner speaks on the moral quality of pure green. In this color, the pure cosmic force of thought takes on life for suprasensory vision, if this vision can permeate the sense-perceptible green with moral sensing. One then has the experience: "Now I understand what I experience when I call forth mental pictures, when I think, when I am active within myself." If the person then goes on to control what he thinks and to be alert in controlling not just his thoughts, but also his tongue, he gains the strength to grasp not only the profoundest of life-processes at work in his metabolism, but also the ones that flash up in his understanding thinking. The sense of balance active in such control merges with the thought sense whenever the human being consciously and livingly determines what to think and not to think, what to say and not to say. In this control of thought and word, emerald-green takes on suprasensory life in the human being.

V. Spiritual future: It is chiefly out of the power in the upper arms that the human being is able to make the arms and hands into organs of expression for his soul. Moreover, it is the power in the thighs that enables him to stretch and to bend his legs and thus to walk and to stand upright, as an expression of his "I." These fundamental forces, which are active in an entirely bodily way, proceed from the stream of the life forces and their perception, whose source is the "I" itself and which are perceptible by the solar plexus as health and illness. These basic forces live as an unconscious source of life, an unconscious sun in the human metabolic system and limbic system. This is why thought control can lead to control over one's life and thus the determination of a way of life capable of transforming itself over and over into pure and free sensing of the truth and of reality, and thus capable of overcoming illusions and weaknesses. Such a lifestyle becomes the life sense that imparts sense to life. This can happen, however, only if we have established balance among all of our forces. In the green of the Apocalyptic image of emerald, an element manifests through which all of life's ideals receive the strength that fills them with "being's might,"* which enables them to pass over from ideal to reality, from becoming to being. It is an existing, "constant" green, such as exists in the plant world. It is meaning flashing up in all being. It is the "Archer" (Sagittarius) of the Heavenly Jerusalem.

An aspect of symmetry, however, is at work in human beings, precisely within the limbs. Between both arms and hands, legs and feet, there always occurs balance, a process attuned toward equalization. The life sense must be permeated by the sense of balance, if

---

* "Being's might" refers to Steiner's "Sagittarius" verse of his "Twelve Moods of the Zodiac."

the experiences one has in life are to be processed spiritually, brought forth actively, and elevated to "eternal life." Through decisions made in the controlled, guided balance of one's consciousness, there arises the incorruptible sense for truth—above all inner truthfulness before oneself and the spiritual world—that guarantees a person's healthy spiritual development.

Sardonyx

I. Name: Combined from *sard* and *onyx,* with the main emphasis on *onyx.* The ancient commentators interpreted the name *sardonyx* to mean that the stone's full picture is three-colored: red sard, accompanied by black onyx, and between white or light gray chalcedony. In this way, the hidden rhythm of the formation of agate was augmented by the rhythm of the three colors red, white, and black.

II. Scientific Research: Both sard and onyx are members of the agate family. They belong to the finely fibrous silicon minerals; hence they are actually varieties of chalcedony. The only difference between sard and carnelian is a yellowish-brownish tone ranging to carnelian-red. However, the "sard" image is not complete without the adjacent layers of white and light-blue chalcedony. The term *sard* actually designates a type of agate. In addition, the color of onyx is a deep dark brownish-black. The latter stone is often nearly opaque, only weakly to moderately translucent, in which case the black passes over into a dark, earthy brown. The chapter on rock crystal deals with the mineralogical research results that pertain here. Sard is associated with the zodiacal sign of Libra (the same is true of sardonyx), thus the reader is referred to appendix 26, in which current concepts of the agates' origin are described.

III. Origin and habitats: In his book on gemstones, Cloos dedicates an extensive chapter to the agates (pp. 35–41). He counts them among the "mothers of rock crystal." The special thing about the agates is that in them the different varieties of silicic acid belonging to the chalcedony group are structured in alternating layers and deposits. They are rendered rhythmic through and through and display a resonant orderliness. The mineral and plantlike nature of their substances and additives acquires a rhythmic arrangement that has sentient, animal, or soul characteristics. Cloos states:

> "The life," which is the basis of agate formation and reflected in the great delicacy of its layering, was from the order of the animal-plants; the hollows point to the "animal nature," the substance-providing silicic acid to the "plant" aspect. The filling in of these hollow spaces with silicic substance from the outside inward; in the innermost place, either rock crystal or amethyst was formed, as long as any hollow space was left for the crystals' free formation. According to the latest research, the layering of the silicon substance was already finished before any differentiation into fibrous chalcedony and colloidal opal occurred.*

Agates are found in this kind of bubble-formed hollows in melaphyre. In German, they are called "almond stones" (*Mandelsteine*). The dimensions of these "bubbles" range from less than an inch to several yards. In larger ones, the agates lie upon the walls of the bubbles, the space is empty, and frequently the largest and most beautiful rock crystals or amethysts sit on top of them. Thus sard and onyx are each based on a double element of rhythm. It is the rhythm of the structure, on the one hand, and on the other the rhythm of the positioning. When sard and onyx converge to form sardonyx, a third rhythm manifests, and this rhythm then displays itself in three colors: orange-red, white, blackish-brown. Awareness of this threefold rhythmic element-become-stone leads to a dawning understanding for the essence of these precious stones, thanks to an indication given by Steiner—according to which onyx is originally connected spiritually with the predisposition for the human sense of hearing.

---

*   Cloos, *Kleine Edelsteinkunde*, p. 40.

IV. Soul virtue: The question might arise as to which spiritual power the sense of hearing is based on. Hearing is, after all, quite different from seeing. In the act of seeing, the life force and the soul force of the human being stream forth out of the eyes' organization, melt together with the chiaroscuro (light/darkness) and the colors out there in the world, and create the complementary counterimage within one's own soul: a bright counterimage for what is dark and a dark counterimage for what is bright; and for the color nuances an amazingly exact counterimage in the form of the complementary color, which "reverberates" for a time in the eye. With the ear, it is different. The tone, the speech sound, or the noise of what is heard is not answered by a complementary response in the ear; rather, the larynx is the place where this process takes place. The larynx replicates what is heard by means of delicate vibrations both of the vocal chords and of the entire laryngeal position (higher or lower), but also by means of the life forces of the larynx. The ear is only half an organization; the speech organization is the other, complementary half. This means, though, that the human will enwoven into this sense organ is engaged between what is perceived and what is replicated in an entirely different way than it is in the eye. Precisely because the ear cannot be closed, as can the eye, the will can be inwardly engaged in the process of perception in a more or less strong manner; it can inwardly open or close itself, thus even enabling it to hear without hearing, because the "I" lives more freely between the ear and the larynx than it does in the eye.

On the other hand, the ear can hear much more deeply and essentially, above all more intimately, if the "I" is more strongly concentrated between the ear and the larynx. The ear hears deeper and more intimately than the eye sees. Genuine hearing and listening requires an "I"-aware devotedness that does not influence what is to be perceived, but rather patiently accepts and participates in the entire process without being forced to. It is an activity that joins in with and takes hold of what is to be heard—patiently, with perseverance, and with presence of the "I." There is a path leading from hearkening to hearing to listening intensely, along which what is heard can utter and articulate itself within. This makes for the beginning of the transition of the soul force of patience into the spiritual power of inspiration. In spiritual terms, to be patient means to be capable of inspiration. This comes to expression in the color rhythm of sardonyx. The two colors, the selflessly active patience of the soul-red and onyx's black-brown with its yet-unknown contents of perception, these two colors are connected through the selfless white, which observes silence and oscillates, mediating, as the virtue of patient, intense, and participatory hearing between the subject and the object.

One can learn to take hold of the entire soul sphere that lies hidden within the entity of sardonyx only if one adds to the qualities of soul discussed up to now (the forces of actively listening–perceiving) a very different, seemingly opposite one. In the polarity of the imaginative pictures of the eagle and the scorpion assigned to one and the same zodiac sign, a profound mystery is hidden. This pertains to the sense spheres, as well. For the sense that is actually connected with the sardonyx-Scorpio entity is the sense of smell. As opposed to the outwardly directed sense of hearing, the sense of smell is directed entirely inward. Everyone knows that odors have something irresistible about them and are deeply connected with the instinctive and desire-oriented life of the soul. In fragrance and stench, what we perceive is not the essence of the respective substance, as with tone, resonance, noise, but rather the substance's relationship with the world. If a thing or a being has a harmonious relationship with the world, then it is fragrant. If it has a disharmonious relationship to the world, it is experienced as stinking. These are the two poles of the world of odors. As hearing leads to conscious understanding, so also does smelling lead to an instinctive, direct encounter. This encounter can be repulsive or enticing, but it can also be purifying, enlivening, balmy. Here we are reminded of the words that characterize the purifying effect of the roses strewn by the angels in the ascension scene of Goethe's *Faust*. This points to what arises not only physically, but also on a soul level, if a being transforms

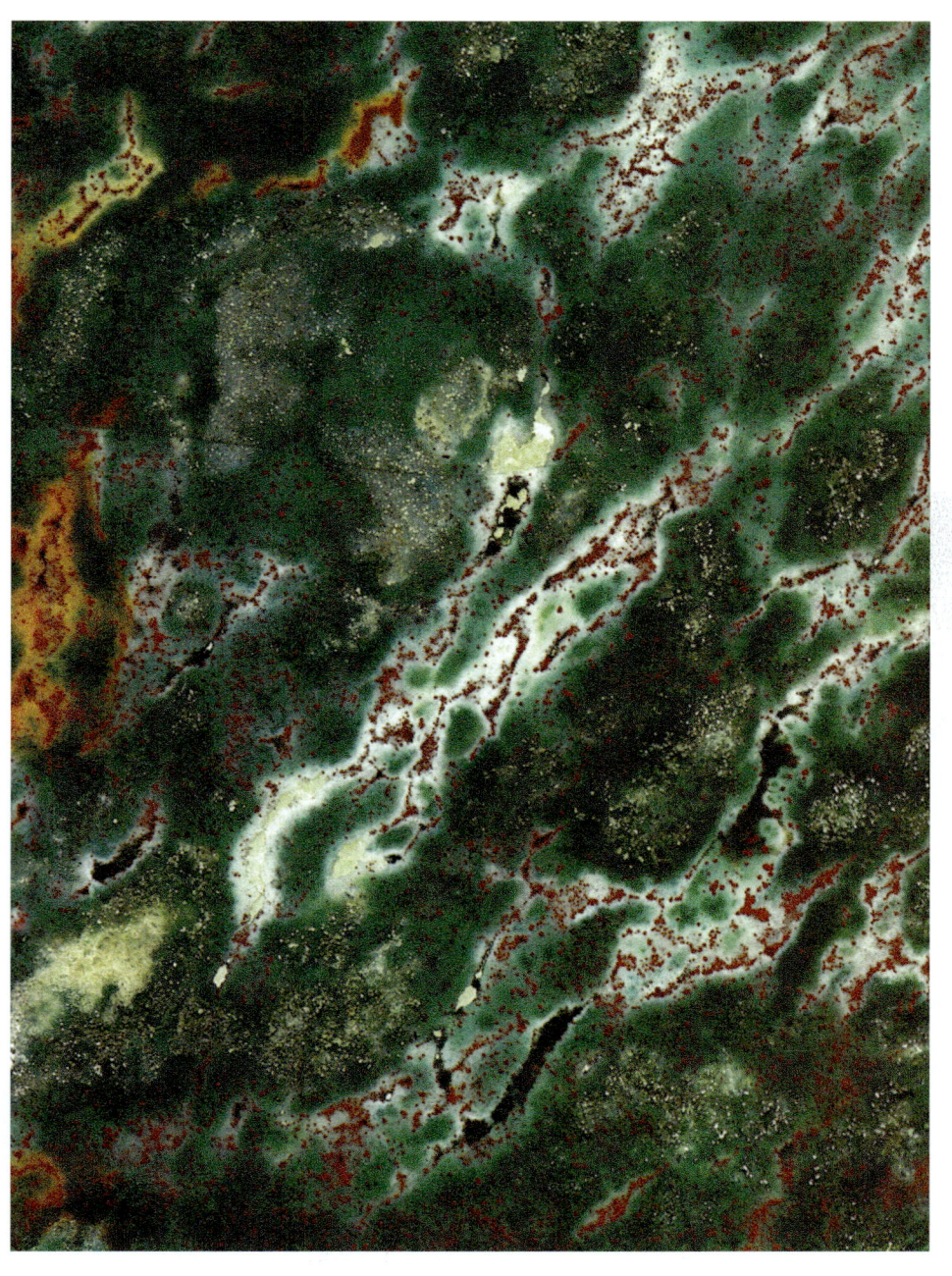

*Heliotrope, cut and polished:
red iron-ore veins in green jaspis plasma, enlarged (India)*

Heliotrope fragment (India)

Sapphire crystal, tumble-polished (Sri Lanka)

Chalcedony fragment (Anatolia, Turkey)

his relationship to the world and patiently comes to the insight that no righteous relationship with the world can obtain without sacrifice. All erring and transgressions can cause the loss of an entity's being and place it at the mercy of the punitive and avenging ruling cosmic might. When those who have fallen learn sacrifice, they lift themselves and attain a new relationship with the world, and in the ascending fragrance of sacrifice, grace approaches them. The soul of Faust receives the strength to sacrifice from the fragrance of the rose blossoms.

V. Spiritual future: It is one of the great enigmas that for the zodiacal sphere comprising November that two such different imaginations can emerge as pictures before inner vision—the scorpion and the eagle. They themselves refer in turn to two so different occurrences in the human being as the head with the sense and nerve systems on the one hand, and the reproductive system on the other. It was not until Steiner that, in the context of directions he gave for eurythmy, attention was drawn to the archetypal relationship that exists between the uterus on the one hand and the larynx and ear on the other, and to the fact that by virtue of this relationship the one is the metamorphosis of the other, and vice versa. This makes understandable how visitation and taking in runs its course in conception, an inner holding takes place in pregnancy, and a speaking out, an uttering takes place in giving birth.

What still occurs physiologically today is intended to assume a completely different character in the future. Human beings will be able to hear inwardly the approaching human soul prior to the soul's birth, and to patiently receive it into the forces of one's own soul and life. Thus receiving, we will be able to bring toward that approaching being devotion that wants nothing and does nothing except what the approaching entity wants. Human beings will develop a higher perceptive faculty, through which they will procreate, because they themselves will have been impregnated by the spirit.

While speaking on the connection between onyx and the sense of hearing, Steiner points to Goethe's fairytale, in which there is a magic power—the Old Man's lamp that has the power to transform whatever its light shines upon. It transforms wood—dead plant matter—into silver; it transforms dead animal matter into precious stone, and the dead pug into onyx. Thus what is dead is not simply subverted minerals; rather, it is refined and ennobled to a higher mineral life of metal and precious stone. The snake's transformation into gemstones, too, once she has sacrificed herself, demonstrates in the fairytale the same character of transformation in the direction of highest, purified mineral substance that we find in the Apocalypse of St. John. The future Jerusalem actually consists of nothing but mineral imaginations. In the future, what came from the spheres of the living—the ensouled, the spiritual, and endured cosmic death as matter on Earth—will become the "noblest of minerals" because of the transformative force of the cosmic Word. The Word appears in the luminous trinity of red, white, and black of the Heavenly Jerusalem's spiritual sardonyx to the eagle-nature of John the Evangelist, human insight impregnated by the spirit; this because insight has sacrificed itself and has fused perfectly with the will of the Godhead.

Sard

I. Name: After the Persian word *serd,* meaning yellow-red.

II. Scientific Research: What here pertains to sard was covered in the previous chapter on sardonyx. Through iron, chalcedony is colored red, to become sard; thus it is actually a carnelian in its lighter, more delicate agate form. In sard, a slightly yellowish shimmer plays into the red, so that when looking at its surface, the stone is brownish, it appears a lively red when looking through it; by contrast, the proper carnelian tends more to flesh red. Carnelian is translucent, while sard is often transparent. In ancient times, it was known to be of Indian origin and introduced via Persia. Since it belongs to the agates, one can derive an understanding of it either solely from the red layer, or else together with the accompanying whitish chalcedony area of the neighboring layer. One can also see sard together with carnelian.

III. Origin and habitat: As mentioned in the preceding chapter, according to Cloos the formation of sard-carnelian is the primeval phase of the plant–animals and mineral–plants, out of which later the minerals, the plants, and the lower animals separated (Cloos, p. 35). According to Rudolf Steiner, the human being developed the yet undifferentiated skin-sense, which originally arose more as a sense of warmth and out of which the sense of touch was then developed simultaneously with sard-carnelian. Seen in the context of the aforementioned undifferentiated phase, one can think of carnelian-sard more in connection with the sense of touch, and think of green chrysoprase more in connection with the sense of warmth.

IV. Soul virtue: The color of sard which, as mentioned above, when gazing through it, displays a milder red than the genuine flesh-red carnelian, and which displays a slightly brownish shimmer when looking at its surface, later became a misunderstanding. Chalcedony of a brownish color later came to be called *sard*. Originally, it was expressly the red mineral that was meant. The delicate brown tone imparts to the soul-filled living red of this stone an earthy character, through which a quiet mood, one more grounded in being, is added to the soul-filled red. The brown brings the power of soul to a kind of harmonious accord with its material existence. This brings the soul force of contentedness to living expression; a contentedness, however, which by no means bears the character of being satiated. It is much rather the attitude of being in agreement with existence, which is only possible, though, if the entity is in agreement not only with its existence, but with itself as well. It is indeed necessary to distinguish between these nuances, in order inwardly to do inner justice to the character of sard's color.

For the designation of circumstances in the world there exist in German two fundamental terms: We speak of the essence of an entity, a thing or a matter, meaning its innermost, most significant, the existential aspect. But we also speak of the entity itself, in which case we are referring to something individual or possessing a personal nature; but here as well we are referring to its actual reality.

We also speak of "world," by which we mean the region common to a group of things or entities, but also to the totality of these entities as such. A world of entities (the plant world, the world of the stars), a realm (the plant realm, the realm of the stars) is addressed here. Uncounted beings of the same nature form a world, a realm, and live and weave in this world. The inverse holds as well, since the world—what everything has in common—also lives in the beings. This commonality, this world of certain beings or entities, is their being or their essence. All philosophies of being are at home in this area.

A being or entity we observe as forming a definite world or a realm with entities or beings of the same kind has a relationship to this world, but it also has a relationship to itself, which can even go so far as to be a self-relationship or a self-awareness. It acquires a taste for itself, but for other beings as well. Through the sense of taste, a person perceives what kind of relationship a substance has to itself within the sensory world (a harmonious one: sweet; a tense one: sour; a disharmonious one: bitter).

The soul's full accord with its own being amounts to the state of inner balance. This state is the good taste, the true equanimity that, pondering or weighing something within one's own being, remains tranquil and does not contaminate or counterfeit, alienate or deny it, but rather asserts itself within this being and within its world.

Cameo carvers and other lapidaries of ancient times used sard to make its brownish-red portion stand out as a pictorial revelation from its background, the white chalcedony. The magic of cameos carved out of sard outwardly manifests an entity's inner taste-relation. If we look inwardly upon the outer figure of the human being, we see the place in the center of the body (the hips and small of the back) where the upright human being is carried, held upright, and supported. In this area and with its help, we become upright in a fully external way and assert ourselves in our true being.

V. Spiritual future: One may ask whether the Apocalypse's imagination of sard reveals only the color aspect, or, in the process of seeing, the whitish chalcedony portion used by the antique cameo carvers as a foundation does not shimmer through, as well. The power of harmony among body, soul, and spirit—which are separate but nevertheless permeate one another—would then lie within the red-over-white (not red-next-to-white, as in sardonyx). Such harmony leads to ensouled spirit and spirit imbued soul, but fully within the body. This alone would be full accord with oneself, but it would also be the highest inner freedom, which not only takes from freedom but also gives it. It is the kind of human behavior that, in deepest affirmation, endows essence—both one's own and essence outside oneself—with its true existence, so that the other entity possesses the freedom to enact what it wants to bring into existence itself. At its purest, this future of true inner and outer freedom manifests in the Christ impulse, which enables the entities of the world to liberate themselves unto themselves—in the highest possible balance between the one-sided errors caused by the adversarial powers. This power shines out toward the Apocalyptist from the "Persian" sard of the heavenly Jerusalem.

Chrysolite

I. Name: Composite of the Greek words for "gold" (*chrysos*) and "stone" (*lithos*), hence "gold-yellow stone."

II. Scientific Research: Chrysolite belongs with the small group of the olivine minerals. Its formula: $(MgFe)_2[SiO_4]$. It crystallizes rhombically and bipyramidally. All types of chrysolite are solid solutions in flowing combinations of 1) magnesium orthosilicate and 2) iron orthosilicate, thus:

Mg_2SiO_4 forsterite, density 3.22, melting point 1,890° C (3,435° F) = Fo
Fe_2SiO_4 fayalite, density 4.43, melting point 1,205° C (2,200° F) = Fa

Olivine in the more narrow sense, 80% Fo and 20% Fa, density 3.43
Hyalosiderite, 66% Fo and 34% Fa, density 3.6
Hortonolite, 30% Fo and 70% Fa, density 4.01

Iron-free forsterite is colorless to bright yellow, olivine bright or dark yellowish-green, oil-green, bottle-green to blackish-green. Iron-rich fayalite is opaque black, often with a metallic shine.

Occurrence: The olivines rich in magnesium are found predominantly in basic and ultrabasic eruptive rock, often as nearly the only rock forming minerals (peridotite, dunite, olivine gabbro). In olivine basalt and olivine diabase, olivine is found as porphyric phenocrysts or in clumps.

The iron-rich sorts of olivine are found pneumatolytically in bubble spaces on crevices or serpentinite rock.

In stone meteorites and mixed meteorites, especially in the various kinds of pallasites in centimeter-sized crystals suspended in a net of nickel iron.

Olivines also occur as eclogite in the schist of deep levels of earth.

In grainy contact metamorphic marbles, one finds both iron-free olivines and olivines rich in brown hematite sediments.

Olivines are found in gemstone form as chrysolite, the mineral is a perfectly transparent olive-green. There are only a few habitats: Brazil, Bohemia, Burma, the island of Zeberget in the Red Sea.

III. Origin and habitats: The greenstones and their precious stone minerals nephrite, jadeite, diopside, epidote, vesuvian, and even diamond come from the Sun state of the Earth (Cloos, p. 126). In basic and ultrabasic greenstone rock (gabbro, serpentine, diabase, kimberlite), magnesium plays the most important role, aside from silicon. In these minerals, a primarily plantlike life process has been mineralized, that of the hovering, oscillating mineral-plants of the time when the Sun and the Earth were still united, so that these plants were the results of an inner Sun influence. Magnesium, a mediator of the light influences of the Sun in the plant, and iron, the mediator of the Sun's life in oxygen, unite in the light mediator silicon, which, as we know, has the greatest of significance for the sense organs, especially for the eyes and the skin. In this trinity of magnesium, iron and silicic acid, the primeval influence of the Sun is replicated. This same solar activity manifests even today in rhythmic form in the different types of olivine and the meteorites, in which chrysolite is also found.

IV. Soul virtue: The plantlike gold-green of pure chrysolite-olivine is a remarkable color. In it, the existence of a delicate, life-filled green tone and a sun-like gold tone both next to each other and within one another manifests in such a way that in turn each of these color nuances can be seen freely for itself and yet connected one with the other. It is like a kind of active and yet restrained mutual influence between the Sun (golden yellow) and the Earth (green). The way the Earth rotates around its own axis, again and again, placing its own powerful life at the disposal of the Sun throughout the years and the days, only to withdraw from it once more, is one of the most comprehensive of cosmic facts. And the Sun behaves similarly toward the Earth. Unlike the ear, the human eye is capable of something similar. It can stream outward in its gaze, and also hold itself back in a chaste downturn of the eyelid. The soul virtue displayed in this gesture is courtesy. It is understandable that so active an organ as the eye must be based on such a virtue, if it is to look into the world without any desire whatsoever. It is understandable why Rudolf Steiner indicates that the sense of sight originated at the same time as chrysolite.

V. Spiritual future: In the dark, consciousness-withdrawn life of the metabolic sphere located in the lower human body, the highest of human forces are at work with one another. These forces possess the ability to divest earthly nourishment of its earthly properties, thus to purify them and conduct them back, as it were, to their cosmic origin, for the purpose of placing them, thus restored to their virginal state, at the disposal of the human being and the makeup of his individual body, whether to build it up, to stimulate its life through the secretion of materials, or ultimately to spiritualize these substances inwardly. In the solar plexus, this mysterious world of the metabolism has formed a brain of sorts, and in the kidneys a kind of inward-gazing eye, which "sorts through" the stream of the blood and returns it, free of slag, to the organism. In the sphere of the soul, this capacity means the virtue through which, out of genuine courtesy, one's own will can come to meet the will of the other. In this process, though, the other entity always remains on the outside. If courtesy becomes heart's discretion, if courtesy of the soul becomes heart's discretion of the "I," the entity, the chrysolite being of the future, becomes active in the worlds and worlds become active in the entities. The one is the preserving, maintaining milieu for the other. A behavior of this kind can wrench a person from "the death of material substance." In the chrysolite image of the Heavenly Virgin of the Apocalypse, there shimmers something of a future world that has become virginal, which in the whole book is then designated as the "Bride of the Lamb": the soul of the world of humanity, in which the Son lives.

The same holds, however, not just for the way in which the soul in itself can become virginal, but also for the way the eye, and through the eye the spirit beholds the whole world. The Gospel contains the following words: "The eye is the lamp of the body. So, if your eye is healthy, your whole body will be full of light, but if your eye is bad, your whole body will be full of darkness. If then the light in you is darkness, how great is the darkness!" (Matt. 6:22–23). The spirit eye's unprejudiced view of spirit, directed through the eye of the body toward the outer manifestation of the world, gives rise to inner light that can find the spiritual essence of world appearance in these appearances themselves. The soul takes hold "of worlds of the entities."* It recognizes the revelations of the spirit in sensory existence. Through one's inwardness having become virginal, the spirit also renders the outer world virginal.

---

*   This phrase suggests to the "Virgo" verse in Steiner's "Twelve Moods of the Zodiac."

This "bridal state" lives in the chrysolite being of the Heavenly Jerusalem both for the entities and for the world of the future.

Beryl

I. Name: *veruliyam,* meaning "stone," from the Indian Prakrit language.

II. Scientific Research: The different types of beryl belong to a group of minerals and precious stones in which the element beryllium plays the deciding role. There are a whole series of them: beryl, chrysoberyl, alexandrite, phenakite, gadolinite, milarite, euclase, and beryllonite. Beryllium oxide is very rare. These minerals also contain iron, manganese, calcium, potassium, sodium, and yttrium. Chemically, beryl is $Al_2Be_3[Si_6O_{18}]H_2O$; hardness 8, density 2.6 to 2.8. Its crystals are developed as prismatic columns and can reach lengths of up to several meters. They are dihexagonally bipyramidal. The crystal matrix carries a sixfold ring of SiO_2 tetrahedrons. Beryllium itself is an alkaline earth metal, steel-gray, very hard and brittle, and has the highest melting temperature of all elements; it takes 1,128 calories per gram (iron takes 315 calories per gram). At the same time, it is very light (specific weight 1.84). It is similar to aluminum and magnesium. Frequently the metals caesium, rubidium, sodium, lithium, chrome, and vanadium join it as pigments.

Common beryl is often quite opaque, colorless, whitish-yellow, and cloudy. The precious beryls emerge from the likewise fully colorless, water clear and transparent pure beryl. Eyeglasses were ground from it in ancient times; hence the German word for glasses, *Brille*. The colored precious beryls are among the most beautiful precious stones—aquamarine (blue with iron), morganite (pink with caesium, manganese, nickel, copper, iron), golden beryl (yellow with uranium), and heliodor (greenish-yellow with iron and uranium). These varieties are all characteristic for a stone's origin in pegmatites that carry beryllium. By contrast, green beryl, the emerald (with chrome) is formed by contact metamorphosis in pneumatolytically permeated schist and grainy limestone. Its color is created by sparse substitution of Al_2O_3 with Cr_2O_3 and/or V_2O_3. In very rare cases, though, it also occurs in pegmatite. This has been dealt with thoroughly above.

III. Origin and habitats: Similarly to alumina (Al_2O_3), beryllium oxide (BeO) stems from the processes that played a large role in the original mineral plant of Earth's past (Cloos, p. 95). These belong to the leaf and fruit-forming parts of this primeval plant, out of which they were then crystallized into mica and feldspar. The totality of all beryl minerals gathered together demonstrates in their elements an indirect relationship with the clay-mica minerals (aluminum, calcium, potassium, sodium, iron, manganese). Together with the other pegmatitic precious stones (such as topaz), their formation in the hollows of pegmatite points to the blossom-like sensory organ characteristic of the primeval plants. The pegmatite beryls stem from a mineral-plant evolutionary process that is of common origin with the human senses in the microcosmic process of the human being's formation (topaz originated at the same time as the sense of taste, beryl simultaneously with the development of the intellect and thus the thought sense).

IV. Soul virtue: Just as in corundum and topaz aluminum is elevated to light and to color, in beryl it is beryllium that is lifted up. However, it is characteristic that the later permeation with light takes place in beryl. The clear transparency of water-bright colorless pure beryl reveals this permeation of the alkaline earth metals beryllium and aluminum with silicic acid. The human sense of thought, whose development began at the same time as beryl, is marked by the fact that it can identify itself fully with its object as no other sense can. One could never really understand other human beings otherwise. The sense of thought develops a power, however, that can also take hold of sensation and feeling. This aids the transition from self-awareness to empathetic awareness of and with the spiritual and soul being of the other entities of the world. In an understanding that thinks along with the other, compassion is ignited, and out of compassion all-encompassing, genuine pity. This virtue, which manifests sensually in clear, pure, transparent, but also very hard beryl, is conscious, thoroughly considered, understanding empathetic thinking and feeling; indeed, even empathetic willing. Here, thought is based on a power of the heart, the intellect on reason. This is only possible, though, by there being three totally different modalities open for the human life of thought.

The first modality one could call that of naïve thinking. It unites the world of the senses, the soul, and one's own self with concepts, initially in the form of names, and permits itself to be guided by the language one has learned from earliest childhood on. A person thinks, in a naïve way, the appearances of the outer world and the thoughts of his fellow human beings; he learns to think from language, he transforms spheres of experience into acts of thinking, but he allows his thinking to be guided not only by the appearances of the outer world, by the properties of language and the thoughts of other people, but as well by his own feelings, motives, needs, inclinations, passions.

Gradually, the reflexive mode of thinking lets go of all this. Thinking becomes more and more abstract, sophisticated, and theoretical. It goes through a kind of death process. Concepts become more and more keen-witted; but more and more lifeless, as well. They are no longer living beings full of content, but rather abstract mirror images and models of the real, living world. When this is taken to an extreme, the human being becomes a rationalist, a skeptic, and a cynic. The only purpose thinking serves today is to keep the world away from ones body, but also to command it; such thinking is self-centered and self-serving. However, there is no longer any reality as such in this thinking; it is merely a means of communication and information. Cold and sober, it contains nothing of what moves the soul, the human heart.

Now something can be added to this thinking. The human being can now reawaken just this dead and abstract thinking to its true being. Concepts and thoughts become essential realities, ideas, if a person discovers that within them a fully intrinsic, ideal, essential content can be brought to life. If spiritually warm life is breathed into this content, it begins to shine forth for the ideal reality of the world as a revelation. This thought-enlivening power must proceed from the heart, though, because it is no mere feeling, but rather spiritually creative power. Just as in the warmth sense we outwardly perceive the inner condition of external substances, as well as our own bodily warmth; through the creative force of the heart, through the ability to be genuinely enthusiastic, we can breathe life into dead abstract concepts. We now experiences with our heart the spiritual power of thoughts and the idea, just as they were reflected to us as pure form by the brain. This higher sense of warmth, which exalts the concept to the idea, then displays the spiritual origin from which the world was brought forth, finding a world of spirit in both the outer and inner perceptive world.

Ultimately, however, this same heart-organ also perceives us ourselves and other human beings—those who are on the way from their originary divine spirituality to independent fallen existence as creatures, just as they previously experienced the path of the idea to sensory manifestation. Now we can be deeply enlightened to the fact that this path of darkening is also a path of suffering, and from our deepest understanding emerges as an organ of the human heart, compassion, and long-suffering, from which an inner need develops to become active in a way that thinks with the other. It leads to the matter of the prerequisite of all this—that is, the issue of freedom.

V. Spiritual future: One of the greatest enigmas in the human being is freedom. What, in fact, is freedom? It is always a relationship free from what? Free through what? Free for what? Free to what end? The freest person is the one who can think along with the thoughts, feelings, and volition of the other as fully as if they were one's own—that is, from the heart. The greatest example of this is Steiner's book *The Riddles of Philosophy*. In that book, the thinking from each thinker deeply grappling with world enigmas—their most profound depths—is understood and reproduced by the author. In this kind of "might of reason,"* the future power of beryl flashes forth to the Apocalyptist at the brightest place in the precious stone imaginations: "bright heart in Leo," born by enthusiasm and in freedom, one might add. If the heart becomes empathetic without sentimentality, it develops an understanding through feeling. Here, feeling becomes thinking and thinking becomes feeling.

Topaz

I. Name: from the island of Topazos in the Red Sea, one of the most important habitats in ancient times.

II. Scientific Research: Topaz is a fluoric mineral. In several fluoric minerals occurring in pegmatite (mica, tourmaline), the hydroxyl group OH is replaced by fluorine to a considerable extent. The formula is $(OHF)_2 Al_2 SiO_4$. Its crystallization is rhombic bipyramidal, often with many surfaces, or solid, dense, and sometimes with coarse shafts. Hardness 8, density 3.5 to 3.6. Pure topaz is colorless, mostly transparent, or translucent. The range of coloration is wine-yellow, honey-yellow, pink, violet, blue, sea-blue, and sea-green, green. Its color diversity is caused by iron in its various oxidation levels; the pink and red tones are caused by chrome. One famous habitat in the eighteenth century was at the Schneckenstein in Saxony; today most topaz comes from Brazil. It fades in sunlight. Certain yellow topazes turn pink when heated to a glow. It is often rich in fluid enclosures, and is found pneumatolytically in granite pegmatites and granites, sometimes in sedimentary gneiss and as a conversion product from feldspars into gneisses of the granites and pegmatites. In contact metamorphosis it can occur in tourmaline rock or even as topaz rock. On the whole, its occurrence is limited.

III. Origin and habitats: If one bundles together the entire hydrothermal geochemistry in which topaz as a fluoric mineral occurs, the elements fluorine, phosphorus, calcium, and tin are found in the greenish

---

* "Might of reason" is the translator's rendering of the German *Sinngewalt*, coined by Steiner for the "Leo" verse in "The Twelve Moods of the Zodiac."

fluorite of pegmatite cavities, and also in apatite, topaz, and cassiterite. This material environment corresponds to the same processes and substances as are found in the human being in the teeth, tongue, and liver. In this area, the portion of the metabolism active is the one mainly pertaining to the intake of nourishment. This is associated chiefly with the sense of taste. According to Steiner's indications, topaz arose at the same time as the human sense of taste.

IV. Soul virtue: There is also something deeper underlying the sense of taste. In tasting, the "I" experiences the relation in which the things it takes in stands to and within themselves (sour, bitter, salty, etc.). A sour-tasting substance has a tense relationship with itself, a sweet one a harmonious relationship. There is also something like the sense for "taste" in the soul realm. To arrange something tastefully means to integrate it into the world according to its own relation to itself, in the same way as the tasted food is integrated into one's own organism. This calls for an ability to be fully responsive to the inner relationships and tensions active in a substance, an object, or in some other entity, which in turn occurs only under the prerequisite of complete selflessness. It is similar with the intake of air into the human chest, above all when breathing in. Thus, when human beings, through taste, imbibe, spiritualize, or excrete nourishment, something else occurs with the stream of the breath. A strong chest can process much through breathing; a good stomach can tolerate a lot. This strength of soul and quality of goodness is the virtue of the soul permeated through and through by the "I," and it is out of just this "I"-strength that the soul unfolds selflessness. In the delicate honey-yellow of topaz, the taste of selflessness manifests to the senses as "gleaming luster"* In the end, though, it is also the same with spiritual nourishment and breathing. If the soul can imbue itself selflessly with spirit and gain strength through it, it will also become a source of spiritual nourishment:

---

*   This phrase suggests the "Cancer" verse of Steiner's "Twelve Moods."

> For in the celestial field
> That becomes the spirits' food:
> Timeless loving is revealed,
> That unfolds beatitude.
>
> (Goethe, *Faust*, Part 2)

Before this soul state of selflessness as depicted in topaz can develop into refinement and purification into catharsis, the soul must first have taken in the content of spiritual nourishment to be tasted: it must have given the spirit beings space, it must hear them and itself be heard. The soul's spiritual ability to hear is also hidden in the topaz being, or entity. What in tasting spiritual nourishment leads to interpenetration of being, that must first be prepared through spiritual answering and being spiritually answered, as in prayer. Whoever does not hear the divine in his or her soul can also not taste it. For this reason, cancer-topaz being originally correlates with the sense of hearing. Upon deeper scrutiny, transparency manifests in topaz in a different way from the way it does in, for example, rock crystal. In rock crystal, transparency is perceived as the ability to be seen through, whereas in topaz it is a subtle ability through which to be heard. It is finely nuanced through the color element that permeates gold-yellow topaz and gives it its "taste."

V. Spiritual future: What remains hidden in the virtue of selflessness ultimately unfolds out of its deep foundation to become what gives all action and behavior its character, as selfless "impetus to deeds," as motivation. Selflessness makes the motives of human soul stirrings sincere and pure. Goethe says this in his "Marienbader Elegy":

> Within our bosom's pureness striving surges
> To give ourselves in freedom, out of gratitude,
> To something higher, purer, unknown,
> Unriddling for oneself the ever-unnamed one;
> We call it "being pious."

In the topaz image, purified piety, or devotion, has become the future reality of the Apocalypse. It is the future cancer entity that is able to harbor the world within its own breast in devotion and piety.

Chrysoprase

I. Name: *Chrysos* means "gold" in Greek; *prason* is Greek for "leek," referring to the leek family in general. The Greek word *chrysos* (gold) stems from the Hebrew word *charuz* (gold). Hence *chrysoprase* means literally gold-colored leek or leek gold. A metal and a plant are connected in the name. Actually, though, the color of chrysoprase is no warm gold tone, but rather a cool, more plantlike, watery green. For centuries, the only known habitat was Silesia; today it comes mainly from Australia.

II. Scientific Research: Regarding the place of chrysoprase among the totality of the silicon minerals, the reader is referred to the above exegeses on chalcedony. Chrysoprase is a green (apple-green, leek-green) chalcedony; it is green-colored due to admixtures of nickel compounds. Thus its pigment is a substance, and this is the reason it occurs almost exclusively in deposit sites carrying nickel ore. So it is a one-sided occurrence among the chalcedony varieties. The nickel that gives it its color, which is a relative of iron, is geochemically relatively widespread, with a dispersion of about 0.01%. As a representative of magnesium, it is mostly found in the magnesium silicates of magmatic rock; consequently, it is scattered throughout over such rock, especially the olivinites and serpentinites. In magnetite, it is then enriched, but nickel minerals are only present in pneumatolytic and hydrothermal ore veins. Here, chrysoprase is also formed alongside such minerals as the likewise apple-green annabergite (Ni_3—[a_5O_4]SH_4O). In cases in which it is especially rich in nickel, chrysoprase is even used in nickel production.

Emerald crystal, double-ended in slate with pyrite crystals (Colombia)

Sardonyx as almond agate cross section; black onyx, whitish chalcedony, reddish-brown Sardius, with sardonyx (Brazil)

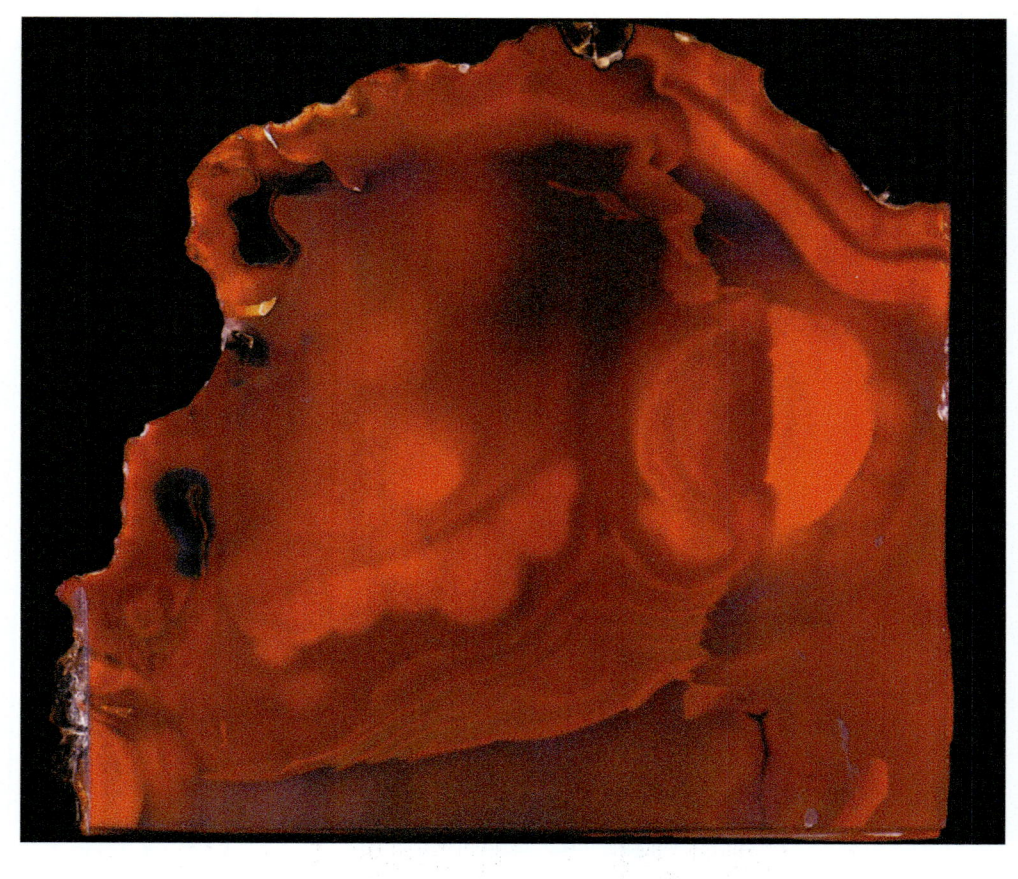

Sardius (slice)

Chrysolite fragment (St. John's Island, Red Sea)

Beryl double crystal; fused in parallel

Light-yellow precious topaz crystal on quartz crystal (Schneckenstein, Saxony)

III. Origin and habitats: As chalcedony, chrysoprase is a product of the mineralization of the primal plant-silicon processes proceeding from the primeval protein of the Lemurian epoch; in the course of this mineralization, chalcedony bonded with the nickel metal process. Chemically as well, chrysoprase is plant (silicic acid) and metal (Cloos, p. 38).

IV. Soul virtue: The tranquil, life-filled green of chrysoprase has something solid, mature, constant about it, something with an equalizing, calming effect. The color green is peculiar, inasmuch as one is aware of how it proceeds from the interaction between yellow and blue, but does not readily see these primary colors in it. How different this is from orange or purple. One has the impression that in green the colors yellow and blue have descended so deeply into sensory nature that they completely conceal their respective characters. If, then, a precious stone is designated as the color apple-green or leek-green, it is an indication that one also has some kind of experience of the colors in the area concealed within it—in this case, yellow and blue. The process that makes yellow shimmer from the green of an apple is, of course, its ripening. One does not notice that, in the green of chrysoprase, a process of becoming is concealed that has ripeness and ripening as its goal. However, no ripening can take place unless it possesses the potential to do so even in sprouting and greening. Moreover, this potential must persevere for it to manifest.

Thus, the virtue of perseverance, staying, and constancy lives in chrysoprase. And in the presence of this virtue, the will both to ripen and to cause ripening to take place can call forth the activity of an inner sun. The innermost being of all ripening is warmth. The generation and perception of warmth prevent the carrying power of perseverance from being torn between the seeming opposition of sprouting and ripening (as can happen to the human being who can become hardened in doubt or despair, or in defiance), and endows it with the strength to stand up under the inner processes of transformation. In truth, all dualities, all polarities are not oppositions, but rather poles between which a third, middle element can transform and unfold itself. In germination, ripening is already contained, and in ripening germination; the feeling for this reality causes all doubting and despair to be overcome within one's soul and spiritual being through patience and perseverance.

However, the thing that actually conceals itself when persevering growth and ripening take place is a slow declaration of what is enshrouded during the growing process. Gold is hidden in the green; the seed in turn is hidden in the gold of the fruit; this path from green to seed via gold is language. In his *Fairytale of the Green Serpent and the Beautiful Lily*, Goethe says:

> Hardly had the serpent set sight on this dignified effigy, when the king began to speak and asked, "From where have you come?"
> "From the crevices," replied the snake, "where the gold lives."
> "What is more splendid than gold?" the king asked.
> "The light," was the snake's reply.
> "What is more quickening than light?" asked the king.
> "Conversation," responded the snake.

The green snake, the gold of the crevices, the light of the question, and the interlocution of the answer—the light of revelation manifests in all germinating, growing, and ripening.

The corporeal manifestation of the spiritual content of the word is the sound of speech—vowels and consonants. A speaking sound is not noise, nor is it tone. It is perceived by human beings through the ear via the sense of hearing by means of a sense that, to be sure, is intimately interwoven with hearing but not identical to it. In the speech sound (vowel, consonant, sound shift), this sense perceives an entity that contains the creative force of reality in it, along with the thought-content. Within its green, chrysoprase conceals gold as the ear conceals the word sense that lives in it and, through what it hears, can experience the light of the creating spirit—the cosmic Word, the Logos.

V. Spiritual future: Now, duality, doubling, and polarity not only become space for an oscillating middle that connects the one pole with the other, but if this oscillating middle is also permeated with perseverance, a third new and promoting element arises; thus a process of heightening develops from the inner identity of "twin" duality. An eagle of the future lies hidden in the human pectoral, or shoulder, girdle, which leads to the maturation of a "Sun's luminescence" from the alternation of the opposites. This resplendency no longer needs to be attained; rather, it has now become intrinsic; it shines out toward the Apocalyptist as the Sunlike golden eagle from the inner golden-green of the chrysoprase image. It is the true "double-headed eagle" of all heraldry—the true Gemini as birth-giver of itself. In this process of becoming, a our lower being is escorted with loving kindness by our higher being because of our faithfulness to spiritual becoming. This gives the higher, future human being a say within the lower, natural person. The Apocalpticist experiences the eternal luminous shine in the gold-permeated green of the chrysoprase image. Thus Goethe can also say, "Green is life's golden tree."*

Hyacinth

I. Name: King Amyclas from Amykles had a son whom Apollo loved. His name was Hyacinthos. This youth was killed by an unfortunate throw of the discus. From his blood there grew a plant, the hyacinth. Every summer for three days, the Spartans celebrated the festival of Hyacinthos and Apollo, the festival of the love of a god for a human being. The name of the plant was transferred to the precious stone.

II. Scientific Research: Hyacinth belongs to the group of the zircon minerals. The element zirconium, a hard, white, and shining silvery metal occurs together with hafnium as a mineral-forming component in syenite pegmatite. On occasion, zircon silicates and zircon

---

* Pertaining to driving force and motivation, cf. Steiner, *Intuitive Thinking as a Spiritual Path*, "The Idea of Freedom," pp. 135ff.

dioxide (ZrO_2) occur in considerable quantities in certain types of rock, sometimes even forming it. The most frequent zircon silicate is zircon ($ZrSiO_4$). In place of zircon, it can contain quantities of hafnium exceeding 10%, and sometimes thorium and uranium. Nearly all types of zircon contain yttrium, niobium, tantalum, and phosphorus pentoxide (P_2O_5). It crystallizes ditetragonally and bipyramidally, and is almost always fully crystallized—never solid or in bulk. The crystals always grow inside or on top of their accompanying material. Hardness 7.5, density 4.8.

Because of its share of thorium and uranium, zircon also carries the radioactivity of nearly all stones and is distributed as macroscopic, accompanying material in all acidic rock (granite, syenite). It belongs in the ranks of the pegmatites and the contact zones of this rock, and is accompanied by ilmenite, rutile, monazite, spinel, and the corundums. In volcanic bombs, as well as in schist, limestone schist and chloritic schist, it occurs in crevices. Its colors are yellow, straw-yellow, yellowish-green, gray, blue-green, and green. It can also be colorless in appearance.

Hyacinth, the precious stone of the group, is yellowish-red. Its light refraction is very high; it often has the sparkle of a diamond. The crystal size does not exceed a few centimeters. Colorless, diamondlike zircons, yellowish-red hyacinths, and yellowish Jargon are esteemed gemstones, as are the blue zircons from Thailand. The color can be both removed and changed by irradiation and heating. Zircon is the heaviest precious stone, with a density ranging from 4.6 to 4.8. It often contains uranium or radium minerals in its crystal, which form halos through their radiation. The precious zircon–hyacinth, however, also varies in color from rose red to brownish-red, yellowish-red, and a fiery yellow-red, also between green and blue. Main habitats: Sri Lanka, East Africa, Madagascar, Brazil.

III. Origin and Habitats: What holds for sapphire, ruby, and spinel also holds true of hyacinth. In the interplay between the blossom zones of the limestone variations stemming from the "tree trunks" of granite and syenite; limestone condenses into "tree trunks" from the primeval mineral plant-leaf processes; and the limestone, marble, and dolomite deposited by the lower plant–animals. This bearer of the greatest weight and radioactive deterioration is purified to become a precious stone, liberated from deterioration and heightened to a diamond flame of yellow-red. Here, too, higher life forces intervene to harmonize and heighten. Zirconium and *Silicium* are related to each other; thus, zircon and, with it, hyacinth represent a kind of highly condensed silicic acid, exalted rock crystal (Cloos, p. 115).

IV. Soul Virtue: In the fiery yellow-red of hyacinth, two colors are united (as is also the case with amethyst): the soul-bearing red, with its will character, is united so purely with the consciousness-bearing, more spiritual yellow, that an inner balance manifests between "driving force" and motivation* in a fiery shine of the will. It is no orange created by a melding of yellow and red; rather, it is a balance of both colors in free cohabitation and interpenetration. The virtue of inner balance is the power of a soul in which the elements of will and of thought can each remain independent of, yet enter free interaction with each other. In this interplay, in this balance of soul, there manifests the actual source of inner human freedom.

V. Spiritual Future: The human larynx, and with it the surrounding organization consisting of throat, nose, ears and mouth, bears within it the mystery of language. The same organization that hears also speaks; and the one that speaks can observe silence and listen. What human beings can say can also be spoken using all of the limbs through gesture and form. This might be eurythmy, but a person also does this with every act. The act is itself *word*, as long as the word remains silent. However, an action is fully itself only when, within

---

*   "Shine of essences" (Ger. *Wesensglanz*) is connected with Steiner's "Taurus" verse in "The Twelve Moods of the Zodiac." *Future word* is from the Pentecost Epistle of The Christian Community "Act of Consecration of Man."

it, soul and spirit, will and consciousness, are in balance. In this way, it does not become a forceful act but action in silence and silence in action, so that real inner progress can manifest deeper volition and being. In the fire of the spiritual hyacinth being, there appears the pulsing strength of the Word of worlds, which is what causes all progress. Those who can hear the Word of worlds within themselves will cause true world progress to work within through a deeper word sense. In their own progress, what reveals the future influence of hyacinth in the "shine of essences" will appear in human beings "Those who have ears, let them hear what the Spirit says" (Rev. 3:22). The word always speaks the future when the spirit speaks it from the past through the present. Such speaking is "future word."* This is hyacinth virtue; this is the "Taurus entity" of the future.

Everything that is "word" has sense. Word is not merely power or will; it is also always meaning, sense, and thought. The spoken word is understood. The transformation proceeds and advances true progress in spirit from the soul virtue of balance. This transformation is eternal becoming, and it occurs through the creative act of a freedom that hears and understands. Those who speak themselves and the world are not those who are advancing; what is concealed in them by the world reveals itself, and what appears in them hour to hour, day to day, year to year, and life to life advances within them.

Amethyst

I. Name: The Greek word *methyo* means to be drunk, inebriated, intoxicated, satiated, or soaked; *amethystos* means sober or capable of resisting the exhilaration of insobriety.

II. Scientific Research: On the place of amethyst within the silicon minerals, the reader is referred to the chapter on rock crystal. The materiality of amethyst can occur in two forms: in solid, bulk form, crystallized in deposits or layers, or hexagonal columns, opaque to translucent, but

---

* Lehrs, *Man or Matter*, London: Rudolf Steiner Press, 2014.

of dark purple color as amethyst quartz; in pure, clear crystal forms in hexagonal columns, as amethyst.

Hardness 7, density 2.65: In contrast to rock crystal, amethyst displays a special structure; right and left quartz alternate with each other, whereby substance and color are arranged in fine lamellae. Its color is more or less deep purple, sometimes taking on a reddish or bright pink tint. The color disappears in some amethysts under prolonged influence of the Sun and of light, and when heated between 300° C (575° F) and 500° C (935° F).

Amethyst contains traces of iron, manganese, titanium, and rhodan iron. The place of these minerals in the crystal matrix can be loosened by radioactive irradiation and converted into the colloidal state. The latter is what actually causes the coloration. Of late, it has been presumed that a minute admixture of isomorphic boron phosphate (BPO_4) plays a role, which can be proved spectroscopically (0.1% BO_2, corresponding with 0.2% BPO_4). Amethyst has a slightly higher light refraction than rock crystal, and is optically bichromatic. When carefully heated, amethyst turns yellow, like citrine. The color of altered amethysts can be restored by means of irradiation with radium. Its closest relatives are fully crystallized quartzes. Amethyst occurs in two different forms of origin; on one hand in crevices of granite, sandstone, and ore veins; on the other hand in melaphyre grown on top of agates in geodes. Habitats: mainly South America (Brazil and Uruguay), Madagascar, South Africa.

III. Origin and Habitats: Lamellar fusing, layering, and frequent twinning point to an origin in precursors of plant form (Cloos, p. 29). The rhodan iron, fluid carbon dioxide, petroleumlike fluids, hydrogen supplied, and, according to most recent research, boron phosphate contained in amethyst indicate the proteinlike atmosphere of the early formative phases of amethyst out of mineral-plant processes. It brought all these components along from the ancient atmosphere. So within the silicon processes it must have had a special relationship to just this atmosphere, thus to the "light" and to the "air" of that age.

IV. Soul Virtue: The purple of amethyst is of a unique quality. The two components of red and blue (actually magenta and blue) are in a very sensitive, hovering mutual balance with each other, one marked by restraint. Each component selflessly withdraws in order that the other may manifest. In this delicate interaction there is, on the one hand, the highest sensitivity in a mutual sensing one another, and, on the other hand, the highest consideration. In this sensitivity and considerateness, the virtue of reverence, veneration, and humility is revealed in a sense-perceptible way. Each partial process fully acknowledges the other, and this is the cause of amethyst crystals' pleasing effect on the eye. The virtue of reverence is no natural predisposition in the human being. Goethe points to this in his description of the Pedagogical Province in *Wilhelm Meister's Apprenticeship*. All four types of reverence must be consciously developed in the human being, but are the indispensable prerequisite for a true encounter between "I" and "I," between entity and entity. This connection has to do with what provides the content of the "I"-sense, the faculty to perceive another person's "I." If the perception of another person's "I" is not based on reverence and veneration, this perception remains empty, unfulfilled, unconscious. The play of amethyst's color can stimulate a person to awaken reverence within his soul.

V. Spiritual Future: The future-mystery of amethyst is its existence as a semiprecious stone. It is still underway.

The head is the most perfect member of the human being. It is also the most independent one, and can harden in an intellectual self-will capable of becoming narrow-mindedness, even idiocy. But it can also fully open itself if, in amazement and reverence, it allows the light of the world, as another entity's "I"-being, to flash up as the shining light of the cosmic thoughts. Human beings are capable of sacrificing their thoughts to the divine thought essence of the world and thus of having the world think within them. This is where the transition from all reverence to the true power of sacrifice exists as one's insertion into cosmic laws and into the kind of accord with cosmic necessity that accomplishes the prerequisite for a being to be fully perceived as an "I"-being by another "I." The highest step on this path is the perception of the "I" of Christ, in which case human beings can receive the Mystery of Golgotha into their own thinking, in which the human "I," the Christ-"I," consummates the true sacrifice to the fatherly ground of the word. This state shines out toward the Apocalyptist from the amethyst image of the Heavenly Jerusalem. It is the virtue of Aries, the sacrificial lamb of the Apocalypse—and it is the "virtue of human beings" in connection with this entity.

Summary

If we now survey the twelve stones of the Apocalypse, we ascertain that half of them are semiprecious gemstones of the quartz family (amethyst, chrysoprase, sard, sardonyx, chalcedony, and jasper). Based on indications from Rudolf Steiner, Cloos shows in his book the significance of the silicon-quartz process in the sensory and perception processes of the Earth, plants, animals, and human beings. Thus, in the quartz group of the precious stones, the relationship between the human senses and the formation of precious stones is most clearly expressed. With "semiprecious stones," we have, on a purely feeling level, an initial sense of something not fully attained; but precisely this might mean that something will be attained later. This indicates the Apocalyptic twelvefold precious-stone entities that unite future forces with themselves. According to Steiner, six of those precious-stone entities originated at the same time as the "I"-sense, the senses of hearing, smell, movement, touch, and warmth. If we consider the other six precious stones of the Apocalypse, we notice that the semiprecious stone character is hidden in them, as well. The relationship of hyacinth to zircon, topaz to the other fluorine minerals, beryl to aquamarine,

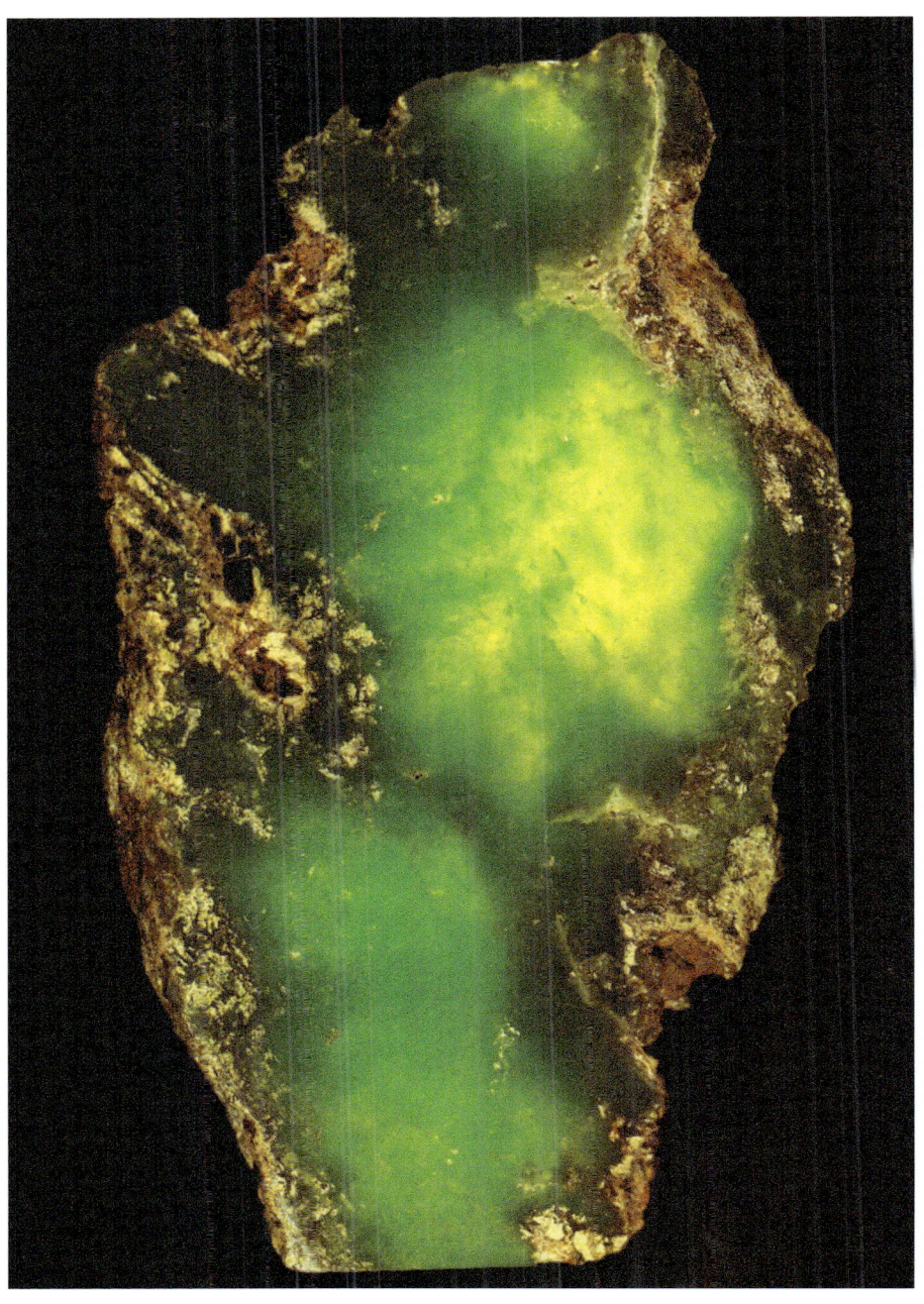

Chrysoprase (Africa)

Hyacinth zircon crystal (Eifel, Germany)

Amethyst cluster (Mexico)

chrysolite to olivine, emerald to beryl, and sapphire to ruby, all touch on these mysteries of transformation.

The future forces of the other six human senses appear in these last six precious stone images of the Apocalypse. They are the life sense, sense of balance, thought sense, sense of sight, word sense, and sense of taste. The correlations depicted to the signs of the zodiac correspond to the future aspect of the senses, whereas the originary aspect would acquire a completely different assignment to the sense spheres of the zodiac. This was previously considered in the descriptions of the precious-stone entities, when we described one sense area as more in the foreground, whereas a second was described as more in the background.

If we try to feel our way into the future sphere of the twelve "world initiators," we will be able to look for the moral qualities that flow from those entities. The corresponding indications can be found in Steiner's guidance for a meditative life; however, it is significant that an inner movement is addressed there that conducts each individual virtue out beyond itself, provided the respective virtue has been developed sufficiently. Thus, for example, in the future development of humankind, reverence (the virtue that correlates with the Aries impulse) becomes the power of sacrifice. An inner view of such processes leads to the attainment of an inner orientation for the way one beholds the respective precious stone. In this way, one can move from the spiritual to the material and from the material to the spiritual.

In the Apocalyptic vision, the arrangement of the twelve precious stones next to each other is not random. There is life in them, movement. Despite their crystalline order, we nevertheless may imagine them as raying and passing over into each other, so that, say, the one color can be transmuted into the other. As we behold our earthly precious stones in this way and perhaps even place them next to each other accordingly, we ought not to remain standing at the specific aspects of the individual entities of this twelvefold. They are members of a higher commonality. The twelvefold is not a sum; rather, it represents the members of a unity, the virtue-entity of the Son God in the Father God, in the cosmos of the future, in the Heavenly Jerusalem. They are the members of a whole.

Living, flexible thinking and seeing will come to develop this inner life of spirit and soul transformations and thus attain an actual experience of the twelvefold as a higher unity. The twelve Cherubim shining from the stones as Spirits of Harmony are united in the hierarchy that, to them, is higher—the Seraphim, the Spirits of Love. In seeing the luminous twelvefold, the Apocalyptist endures, as it were, the highest jasper experience, the experience of all-encompassing and all-permeating godly love.

Chapter 6: Gold

Sevenfold Unity in the "I"

> The mountain folk, they think and simulate;
> In scripts of rock and nature are they learned.
> These spirits, long withdrawn from level land,
> Are more than others partial to the mountains.
> They mutely toil through labyrinths of crevice
> In precious gas of metal-fragrant odors;
> In constant isolating, testing, pairing,
> Their only impulse is to make things new.
> With mighty spirit powers' silent, gentle finger
> They build transparent forms and shapes and figures;
> And then in crystal, its eternal silence,
> They glimpse the event of worlds above the surface.
>
> (Goethe, *Faust*, part 2)

Gold in the Book of Revelation

Who does not know what gold is? As jewelry, a ring, a fitting, an altar chalice—we all know it. Of course, if we have ever had the opportunity to hold a bar of gold, we are startled by its heavy weight. Its bright, cheerful shine, which makes it so attractive to the eye, is overpowered by the impression of a concealed might that immediately dampens cheeriness and shrouds it in darkness, somehow giving an inkling of mysterious levels hidden beneath the golden shine. At the same time, a feeling of value comes over one's heart, which is not because we are aware of its current money value on the world market; rather, it is an impression that arises quite spontaneously, and we wonder either consciously or subconsciously about its manner of bright, dark, strong nature.

It is different in the Revelation of St. John. Whenever gold appears in its images, this originary feeling of magnificence occurs—the feeling of a most exalted thing, a Sunlike luminescence, of something imparting, giving of itself. From beginning to end, gold shines from the Apocalypse, beginning at the start of the first chapter, in verses 12 and 13—"on turning I saw seven golden lampstands." These seven candlesticks return in verse 20: "As for the mystery of the seven stars that you saw in my right hand, and the seven golden lampstands, the seven stars are the angels of the seven churches, and the seven lampstands are the seven churches." And immediately again: "To the angel of the church in Ephesus write: 'The words of him who holds the seven stars in his right hand, who walks among the seven golden lampstands" (Rev. 2:1). "In the midst of the lampstands one like a son of man, clothed with a long robe and with a golden sash around his chest" (Rev. 1:13).

In the epistle to the church in Laodicea, it says, "I counsel you to buy from me gold refined by fire, so that you may be rich" (3.18). In the grand vision in chapter 4, it says in verse 4: "Around the throne were twenty-four thrones, and seated on the thrones were twenty-four elders, clothed in white garments, with golden crowns on their heads." In Revelation 5:8: "And when he had taken the scroll, the four living creatures and the twenty-four elders fell down before the Lamb, each holding a harp, and golden bowls full of incense, which are the prayers of the saints." In Revelation 8:3, when the seventh seal is opened, it says, "And another angel came and stood at the altar with a golden censer, and he was given much incense to offer with the prayers of all the saints on the golden altar before the throne."

The golden altar appears again in Revelation 9:13: "Then the sixth angel blew his trumpet, and I heard a voice from the four horns of the golden altar before God." Even the counterimage is veiled in golden glow in Revelation 9:20: "The rest of humankind, who were not killed by these plagues, did not repent of the works of their hands nor give up worshiping demons and idols of gold and silver and bronze and stone and wood."

After this, gold is not mentioned for a while. After many transformations in the interim, gold reappears in chapter 14, verse 14: "Then I looked, and behold, a white cloud, and seated on the cloud one like a son of man, with a golden crown on his head, and a sharp sickle in his hand." Then the image of gold passes to the angels: "And out of the sanctuary came the seven angels with the seven plagues, clothed in pure, bright linen, with golden sashes around their chests. And one of the four living creatures gave to the seven angels seven golden bowls full of the wrath of God who lives forever and ever" (Rev. 15:6–7).

In the appearance of the great whore of the city of Babylon, gold appears once more in its counterimage: "The woman was arrayed in purple and scarlet, and adorned with gold and jewels and pearls, holding in her hand a golden cup full of abominations and the impurities of her sexual immorality" (Rev. 17:4). Similarly: "And the merchants of the Earth weep and mourn for her, since no one buys their cargo anymore, 12 cargo of gold, silver, jewels, pearls" (Rev. 18:11–12). Finally: "Alas, alas, for the great city that was clothed in fine linen, in purple and scarlet, adorned with gold, with jewels, and with pearls! For in a single hour all this wealth has been laid waste" (Rev. 18:16).

With this image, the series of the appearances of gold in the transitions and transformations end and flow into the final images of the Heavenly Jerusalem. There, of course, the golden shine is different from that of previous appearances of the transitions. First, a golden reed shines in the hand of Him who shows the Apocalyptist the city: "And the one who spoke with me had a measuring rod of gold to measure the city and its gates and walls" (Rev. 21:15). And the gold motif changes for good in the place where the city itself is described: "The wall was built of jasper, while the city was pure gold, like clear glass" (Rev. 21:18).

Now gold is suddenly no longer shiny, but fully transparent, divested of its dark heaviness and fully spread out throughout the entire image of the Heavenly Jerusalem. We can no longer think of the metal we can hold in our hands; we are lifted unintentionally in our imagination to the images we know in the earthly realm at the special moments of sunrise and sunset. What sometimes shines into the eye like bright-yellow gold, fully transparent and in surging motion, corresponds roughly to what occurs in the Revelation image as the final gold motif. The only nature impression possibly capable of bridging the stark contrast between a bar of gold in the hand and the golden shine in the sky of the rising or setting Sun might be the image offered the eye in midsummer fields of grain shone on by an afternoon Sun. This is the motif that moved the poet Christian Morgenstern to say, "The world turned into gold."

To clear a path to an inner understanding of the nature of gold, it first needs to be situated within the full context of earthly materiality; gold is, after all, a metal.

Crystalline and Metallic

Scientific research of the material world runs its course in a systematic and consistent process of analysis. This process leads ultimately to substances unable to be chemically reduced any further. These substances, the ninety-two so-called chemical elements, are simply there. On account of their chemical behavior, it was possible to arrange them in lawful groups and series, which yielded the brilliant invention of the periodic table of elements in 1869 by Mendeleev and Meyer, simultaneously and independently of each other.

As substances, the elements are concrete and sense-perceptible phenomena, each possessing its own bundle of properties. Since 1869, ongoing physical analyses have led to the exploration of the fabric of forces, of the molecules, atoms and elementary particles, and of the quantum mechanical lawfulness that comprehend just this periodic system of elements as a kind of overall structure of the effects of the subsensory that enable physical and chemical properties to manifest. However, it should be noted that the analytical exploration of the chemical elements adheres exclusively to one particular angle of interpretation. Its fundamental point of departure is the assumption that two or more of the ninety-two elements have "combined" to form the new substance of a chemical compound.

The sense-perceptible appearance of a substance as a unit of properties and behavioral patterns (whether the substance is an element or a compound) is considered the mere result of some subsensorially conceived and abstractly calculated influences that exert a specific effect on the human senses. There is no room in the thought processes of this approach for the notion that these properties might be a perceptual content pointing to something quite different from some mere quantum mechanical substrate. *Silicium* and oxygen are not hidden in quartz as "substances"; they have much rather withdrawn to a suprasensory sphere and left behind nothing save the subsensory substrate through which in turn the substance of quartz, and not some entirely different sense properties, can manifest. In truth, it is not possible "to produce" *Silicium* and oxygen by separating them out of rock crystal; it is only possible to deprive the quartz entity of the subsensory force field that enables it to incarnate, the same way as one can deprive a living being of its body by killing it. What happens when this is done to quartz is that the two elements *Silicium* and oxygen are then able to incarnate into their own respective subsensory substrates. That is, they reappear to the senses.

So where are *Silicium* and oxygen when compounded in the substance of quartz? They are in its periphery. This actually holds for all elements: either they themselves manifest, or else they are, along with their essential properties, in the periphery of the substances designated as their respective chemical compounds. They are not like bricks of a house that can be laid one on top of the other and torn apart again; rather, they are something like the descendants of earlier mother-substances, with which they formerly existed communally, but from which they were completely different. Unlike organic descendants, though, once the elements are born individually, they can return once more to the communality of their origin. Then, their original predecessors (the compounds) can reappear. Silicium and oxygen are not the original, but rather the quartz from which they are born. Thus the individual metals are not the original; rather, it is a primal metallic quality, a cosmic substantiality from which the metals proceeded—substantiality, however, which manifests along with them as what is common to all metals, as the thing that as it were defines them as "a clan."

The sequence of the periodic table of elements can be regarded, numerically and statistically, as the expression of the order of protons, neutrons, and electrons. This renders them as a fully quantifiable, mechanical framework or scaffolding. And the periodic table does indeed contain this aspect. On the other hand, the substances display something of formation, rhythm, periodicity, structure, and orderliness—a musical element. Mathematics becomes statistics, order, framework, and mechanism or it becomes resonance, tone, chord, and melody—i.e., music.

The periodic system of elements truly contains both. In the first case, the commonality is a sum total; in the second case, it is the structure of a higher mutuality. The numeric aspect of the periodic system easily leads one to forget what one perceives as the sensual manifestation of *Silicium*, oxygen, iron, and gold. This leads to the inkling that the elements with all their sense-perceptible properties and modes of behavior cannot be the first, the original thing, which in turn combine to form the chemical compounds, but that they are rather the final thing, something that has fallen out of a higher commonality and into a spatial and temporal existence, as a mere scaffold.

So-called compounds, too, can be considered something originary, or maternal, something belonging to a former state of the cosmos, out of which later the individual elements were born as the final part. On this path, the elements, and out of them the elementary particles and quanta, are ultimately pressed out of the sensually existing substances. The elementary particles, the elementary quanta, and the four physical aggregate states all belong to the field we carve out of subnature when we treat matter accordingly. They are not truly the first, original thing out of whose infinite combinations everything of a physical-mineral-material nature emerges; rather, they are something final, something produced—something that can fall out of the full reality of nature.

In his book *Man or Matter*,* Ernst Lehrs comprehensively analyses these states of affairs and places the analytical approach to scientific research alongside the synthetic approach, initiated by Goethe and carried forward by Rudolf Steiner. The most important result of Lehrs's exegeses is the following: The ninety-two elements stem from a higher sphere of nature, the fruit-bearing primal protein of former Earth states is the mother-substance, from which the "sons" stem (carbon, oxygen, nitrogen, hydrogen, sulfur, and phosphorus).

Original mother substances similar to alkalines brought forth the halogens on the one hand, and the alkali metals on the other. Original substance-entities of former states of our planetary system, mighty in soul, are the father-level of a kind of primal metallic quality, from which the metals proceeded; and it is out of an original lightlike, form-bearing ether substantiality that the quartz mother-process emerged, which in turn brought forth the quartzes and, in reciprocal interaction with the metal-fathers, the silicates.

---

*   Steiner, *Mystery Knowledge and Mystery Centres*.

What one can see in modern geophysical and geochemical notions of the originally gaseous and fiery-molten magmas are depictions of these mother and father substances in terms of today's 92 elements. And so one can speak in terms of the protein mother and the planet fathers both of the metals and the semimetals. Everything we have today in the way of compounds and elements are the descended, mineralized end stages of those original states of the life of matter.

It is easier to see the phenomenological commonalities of metals. To be sure, they crystallize; but that is not their most pronounced trait. What they all have in common is that they can flow without breaking. One of them is liquid at normal temperatures of the Earth's surface: quicksilver. Of course this fluidity also has to do with the metals' subsensory substrate, the so-called metallic-chemical bonding with freely flowing electrons. This, however, is by no means the cause, but rather the precondition of the manifestation of their original nature, which even in a crystalline state only partially behaves like a crystal. One can characterize the whole of metallic nature as follows: high luster; strong capacity to reflect light and great capacity to absorb color; outstanding ability to conduct heat and electricity (an ability that decreases as the temperature increases); pliability in rolling, forging, pressing, drawing; well suited for producing positive ions, even as a crystal; possessing a highly symmetrical crystal matrix; its crystal matrix possesses coordination numbers—i.e., the possibility to unite with many ions; metallic bonding in the matrix between a kind of freely mobile electron gas and positively charged atomic cores, without semivalences becoming saturated.

All genuine metals crystallize in matrices in which each atom gathers as many other atoms around it as space allows. This yields highly symmetrical crystal matrices. It is characteristic of metals' structures that each atom has a large quantity of neighboring ions (12 for the greatest cubic and hexagonal density of spherical shells, 8 for spatially centered cubic arrangement). In this way, "superfluous electrons" occur, which endows the atoms with the ability to form positive ions, even within the crystal matrix. This causes the crystals' atoms to exist not in a neutral state, but rather as metal ions; and the electrons freed move between the ions' positive atom torsos as "electron gas," to cause what is known as metal bonding.

From the above, it is evident that even the subsensory substrate is fluid crystal all the way down to its quantum mechanical process. Hence no sharp distinction between metals and nonmetals is possible. Under certain conditions, even nonmetals can behave like metals, and vice versa. There are seventeen elements that are nonmetals in the proper sense: hydrogen, helium, neon, argon, krypton, xenon, radon, carbon, oxygen, nitrogen, phosphorus, sulfur, fluorine, chlorine, bromine, iodine, and selenium. Carbon, phosphorus, selenium, and boron, however, can also behave like metals. There are likewise metals of flawed metallic character: *Silicium*, germanium, selenium, arsenic, antimonium, tellurium, and boron. They are called semimetals. Especially in the case of boron and *Silicium*, it depends where they are placed. And there is a further series of metals with particular common properties on account of which they are called metametals: beryllium, zinc, cadmium, quicksilver, indium, and thorium. Finally, among the proper metals, one distinguishes between nonprecious and precious metals: gold, silver, platinum, iridium, palladium, and rhodium. By arranging the entire periodic table according to these behaviors, we arrive at this order:

1. 17 nonmetals
2. 7 semimetals
3. 6 metametals
4. 6 precious metals
5. 6 alkali metals
6. 6 alkaline Earth metals
7. 14 Earth metals (the lanthanides, also called triels, the "boron group," or the rare Earth metals)
8. 3 natural actinides
9. 27 nonprecious metals.

If we inquire, in the spiritual-scientific sense, about the origin of metals, we are led away from Earth to the primal states of our solar system, Sun and planets. The actual "fathers" of metals are the planets from which the metals came to the Earth in a fluid astral-etheric state, to wrap themselves in the nonmetals and conceal themselves inside their "mothers," the metal ores. In connection with oxygen, phosphorus, sulfur, carbon, halogens, and so on, they relinquished their etheric flow and enveloped themselves in ores as their mother substances. That is, in a sense, their myth.

By number they have an absolute majority over the nonmetals. Of the 92 elements, 75 are metals (17 nonmetals). By mass, however, they are far behind the nonmetals in the composition of Earth. The Earth crust consists of two substances—oxygen (46.6%) and *Silicium* (27.7%), at 73.13% of its total weight. The heavy metals not including iron are represented by mere hundredths to hundred-millionths of a percent (chrome 0.022%, gold 0.0000005%). Iron is the leader, with 5%. The light metals are much more frequent (natrium 2.8%, magnesium 2.1%, aluminum 8.1%, calcium 3.6% of the Earth's weight). At the same time, the nonmetals are lower in specific weight; many of them are gases. The metals range from heavy to very heavy.

All of this demonstrates that on Earth the metals are actually foreigners. They stem from an essential cosmic-planetary state, corralled into the Earth by three forces and with the help of the nonmetals. The three forces are, firstly, the gravity from the subsensory world; secondly, the spatially active crystal forces from the suprasensory; and, thirdly, the chemical forces, which guided the metals into their compounds. Rudolf Steiner describes their primal state* as a colored cloud surrounding the primal Earth in an astral state of soul forces,

---

*   Early research based on Steiner's work is documented by Lili Kolisko in *Sternenwirken in Erdenstoffen, Saturn und Blei. Ein Versuch, die Phänomene der Chemie, Astronomie und Physiologie zusammen zu schauen* (Stellar influences in Earth substances, Saturn, and lead: An attempt to gain a comprehensive view of chemical, astronomical, and physiological phenomena; published privately, 1952; no English translation).

from out of which they then passed over into a colored etheric stream, which flowed like glowing brooks into the nonmetallic environment of the Earth. It is for this reason that on one hand they are distributed over the entire world and that, on the other, they are particularly strongly localized in ores. The fact that metals are heavy and hidden in ores, and are crystallized in their pure state is not in keeping with their nature, but rather with their devotion to circumstances on Earth. Their nature shows on one hand in the above-mentioned flowing state, even when they are solid, and on the other hand in their colorfulness. In their pure manifestation, they themselves always have the aforementioned shine; but their intrinsic colors indicate a certain restraint (yellow, red, gray to dark gray). Only their ores reveal their tremendous colorfulness, which is even maintained when they are in their gaseous states, in which they are capable of displaying the most magnificent flaming colors.

Movement (flowing) and color (mood), though, are always a sense-manifest expression of soul. What manifests in the mineral realm as metal ores and metals is an extraordinarily genuine soul aspect. These soul qualities are like unambiguously noble forces of soul or tendency that feed into the metallic phenomenon. The austere or dry disposition of the metal lead with its white and yellow ores; the active tendency of iron, which oscillates between two valences; the bright inclination of silver, which mirrors all the world; the shine of gold, which is born by the strongest "I"-being; all of these qualities of soul are materialized in the metals. As matter, the metals with their properties are more genuine than the nonmetals.

They have their origin in the outer cosmos of the planets. Both the old tradition and modern Spiritual Science speak of the dispositional characteristics of the planetary intelligences. The correspondences are quite clear in all esoteric traditions for the so-called main metals—silver belongs to the Moon; quicksilver to Mercury; copper to Venus; gold to the Sun; iron to Mars; tin to Jupiter; and lead to Saturn. The planets and the metals are, in the material-phenomenological sense, carriers of the same dispositional strengths; herein lies their true relatedness. Even today, the fact that such relationships exist can be clearly proved by experimentation.

The planetary aspect as spiritual point of departure shows that the planetary system is no mere sum of the Sun and the planets, but rather that it is an organic whole that even in its very material sense belongs to the Sun. all the planets together, including the Earth, make up a mere fraction of the Sun's mass. It was Kepler's true and greatest striving to find the harmonies that bring to expression, all the way down to the mathematical quantities of distance and speed, such a spiritually essential unity of the planetary system. It was precisely in his third law of the relation between the distance and the period of any two planets—and thus of them all—that for Kepler the inner unity of the whole, the divine harmony, the whole as the cosmic world soul, revealed itself. He was able to think the inwardly essential and psychic world-content alongside the mathematical world-content.

It is from this point of orientation that it is at all possible to see the planetary system and the human disposition in connection with each other. And it was precisely Rudolf Steiner who never tired of describing and unfolding such connections over and over; after all, the human soul in its manifold possibilities is also an inner unity that is vouched for by the Sun-nature of the human "I." The planetary system and the human disposition are at once parts and a link, and at the same time they are both a totality and a unity. Only in states of illness does the disposition fall apart or become lost in one-sidedness.

If we turn from the planetary system and the human disposition back to the metals, we find here as well the unity that pervades them, diverse as they are—and this unity is not just external, but also inward. From here one will then be able to comprehend properly the place of gold, both in the midst of the seven main metals and among all the other metals of the periodic table. Gold too is, for one thing, the specific entity that is it is; for the other, it is the most precious of metals precisely because by virtue of its purity and perfection it is best able to mediate the manifestation of metallic qualities. In gold, all other metals can feel just as accommodated as the individual stirrings of the soul disposition are accommodated in the "I." In a certain sense, gold is also silver, quicksilver, copper, iron, tin, and lead.

The peculiarity of everything metallic becomes more definite if we regard the seventeen nonmetals (the place of *Silicium* is ambiguous):

1. The six protein producers: carbon, oxygen, nitrogen, hydrogen, sulfur, phosphorus
2. The six noble gases: hydrogen, neon, argon, krypton, xenon, radon
3. The four halogens: fluorine, chlorine, bromine, iodine
4. *Silicium* and boron, especially *Silicium,* which plays the greatest role as the mediator for the entire mineral realm and can be assigned a place among the semimetals

The nonmetals, too, have something in common—they are the actual bearers of crystallinity. In this respect, *Silicium* and boron belong to the nonmetals. At the top we have carbon (diamond) and *Silicium* (quartz minerals and all silicates); but as well the four halogens as producers of salt in the stricter sense, and sulfur, phosphorus, and boron, with their abundance of salts, are carriers of crystallinity. In the sulfides, sulfur plays a special role, as oxygen does in the oxides and hydroxides. Hydrogen has a part everywhere. While the metals as material soul-bearers have their relationship with the planetary system, the nonmetals display stronger connections with the inner forces and soul entities of the fixed stars, especially the zodiac. In his books on teaching chemistry in schools, Frits Julius,* among others, tried to establish correspondences: oxygen = Leo; nitrogen = Cancer; hydrogen = Gemini; sulfur = Taurus; carbon = Aries; phosphorus = Pisces; *Silicium* = Aquarius; and one can continue where Julius leaves off: boron = Capricorn; fluorine = Sagittarius; chlorine = Scorpio; bromine = Libra; and iodine = Virgo. The impression can arise that the actual metal substances only assume

---

* Cf. Julius, *Stoffliche Welt und Menschenbildung.*

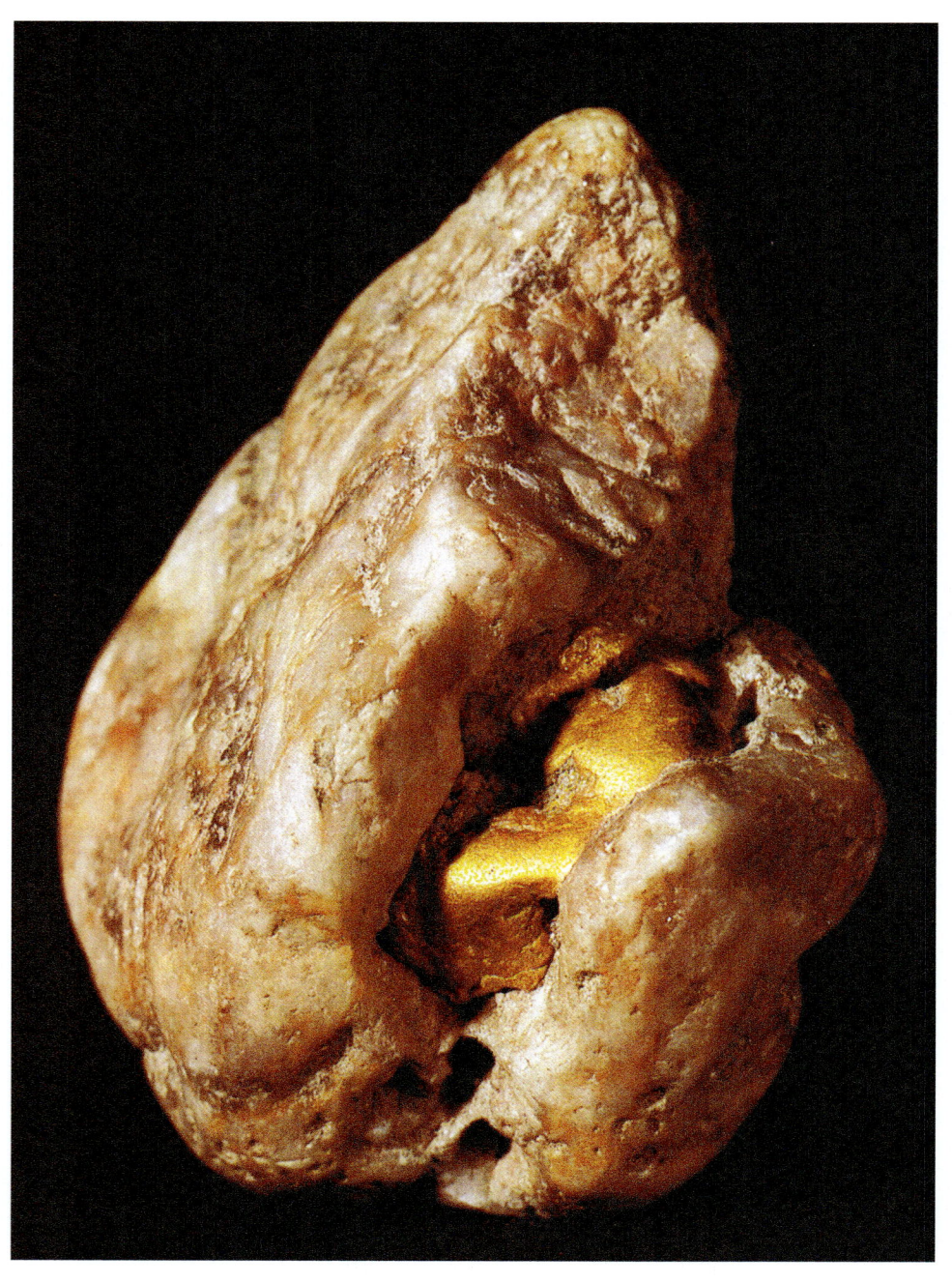

Gold nugget embraced by a rough stone

Gold crystals in various manifestations

Crystallized gold (Transylvania, Romania)

*So-called carbon strips in a quartz conglomerate (Witwatersrand, South Africa).
We see a thin band of Witwatersrandkohle (carbonaceous matter).
The conglomerate contains much detrital pyrite. Carbon-fiber-shaped
gold can be seen (magnification approximately 1.5x).*

the crystalline state because they are forced to. It is part of the overall characteristic of the metallic bonds that even a portion of the subsensory substrates retain metal's flowing, flexible nature, and this manifests as oscillation and resonance. Metallic bonding allows warmth and electricity to flow through as freely as possible. To be sure, they bear the matrix and are still matter, but they permit their form to be completely altered and reshaped by purely mechanical force; they can be forged, or easily melted.

By contrast, the nonmetals are either gas or liquid, or else fully crystalline. They resist being forged, splintering instead. For this reason one can say that the proper joint higher aspect of the nonmetals is crystallinity, just as the proper joint higher aspect of the metals is mobility of soul. The semimetals stand between the two, determined from the one side by crystallinity, from the other by materiality. The metals replicate the soul aspect in the mineral realm: the element of soul as substance, as color. Precisely where they are taken up into crystallinity, they are the actual mediators of the element of color in the entire mineral world. On the one hand, seen spiritually, the nonmetals impart crystallinity; and seen chemically they impart cosmic functions.

In metals, the nature of metal qualities (or soul forces as matter) is contained everywhere. In gold, the most precious metal, this metal-nature manifests the most purely. The fundamental entity of the planetary system that corresponds to this is the Sun. The individual planets are like little shining Suns on the background of the heavens of the fixed stars. Sometimes even the Moon can appear like a paled Sun when it rises or sets. By contrast, the nonmetals are the bearers of cosmic functions not only for the mineral realm, but as well for the realms of life (carbon, as carrier of the framework, such as nitrogen as soul carrier in living nature). In the four halogens, the four elements—fire in fluorine, air in chorine, water in bromine and earth in iodine—attain to the status of bearers of matter.* In crystallinity, the nonmetals dis-

---

* *Tellurides* are binary compounds of tellurium with a more electropositive element or group.

play something of their relatedness to the grand cosmic spatial order of the starry world.

The Question Replaced

The endeavor to interpret the word "gold" (according to how it is used to name images in the Apocalypse) leads to a consideration of both sides of the entity of gold—as a particularity in its sense-perceptible manifestation and as a universal that, by its very nature, is the purest revelation of metal qualities. Herein lies the connection between gold and the human "I," which within the human being's constitution is furnished with a universal capacity that pervades all the details of the soul, makes them an inner unit and unfolds and develops itself ever further. From this perspective, our gaze is directed to the Gospel according to Saint John, in which the divine "I" of the Christ being appears in the human being Jesus in such manner that the "I" of God pervades and fills the human mind and soul, and acquires the capacity to undergo a sevenfold expression of its nature. This actual mystery of the "I" becomes evident in the seven times "I AM" is spoken by Christ according to Saint John's Gospel.

Gold as a Particularity

I. Name: The Greek word *chrysos* is borrowed from the Hebrew *charuz*. There are two words for gold in Hebrew: a) *ZAHAB*, "to shine," "to be shining yellow." However, the same word also exists for gold as a metal, as material appearance. It also means "golden shine of Heaven" (the Sun). b) *CHARUZ*, "yellow," "yellowed," "sharpened," "pointed," "to be sharp." Further, it can mean "excavation of a fortification trench" and "judgment and punishment." The same word also means "zealous," "diligently busy," and "active." In a somewhat different vocalic scripting, it also means "gold." This expression for gold is never used in a profane sense; rather, it is only ever intended poetically, metaphorically—i.e., when conveying matters of a spiritual and soul nature (Psalms 68:14).

The ancient Jewish people's experience of gold is on the one hand entirely material, but on the other hand it is expressed in acute, vehement soul activities, including moral decisions through which the Divine shimmers.

The German word for gold has a threefold root:

a) *GHEL* = yellow, shining, luminously yellow, glowing bright, cheerful, smiling, laughing
b) *GEL* = to be cold, to freeze, frosty, to be closed off
c) *GEL* = to want to devour, to be salacious, prurient, randy

We see again how the outer meaning of the word has a different form from its inward one. The Indo-European folk spirit experienced the inner world in a more volitional manner, in contrast to the Semitic folk spirit, which comprehended it in a more conscious way.

II. Research: Gold is found about twenty times less frequently on Earth than silver. Together with copper and silver, it constitutes heavy-metal series 1; and along with quicksilver and lead, the sixth period of the periodic table. It is a kind of corner point, flanked on either side by a different classification criterion. In gold, all physical and chemical properties of a metallic nature manifest in ideal form. Geochemically, it is assigned to the so-called siderophilic elements, which are those that have less of a chemical affinity to oxygen and sulfur than to iron. They are more starlike. Most frequently, it occurs as native gold, either alone or along with silver. It stems from the hydrothermal crystallization phase, along with quartz, arsenopyrite, and pyrite or marcasite, but also with rhodochrosite, barite, and other manganese minerals. Native gold in its natural habitat is never absolutely pure. It nearly always contains two to twenty percent silver, but also rhodum, copper, bismuth, barium. The silver is perfectly interpenetrated with the gold as a solid solution. Natural gold with more than twenty percent silver is white and known as *electron*. Native gold crystallizes in a cubic system, isomorphically with silver and copper, and always mixable with silver as a solid solution. It is seldom fully crystallized. The crystals are often contorted, with curved surfaces, rounded corners, and edges. Oftentimes, several crystals form feathery, stretched, dendritic groups or surfaces. The crystals are cubes or octahedrons, nuggets, sheets, tinsel, wires, moss-like structures, and are sprinkled in or grown on top of or into their host mineral.

Even when cold, gold can be stretched to extremes by hammering. The thinnest leaves have a bluish or greenish translucence. Gold's shine very strong (a high degree of reflexivity); its color is the broadest range of yellow hues. Its hardness is 3, its density is 15 to 19.3, depending on the amount of silver it contains. It is almost twenty-eight times heavier than water. It melts at 1,063° C (1,945° C). It immediately forms an amalgam with quicksilver.

Most of gold's naturally occurring chemical compounds are tellurides,* but it can also be captured by antimony, sulfur, even lead. The following tellurides are known:

1. Sylvanite, $AuAgTe_4$; it forms monoclinic crystals; the crystals form script-like groups
2. Calaverite, $AuTe_2$; monoclinic, whitish-yellow crystals
3. Petzite, Ag_3AuTe_2; cubic gray crystals
4. Krennerite, $(AuAg)Te_2$; rhombic, brass-yellow crystals
5. Aurostibite, $AuSb_2$; similar to galena

There is also a highly unusual gold ore: nagyagite, $Au(PbSbFe)_8(TeS)_{11}$. It consists of monoclinic, thin-slabbed crystals, flexible and soft like gypsum, dark leaden gray. It is astonishing how gold has enshrouded itself in this mineral

The occurrence of gold is bound up with three phases of the Earth's history. The more recent gold-ore deposits are bonded with volcanic rock. In these deposits, the gold cohabitates with silver, copper, rhodochrosite, and barite. The older gold-ore deposits are for the most part poorer in silver, and are bonded with bedrock (granites). Here it

---

* Schiffers (in Harms, *Afrika*).

cohabitates with quartz, pyrite, and arsenopyrite. There are two phases of this older formation of gold. In addition to these gold habitats, there are the gold placers, where gold nuggets are deposited in conglomerates, gravel, stones and sands that have eroded from ore deposits.

Today, the price of gold is so high that even two grams of gold per ton is profitable. Currently about 1,000 tons are mined per year (the leading countries are Russia, the United States, Canada, and, above all, South Africa, with a third of the entire production). The most remarkable occurrence of gold on Earth is the South African quartz conglomerate of Witwatersrand near Johannesburg in Transvaal.

Appendix 29 contains more details on the origin of the gold found in the Witwatersrand Reef in South Africa. Consideration of these most recent research results can be an impulse to make the process of nature that created this geological formation a parable for the main idea represented in this book on the esoteric mineralogy of the Apocalypse. The "primeval lichens" of the primeval ocean that was the South African continent performed the enlivening (colloid formation) and the assimilation into their life of quartz, gold, uranium, and so on from the primal colloidal state of the latter. The lichens digested them before redepositing them in mineralized replicas of the organic structures of the lichens. This primal gold has lain in the Earth for millions of years. It has been mined for about the last century (five to seven grams of gold per ton of rock).

> Hundreds of thousands of tons of ore must be mined, crushed, washed, and subjected to a chemical separation process.... The gold filtrate undergoes numerous chemical processes, among them the admixture of zinc dust and other chemicals, before it reaches the smelting furnace, after which it is poured into bars in graphite molds. These bars contain only eighty-eight percent gold. They are transported to the Rand Raffinery, Ltd., in Germeston, the largest gold refining facility in the world... The bars are resmelted, in which process the last foreign matter is removed, until 4.5 parts silver per 1,000 parts gold remain. When the pure gold flows out

of the smelting oven as a boiling mass, it glows in all colors of the spectrum. South Africa produces seventy-three percent of the world's gold outside the Iron Curtain.*

This gold, cast in the shape of bricks, then goes to the gold treasuries of the states, banks, and private individuals; to the greed, addiction to economic power, the egoism, and finally people's jewelry addiction. Only a fraction is sacrificed for use for cultic purposes, hence for the divine-spiritual world.**

Nevertheless, this gold also bears not only the outer stamp, but also ultimately the spiritual stamp of human work: it is mined, refined, and processed by human beings and itself awaits its spiritualization in the future, as does the entire mineral world.

"All that is transient is but a parable." (Goethe). The gold of the Heavenly Jerusalem passes through humanity along the path of spiritualization, and like a natural parable, its physical path through the mineral gold of the Witwatersrand Series led through the primal lichens of the primal sea of the primal continent. Is it coincidence or parable that these ancient organisms containing silicon, "rock crystal," and gold allowed uranium, of all things, to pass through them? Might humanity be able to impart a different direction to the technological processes wrenched from nature through nuclear technology—a direction different from that of irreparable disintegration, toxification, and destruction? What spiritual or even godly forces would it take to transform even uranium into a building substance of the Heavenly Jerusalem?

III. Origin and Habitat: It is one of the greatest of world enigmas that, in all the old traditions, gold was always associated with the Sun. Spectral analysis finds hardly any gold on the Sun. Apparently, the circumstances there are not such that this metal can materially manifest outwardly in more than mere traces. This does not mean that the Sun is not the cosmic origin of all gold nevertheless; but it is the origin of the

---

*   Cf. Klockenbring, *Geld-Gold-Gewissen*.

**   Goethe, from the conclusion of *Faust*, part 2.

gold process, which only gets as far as etheric substantiality, without becoming physical. In the Sun, a process is at work that outwardly emanates light, warmth, electromagnetic waves, and a solar wind. On the other hand, though, there is something formed inwardly (into the astral-etheric element of the Sun), which amounts to gold's inner quality as the life of the spiritual entities that inhabit the Sun. In the spirit of the esoteric traditions and of modern Spiritual Science, the gold in the Sun is definitely still in a suprasensory, etheric and astral state, and is therefore perceptible only to suprasensory vision.

It was also in this state when the Sun and the Earth were still united. When the Sun separated from the Earth, an element of its nature was withheld within the Earth and was able to permeate and pervade the granite-mineralization process. Thus, at that time there were definitely areas where the forces of the Sun were concentrated. In these places, gold streamed along in fluid, etheric form. From there, it became solidified and mineralized as mountain gold in the crevasses, and through it erosion landed in placers. Hence we can say that gold stems from the former cosmic life-process of the Earth, and this is the way Steiner describes it in *Mystery Knowledge and Mystery Centres*. That is the origin of gold's life in its association with the Sun. If one proceeds from the organic aspect of the Sun to that of the human being, one finds something similar: it is in the physical heart where one finds the very least physical gold. All the same, gold is a medicinal remedy for the heart, able to heal quite specific heart ailments. From these two points of view, the question arises pertaining to the inner properties of gold, and these can shed light on the transparent gold that appears in the Revelation of St. John.

IV. Soul Virtue: Nothing in the world or in the human being that is of a soul nature can be understood unless its proper spiritual essence is attended to, that is, unless its unifying aspect is sought in the tremendous manifoldness of the substances of life and of the soul. But there is no manifoldness either of the mineral or of the plant world that can reach the soul wealth of the human being. This is because the soul is always in motion. In the animals this motion is one-sided, depending on the specifics; in the human being it is comprehensive. Whether from the inside outward, from oneself out into the world, or from the outside inward; from the world back to oneself; or whether completely within oneself in instincts, desires, and passions; in sympathies and antipathies, pleasure or disgust; in thousands of moods, motivations, and soul states; in the finest of sensitivity and excitability, irritability, susceptibility—to the past, the present, to the future, the soul is always motion, both intensively and extensively.

This yields the fourth, the actual fundamental property of the soul element: its inwardness. This character of the soul's inwardness is unlimited. The soul is deep, but it is always capable of further deepening.* Everything of a soul nature is movement, intentionality, subjectivity, and inwardness. All this leads to soul autonomy and selfhood, to soul existence from itself and for itself. It is "I"-being of soul—as true reality, the indestructible continuance, the genuineness and immortality of the soul.

But all metals, too, are based on genuineness, on solidity, soundness, substantiality. They also occur this way in nature, whereby gold is the front runner (and after it platinum, silver, copper, quicksilver). Besides these qualities, all metals also have other properties of soul. However, the named characteristic is the virtue of gold. Gold is, in its very existence, saturated in itself, and does not want to be anything other than what it is through itself: yellow, shiny, heavy, pure, consummate, certain, and untouchably resting within itself. The pure virtue of gold is its "I"-being. It can be hammered, stretched, leafed, cut, melted, vaporized; it always displays the noblest inapproachability, through which it always returns to itself, rests within itself. "I"-being, genuineness, solidity, soundness, substantiality, and reliability are its

---

*   Nietzsche says, "The world is deep, and deeper than the day thought."
    Novalis says, "Inward goes the enigmatic path."

soul virtues. It can also become involved with other elements, but the way it does so shows that its will to be itself prevails.

V. Spiritual Past and Spiritual Future: the demonic nature of gold is also in its "I"-being. Its outer gleaming beauty, its unapproachable, proud, and noble inner nature, and its constancy arouse a craving to possess it ("Gold doesn't rust," says the German proverb). Outer material ownership of it affirms in a remarkable way our "I"-being and sense of self. Addiction to gold is also real. This side of gold shows today in the human economics, in which gold is either the standard for money or hoarded as hard reserves or capital, serving no real purpose.

There is a kind of magic at work here. This magic merely represents the final conclusion of a millennia-long development from those beginnings in which for humanity gold still stood entirely in the service of the magic that was at home in the ancient mystery cultures. There, material gold was still experienced in an entirely spiritual way; it was considered the material effigy of the gods, of the initiates' and the wizards' will forces, who through exalted life-achievements, experience, and knowledge were purified and refined, and who in wise will and knowledge administrated this most precious spiritual good, the most lasting substance in the world—the Sacred. "I"-being, will, feelings, and thoughts coagulated into wisdom gained through world experience; that was the gold tended in the mysteries in the sense of spirit achievement and spirit legacy. People had the conception that material gold can never be human property; instead, it is the property of the gods, and must only be administered as material gold by initiates, priests, and kings. It was allowed to be used only for cultic purposes for instruments, insignias, images, cultic garments, especially for the heart and the head—and macrocosmically for the Sun and the universe.

The classic example of this kind of gold culture was the Andean Inca culture insofar as it adhered to its pure origins. Others include the Indian, Persian, Babylonian, Egyptian cultures, as well as the primal cultures of the European Celts, Germans, and Slavs. Originally, they all understood gold as the bearer of soul "I"-being and divine will as wisdom. This is the spiritual past of gold; it is also its magical power. When employed correctly in a ritualistic way, it had the power to conduct one to the golden wisdom of the Godhead. However, because that ancient wisdom was always connected with a certain heightening of "I"-being, it was easy for luciferic deities to participate in the mysteries, inasmuch as magic and wisdom passed into outer shine and earthly power.

From this its original spiritual-divine past, gold fell into the abysses of all different kinds of demonic nature. Today, gold is cursed with the curse uttered by the dwarf Alberich in the *Nibelung* saga on the gold of the daughters of the Rhine.* It becomes the property of the dragon. Wisdom and Sun-luminous volition are overcome by egoism, hunger for power, and greed. Gold goes from hand to hand, but ownership is illusion. It endows not only wisdom in the service of the gods, but also darkening of the human spirit in the service of matter. Nonetheless, gold also has a spiritual future: "I counsel you to buy from me gold refined by fire, so that you may be rich" (Rev. 3:18).

The soul force of "I"-being, as well as the spiritual force of wisdom and might, require smelting or purification. The will of selfhood and own-ness, wisdom and might, needs to be recast as a force that not only endures and wants to endure and knows that it endures, but also becomes a force willing to take part with wisdom that makes the experience of other beings and worlds its own, taking up the will of other entities into its own will, which is capable of dying into the other entity, thus permitting this other to unfold in its own being, and a force that puts itself at the disposal of others—all this is love. Love as substance is the spiritual gold of the future.

Gold of this kind appears at the beginning of the Book of Revelation in the seven golden candlesticks, which are no more or less than

---

* The German *Nibelungen* (Old Norse, *Niflungr*) is the Germanic mythology of the royal lineage of the Burgundians.

the seven angels of the seven churches. In the middle of the Revelation, this germinal force of angel-guided community building becomes the golden censer of the angel at the altar, in which love is worship, and this germinal force appears as the golden altar itself in which love is the power of sacrifice. After that, gold emerges in the middle of the Apocalypse from the Sun with which the woman is clothed. However, even the counterimages of the gold that has succumbed to the demonic nature shine forth over and over from the darkness of errors for the last time (Rev. 18:16).

Then, the gold process of the world passes over into its own future. The angel who lets the Apocalyptist behold the Heavenly Jerusalem carries a golden reed of the true measure of all wisdom, for the true measure of all wisdom is not wisdom itself, but rather the love holding sway within it. It is the measure of the human being and humanity. It is the measure that becomes active in the image of the cubic shape of the Heavenly Jerusalem. This leads to the future image itself as transparent gold. The wisdom pervaded with love, the will shined through by wisdom causes the gold-permeated inward interconnection of all forces of soul and movements of soul, down to its deepest inside—the inwardness from which the Sun-gold of love springs forth. Here we can no longer distinguish whether love stems from human beings or from God; in the soul and the world pervaded by the Christ impulse, each has become gold of the future.

> The Sun wants to reflect itself sevenfold,
> In all the seven members of our body:
> That they can feed her image back seven times.
> The Sun wants seven times us to unseal
> (CHRISTIAN MORGENSTERN)

Longitudinal section through a piece of Witwatersrand coal. It was oxidized in the cold oxygen plasma and shows the individual columns with fine gold threads inside. The lower section of the sample is formed by a part of the slate. (from Carbon Leader Reef, Blyvooruitzicht Gold Mine, Carletonville, Gauteng, South Africa; magnification approx. 2.5x)

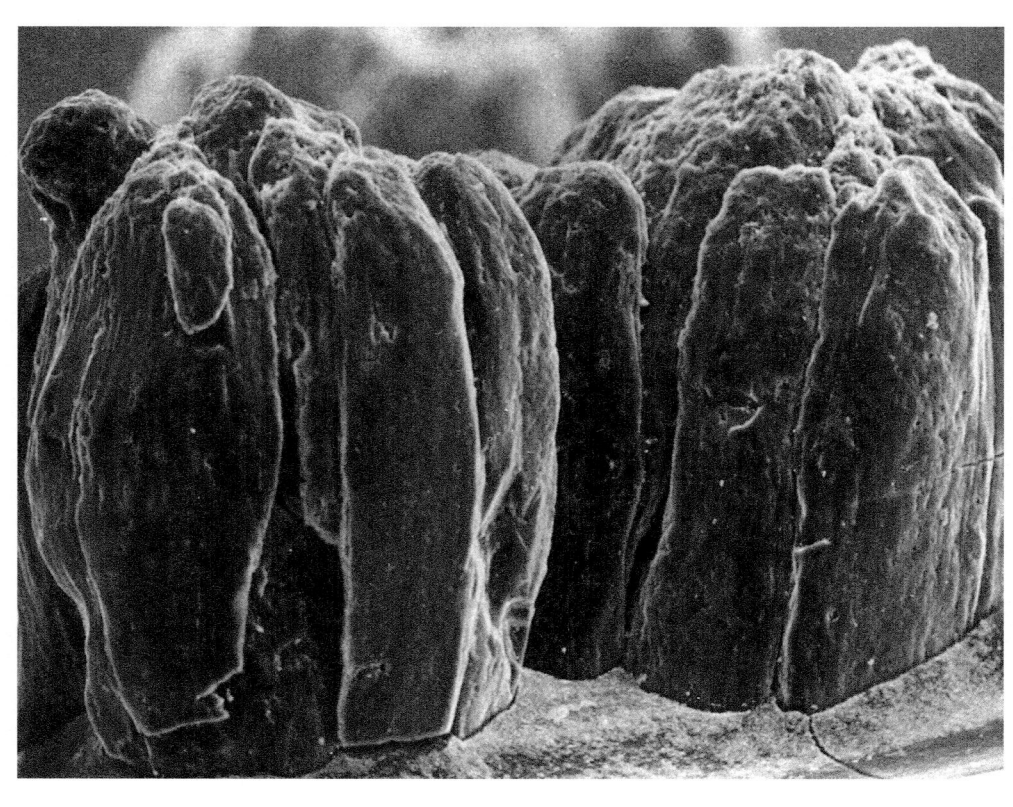

Electron-microscope image of carbon particles. They form a kind of lawn and consist mostly of carbon. Prepared with hydrofluoric acid. (Cross section 400 to 700 nanometers)

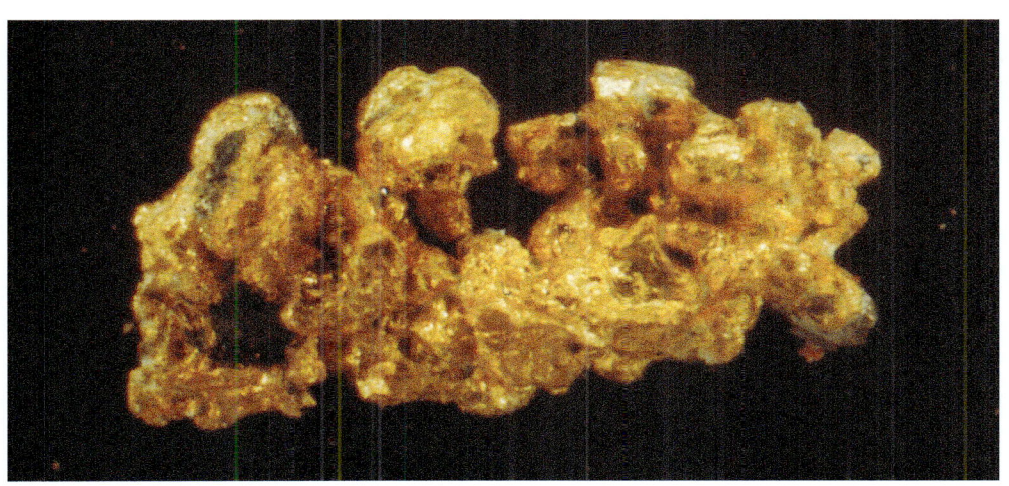

*Gold grains from the inside of lichen; the shape is due to the organics
(magnification approx. 120x)*

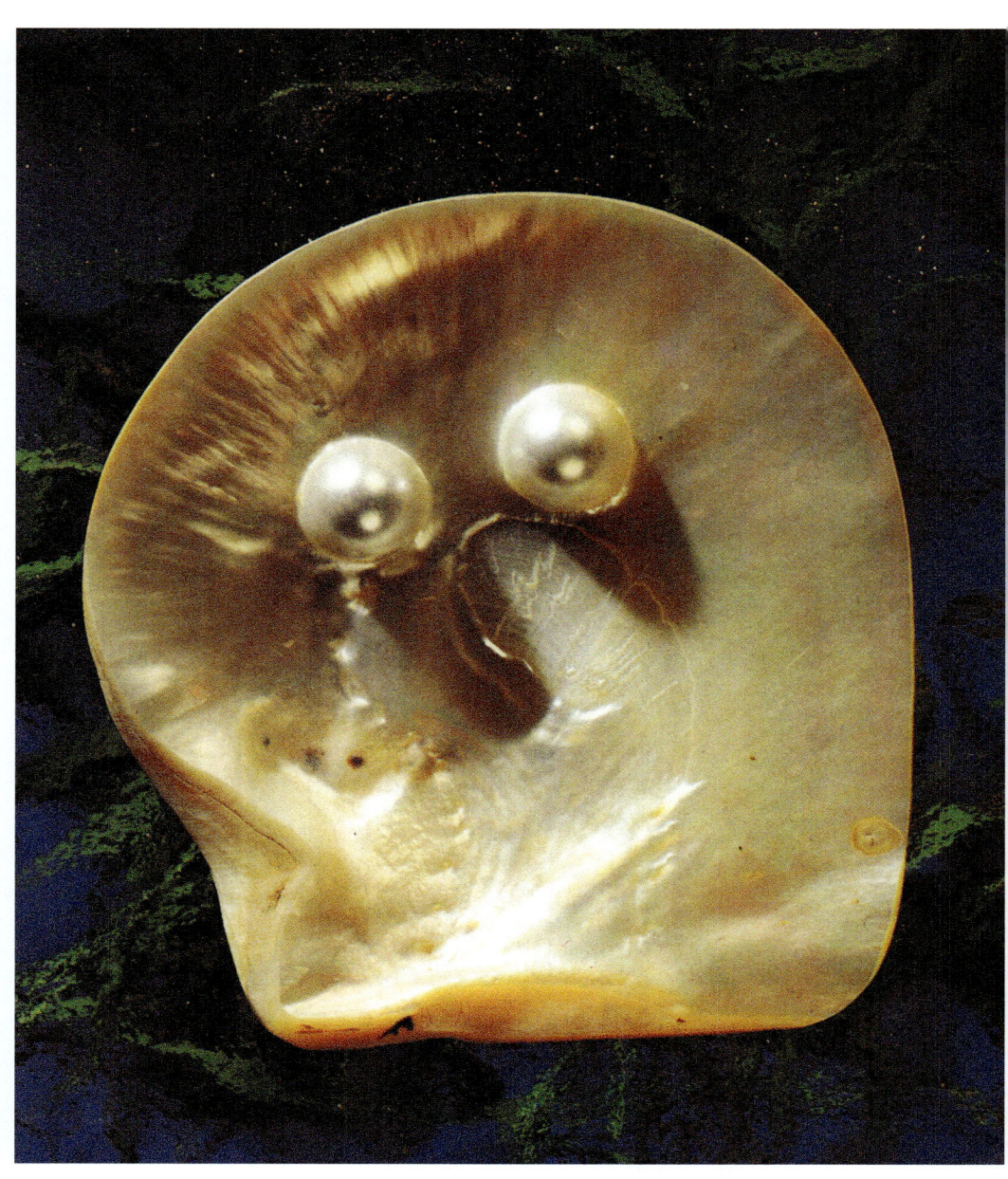

Two pearls in a mussel shell

Chapter 7: Pearl

Purified Pain—Sense Organ for the World Essence

I. Name: From the Latin *pirula,* "small pear." Thus, the name is derived from a fruit.

II. Research: Pearls are growths inside a great number of mollusks. Pearls are found in blue mussels and nautiloids; precious pearls in the pearl oyster. Sea pearl oysters (*Meleagrina*) and some of their relatives such as mussels (*Mytilus*) live in the coastal regions of warm oceans at depths of 6 to 30 meters (20 to 100 feet). Mussels lie flat on the ocean floor, and use secreted threads of byssus to fasten themselves to the substratum. The shells of the genuine sea pearl oyster can reach diameters of up to 30 cm (12 inches).

Mussels have a soft, slimy, two-leaved mantle surrounding their soft organs. The surface of this mantle is covered with countless glands, one kind of which secretes, in the form of thin lamellae, calcium carbonate ($CaCO_3$) taken into the blood from the seawater. The lamellae then crystallize. The second type of gland secretes a protein substance, conchiolin, which dries to form lamellae after being secreted, and is yellow to brown in color. A third type of gland secretes diagonally oriented prisms of calcium carbonate, which form the ostracum in the seashell. The forth type of gland secretes conchin, likewise a kind of protein found only in mussels. Thus the mussel shell has three layers: the outer layer is brown conchiolin; beneath it is the conchiolin layer, consisting of diagonally set calcium carbonate crystal prisms; the inner layer consists of ultrafine calcium carbonate lamellae, between which the very thin layers of conchin are deposited.

This is mother of pearl. The mantle with its glands is firmly attached to the mother of pearl, but not grown together with it. Thus, foreign bodies can trespass into the space between the mantle and the shell. These are usually tiny parasites (larvae from worms or mites), and occasionally minute grains of sand. These injure the highly sensitive mantle, which reacts to the injury by forming a small indentation in its tissue, into which it draws the foreign matter. The indentation is able to separate off inward from the outer layer of the mantle, and even to migrate into the conjunctive tissue beneath it, where it then fully engulfs the foreign particle, so that now the cells of the mantle's glands surround it entirely and it is suspended in the conjunctive tissue. This is how the pearl sack is created. Now a slow secretion of mother of pearl around the foreign body begins, and the pearl is developed. The foreign body is embedded at its center, and the mother of pearl begins to be deposited around this center point. Pearls grow very slowly; those smaller than a pea in size take 4 to 10 years, larger ones 10 to 50 years. Ninety-two percent of the pearl consists of the lamellae of calcium carbonate, about six percent conchin and two percent water. Pearls and pearl sacks are the results of an injury, a kind of permanent wound, in the detached mantle; and of an ongoing healing performed by mother of pearl over against the wounding foreign particle, which, in tranquil patience, is gradually engulfed. The little sacks that secrete the mother of pearl (calcium carbonate and conchin) are closely connected with the pearl's substance (mother of pearl), but similarly to the mantle on the mother of pearl of the seashell, are not fused with it.

III. Origin and habitat: While other precious stones' origin is understandable only on the background of earlier phases of the Earth's development with its mineral-plants and plant-minerals, the pearl's origin is immediately recognizable (Cloos, p. 141). It stems from a wound-healing process brought forth by animals, which themselves are in turn among the lowest, most primitive of animals, and which display growth and living circumstances that are largely still plant-like. These animals are the coelenterates (sponges, jellyfish, polyps, and corals) and the mollusks (mussels and snails). They all have a special relationship with calcium carbonate. They constantly take dissolved calcium carbonate from the water, sometimes silicon as well, conduct it through their own soft, jellylike, often transparent body, and deposit it in crystals, solid or colloidal lamellae, and layers surrounding themselves. Out of their soft body, they form their own solid housing, in and on which they live. They do the same thing as the plants do, which likewise deposit living matter in the form of bark and wood. Their accomplishments in the course of geological epochs are enormous, since almost all limestone mountain ranges and all limestone on Earth were deposited by these entities.

Coelenterates and mollusks behave differently from each other, though. The coelenterates (corals and polyps) first deposit calcium on their interior and then lift themselves away from this foundation, abandoning what they have secreted, so that growths of treelike appearance arise. The mussels surround themselves with these calcium processes, in this way sheathing and enveloping their softness in a living way. This is the group to which the pearl oyster belongs. It takes an injury from a foreign entity into its enveloping force, transforming the pain of the wound into the healing sheath.

IV. Soul Virtue: The deepest and most all-encompassing mystery of the human being is the "I." Since primeval times, the mysteries have known that the human "I" exists in repeated earthly incarnations. After death, man's inside always becomes his outside. This was discussed in the chapter on the construction of the Heavenly Jerusalem.

In earthly life, the mystery of the "I" is not easy to understand, because the human "I" lives out its life from two entirely different sides. On one hand, it is connected with its bodily organization and emanates into it as the will from the metabolism into the heart, becoming a person's sense of self. The "I" radiates as thinking from the head and into the human being's heart, where it becomes power of judgment. Moreover, in the heart itself, the "I" lives in feeling and the conscience. The will to development, the power of judgment, and the conscience are the expression of the "I" in the heart.

On the other hand, the actual, true human "I"-being also lives on the Earth in everything that seems to encounter the human being from without. In sensory impressions, our own "I," connected with the qualities of the world's contents, streams toward us as the carriers of our consciousness. Earth-consciousness forms within us in this process. In all encounters with other human beings, our own "I" streams toward us as our karma, carried by the other person. The "I" lives within human beings as spirit seeking and striving, and its own interior confronts it as inner destiny. This is where the encounter with Christ can also occur as inner destiny. As the "I" confronts itself from the inside outward and from the outside inward, in the wielding of destiny, in thinking, feeling, and willing, everything that causes suffering and inner joy is set in motion. After all, all experience is support and demand, fortune and misfortune, gift and task, gain and loss. Receiving everything that is positive in life heightens, as a gift, the entity a human being has become to date.

As suffering, all ordeals that the higher "I" causes for the lower "I" cause our further development. It is only through this side of fate that we can become higher, deeper, purer, freer, richer, stronger, and greater than we are. Human beings want to develop in their deepest foundation; we strive. Rudolf Steiner calls Goethe's *Faust* the world's greatest literary work about striving. Nevertheless, precisely what Goethe's *Faust* isn't is a series of successes and victories; instead, it is a series of catastrophes and defeats. The tragedy of cognition is followed by the tragedy of Gretchen and Valentin. The tragic collapse at the emperor's court, to the point where Faust is paralyzed, followed by the powerful new beginning of classical Walpurga's Night, which in turn leads to the tragedy of Helen of Troy; Faust's endeavor to work outward into the world results in the bitter tragedy of Philemon and Baucis.

Nevertheless, a gain is couched in every loss. What Faust derives from the tragedy of knowledge and carries further as the power of thought becomes the capacity for him to know spiritual matters. In the Ariel scene at the beginning of *Faust,* part 2, what he has had to endure in the Gretchen episode becomes the ability to grasp life in and as its pictures. Moreover, what ultimately emerges from Helen of Troy's fate and leads to a catastrophe of social willing, that becomes the capacity to love in Faust's apotheosis after his death. What has become of all the striving, struggling, losing, and failing? Pearls, forces of the future, are the result of being wounded. In the images of the Paters and the penitent women, these newly won forces and abilities surround him as mirror images of his own essential being. In the blessed boys and the transfigured soul of Gretchen, the very highest reflects itself in his direction. Thus, what has come of suffering? Experience. Experience, though, becomes the sense organ for what is essential in the world, for the spiritual. Life experience born of pain becomes organ of spirit ("organ fit for world and spirit").

V. Spiritual Future: In dealing with silicic acid as a mineral reality, and as selflessness of soul in mediating the world, it was shown how, by its nature, the entity of quartz bears within itself what enables it to become a carrier of sense processes and activities in all areas. In a way, the physical-etheric-astral substrate within our twelve senses are the twelve gates to the world of the current planetary stage of cosmic development—that is, nature. All the painful experience, as much as personal schooling and self-education, we purify onward to become organs of spiritual matters—all that appears to the Apocalyptist in the image of twelve gates that are pearls. This means, however, that in a future world it will no longer be the silicon process that carries everything to do with sense activity; rather, this role will pass on to the calcium process. In the noblest of calcium's manifestations found today, calcite, light is as yet refracted doubly, and the calcium entity is still a carrier of desire today. It cannot yet be a mediator of perception, as silicon can. In a future world, everything will be purified desire-being—pearls, all developed from life and sensory activities; all will be pearl, the mediator of the perceptive activity of the twelve gates, the future senses. It is with the sense forces (which have been purified and become selfless) that the human being of the future will perceive. Thus it is the forces of pearl that will constitute the twelve senses. This reveals the spiritual future of the pearl entity. This entity will be the basis of twelve senses, in which the sensible percept and the suprasensory can be perceived simultaneously. Just as today the silicon process can only perceive sense impressions, but is nevertheless capable of consciously guiding their spiritualization (a process in which precisely Goethe can be the best guide), in the same way, the pearl-future is preparing itself now in our souls and our senses.

Chapter 8: Wood

Death from Life—Life from Death

> Let us love the trees,
> They love us, after all;
> Within their shooting greens
> Christ's life-blood climbs and falls.
>
> Wood nearly ceased to flourish,
> Upon it Christ did hang,
> That we ourselves might nourish
> Anew: new life began.
> (Albert Steffen)

I. Name: The word *wood* means both the substance of trees and shrubs, as well as the forest as a whole. In the ancient Greek, the word *klados* means "twig," "branch," or "branching." This refers to an aspect of the wood process experienced in growth that branches or fans out. The word also has a connection with holding and fetching, in which the experience expresses how the way a plant draws something together from its surroundings, makes it into wood, and holds itself with it. Both meanings are livingly united in the original word stem.

II. Research: Roots, trunks, branches, and twigs of the Earth's trees and shrubs contain wood. It is the central part of their three fundamental tissues: bark on the outside, wood on the inside, and in between a delicate transparent veil—cambium—a mere few cells thick, tender tubing or hose, that envelops the wood down to the finest of its branches. It consists of polyhedric, thin-walled cells filled with translucent, living protoplasm, flowing and circulating in every cell with its respective organelles. The cells constantly exchange fluids with one another, keeping as much as ninety percent of the tree's water in its protoplasm and its fluid cavities under pressure, which helps in the exchange of those substances. The cells multiply unceasingly in annual rhythms by cell division. One cell drips out of the other, one cell layer out of the other, not only within the cambium, but also outward toward the bark and inward toward the wood. At the tips of the roots and the sprouts, the cambium cells form tiny cones like caps, or miters, the tips of which contain the apical cells that drip the cambium cells backward, causing them to be carried on forward. Where leaves are formed, the cambium flows out and apart into flattened layers, thus producing the leaves' embryonic tissue, depositing on top the palisade cells instead of wood, and on the bottom the spongy parenchyma tissue instead of bark. This delicate veil is the centuries-long life of trees and shrubs, a kind of milk organized as cells.

According to their elongation, lumen expansion, and thickening walls, the cell layers that the cambium deposits inwardly change and vary into the following types:

1. Vascular cells (spiracles) with thin cell walls. These are capillaries; water flows through them from the root hairs to the leaves, and into the cambium.

Giant sequoia, the largest tree in nature

2. Fiber cells with thick walls, called *sclerenchyma* cells in deciduous trees and *tracheids* in conifers.
3. Wood "ray cells" are storage cells, parenchyma cells, and transverse tracheids. They penetrate the body of the wood radially and perpendicular to the direction of the wood's fibers. The annual rings are formed by the cells producing greater diameters and larger lumina in the spring and smaller ones in the autumn.

The wood cell walls are made of a middle lamella, the border between neighboring cells. Connected to it is the primary wall, a network of tiny fibers, microfibrils made of cellulose. Then comes the secondary wall, in which the cellulose fibrils run parallel to the cell's axis. The third wall covers the other two. The density of the cellulose fibrils and their enmeshing is part of what determines the wood's hardness. Chemically, the wood substance consists of forty to fifty percent cellulose, twenty to thirty percent wood hemicelluloses, and twenty to thirty percent addition of lignin, resin, oils, tannin, and mineral substance. The sum total is fifty percent carbon, forty-two percent oxygen, six percent hydrogen, and two percent other elements.

Crystals have no place in a discussion of trees. Wood is formed into fibers and deposited by the living protein in the cells. This creates an infinitely intricate and dense fabric, similar to the cryptocrystalline filaments of the fiber quartzes such as chalcedony. Silicon is not present; instead, carbon plays the key role as the foundation of wood.

III. Origin and habitat: It is possible to designate wood as a mineral, despite the fact that it remains part of a living plant or one that has died; even after centuries, the cambium gives up its life and only the wood remains. We need to consider only that, in the geological past, wood has mineralized into turf, brown coal, bituminous coal, anthracite, and graphite. In a way, wood is a mineral substance that has fallen out of the condition of life. The life, the cambium, always sets

Giant sequoia; the massive base of the tree trunk

Tree cross section; wood rings inside, cambium and bark outside. The years of "life" and "death" are depicted in the rings. Between death (wood) and death (bark) is the tender ring of life, the cambium.

Exposed and weathered wood grain

itself off against what it has caused to fall out of its life into death. As the plant does this, it gains the ability to endure for decades and centuries as a living being. In order that it can live, it must build death into itself, cause its own corporeality to become a mineral.

If we dwell on the other meaning of the word *wood,* that of a forest branching out as it grows, we get a somewhat different picture. We can compare an individual tree or shrub with the mineral Earth as a whole, which is distinguished by the fact that life develops on it, but only in those places where this mineral Earth has eroded and commingled with organic waste material to become the fabric of that thin layer, in which an infinite life of bacteria and small living organisms creates the partially alive humus without which the plants cannot live. The thin layer of earth on which the life of the plant world thrives—the humus—lies on top of the mineral and dead foundation of the rock layer. We can compare the cambium with this humus layer. The humus layer is the portion of the mineral Earth that is still alive today, and when the cambium precipitates wood inward, it means, in a figurative sense, that a part of the mineral Earth has been lifted above the surface of the Earth, and that the greening and blooming, leaf, blossom, and fruit nature of the plant grows on this uplifted portion in the same way as the annual and biennial green plants grow and thrive in the soil of a meadow or a field. Wood is a mineral brought to death from a living state so that more life can thrive on its foundation. Wood interacts with the humidity and dryness of the air by welling up and contracting, thus showing that it has maintained its ongoing connection to its living origin, and that it is even still alive in a sense. Thus, we can say that wood is the death that enables life; it does so only so long as it remains constant in its woody state within the plant, which is how the difference arises between sapwood, which conducts water, and heartwood, where other deposits are worked in as well.

IV. Soul Virtue: In wood, the emergence of death from life for the sake of becoming a foundation of life is a process that runs in a quasi-temporal sequence. First, wood must exist; it must have died to carry life. Similarly, in human beings there are soul processes in which self-restraint, self-conquest, sacrifice, and transformation can become a lasting, subtle condition of death that enables the development of more delicate and exalted soul forces. When human beings overcome themselves, it is never an act that, once accomplished, serves as the basis for something higher; rather, it is an ongoing, uninterrupted process running its course in the interpenetration that consists in overcoming something lower in favor of something higher—a transformation of error into truth, evil into good, ugly into beautiful. Dying out of life becomes living out of death.

V. Spiritual Future: As he sees the Heavenly Jerusalem, the Apocalyptist calls this living in dying the wood of life, which appears on both sides of the stream: "On each side of the river stood the tree of life, bearing twelve crops of fruit, yielding its fruit every month. And the leaves of the tree are for the healing of the nations" (Rev. 22:2). From the spiritual stream of the water of life, the wood of life is constantly formed, the interpenetration of living and dying, of dying and living, of being "wood." Only from this can fruits emerge—fruits of soul that in all months, in all directions of soul and spirit, can ripen at a given moment. Since they emerge from such interpenetration of living and dying, they have healing power. Novalis was able to say this in *Hymns to the Night:* "You are Death, who at last makes us whole."

Chapter 9: Conclusion

Talismans

Not only do images of minerals, precious stones, and pearls appear to the Apocalyptist, but he also reads spiritual writing on the stones; he reads names. On the twelve pearls of the city's gates, he reads the names of the twelve tribes of God's people. Moreover, on the precious stones, the foundation stone-jewels, he reads the names of the twelve apostles of the Lamb. A name is always the designation of an "I," an entity, and here certain contents of the Bible merge. In the images, suprasensory vision is active. In the words of the spiritual entities and those of the Apocalyptist himself, suprasensory hearing is alive. In the reading of the names lives a direct encounter with the beings to which the names refer.

In the Old Testament, the names of the tribes are engraved on the shoulder stones (six each), and on the stones of the coat of arms (one each) of the children of Israel. Historically, within the twelve tribes of the children of Israel (as Jacob is called), twelve educational, formational impulses have lived over the course of two millennia; they are woven into the hereditary stream of the twelve tribes. These impulses were fully developed under Moses and Aaron during the years of wandering in the wilderness. They were still present—even settled geographically—when Joshua and the judges took possession of the Promised Land. Nevertheless, they declined and faded out over the millennia. The entire Old Testament is the account of that decline.

In addition, at the time of the Mystery of Golgotha, it had all been reduced to a single tribe, Judah—the Jews and Judaism. Nearly all the rest of the tribal identities had been dissolved into heathendom. When Christ walked the Earth as Jesus, the abundance of the tribal nature was essentially extinguished. Their spiritual impulses had withdrawn, and only the tribe of Judah, the Lion, remained. Seventy years later,

*The Angel shows John the heavenly Jerusalem with the Golden rod.
(Gold leaf miniature of the Apocalypse, West Flemish, 1400)*

through the horrific violence of the Romans, even those remains of its city of Jerusalem—its temple, altar, and Ark of the Covenant—were stolen and strewn over the world.

In the plenitude of what Jesus Christ brought with him when He came, the original twelve educational, formational impulses were returned. He installed twelve individuals, whom he groomed, until after His Resurrection He sent them out into the world as the twelve apostles of the Lamb. What they carried into the world became the seeds of new communities, which pass over and over through the seven developmental levels of the cycles of time, and these in turn appear to the Apocalyptist as the seven churches. Through these ongoing transformations, twelve possible classifications for humankind were created that, in the Apocalypse, bear the names of the tribes. Today, however, they are no longer tribes, but communities whose interconnections arise through twelve spiritual beings newly connected to humanity.

These are the twelve angels above the twelve gates of pearl with the names. Now, however, it is not single, definite human individuals that hover over the names of the former tribes, but rather twelve spiritual beings. From the comprehensive principle of the Christ-being and through the twelve apostles, twelve angels have been connected with humankind (Rev. 21:12). This does not mean, however, that in the future of a new world individual human beings are forever bound to one and only one community; it is precisely the twelve gates of pearl that bear the names and the angels. In each gate, name, and angel an abundance of possibilities are prepared spiritually, and through these possibilities free human beings can, under the guidance of the spiritual beings, carry the formation and development of communities. Belonging to these communities in a committed and responsible way, for the sake of collaborating on building the world, is always the exclusive result of individuals freely integrating themselves into one or the other of these grouping possibilities, or classifications of human beings.

In the gates, the angels and, above all, the names, therefore, the Apocalyptist encounters not arrangements of the earthly world that are predetermined by heredity, but rather arrangements, organizations of a future world that always group and regroup in freedom. The angels open up twelve sorts of creative powers of the future to voluntary participation under their guidance, and they themselves form and dissolve these communities. It is the pearl that emerges from the purification process of suffering at one's own hands—indeed, all suffering is ultimately at our own hands—to become a gate above which the angel stands and acts, a gate to the future, a gate on which is written the name of a community accessible by the capacity for sensing the future. This capacity is the true sense for the angel and for other human beings, the sense of what is purely spiritual being within the other person, and for what leads from person to person to the symphony of sensations, impressions, and joint action in voluntary submission to a cause. The writing on the pearl is no gift of the kind given by the old tribal association; instead, it is a task whose protective and carrying power consists precisely of the fact that it can be taken up in freedom.

Those of Goethe's time drew a distinction between the talisman and the amulet. The talisman was a precious stone on which a name or a verse was engraved. The verse had to be short, as space on the stone was limited. It was general opinion that women should wear them on their belt or bosom. An amulet was also a precious stone, but without engraving. Instead, it was carried in a pouch along with an inscribed piece of paper, on which it was possible to write more. The notion went that men—especially soldiers at war—should carry or wear the amulet, either on a chain around their necks or at their shoulder in the scapular of their uniform.

In the "Book of Singers" in Goethe's *West-Eastern Divan*, the talisman that the poet chooses is sardonyx, the agate with the three zones of color: black onyx at its base, white in the middle, and red (sard, carnelian) at the top. He says:

> From a carnelian Talisman
> The faithful gain glad prosperous days;
> If it rests on an onyx ground
> Let it be pressed to devout lips!
> All that is ill away it will chase,
> It shields you and it shields the place;
> If the engraved word proclaims
> With pure intention Allah's name,
> To love and deed it will inflame;
> And women, more than others can,
> Will vantage by the Talisman.*

This then impels the singer to add:

> Like symbols, but set on paper
> By pen craft, form the Amulet;
> No narrow limit here will hem
> The scribe as with the graven gem,
> And pious souls may thus rejoice
> In longer verses of their choice;
> Men wear such papers round their neck
> Devoutly as a scapular.

Goethe also wrote talisman verses of his own. These contain a reflected splendor, albeit fully human, of the macrocosmic sight beheld by the Apocalyptist in the signs of the spiritual world: worlds in the names and names from the worlds. Only the names on the stone and from the stone unite the world development of the mineral realm intimately with the world development of the human being. Thus, Goethe says in the *West-Eastern Divan* "Book of Verses":

> I mean to strew talismans in this Book
> And thus effect a proper equipoise.
> Prick with a pious needle and expect
> Everywhere some good word to gladden you.**

---

* Steiner, *The Temple Legend*, lect. 8 (from the German edition).
** The "needle" is a means to engaging in a bit of spiritual inquiry.

Therefore, there are five talismans in the "Book of the Singer":

> God's very own, the Orient!
> God's very own, the Occident!
> The Northland and the Southland
> Rest in the quiet of His hand.
>
> Justice apportioned to each one
> Wills He Who is the Just alone.
> Name all His hundred names, and then
> Be this name lauded high! Amen.
>
> Error would hold me tangled, yet
> You know to free me from the net.
> Whether I act or meditate
> Grant me a way that shall be straight,
> If earthly things possess my mind
> Through these I find some higher gain;
> Not blown abroad as dust, but driven
> Inward, the spirit mounts toward Heaven.
>
> In every breath we breathe, two graces share
> The in-draught and the outflow of the air;
> That is a toil, but this refreshment brings;
> So marvelous are our life's commingling.
> Thank God when you feel His hand constrain,
> And thank when He releases you again.

May these talismans also accompany readers once they have read their way through the book on their further paths.

> Pour together chemicals:
> Anon the flames arise.
> But thoughts as well
> Are gas and smoke;
> Turn back again
> And teach the whole,
> Saying, feel
> This heat, this cold...
>   (Christian Morgenstern)

Chapter 10: Retrospect and Outlook

Looking back on the whole, it might now become clear what it ultimately means for us human beings to be able to stand before this enormously outspread breadth: for one, the mineral in our hand; for the other, the mineral images of the Apocalypse of St. John in our soul's gaze. They are the most extreme extremes of our existence. In them, through them, a modern Parzival question articulates itself in the depths of soul: You mute stone, who are you? Let us allow the stone itself to speak:

> I am in the Father-God. In me is pure, unintentional will of pure being, the pure substance of the Father. Within me, the Father is infinitely carrying might. But in me His infinite Being, which pervades the whole universe, has been condensed earthly to become the most extreme density, hardness, heaviness, and darkness.
>
> The Father-God is a volitional entity. His will is condensed in me and has refracted and solidified into the manifoldness of 92 elements, 2,500 types of minerals, 8 times 12 precious stones. He, the Ground of the Universe, is in me the mute ground of the material world.
>
> And the Father-God is a feeling entity. He feels this condensation of his as bodily pain, just as you, too, O human being, sense bodily pain. My being is also solidified pain. Patience and pain of the Father-God: they carry you, in me through all your lives.
>
> And the Father-God is a conscious entity. In the shape of my being, the crystal gestalt, He knows of Himself in me. In countless forms, in pure, clear figures, His consciousness reflects itself in me, is refracted to become me, and in what is refracted He is unbroken, clear, transparent thought, consummate in itself. When you wander over the Earth and tread on me, you set your foot on patience, on pain, on thought.

And the stone continues:

Since 2,000 years ago I am no longer only within the Fatherly Ground, as I was from the beginning. The Son has held His entry into me. Within me, He looks at you. In transparency, clarity, abundance of color, shine—inasmuch as you expose me to the light—this that is inside me can serve the appearance to you of Christ in me. If you have found Him in you, you look at me with an eye through which Christ looks at me; but then Christ sees you through me and me through you, for He has entered me and lives in me as the power of the spiritualization of the future.

> From earth, stone, sea, and light's pure glance
> His childlike countenance shines.
> (Novalis)

In me, too, He is the meaning of the Earth. Even when He is in me, He loves you through me.

And finally, the stone says:

> Lo, I do not intend to stay what I am forever. I wait and wait and wait for you, O human being. You will know me; you will burn me through the power of your working at me. You will transform me into yourself, just as you will transform yourself into me once you have, through the Son, transformed into yourself the virtue the Father-God placed in me. In a light common to you and me, the Spirit-God will illuminate you and me. And we two will be: you divine-human virtue as spiritual stone. When this comes to pass, the City of God will become the seed of the world.

Appendices

Appendix 1
Part 1, Chapter 1

The question of Anthroposophy

The treatment of the contents of this book involves fundamental and comprehensive epistemological questions having to do with the world, the Earth, and the human being. For this reason, it was always an inner necessity to refer to the results of Rudolf Steiner's Spiritual Science. This was because today there is only one direction of research that takes completely and utterly seriously the primacy of the spirit, of life, and of the living organism, of what is meaningful and essential, and of the providence that presides over the world. This path of research is Rudolf Steiner's anthroposophically oriented Spiritual Science. It alone opens the cognitive paths leading from matter to spirit and from spirit to matter. However, what is the relationship of Spiritual Science to conventional science?

An overview of the compass of the life of human knowledge through the twentieth century shows the abundance of what science, in the broadest sense of the word, can accomplish. Such abundance, however, must not distract us from the fact that this science is founded on a magnificent one-sidedness. On the one hand, this one-sidedness relates to how the object of this knowledge is based on recognizing only what is available directly or indirectly from sensory experience, observation, and testing. Only these are allowed and are the possible and legitimate point of departure and endpoint of all science. On the other hand, it is the intellectual life of human thinking that systematizes, analyzes, and interprets this object in terms of causality. Hypotheses, theories, and models come from this methodology and represent the final result of this mode of knowledge. This alone is so-called science. Of course, such science can inquire into also the objective or subjective substance of the sensory substance of ordinary naïve consciousness itself; but for this it is absolutely necessary that such contents have a bearing on—and are perhaps even reduced to—some circumstance or other beyond human subjectivity, and this (objective) circumstance must be unarguably present for all hypotheses, theories, and models.

Since Kant, scientific consciousness has become definitively critical, that is, it monitors its own facts and methods. This is the basis for scientific theory: the science of science.

Here, it is basically a matter of a mere three, albeit overlapping, categories of cognitive life. The first we can call a more or less naïve, uncritical attitude toward knowledge. Humanity, with its perceptions and experiences, reflects on everything according to acquired categories. Those categories are derived from language, childhood experience, education, the judgments of others, dogmas, slogans, and habits of thought assimilated from the mass media and popular science. A person's own ideas also play a role here, but they, too, are formed in a naïve way. The naïve person forms views of the world and of life, into which are integrated individual experiences, and so on, depending on individual intelligence. The characteristic of this process is that the person believes these experiences and judgments naïvely and implements them naïvely in life.

Those who undergo scientific training rise step by step above this. They develop a more or less critical consciousness, reflect on and test their media and methods, and open themselves to the critique of scientific peers. Here, logic and facts play the decisive role. Here, too, there are many possible abilities, depending on intelligence and capacity for critical consciousness. Naïveté, dogmatism, blind faith in authority, and intellectual idiocy resulting from one-sided specialization are, however, constantly at odds with impartiality, intellectual freedom, and self-criticism. This makes for clearly delineated levels within the pursuit of science. Even as a scientist, a person can be to some extent quite naïve and remain that way.

Connected to the life of scientific knowledge arising from research in the broadest sense, is its teaching. Prerequisite to this teaching is skill on the part of the teacher to see things from the perspective of his pupils' consciousness in such way that a bridge may be built from the contents of one consciousness to those of the other.

Finally, the results of scientific research are applied in practical life, and science and teaching pass over to the one who brings them to practical application.

Naïve persons can *know* without being scientists; they can investigate without being critical; critical and self-critical scientists can know without being able to instruct. These three categories—those who acquire knowledge naïvely, scientific researchers, and teachers—cover the whole scientific range of human cognitive life. On one hand, insurmountable barriers lie in the world of sensory experience and, on the other, they lie at the boundaries of consciousness and in the thought categories of the intellect. In this sense, it is characteristic of the life of knowledge that all concepts belonging to its theories and models must ultimately bear on sense-perceptible experience and/or interpretations of it. Objectivity, precision, logic, and verifiability are its methodological postulates. Moreover, anything that goes beyond these areas is no longer an object of science; rather, it is metaphysics, mysticism, occultism, esotericism, parapsychology, magic, religion, or simply illusion, hallucination, pathology.

At these limits, there is completely unnoticed naïve dogmatism. As sensory perception, soul experience, and intellectual conceptuality cast in language are facts that can be tested critically; in the same way clairvoyance, second vision, inkling, and prophecy exist outside the boundaries of the senses. They are certainly facts available to of human experience, within which the human being is confronted by a world dimension that is not accessible to the ordinary senses, normal soul experience, and logical thinking. If we call these facts "spheres of a suprasensory world," this says nothing about whether they are objective and factual, on the one hand, or subjective and unreal on the other. There are far more clairvoyant people in the world than generally believed.

It is important to note, however, that most clairvoyants are present to their experiences in just as naïve a way as "normal" people are to the sensory world. Here, the scientific question is a twofold one: does a person's relationship to suprasensory experience have to remain a naïve one, or is it possible for a clairvoyant to undergo scientific schooling whereby suprasensory experiences can be monitored, ordered, explained, or justified as critically and rigorously as the scientist investigating the sense-perceptible world? And the other part of the question is: Can researchers of the suprasensory take their own perceptive possibilities in hand, school them, consciously guide them, refine, expand, and deepen them, and above all test them by reshaping and training their own constitution through such means as self-monitoring, meditation, concentration, and so on? Such measures would be able to preempt everything illusionary, hallucinatory, and pathological.

If this is so, it is possible for the natural clairvoyant to become an explorer of the spirit, a scientist in the field of the suprasensory, able to comprehend, critically and conceptually, suprasensory experiences. One can neither trust nor control the naïve clairvoyant. Nevertheless, does the same hold true for spirit researchers? If we can pass on the results of such research in a scientifically verified way, then these results are understandable, explainable, and justifiable to others, even if not perceivable by them. The prerequisite is simply that the spirit researcher be in a position to confront, connect, and penetrate critically tested research results with the experience of normal consciousness, both naïve and scientific. This means, though, that such a person must also be a teacher of the spirit, able to make suprasensory research absolutely comprehensible to anyone, and be able to connect suprasensorily expanded contents with already existing ones in a way that the latter supplement what cannot be found on the normal path. Finally, such a one needs to be able to show how the results of suprasensory research are applicable to, and fruitful for, practical life.

But there is yet something else that enters the suprasensory sphere. In the field of the senses, the researcher performs his or her own interpretation of nature. It is only with one's fellow human beings that this is not possible. An encounter with another person who thinks and speaks always means that one has to wait and discover what that person says about himself or herself and the contents of the person's consciousness. Here the researcher has to learn of something through personal communication; otherwise he will not learn it at all.

This circumstance as well can be applied to the spiritual world. In the spiritual world, spiritual researchers encounter individual spiritual entities. Researchers can observe and interpret them, but they can also receive communications from them, which they can access only when these beings say something on their own. The beings can communicate their intentions to them. Researchers will then learn something that is never accessible to ordinary consciousness. Persons of this kind become what for ages have been called "initiates." As such, they live in the recollections, the current actions and future intentions of the spirit beings who are not natural entities and do not manifest sense-perceptibly, as do human beings. These contents, too, spirit researchers can communicate to nonclairvoyant individuals.

At this point, the objection could be made: Why then is exact natural science necessary for true knowledge of the world in the first place? Everyone would just need to do exercises, become clairvoyant, and do spiritual research.

But this is not the case. First, training in exact, scientifically critical consciousness needs to be gained through work in and at the sense world. Philosophy, mathematics, and exact natural science are the educators toward a specialized knowledge needed also by clairvoyants if they are to become spiritual researchers. Second, the results of physical science of the senses on one hand and science of the spirit on the other belong to each other as one glove to the other. They do not overlap perfectly, but they do complement each other in existential symmetry. This has to do with human existence as such. Whether we are aware of it or not, we always live in three worlds—the worlds of the senses, the soul, and the spirit. In keeping with the whole of our nature, we are citizens of three worlds. We can restrict our inquiring consciousness to only one of those worlds, but we can also apply it to all three, depending on the knowledge we seek. Only these three together—natural science rationally, soul science after the way of the soul, and Spiritual Science in a spiritual way—open paths of knowledge for the whole world and for the past, present, and future.

We can encounter one such clairvoyant, spirit researcher, spiritual teacher, helper in practical life and initiate in the figure of Rudolf Steiner. Because suprasensory facts are the subject of the Revelation according to Saint John, it is advisable to seek advice where paths of knowledge exist for such facts. For these reasons, as a matter of principle it has been indispensable to take recourse to Spiritual Science over and over. This is why these appendices quote the corresponding works and lectures by Rudolf Steiner.

Appendix 2
Part 1, Chapter 2

One understands the details of the Apocalypse in terms of the whole; the inverse does not hold. The whole, in turn, presents itself to us in terms of the dynamics and the lawfulness of the course of its development, which proceeds by building and releasing tension. Only via dynamic, non-static concepts is it possible to see how the grand figures and cycles of development emerge one from the other. The only reader who can keep up with this process is the one capable of exerting an imaginative activity that is painterly, musical, and sculptural in nature. At the beginning, the seer encounters Christ at a moment that might well be called his Damascus. This encounter awakens in him a new consciousness. The Johannine Eagle now begins to soar aloft and to rise in spiral movements, as it were, into the world behind the curtain.

The first cycle remains still close to the Earth. It is reflected in the Seven Messages (ch. 1–2). Seven perhaps insignificant early Christian congregations in Asia Minor appear as a quintessence of humankind, arranged in a circle, like a cyclical collection of phases of history. It is in seven stages that both the fruit of the great pre-Christian cultural epochs and a seminal anticipation of future phases of evolution become visible. This preparatory round is followed by the Seven Seals (ch. 5–8), the Seven Trumpet Blasts (ch. 8–14), and the outpouring of the Seven Vials of Wrath (ch. 15–18). The Seven Seals contain spiritual pictures, indicating that an inner faculty of seeing has been developed. The Trumpet Blasts are a higher form of speech, presupposing an inner faculty of hearing. In the last and holiest cycle, reality follows picture and word. Real contact with super-earthly forces and beings opens up inner organs, which are a spiritual octave of the sense of touch.

Each of the three higher stages contains a main theme: the Seals are connected with the Book, the Trumpets with the Altar, and the Vials of Wrath with the Temple in Heaven. We begin to sense how, in the fabric of its images, the Book in Heaven contains the divine knowledge that can become the source for a consecration of our own thinking and knowing. The Altar and the Temple in Heaven contain the religious worship, the "sacred act," whose performance comprehends everything that goes on in the divine worlds. It is for this reason that such cultic enactment can in turn become the source for the consecration of our willing and our actions.

The description found in Steiner's writings of the three stages of suprasensory knowledge, which he calls Imagination, Inspiration, and Intuition, supplies an important key to the architecture of John's

Apocalypse. In Steiner's teaching, he replaces dogmatic talk of inspiration and the supernaturally inspired origin of the New Testament Scriptures with a concrete description of three realms of higher perception, to which the human mind, raised by the grace of God, can ascend. This provides an answer not just for the well out of which the Apocalypse is drawn. The structure of the Apocalypse is a veritable map of these provinces and spheres of increasing suprasensory knowledge. What awaits a person first, if he grows beyond mere earthly sense perception and rational knowledge, is spiritual seeing, cognition in images: the level of Imagination. As one progresses, one surpasses vision and attains to suprasensory hearing, to the tonal and verbal experience of Inspiration. Here, the word *Inspiration* no longer refers to a vague collection of archaic dogmatic concepts, but rather to an exact and specific spiritual condition of being. The third level is Intuition, that of real touching and interpenetration. Oftentimes, intuition is referred to in a superficial sense. In the spiritually exact sense, though, intuition is a higher kind of touching and tactile perception. A person able to sense the psychic atmosphere surrounding him, or the essence of what people around him emanate, is in possession of an earthly shadow of the spiritual experience of intuition.*

Appendix 3
Part 2, Chapters 2, 3

We must be quite clear that the humanity of the ancient times of which we are speaking did not have a full "I"-consciousness, as we do today. In their dreamlike consciousness, there was no full "I"-consciousness;... Thus the people of that period did not perceive what existed in dead nature, in the mineral nature....

---

*   Bock, *The Apocalypse of St. John.*

But there were ceremonies originating in the mysteries that, in the course of the year, brought to humankind something approximating human "I"-consciousness, on the one hand, and perception of the general mineral kingdom on the other.*

Appendix 4
Part 2, Chapters 2, 3

Consider what is happening now. We call the current cycle *the mineral cycle,* because in it the human being has to do with the mineral world. The natural scientist says: we cannot comprehend the plant world yet; this is because he considers the plant to be a sum of mineral processes. And he does the same with the animal. If this seems like a caricature of a worldview, there is a reason for it. The natural scientist uses his intellect to combine things arranged next to each other in space and one after the other in time. Everywhere it is the intellect that is at work on the dead, the nonliving, that assembles the parts. Start with a machine and progress to a work of art, and you have the human being's task in the current cycle of development; and he will proceed through to the end, to the point at which he has transformed the whole Earth into his artifice. This is the task the human being has for the future. The human task on Earth is incomplete as long as there exists a single atom that humanity has yet to work through by means of its power. Anyone who keeps up with the latest progress in electricity knows how the natural scientist is able to cast his gaze into the mineral world's smallest particles. This is because he has mastered electrical power, which fifty years ago was nearly unknown. His task consists in transforming the nonliving into a great artifice. It is for this reason that there were works of art long before historical times, long before the Egyptians. Follow through on this and you will understand that the current cycle means

---

*   Steiner, *The Cycle of the Year as a Breathing Process of the Earth*, lect. 4.

the permeation of all of mineral nature with spirit. Even reasonable natural scientists tell us that it is not unthinkable—according to what we know today—that a time will come when people will be capable of entering into the being of the material world even more deeply. That is an outlook on the future that is certain. Those of you who know a thing or two about physics might recall this thought: a perspective on the future is being gained by a large portion of our technological work being devoted to the production of heat, the transformation of warmth into work. Heat theorists show us how only a certain portion of any amount of heat generated can be transformed into work or into something of any technological value. If you heat a steam engine, you cannot apply all the heat toward the creation of forces of movement. Now just consider that work of any kind always involves expending heat, but that not all heat can be transformed into work; so that there is heat left over, which is the state of heat the heat engineers, the heat theorists can present as a kind of death state of our physical Earth. The person who deals with the phenomenon of life, though, objects that at this point it is possible for life itself to intervene, the living machinery that rules over molecules and atoms in an entirely different manner, through which we move our arms, set our brains in motion. If our forces of transformation are not enough, this force could then work more deeply into the nature of matter than even the powers we are capable of imagining today.

This shows you a perspective, though, that for the seer in a position to follow the spirit of development is no mere image, but rather something concrete and real: he sees how the whole Earth will have become transformed into an artifice. Once this has been accomplished, the human being has nothing more to do with the mineral world; then he will be free on all sides to move as he wants; his soul will no longer be at odds with objects. That will be the time when the Earth enters the so-called astral state. Just as today mechanics are masters of the outer world when they manufacture machines permeated by their minds, so also will it be with human beings. Everything that exists will be the direct product of their deeds. What our deed is, what we ourselves have formed, that we no longer need to perceive. Our senses will have been transformed then, and the astral state will begin. This is the point of view: the mineral world will end with our Earth cycle, and this is why we call the next cycle the human being will absolve the cycle of plant existence. The Earth will have been stripped of its mineral nature and humanity will take hold of the world of life with its soul force, in the same way that the mineral world is taken hold of by the intellect. Humanity will then be on a higher level than the plant world, just as today we are lords of the mineral world. Then we will arrive at the level where we will live on an utterly living Earth. But we only want to use this image as an approximation; we want to be content with having gained an outlook on the next cycle.*

Appendix 5
Part 3, Chapters 3, 9

We need to distinguish between the human being's initial inner life on Earth and what separates off from the individual as a kind of outer life. Inner life—we can refer first to the feelings, to the inner content of sensations the human being goes through between birth and death. This is the inner life proper. What a person feels toward the impressions of the outer world, toward one's own inward experience, including approval or reproach toward the expressions of one's actions; all that is something a person comes to terms with more or less on his own, something he can allow others to see into, to be sure. But the essential thing about it is the way a person comes to terms with all this on his own.

What humans experiences in perceiving, as we know from our considerations of late, is not actual, real experience; rather, it is a world of mere appearance spread out around us. It is the world in which we

---

* Steiner, *The Temple Legend*, lect. 3.

participate that is basically neither inward nor outward, and that we make into our inner world only by forming thoughts about it, by developing feelings about it, by its instigating us to do this or that....

But we need to consider something else that connects us with the outer world: what has its roots in our willing and passes over into our actions becomes a piece of outer world. Everything that occurs through our doing changes the outer world. The smallest thing we do contributes one thing or the other to the outer world, thereby changing it.

Now we can say that this outer world, which we ourselves produce through our doing, this outer world has its roots in our willing. It stands in the same relation to us as the events during our sleep. We see with our consciousness into the depths of our world of willing just as little as we see into what goes on during sleep. Thus, what actually happens in the world of willing remains outside our consciousness. I've often stated that, when we simply move our arm, our hand, the entire process of willing, this accumulation of force at work in the arm or the hand brought into motion, is withdrawn from our consciousness. Nevertheless, we watch our hand as it moves. We see the change we create. If all we do is move an object from one position to another, we take in the changes through our perceiving. Thus we can say that through our perceptions we are aware of our own expressions of will. Our willing and its effects flow, as it were, into the world of our perception....

This world of willing—in normal consciousness it cannot be distinguished from the "I." It connects itself completely and utterly with the "I." However, nothing of that happens within the "I" when the "I" wills, when it acts; nothing enters directly into normal consciousness. For normal consciousness this is like the events of the state of sleep.

In our physical body we have our sense organs, and the sense organs are what have the perceptions. Through these perceptions we perceive the expressions of our will. Therefore, in our physical body we have eyes and ears, and what unfolds out of the "I" and our world of willing is, basically, perceived by the senses. Hence what is outermost in human beings, perception, unites with what we experience through our will and our "I"-being.

Whenever we motivate our "I"-being toward volition and apply those will impulses toward actions, we experience those actions, regardless of whether we accomplish them through walking or grasping; we experience all our actions through perceiving. In our will, we actually belong to the world of our outer perceptions. Let us bear that firmly in mind; with our will we belong to the outer world of our perceiving. We do not gain access to our proper interior when we unfold what we observe in the way of our expressions of will, the revelations of our will. So doing, for our consciousness we actually perform an external process, or to put it more exactly, an accumulation of external processes, within our body—notwithstanding the fact that the will flows from our deepest interior.

Now let's have a look at the interior. Here we have, to start with, the weaving world of thought. The way this weaving world of thought takes outward effect can be of no proper interest to us in this context. This thought world lives outwardly by importing a certain logical, lawful coherency into the perceptions. We classify nature. We see plants that are similar to each other and assign them to a particular class; we see animals that are similar to each other and assign them to a particular class. We look for other laws of nature; none of the things we structure in this manner properly belongs to our actual inner life. It is what is common to all people as science. It does not belong to our inner life....

These thoughts permeate the etheric body first, but continue on to connect with our feeling, the astral body. All this is something that happens within. This inner side of our thought life, including the world of feeling, is the proper inner human world....

And we can now distinguish precisely between what is external life by virtue of humanity constantly exporting its interior into the outer world, and what is the inner world....

Thus if we want we can exactly differentiate between what is humanity's proper interior, woven in soul of thoughts and feelings, woven in body of the rhythmic interpenetration of the etheric and the astral bodies. We can distinguish from that what, in a sense, is outer world, woven in soul out of the content of our will and our perceiving, woven in body out of our I and our physical body. After all, we take our physical body along with us, we observe it, it enters various relationships with the environment. We can distinguish the inner from the outer in the way I just described. This distinction is very important, though, when we now want to contemplate the life that humans carry through the portal of death. We can utter in a quite comprehensive way how what we have just characterized as interior and exterior will behave after death, by saying

> The outer becomes the inner.
> The inner becomes the outer.

This indeed is the enormous change that takes place as we pass through death. The outer becomes the inner. Just as we now sense the interior of our soul, as we say "I" to our inside—we need only call to mind how this soul-interior is a fabric of our thoughts and feelings—in the same way, after death everything we have experienced in the way of the perceptions of our actions becomes our interior. Thus it is as it were a complete inversion: what was on the outside, what we could only perceive by seeing what we did, then becomes our inside. As we live in the sensations, the feelings of outer impressions now, we will then live in our deeds. Our actions will be our very interior then. Whoever did anything good or anything bad to someone else is himself the good or the bad he did. He truly is that after death. We must not imagine these things abstractly—as if some vague "I"-being slips through death and is then something else, or only a bit different—rather, we ourselves are what we have done, right down to the details. After death, we are our actions. We are each one of our experiences, and we call it all "I."

Conversely, the inner becomes the outer. All thoughts, the world of thought and the world of feeling, become something external. Just as now the sunshine, the clouds, or the night's starry heavens and all their movements surround us, after death our thoughts and sensations surround us as our outer world. Therefore, what we bear intimately within us integrates itself into the outer world after death, manifests to us in mighty pictures in the outer world. In the same way as now we see a sky in which the Sun shines, after death we see a sky in which there shines what here was our inner human nature.

If I am to depict the matter in its particulars, it is like this: I said before that we feel our deeds as if in a sphere, as our interior. What we have accomplished in the world we rehearse over and over; the way we always have walked, we go on walking. In a way, after death we are something that goes through its own deeds in a sphere, but always in a magnified way. And we always gaze back at the Earth. The way we now look outward into space at the stars, the Sun, in that way we look back at the Earth then. Moreover, the Earth is surrounded by images of our previous inner world. It is not as if we would experience the mere appearance of our inner world; rather, from the place we have left we experience those things that earlier were our inner world as if they were shining after us, in the way that cloud formations, star figures and so on radiate from where we are now. We feel as if inside the former peripheral world, and we feel the former world of the Earth, on which we stood, as our central outer world. We look down onto it. We are then the ones who are in orbit, and the centrally situated Earth is what we gaze upon and what opens unto us in mightily unfolding images.

> The outer becomes the inner.
> The inner becomes the outer.

This holds for every detail.

If one then looks back down to the Earth from out of the ever-widening sphere, one sees streaming back from the Earth all the feelings, sensations, and impressions one imparted to others. What one experienced inwardly that was not associated with other people appears more as cloud formations, but the sensations one had for other people appear starlike. The people themselves, though, one sees as figures in the life between death and a new birth whom one actually encountered as experience caused by deeds—this becomes a world. So all people with whom you had relationships become part of your inner world.

This is mutual, of course. Between death and rebirth, all human beings carry within themselves, along with the figures of the other people they encountered, everything that happened between them those people both externally (spatially and otherwise), just as here we carry our feeling or even our heart and stomach within us. Of two people who were close in life on Earth, one, person A, bears the image of person B, and person B that of person A, as each one's respective own inner substance. The outer becomes the inner; the inner, or feelings we experienced, become something outer; they become cosmic content. What we felt for people—everything we received from them—emanates toward us from Earth.

In this way, human beings actually create what surrounds them after death. Here is how it is during life: We always stand at some point in the world, do we not? I am not talking in a trivial sense about standing in Basel or Dornach; I mean some point in general, some standpoint we have in the world, both in a physical and in a moral sense. We see the world from that viewpoint. So we can say that we stand at a certain point and we see the world from the perspective of this point. That is something subjective. Everyone else has one's own, different standpoint. After death it's different. There, people have something in common, a sphere common to all. But on Earth they all had different inner lives. In addition, for this reason the Earth emanates round each soul differently, with different clouds, different star formations. It is as if all human beings would stand on the same single point on the Earth, but for the one person this image would present itself, for the other person a different one. This is how I can put in terms of sensory perception the state of existence after death.

Human beings shed their physical body after death. The physical body...is dissolved by the earthly realm itself, but what remains is the fabric that arises from our actions as we trace our acts, or revelations of our will, with our perception. Just consider all the paths you have taken on Earth (for example, as a child you just crawled around somehow, then you walked, then you took a long journey—all sorts of activities). All of this becomes your inner life at that point. But this is merely the outermost scaffolding.*

Appendix 6a
Part 3, Chapter 3

Now every single thing you've done all weaves together to a fabric; it expands, it becomes a sphere, it becomes inner life. It becomes inner life, and the fact that it becomes inner life guarantees human beings an "I" during Earth existence. For a person has an "I" from the Earth or through the Earth. The fact that after death one receives a memory-image woven of everything one has done on Earth enables us to carry our "I" into death. By contrast, the actual inner experiences are gone through in retrospect shortly after death by the etheric body dissolving only a bit later. The etheric body is dissolved out into the cosmos, and this provides the foundation for all that is woven out of thought and feeling from out of the etheric body—it also includes an astral influence—to become the cloud form or, as I have indicated, that configuration of stars that surrounds the Earth. What falls off of us in two directions, to the Earth and out into the space of the atmosphere, as it were, constitutes our inner and our outer makeup as we pass through life between death and a new birth.

Thus, imagine as vividly as you can what kind of environment you have between death and rebirth. As your inner life, you have your doing,

---

* Steiner, *Cosmosophy*, vol. 2, lect. 12.

inasmuch as it flows from the will. You have your feeling and thought life as the cosmos, as the outer world. Except you do not look out into the cosmos, but rather inward from the cosmos at the Earth, which emanates these inner thought aspects of yours back to you. When we live here between birth and death, we have the life of the Sun on the one hand. The Sun is on the outside. We stand on the Earth. After all, we ourselves are the Earth, and what we are ourselves, we do not see. We simply pass over into the life of the Sun, and what I described before is the transition into the life of the Sun.

The fact that we ourselves become our actions is connected with our passing over into the sun-life. And in distancing ourselves from the Earth, what we experienced through it now becomes what we behold. Here we stand on the Earth and behold the Sun. We see the Earth beneath us. This is because of the Earth's particular material constitution. The Sun has no material constitution. What physicists have to say about it (I've stated this before on occasion) is pure fantasy. If we ourselves were in the Sun and looking back, so to speak, we would have behind us the entire spiritual world, the world of the hierarchies. Therefore, we are Sun and we see the true Sun, which is of course spiritual.

We could call the Earth "Heaven." However, now it is the heavens that the human beings produce from what they live inwardly. That will also be the future; it will also be Jupiter existence. I gave a graphic depiction of it. All the things people weave around the Earth through their feelings, their thoughts, will remain. What will disappear is what exists today as the material Earth, for that will decline. Today the human being between death and rebirth can see what he inwardly weaves here. Later, that will become reality when the Earth nears extinction; that itself will become a new Earth; then the old Earth will melt away, and everything people have inwardly lived through will become the future of Earth.

This is how the real metamorphosis is accomplished. All we have to show is something external and abstruse if we say the Earth will pass over into Jupiter. We only comprehend the process if we know that what is outer, earthly matter will melt away into cosmic space; it will atomize. What will be woven around it from our feelings is what will become the future Earth. It will become increasingly dense; it will become, in fact, the planet Jupiter (ibid.).

Appendix 6b
Part 3, Chapter 3

Last time, I read to you the speech given by the English prime minister Balfour, in which he points to the fact that certain matters of ancient occult knowledge have become physical truth today. If you read H. P. Blavatsky's *Secret Doctrine,* you will find a passage about electricity that says literally the same thing as what physicists are gradually discovering today. However, what you find there is a mere inkling of the matter in its entirety. It concerns the physical atom. Until four or five years ago this was rejected by all external science, but not by esoteric science. The atom was considered a space-filling mass.

Today, people are starting to recognize this physical atom for what it really is. They are finding out that the physical atom behaves toward the force of electricity in the same manner as a clump of ice behaves toward the water out of which it congealed. If you imagine water freezing into ice, then ice is water, too. Similarly, the physical atom is nothing more than frozen electricity. If you comprehend that and go through the communications pertaining to the atom that were contained in all the scientific writings until a few years ago, and if you consider these writings rubbish, you will have an approximately correct idea. Only since very recently has physics been able to form a notion of what the physical atom is. That is, it behaves the way a clump of ice does toward the body of water out of which it congeals. The physical atom is electricity condensed. Balfour's address may be considered to be extraordinarily important.

It is something...that has reached public attention since 1875. This fact has been known to occultists for millennia. Now people are beginning to realize that the atom is condensed electricity. But there is a second thing involved, as well: knowing what electricity itself is. That is still unknown. There is still one thing they don't know: where to find the nature of electricity. This essence of electricity cannot be found through any kind of external experimentation or outer research. The secret that will be found out is that electricity is exactly the same thing as the human thought. The human thought is of the same nature as electricity: considered in the one case from within, the other case from without.

Now anyone who knows what electricity is knows that something inheres in it that, when frozen, forms the atom. Here you have the bridge from the human thought to the atom. The building stones of the physical world will be found out; they are minute condensed monads, condensed electricity. The moment that people have discovered this most elementary of occult truths concerning the thought, electricity and the atom, that very moment they will have recognized something that will be of the utmost importance for the future and for the entire sixth epoch. They will through the power of thought be able to use the atom for the purpose of building.

This is the great thought, that...all progress is based on involution and evolution. Involution is sucking in, evolution is emitting. All stages of the world alternate between these two ascending and descending phases. You breathe nature in by seeing, hearing, smelling, tasting. What you see does not go by you without an effect. The eye will be destroyed, the object will be destroyed, but what you have seen will remain. Now you will understand that at certain times it can be necessary to awaken an understanding of such things. We are nearing a time in which, as I recently indicated, understanding will get hold of the atom. People will comprehend—even in popular conception—that the atom is nothing more than congealed electricity; thought itself is of the same substance. In fact, it will go so far that before the end of the fifth cultural epoch humanity will be able to exert an influence even into the interior of the atom. All one needs to do is understand the material nature common to both thought and the atom, and one will not be far from understanding how to exert an internal influence on the atom. And then no access will be barred for certain kinds of influence: I will stand here and, unnoticed by anyone, press a button in my pocket that causes something at a great distance—say in Hamburg—to explode! Just as even now you can send telegrams wirelessly by generating wave movements here and causing them to manifest in a certain way at a certain different place, in the same way what I just described will also be possible. That will be able to occur the moment the occult truth is implemented in practical life that the thought and atoms are made of the same substance.*

APPENDIX 7
PART 3, CHAPTER 4

When you contemplate this thought—that the human being, as a being with senses, of glands and of digestion, has by virtue of these activities no worth for eternity—then you will easily be able to unite it with the thought we expressed yesterday in a general way and that we can, unfortunately, only indicate very slightly in this short course of lectures; the thought, namely, of scattering form, of form that is breaking and scattering and dispersing. When form sprays into these activities, when shattered form, that is to say matter, is driven into the organism it brings about sense activity, gland secretion, and metabolic activity. Hence it is evident that in these activities we have to do with breaking form, with a form that breaks to pieces. It is nothing more than special

---

*   Steiner, *The Temple Legend*, lect. 3.

manifestations of the destruction process in form that meets us in sense activity, gland secretion, and the activity of digestion. They are particular processes of what we can describe in general as the destruction process in form, or as the shooting of form into matter.

When, however, we come to nerve activity, muscle activity, and the strength and effective virtue of the bones, the case is altogether different. We were able to show yesterday that in the bony system we have Imagination that has become material; in the muscular system, Inspiration that has become material and manifests in movement; and in the nervous system materialized Intuition. And now we have reached a point where we can go on from this and give a fuller description of a truth that can only be partially described in more general anthroposophic lectures. When the human being passes through the gate of death, little by little, through decay or combustion, or however it may be, the bony system falls to pieces. But what remains when the bony system crumbles away in the material sense is the Imagination. The Imagination is not lost. It remains in those substances, which we still have in us even when we have passed through the gate of death and enter Kamaloka or Devachan. We retain in us a picture form that the thoroughly experienced clairvoyant does not indeed find to be quite like the bony system; but when a less trained clairvoyant lets it work upon him he finds an outward similarity in the form to the bony system; and on this account is death, not without some justification, represented in the Imagination of the skeleton. The picture goes back to an untrained, but for all that, a not-altogether mistaken clairvoyance.

What remains from the muscles is combined with this Imagination when they decay in the physical sense. From the muscles remains the Inspiration, of which they are in reality only the expression; for the muscles are Inspirations steeped, soaked in matter. The Inspiration remains for us when we have passed through the gate of death. That is a very interesting fact. From the system of nerves, when the nerves themselves have undergone their process of decay, we are left

Appendix 7 ∞ Part 3, Chapter 4

after death with Intuition. All these are actual constituent parts of our astral as well as our etheric body.

You know that the human being does not lay aside the etheric body completely; an extract from the etheric body we take with us when we have passed through the gate of death. However, this is not all. There is something else we have now to discover. The human being carries its system of nerves continuously through the world, and this system of nerves is nothing else than Intuition interspersed with matter. As we bear this system of nerves through the world it is really so that in the places where the nerves are situated in the human organism there is always Intuition, and this Intuition rays out a spirituality that we have perpetually around us like a kind of radiating aura. It is thus not only a question of what we take with us when we go through the gate of death; but we must also consider the Intuition that we are sending out from us all the time, in proportion as the nerves decay. A process of decay is going on in you all the time; you need to be continually formed anew—although in the case of the nerves there is a greater measure of durability than elsewhere.

A constant outflow takes place that can only be perceived by means of Intuition. We may say that spiritual substance—a substance that is perceptible to Intuition—is perpetually raying out from a person in proportion to the physical nerve system going to pieces. You will see from this that we are not without significance for the world, inasmuch as we use our physical system of nerves and inasmuch as we use it up and bring it to destruction. We have, in fact, great significance. For it depends on the use we make of our nerves what kind of intuitively perceived substances stream Inspiration. This outward flow takes place in such a way that it is continuously populating the world with finely, infinitely differentiated processes of movement. Inspired substances flow out from human beings into the world. (These words are ill suited to describe what actually happens but we have no others.) From our bones streams out what we may call "Imaginatively perceived substance." There you have the most extraordinary and interesting fact.

Let me enlarge on it a little, not to overwhelm you with the results of clairvoyant research, but because it is truly interesting.

Through this radiation from the bones as they decay, we literally leave behind, everywhere we go, pictures—that is, spirit images perceptible through Imagination. Fine shadow images of us remain behind wherever we have been. After you have left this hall, a finer and well-trained clairvoyance would still be able to perceive fine shadow images on your chairs. They would be perceptible for a while, until they are received into the general world process—delicate shadow pictures of individuals that have been radiated out from their skeletal system. Those Imaginations are the cause of that unpleasant feeling we sometimes have when entering a room that has been lived in by a disagreeable person. The feeling is caused mainly by the Imaginations that person left behind. We meet that person in a kind of shadow image. In this sense, sensitive people are not far behind a clairvoyant; they get an uncomfortable feeling about what that other person has left behind in a room. Clairvoyant have only the advantage that they can see in an Imaginative picture what the other only feels somewhat instinctively.

Now what happens to all that we let radiate out of us in this way? All that rays forth from us in this way, my dear friends—take it altogether and you have, in very deed and truth, the whole influence that is exerted by us on the world. For whatever you do, when you do it, you move, you bring your system of bones and muscles into movement. Not only so, but even when you only lie and think you are still raying forth substance that is perceptible to Intuition. In short, whatever activity you engage in you are sending out this spiritual substance into the world, it is perpetually passing over from you into the world. Now the fact is, if these processes were not taking place there would be nothing left of our Earth when it came to the end of its evolution, nothing left of it but pulverized matter that would pass over like dust into universal space. Nevertheless, something is saved through humanity from the material process of the Earth and lives in the general cosmos, in the universe; and it is what can arise through

Inspiration, Intuition, and Imagination. In this way, humanity gives to the world what the world uses to build itself up anew. Humanity provides, as it were, the building-stones. This is what will continue to live as the soul and spirit of the whole Earth when the material substance is torn from this Earth and shattered like a corpse—even as the individual soul and spirit nature of a person lives on after death. We bear our individual soul through the gate of death; the Earth carries over into the Jupiter-existence what has come of the Imaginations and Inspirations and Intuitions of humanity. There you have the great difference between the two sides of our dual nature: the part of us that perceives with our senses, secretes in our glands, and digests and nourishes—this is the part of us that is destined to be cast off, for it belongs to time and passes away. But all that is the result of the presence of nerves and muscle and bone—all of this is incorporated into the Earth, so that it may thereby continue to exist.*

Appendix 8
Part 3, Chapter 4

Now we come to something that stands like a great mystery in our whole existence, and that, because it is in very truth a mystery, cannot be grasped by the intellect; rather is it for the soul to believe it and penetrate to its depths. It is, nonetheless, perfectly true. What human beings allow to flow out into the environment divides itself into two distinct parts. First, there is the part of the Inspiration, Intuition, and Imagination upon which general cosmic existence, so to speak, depends. The cosmos receives it, and drinks it in. However, there is another part that cosmic existence does not receive but rejects. Cosmic existence makes its attitude clear, as if to say, "I can use these Inspirations, Intuitions, and Imaginations. I absorb them so that I can carry them over to

---
* Steiner, *The World of the Senses and the World of the Spirit*, lect. 5.

Jupiter existence." However, cosmic existence rejects others; it refuses to receive them. The result is that the other Intuitions, Inspirations, and Imaginations, not being received, remain as such for themselves; they remain, spiritually, in the cosmos and cannot disintegrate. Thus, what we radiate from us falls into two parts: what is received gladly by the cosmos and what is rejected by the cosmos. The cosmos is not satisfied with the latter and leaves it alone; it remains where it is. How long does it remain? Until the human being comes and destroys it by means of outward flows that are able to destroy it.

As a rule, no human has the power to destroy out-flows that are rejected by the cosmos other than the person who sent them out. Here you have something of a karmic technique and why we must ourselves meet again, in the course of our karma, all the Imaginations, Inspirations, and Intuitions that have been rejected by the cosmos. We must ourselves destroy them and annihilate them; the cosmos receives only what is correct and right in thought, beautiful in feeling, and morally good and sound. It rejects everything else. That is the secret, the great mystery. A person must erase whatever is false in thought, ugly in feeling, and morally evil from existence if it is to disappear. We must do so through the necessary thoughts and feelings or will impulses or actions. It will follow us forever until we have erased it.

Therefore, you see it is untrue to say that the cosmos consists of and expresses only the neutral laws of nature. The cosmos around us, which we believe we can perceive with our senses and grasp with our intellect, has other forces in it, as well. If we may put it in this way, the cosmos vigorously repels and repudiates evil, the ugly, and the false and is eager to receive into itself the good, the beautiful, and the true. It is not merely at certain times that the powers of the cosmos sit in judgment; it sits in judgment throughout the whole of earthly evolution.*

---

*   Steiner, *The World of the Senses and the World of the Spirit*, lect. 5.

Appendix 9
Part 3, Chapters 4, 7

You see, in this way the life of the individual human being connects with the life of the entire cosmos. Living here between birth and death as we do, we see what former worlds have left over for us, what is left over from Saturn, Sun, and Moon existence, or past Earth existences. When we are here we see all that shone round by the manifestations surrounding us as phenomena. That points us more or less in the direction of the past. Everything we carry within us and everything we perform on this Earth points us to the future, and we see this future reflected into the present in our experiences between death and a new birth, as the inner becomes the outer and the outer becomes the inner.*

Appendix 10
Part 3, Chapter 4

The esoteric science of all eras says the following about the Earth's interior. We must think of the Earth as consisting of a series of layers, not completely separated from one another like the skins of an onion, but merging into one another gradually.

1. The topmost layer, the mineral mass, is related to the interior as an eggshell is to the egg. This topmost layer is called the Mineral Earth.

2. Under it is a second layer, called the Fluid Earth; it consists of a substance to which there is nothing comparable on Earth. It is not really like any of the fluids we know, for these all have a mineral quality. This layer has specific characteristics: its substance begins to display certain spiritual qualities, which consist in the fact that as soon as it is brought into contact with something living, it strives to expel

---

*   Steiner, *Anthroposophy as Cosmosophy*, lect. 12.

and destroy this life. The occultist is able to investigate this layer by pure concentration.

3. The "Air-Earth." This is a substance that annuls feelings: for instance, if it is brought into contact with any pain, the pain is converted into pleasure, and vice versa. The original form of a feeling is, so to speak extinguished, rather as the second layer extinguishes life.

4. The "Water-Earth," or the "Form-Earth." It produces in the material realm the effects that occur spiritually in Devachan. There, we have the negative pictures of physical things. In the "Form-Earth" a cube of salt, for example, would be destroyed, but its negative would arise. The form is as it were changed into its opposite; all its qualities pass out into its surroundings. The actual space occupied by the object is left empty.

5. The "Fruit-Earth." This substance is full of exuberant energy. Every little part of it grows out at once like sponge; it gets larger and larger and is held in place only by the upper layers. It is the underlying life that serves the forms of the layers above it.

6. The "Fire-Earth." Its substance is essentially feeling and will. It is sensitive to pain and would cry out if it were trodden on. It consists, as it were, entirely of passions.

7. The "Earth-mirror" or "Earth-reflector." This layer gets its name from the fact that its substance, if one concentrates on it, changes all the characteristics of the Earth into their opposites. If the seer disregards everything lying above it and gazes down directly into this layer, and if then, for example, he places something green before him, the green appears as red; every color appears as its complementary opposite. A polaric reflection arises, a reversal of the original. Sorrow would be changed by this substance into joy.

8. The "Divisive" layer. If with developed power one concentrates on it, something very remarkable appears. For example, a plant held in the midst of this layer appears to be multiplied, and so with everything else. But the essential thing is that this layer disrupts the moral qualities also. Through the power it radiates to the Earth's surface, it is responsible for the fact that strife and disharmony exist there. In

order to overcome this disruptive force, men must work together in harmony.

That is precisely why this layer was laid down in the Earth—so that men should be enabled to develop harmony for themselves. The substance of everything evil is prepared and organized there. Quarrelsome people are so constituted that this layer has a particular influence on them. This has been known to everyone who has written out of a true knowledge of occultism. Dante in his *Divine Comedy* calls this layer the Cain-layer. It was here that the strife between the brothers Cain and Abel had its source. The substance of this layer is responsible for evil having come into the world.

9. The "Earth-core." This is the substance through whose influence black magic arises in the world. The power of spiritual evil comes from this source.

You will see that humanity is related to all the layers, for it is continuously radiating its forces. Humanity lives under the influence of these layers and has to overcome their powers. When human beings have learnt to radiate life on Earth and have trained their breathing so that it promotes life, they will overcome the "Fire-Earth." When spiritually they overcome pain through serenity, they overcome the "Air-Earth." When concord reigns, the "Divisive" layer is conquered. When white magic triumphs, no evil remains on Earth. Human evolution thus implies a transformation of the Earth's interior. In the beginning the nature of the Earth's body was such as to hold subsequent developments in check. In the end, when human powers have transformed the Earth, it will be a spiritualized Earth. In this way the human being imparts its own being to the Earth.

Now there are occasions when the very substance of the passions of the Fire-Earth begins to rebel. Aroused by human passions, it penetrates through the Fruit-Earth, forces its way through the channels in the upper layers and even flows up into and violently shakes the solid Earth: the result is an earthquake. If this passion from the Fire-Earth thrusts up some of the Earth's substance, a volcano erupts. All this is closely connected with humanity. In Lemurian times, the upper layer was still very soft and the Fire-layer was near the surface. Human passions and the "passion-substance" of this layer are related; when humans give rein to evil passions they strengthen its passions, and that is what happened at the end of Lemurian times. Through their passions the Lemurians made the Fire-Earth rebellious, and in this way they brought the whole Lemurian continent to destruction. No other cause for this destruction could be found except in what they had themselves drawn forth from the Earth. Today the layers are thicker and firmer, but there is still this connection between human passions and the passion-layer in the interior of the Earth; and it is still an accumulation of evil passions and forces that gives rise to earthquakes and volcanic eruptions.*

Appendix 11
Part 3, Chapter 5

In modern textbooks the nature of the cause of physical movement is usually defined as follows: "Any change in the state of movement of a portion of matter is the result of the action on it of another portion of matter." This represents a truth if it is taken to describe a certain kind of causation. In the axiomatic form in which it is given it is a fallacy. The kind of causation it describes is, indeed, the only one that has been taken into consideration by the scientific mind. We are wont to call it "mechanical causation." Obviously, the human being's onlooker-consciousness is unable to conceive of any other kind of causation....

We cannot rest content with this state of affairs if we are sincerely searching for an understanding of how spirit moves, forms, and transforms matter. We must learn to acknowledge nonmechanical causes of physical effects, where such causes actually present themselves to our

---

* Steiner, *Founding a Science of the Spirit*, lect. 14.

observation. The fact that this word has gathered all sorts of doubtful associations must not hinder us from adopting it into the terminology of a science that aspires to understand the working of the suprasensory in the world of the senses. The falling into disrepute of this word is characteristic of the onlooker age. The way we suggest it should be used is in accord with its true and original meaning, the syllable mag, signifying power or might (Sanskrit, *maha;* Greek, *megas;* Latin, *magnus;* English, *might, much, master*). Henceforth, we will distinguish between mechanical and magical causation, the latter being a characteristic of the majority of happenings in the human, animal and plant organisms....

Earlier in this chapter, we said that if we want to understand how spirit moves, forms, and transforms matter, we must recognize the existence of nonmechanical (magical) causes of physical effects.*

Appendix 12
Part 3, Chapters 7, 11

The first observation that I have to make is difficult, indeed hardly understandable at all for modern consciousness, but it is good if one is aware of it. It relates to the question of how planetary structures, once they have appeared, disappear again. From a spiritual point of view, it is clear how the course of development occurs. Beings ascend to higher stages, and, as they advance, they have to leave their previous places of activity, that is, they must leave their former dwelling places that enabled them, for a period, to develop certain faculties that they would not otherwise have been able to acquire. When, in the course of evolution, that time we call the old Lemurian period drew near, humanity had come so far in its development that it had recapitulated all that could be achieved through the stages of Saturn, Sun, and Moon. Then

---

* Lehrs, *Man or Matter.*

humanity appeared in the environment of earthly evolution, which had just been made ready for our further development. We developed through Lemurian and Atlantean times on into our own period, and, moving from incarnation to incarnation, we will develop further in the future. Then, after a time, humanity will have to leave the Earth again. The Earth will have nothing further to give humanity, for it will not be able to offer further possibilities of development.

You could imagine that after the departure of humanity our Earth would become a desolate ruin. You could compare it with a city that had been deserted by its inhabitants. You know what such a city looks like after only a short time—how it gradually turns into a mound of earth. Seeing ancient cities taken over by the forces of nature gives us a graphic picture of the process. So it is today in reality. But this will not be true for the future of the Earth. The following observation can guide you toward an answer to the following questions: How will it be in the future of our Earth? What is the significance for the development of the Earth of such persons as Leonardo da Vinci, Raphael, or any of the other great geniuses in this or that field? What does it mean for earthly development that Raphael or Michelangelo produced wonderful works of art that are still enjoyed by thousands and thousands of people to this very day? Some of you may have felt certain sadness on seeing Leonardo's *Last Supper* in Milan, and you may have wondered how much longer this magnificent work will last. We should remember that Goethe, on his first Italian journey, still beheld the work in its full glory, and that we can no longer see it in that state. From Goethe's time until today, the fate of this work of art within its outward material environment is such that it now calls forth feelings of sadness in us. For people who will live as long after us as we live after Goethe, the work will no longer be in existence. Thus it is with everything that human beings have created and embodied in physical matter on Earth. *

---

* Steiner, *The Spiritual Hierarchies and the Physical World*, lect. 10.

Appendix 13
Part 3, Chapter 9

The animal and plant kingdoms are imbedded in the other kingdom of nature, the mineral ground of the Earth. In all this live the forces that manifest in varied forms of appearance through the seasons. Consider the plant world. In autumn and winter it manifests physically dying forces. In this form of appearance, the consciousness of the seer perceives the nature of the forces that have brought about the gradual death of the macrocosm. In spring and summer, forces of growth—springing and sprouting forces—reveal themselves in plant life. In the growing and sprouting process, a seer's consciousness perceives not only what brings forth the abundant blessing of the plant life for the given year, but also an excess—an excess of germinating force. The plants contain more germinating force than they spend on the growth of foliage, flower, and fruit. For a seer's consciousness, this excess of germinating force flows out into the supra-earthly macrocosm.

Similarly, a surplus of force radiates from the mineral kingdom to the supra-earthly cosmos. This force must carry the forces from the plant world to the proper places in the macrocosm. Under the influence of the mineral forces, the plant forces become a newly fashioned picture of a macrocosm.

Likewise, there are forces that proceed from animal nature. These however do not work as do the plant and mineral forces that radiate from the Earth. They work in such a way that plant nature, which the mineral forces carry in clear formation into the great universe, is gathered into a sphere, so that a picture arises of a macrocosm compacted and self-contained on all sides. It is thus that spirit-seeing consciousness beholds the essence of the earthly realm, which stands as a new, life-kindling element within the dead and dying macrocosm. As when the old plant has died and fallen away, a new plant, however large, is formed again from the seed in space so insignificant and small—so while the old dead macrocosm falls away, a new macrocosm comes forth from this "speck of dust," the Earth.

It is a true contemplation of the Earth nature that sees in it on all hands a germinating universe. We come to understand the kingdoms of nature around us only when we feel the presence of this germinating life in them.*

Appendix 14
Part 3, Chapter 10

The threefold adornment that the Woman wears—gold, precious stones, and pearls—is the heavenly Trinity of Sun, Moon and Stars, debased into earthly ornamentation. While the Mother in the heights bears the golden heart of the world radiating from within her, the debased figure completely abandoned to this world adorns herself with the glittering material gold that is the materialized earthly shadow of the Sun. And just as the Woman in Heaven has the stars as a crown about her head, so the Whore adorns herself with precious stones, which are like the thoughts of the stars imprisoned in matter. Not until we consider the heavenly Jerusalem, in the fashioning of whose body gold, precious stones, and pearls also play a part, shall we recognize fully what infamy lies in the fact that the Whore Babylon also adorns herself with pearls. Pearls are not minerals. They grow through the reaction of living beings to pain in the overcoming of pain caused by the incursion of a foreign body; the oyster develops the pearl. Thus the pearl is a wonderful symbol of pain overcome in the soul. In the language of Apocalyptic symbols it is equivalent to the conquest of the dark and oppressive forces of the night, which the Heavenly Woman masters when she keeps the Moon under her feet. I the spiritual-physical body

---

* Steiner, *Anthroposophical Leading Thoughts*, "What Is the Earth in Reality within the Macrocosm?"

of the heavenly Jerusalem, pearls as well as gold and precious stones are tokens and results of inner discipline and spiritual victories, tokens of inner mastery. The Whore Babylon has not herself suffered the pains whose results she hangs about her as ornament. She is the antithesis of the Woman who has the Moon beneath her feet. Gold, precious stones and pearls in her are tokens of outward show, unearned and unintegrated. The Woman and the Dragon are not clearly distinguishable; the glaring red of passion and greed envelops both in equal measure. Out of the golden cup that she holds in her hand, "full of abominations and filthiness," the Whore Babylon dispenses an unclean wealth, which binds those who accept it to the dark depths and forces of the world. It is often said of a man that "two souls dwell in his breast." This is true also of humankind as a whole. Since the Woman in Heaven, the higher soul of humanity, bore her son, Humanity has had the choice between the higher and the lower ego. The free decision between above and below, maturing during the ages of the life of the Earth, must lead to a parting of the ways. In the picture of the Whore that part of humanity ultimately appears in which the lower soul, earthbound and heavy, has arrogated all power to itself.*

Appendix 15
Part 3, Chapter 10

The image of the mountain occurs so often in all the Biblical Scriptures that it points unmistakably not to an earthly, but to a spiritual sphere. For example, even Christ's words about the "faith that can move mountains" may become a truly Apocalyptic expression. Of course, this does not mean that faith can do the work of the spade. The mountain before which I stand blocks the view behind it. Not until I climb to the top of it can I see the view again. The magic of faith consists of moving

---

* Bock, The *Apocalypse of St. John*, pp. 147–148.

the mountains that block the view into the world of the spirit from the human soul. The faith that moves mountains also lifts the soul to a level where nothing obscures the horizon. We recall that, at the sound of the Second Trumpet, a burning mountain fell from Heaven. At that stage, Heaven itself caused human beings to "come up against a brick wall"; they fell into a kind of consciousness wherein they lost sight altogether of the spiritual sphere—the mountain of materialism towered up in front of them.

According to the book of Daniel (ch. 2), a similar vision seized the soul of Nebuchadnezzar. An invisible hand broke of a stone and hurled it against an image. As the stone fell it grew into a gigantic rock. It was a prophetic vision of the fact that the human race, which once saw into the sphere of the gods with innocent forces of clairvoyance, had to descend into the dark valley, surrounded by nothing but mountains. Physical sense perception is the mountain that no longer allows a view into the inner realms of existence.

In Grimm's fairy tale of Snow White, the Apocalyptic motif of the Seven Mountains occurs in a characteristic context. The proud queen, Snow White's wicked stepmother, stands in front of the magic mirror to be assured that she is the most beautiful being in the whole country. However, at a certain moment the mirror answers, "Your Majesty, you are the most beautiful here. But Snow White, across the seven mountains, with the seven dwarves, is a thousand times more beautiful than you are." The world in which Snow White lives is not the same as the world of the stepmother. The queen is in the world of matter and of the physical senses; but Snow White moves in the world of the elements and elemental beings that are not physical. The towering boundary zone appears in the picture of the seven mountains, which must be surmounted by anyone who wishes to pass from the sensory world to the suprasensory world.

The Seven Mountains of which the Apocalypse speaks are also a boundary range between this world and that. Clearly, it is not a coincidence that a city such as Rome is built on seven hills. Indeed,

Rome is not the only town that has had similar mythological scenery for its foundation. Prague, also a city on seven hills, has frequently been called the "Eastern Rome." Apocalyptic motifs can stray, as it were, into physical geography when world history turns cities into symbols, causing them to spring up in places where, through nature and destiny, special possibilities of a connection between the two worlds exist. For Prague, the secret of the seven hills is brought out by the name of the city, which means "Threshold." Such places and centers, however, are also dangerous points. The enchantment of a magnificent material civilization seduces human souls until, eventually, the Seven Mountains and the seeming glory of this world blind one's eyes to the world beyond. When the Apocalypse shows us the proudly adorned woman sitting on the Seven Mountains, it presents to us a power whose will is that humankind wall be separated from the spiritual world.*

Appendix 16
Part 3, Chapter 10

With its concepts and ideas, humanity still lives in nature, even though it carries its habitual mechanical thinking into its theories of nature. However, humanity lives in the mechanical processes of technology and industry with the life of will, to such an extreme that it has long imbued this age of science with an entirely new quality.... Through our senses, we perceive the cosmic at work on the Earth; through our thinking we conceive and think the cosmic influences that work downward to the Earth from the encircling spheres.... All that human beings experience in their souls by way of purely mechanistic laws has been discovered inwardly through this relationship of orientation toward the earthly world.

---

* Ibid., pp. 149–151.

The mechanical is thus characterized as having a purely earthly nature. The laws and processes of nature as they rule color, sound, and so on entered the earthly realm from the cosmos. It is only within the earthly realm that they, too, are imbued with the mechanical element, as does a person who does not confront the mechanical in conscious experience until coming within the earthly realm.

By far, most of what works in modern civilization through technology and industry—within which human life of humanity is so intensely woven—is not nature at all, but subnature. It is a world that frees itself from nature...in a downward direction.... Humanity needed this relationship to the purely earthly to unfold the spiritual soul.... Entering the purely earthly element, we strike upon the ahrimanic realm....

Nevertheless, in the age of technology thus far, the possibility of finding a true relationship to ahrimanic civilization has escaped humanity.... We must understand subnature for what it really is. We cannot do this unless we rise, in spiritual knowledge, at least as far into supra-earthly supra-nature as we have descended into technology and subnature.... Electricity, for instance, celebrated since its discovery as the very soul of nature's existence, must be seen in its true character—in its peculiar power to lead down from nature to subnature.... The purely ahrimanic dominates this sphere.

In Spiritual Science, we now create another sphere in which there is no ahrimanic element. Humanity is strengthened to confront Ahriman in the world simply by receiving, in knowledge, this spirituality to which ahrimanic powers have no access.*

---

*   Steiner, *Anthroposophical Leading Thoughts*, 29th letter.

Appendix 17
Part 4, Chapter 4

In the course of earthly evolution, humankind must become ever freer. Only by our growing freer will the Earth reach her evolutionary goal. During a certain period, intellectuality was necessary to this end. That period is, of course, our own. Look back to earlier times and conditions on Earth, when human beings still enjoyed a kind of dreamy clairvoyance. There were always spiritual beings living in that dreamlike clairvoyance. A human being at that time could never say, "I have my own thoughts in my head." That would have been untrue. In very ancient times, one had to say, "I have the life of angels in my head." Then in later times, "I have the life of elemental beings in my head." Then came the fifteenth century, and at long last the nineteenth and the twentieth centuries. Today, we no longer have spiritual beings in our heads, but only thoughts—mere thoughts. By not having any higher spiritual life but only thoughts in our head, we can make our own pictures of the outer world.

Could human beings be free so long as spirits were living in them? No, they could not; those spirits directed them, and everything was owed to them. Individuals could become free only when spiritual beings no longer directed them—when they had mere pictures, or images, in their thoughts. Thought images cannot compel you to do anything. Say, for example, you face a mirror; the reflected images of other people, regardless of their ill will, cannot strike you, since they are not real but mere images. If I am resolving on some action, I may cause the mirror image in my thought to picture the resolve, but the picture cannot of itself create a resolve.

Thus, freedom is born in the epoch when intellectuality puts only thoughts into our heads, inasmuch as thoughts lack power to compel. We can achieve true freedom today because we hold our moral impulses in the form of pure thoughts (as described in my *Philosophy of Freedom*). The intellectual age, therefore, is a necessity.

Yet, strange as it may sound, this age is essentially already past. The age when it was right for humanity to develop mere intellectuality, or thinking in images, has run its course. It has become a thing of the past with the nineteenth century. If human beings continue to develop mere image thoughts, their thoughts will fall a prey to ahrimanic powers. Those ahrimanic powers will then gain access to humanity and, having reached freedom, we will lose it to the ahrimanic powers. Humankind is at the threshold of this danger now. We are faced today with a choice: Comprehend spiritual life—the reality of what I have been describing today—or deny it. If humanity persists in denying what is spiritual, free thought will no longer be possible. On the contrary, Ahriman— the ahrimanic powers—will then think in humankind, and all humanity will undergo devolution.*

Appendix 18
Part 3, Chapter 11

What must first of all be considered from a spiritual worldview is individual evolution. Leonardo da Vinci has risen higher by means of what he accomplished. That constitutes his ascent. We ask ourselves: Are the great thoughts, the great impulses that the great creators imprinted on the substance of the Earth, of any significance for the future of the Earth? Will the future reduce the Earth to dust, and will everything that men and women have made out of the Earth disappear when the planet no longer exists? You admire Cologne Cathedral. Certainly, in a relatively short time, not one stone will rest upon another. Does this mean it is of no significance for the Earth as a whole that human beings embodied the idea of the Cologne Cathedral in stone? We are not now considering what human beings take with them from Earth; we are looking at the Earth itself. A planet actually becomes smaller

---

* Steiner, *The Mystery of the Trinity*, lect. 9.

and smaller in the course of its development. It contracts. That is the destiny of the material part of a planet—but that is not the whole story. It is, so to speak, only the part that can be observed by means of physical eyes and instruments. There is also an evolution of matter that proceeds beyond what can be so observed.

I now want to consider the evolution of matter beyond this point, and thereby I come to what I previously described as difficult, indeed almost incomprehensible, to contemporary understanding. The Earth is constantly contracting. Matter is being pressed from all sides into the center. Now I can say, with full awareness of course, that there is a law of the conservation of force, but I must also say in full awareness that there is another fact known to every esotericist—that matter presses increasingly into the center and, remarkably, disappears into the center.

Imagine a piece of matter pressed more and more into the central point, where it disappears. It is not being pushed through to the other side. At the center, it actually disappears into nothingness! In other words, eventually the Earth, as its material aspect presses in upon the middle point, will disappear into the center. That is not all. As much as disappears at the center, so much reappears at the periphery. It reappears at the extremity. Matter disappears at one point in space—the center—and reappears at another, the circumference. Everything that disappears into the center emerges again at the periphery. Everything has been worked into this matter. The beings who were at work on the planets impressed everything into the matter. Naturally, the matter is not in its present form, but in a form that it received by means of this process of transformation. So you will see Cologne Cathedral, whose material particles disappeared into the middle point, reappearing from the other side. Nothing, absolutely nothing of what has been accomplished on a planet is lost; it returns from the other side.

All that came to us during the earliest phase of earthly development before Saturn was thus transferred outside, beyond the zodiac. In primeval wisdom this is called "the Crystal Heaven." It is where the deeds of beings belonging to a previous evolution were deposited. They formed the basis on which new beings could become creative.

As I said before, it is difficult to understand these things with contemporary understanding, because we are accustomed to considering only the material aspect. We are not used to acknowledging that matter can disappear from one position in three-dimensional space and come back again somewhere else after it has gone through another dimension. As long as you remain in your thinking in the context of three-dimensional space, you cannot grasp it, for this phenomenon goes beyond three-dimensional space. Thus, it cannot be seen until it again reenters three-dimensional space from the other side. In the intervening period, it is in another dimension. This is something that we must understand, for aspects of cosmic creation are bound together in the most complex manner. Something in one place is connected in a complicated way to something else found in an entirely different place in three-dimensional space.*

Appendix 19
Part 3, Chapter 11

You all know of course that in this fifth post-Atlantean epoch people gradually began replacing the old clairvoyance inherited from the ancient Moon with the genuinely outward objective observation of things, which gradually became the scientific mode of regarding things, which in turn led to the materialistic conception of the world; and that we wish to place within this materialistic world conception the spiritual-scientific one. Gather everything together we can conceive of and know about the world; consider everything a person can have in the way of perceptions, concepts, ideas.... We have often discussed, haven't we, how it is that we actually have all this. We have it because our spiritual

---

*   Steiner, *The Spiritual Hierarchies and the Physical World*, lect.10.

and soul element is reflected in the physical-bodily element in such a way that today in our waking earthly life we form images through our spiritual and soul element calling forth certain processes in the physical and bodily, and these processes become a reflective apparatus; and this reflective apparatus then forms the content of our consciousness. Thus, when we have a certain content of our earthly consciousness from waking up until falling asleep, such as images, sensations, will impulses, our earthly being is, at first, an apparatus for it all, for the content that we gather in the course of earthly life.

Therefore, during waking earthly life we experience with our physical, earthly human being. However, we also carry within us the human being from the Moon. This "Moon human" is not suited to serving directly us as an instrument for perception. The Moon human was suited to forming the primeval dreamlike imaginations on the Moon. Today it is not suited for forming our bright, earthly perceptions. But this Moon human is inside us, and we should not think that it does nothing. What does this Moon human do? Well, it does the same thing it did during the Moon epoch—it dreams. We do not notice this immediately when we are awake, so we do not normally perceive the dreams at work in our subconscious. We pass through the world with the content of the dreamer, just as we pass through the world with our waking consciousness. Although we know nothing of this dreamer, there are other entities that do. Those entities are the beings of the hierarchy of Angeloi, and what this dreamer dreams becomes image in the souls of the Angeloi; they elevate it to their imagination.

Thus, during the Moon evolution, this dreamer developed the consciousness attainable during it. When earthly humanity arose, this dreamer crept inside of us; but what the dreamer now experiences the Angeloi develop into clear, conscious pictures, and for them these pictures are imaginations. They transform our dreams into imaginations. So the dreamer within us becomes a mental picture for the entities from the hierarchy of the Angeloi, and they make imaginations out of them. Thus we can say: What the Moon human dreams, the angels imagine. Now it will be easy to move on to the admittedly somewhat sketchy next step. But this sketch is true.

The Sun human has even duller images within us, images such as plants have. So we carry not only the dreamer within us; we also carry a sort of plant person, who constantly sleeps, just as the plant does. These dull images become inspirations in the entities from the hierarchy of the Archangeloi. Thus what the Sun human experiences in a state of sleep inspires the Archangels. The Saturn human is in an even duller state of sleep. This one sleeps the deep sleep of the minerals. This Saturn human gives the images of deep sleep to the entities from the hierarchy of the Archai; these images are the substance, the possibility of intuiting. Thus we can say: What the Saturn human is in deep sleep, is intuited by the Spirits of Personality (beings of the hierarchy of the Archai).

But you only acquire a proper notion of this if it is clear to you that imaginations, inspirations, and intuitions are not the sort of abstract figures that our thoughts, mental pictures, and sensations are; rather, imaginations have something real about them, inspirations something even more real. For inspirations do not just sit inside a being, they intone outward into the world and become music of the spheres, and create something in the world. Intuitions enter into the substance of the world and fill it. The Spirits of Personality send what the Saturn human is in deep sleep out into the world as intuition.

That's how it is today. But the Earth will undergo yet another development in the future. Then the intuitions of the Spirits of Personality will become denser and denser, ever denser and denser. Currently, they are extraordinarily thin figures; but as humankind leaves the fifth Earth age and enters the sixth and seventh, these intuitions will become increasingly dense. The Earth will pass away, and these intuitions will be preserved in the souls of the Spirits of Personality. But when Jupiter comes, these Spirits of Personality will ascend to the rank of Spirits of Form; and these impulses they have learned to make during the Earth epoch will be forms; and because they are Saturn forms they will be mineral forms. Hence at the end of the Earth epoch these intuitions will be dense cosmic impulses, and later, during Jupiter, forms.

But when they become forms on Jupiter, they will be its overall mineral foundations. During the developmental epoch following that of the Earth, the Spirits of Personality will exert a constant influx into our Saturn-human; they will attain the impulse that they then radiate out into the world; they will then emanate forms, but these forms are Jupiter; Jupiter will be nothing more and nothing less than these forms. Therefore, we bear a Saturn human within us, but by virtue of the fact that this Saturn-human is engaged in the activity of the Spirits of Personality, he is the seed for Jupiter. Jupiter will have to acquire everything it has in the way of its mineral foundation from what we bear within us as our Saturn human.

Now you have a view into the task of the Spirits of Personality during Earth evolution. However, you also see that if the matter is the way it is, we could develop only a mineral Jupiter through everything we develop in this manner. Moreover, this mineral Jupiter will be developed at all events. That has been seen to, and within the unfolding of the cosmos the prospect is quite certain that this mineral Jupiter will develop. Now, however, consider that this Jupiter would not have anything yet that corresponds to the plants, animals, or human beings; we ourselves as human beings could not exist on this Jupiter, because the hidden part within us, the Saturn human, would be transformed into Jupiter through dreaming during deep sleep of what earthly human beings form as images in their consciousness.

You see, under these circumstances Sun-human cannot accomplish anything real within us. The Archangels would get only as far as inspirations if everything went on as described up to now; and the mineral Jupiter would arise, and inspirations would well up and over this mineral Jupiter—dense inspirations, to be sure, but they would only wash over it. In order for something to come about that corresponds to our plant life, something must be added, and we need to develop something outside of the Earth human. That is simply what earthly humanity can never learn through the physical body: it is what we take in from Spiritual Science. Consequently, I want to call this human being the "spiritual-scientific human," though it might sound peculiar—spiritual-scientific human beings who rally, motivate, and stir themselves to what goes out beyond the Earth.

The Sun human within us really can do something with what we assimilate from Spiritual Science. The Sun human can transform the dull, plantlike images found in sleep into inspirations, and these will become increasingly dense over the whole course of the remaining Earth period, and will cause not only diffused harmony of the spheres to waft over Jupiter, but will also cause that harmony of the spheres to become certain plant growth, as also occurred with the plants on Earth. They were created by the harmony of the spheres and then drawn out by the light.

Thus we can say: If the only development that filled the Earth in the future were the development produced by the Earth itself, which does not lead to spiritual-scientific man, all that would be realized in the cosmos would be a mineral Jupiter. This is the tendency of all materialistic worldviews. The notion that Jupiter might also be of plant nature is an object of hatred in the deepest soul of the materialist; deep down inside, all they want is for Jupiter to be mineralic. And if today one searches through all materialistic science, the laboratories, chambers, and so on one finds that it is all working toward the creation of a mineral Jupiter. And without Spiritual Science, Jupiter would be dead slag, would actually not even contain plant growth.

What the current entities of the hierarchy of the Archangeloi can achieve, which corresponds to plant growth, is being prepared by us through our earnest involvement with Spiritual Science. So we can say: What Sun human experiences in a state of sleep will, by the conclusion of Earth evolution, become ripe to give off cosmic impulses for the plant growth on Jupiter through the Archangeloi.

So let's become aware now of the cosmic task of Spiritual Science: let us learn to know that with what we go about when we operate according to Spiritual Science we are really giving the beings of the hierarchy of the Archangeloi the possibility to carry a plant covering over to Jupiter. What the Sun human experiences within us through spiritual-scientific images, the Archangeloi can use to develop plant growth on Jupiter.

Then will come a time in Earth development when those who have become spiritual scientists will say: Spiritual Science is everything, Spiritual Science is the final salvation, and all those who undertake within their souls anything other than Spiritual Science are dreamers and romancers. Scientists of the spirit will speak of these others as materialists speak of us today. But in the same way as spiritual scientists stand over against the materialists, in the future there will be a small group of people who will surpass this Spiritual Science and go on to something that in the future will relate to Spiritual Science as something every bit as novel as Spiritual Science is in the eyes of mere external science. It will place even greater demands on human activity than Spiritual Science, which is found to be so inconvenient. It will be something that the dreamer in us, the Moon-human, will dream in an enormously more intensive way than the Sun human today can experience. But what the dreamer in us will be able to experience in a future epoch will be taken up and worked through by the entities from the hierarchy of the Angeloi, and they will carry it over to Jupiter in the same way and, based on the mineral and plant realms, will found something on Jupiter that corresponds to the animal realm. Thus we can say: The dream images of the Moon human (or of the dreamer within humanity) will become condensed imaginations for Jupiter— the basis for an animal realm through the Angeloi.

Then, finally, something else will come during Earth development. We see into a future in which we can have an inkling of something this wonderful. Only what comes then will be able to provide the seed for Earth humans to raise their realm on Jupiter and establish something new.

So what can be developed today with the help of the Earth human will progress further. Then, after the time when ever more and more novel things will have been developed, something will come that earthly humankind can now know of as the highest blossom of the spiritual unfolding of the Earth. And out of this knowledge of the highest blossom of the spiritual unfolding of the Earth, the thing will arise that will enable earthly humankind to progress on its own once it has reached the Jupiter stage. Thus through the soul content of the most highly developed human beings on Earth, the earthly human's mental pictures will become impulses for the development of humankind on Jupiter.

Our Spirits of Personality will by then have ascended to Spirits of Form; our Archangeloi will by then have ascended to Spirits of Personality; our Angeloi will have ascended to Archangeloi; the human being will have ascended to the rank of the Angeloi. Then, in the hierarchy of the Jupiter–Angeloi (which we ourselves will be), we will be able to continue the spiritual development of Jupiter out of the loftiest of the Earth-human's mental pictures. Then we will have in what is developed at the end of the Earth epoch something similar to what one had at the end of the Atlantean epoch for the sake of inaugurating a proper Earth-development.

Yes...out of the Earth's stones, out of the Earth's plants, out of the Earth's animals, out of the Earth's human physical bodies nothing new will arise; they are here in order to be sloughed off. But out of the Saturn-human you carry within, the mineral Jupiter will arise. As true as it is that the only thing of the hen walking around in front of you that will exist in the future daughter hen is the tiny seed in the egg, it is just as true that on the entire Earth there is nothing for the existence of the future Jupiter except the Saturn seeds living in the human body. That is all that will pass through the Pralaya to Jupiter; everything else will fall away from the physical Earth. (I am speaking now not of souls, but rather of the physical Earth.) And if anyone should harbor the notion that the physical Earth will also be transformed, then that is a nebulous notion; what is concrete is that everything will be atomized into the cosmos, with the exception of all these Saturn seeds that are taken up by the Archai and out of which the atoms, the mineral atoms of Jupiter will develop. I hinted at something similar many years ago in a small circle in Berlin, trying back then to explain what a childish notion it is to imagine the atoms of the Earth the way the physicists do. We must much rather imagine these atoms as the innermost element of the human being on the former Moon, but utilized by the entities who on the Moon were ahead of humanity and who transformed this innermost being of humanity into earthly atoms. Today it is no longer within the Saturn-human, but rather in the interior of the Earth.

Thus one of these atoms really is something compared to which the physicist's atom is an utterly childish notion. For this atom in fact came about in an enormously complicated way. Consider that the atom must arise out of what humankind developed on Saturn and was maintained throughout the Sun, Moon, and Earth epochs, and what then must be transformed by the Spirits of Personality, which on Jupiter will be Spirits of Form, into atoms for Jupiter. That's how complicated the cosmos is.

I have often referred to the mode of imagination on which these things are based—for example, let us assume it is 3:00 p.m. At that time, two people are standing next to each other; we join them and, say, person A is standing there with person B. Now we go away and tell this to a third person. However, let's assume that person A had been standing there from 9:00 a.m. until 3:00 p.m., whereas person B was walking around somewhere else and did not arrive until 3:00 p.m. Then we discover this—two people are standing next to each other. However, the one who has been there for six hours will be standing differently from the one who walked around the whole time. On the inside, the two are very different from each other, and this is the important matter; people are not the same, but vary.*

---

*   Steiner, *Kunst- und Lebensfragen im Lichte der Geisteswissenschaft*, lect. 5.

Appendix 20
Part 3, Chapter 11

Now our question concerning the beings, who will reach the human level on Jupiter, is connected in very truth with the deepest questions of humanity's Earth evolution. There is something in our Earth evolution that has always been a philosophical problem, namely the relation between human moral behavior and natural existence. As an earthly being, humanity has to decide to what extent it is the kind of being who is ruled by instincts, has to obey and satisfy them, and is at the mercy of natural instincts and their satisfaction, because the laws of nature simply insist on their being satisfied. That is one side of human nature. In this respect we may say: We do these things because we have to; we have to eat and we have to sleep. However, there is another realm of human conduct on this Earth, a realm in which we cannot say "must," since it would lose its whole significance if we were to use the word *must* here. This is the wide realm of *shall,* a realm in which we feel that we have to follow a purely spiritual impulse as distinct from instinct and everything arising out of ourselves on a natural level. "You shall" never speaks to us from our instincts, but directs us in a purely spiritual way. "You shall" comprises the realm of our moral obligations.

There are some philosophers who cannot find any connection between what is implied by the "you shall" and "you must." Today, this is almost bogged down in materialism, especially when moral life is concerned, and will become increasingly bogged down and would like to turn all "you shall" into "you must." We are heading for times where, in this respect, the turning of "you shall" into "you must" will be blazoned forth with a certain amount of pride, and actually called *psychology.* Terrible aspects present themselves when we look at what is developing in the field of criminal psychology. It is already clear that human beings are being thought of in a way that people do not ask whether they have overstepped a "you shall," but try to prove that they were driven to some destructive act through a need of their nature. Increasingly, strange experiments attempt to define crime merely as a particular case of illness. These things arise from a certain materialistic lack of clarity today regarding the relation of "you shall" to "you must."

What does "you shall" the categorical imperative, actually signify within the whole framework of human existence? Whoever obeys "you shall" is known to carry out a moral action. Whoever does not obey "you shall" commits an immoral action. This is, of course, a trivial truth. Now let us attempt to look at "moral" and "immoral," not just with regard to the outer maya of the physical plane, but also with regard to the truth and what actually lies behind physical maya. Here the moral element corresponding to the "you shall" appears to initiation science as something that hits you in the eye, spiritually, to put it rather crudely. If you look at a person (these truths, which the materialistic outlook detests, sometimes have to be stated), someone in certain temperature and weather conditions (we see this even better in horses, but we are not speaking about horses here), you will see that person breathing out and that breath becoming visible as vapor in the air. Obviously, insofar as materialistic science is concerned, that exhaled breath disperses and evaporates and has no further significance. However, it has significance for those who follow up the phenomena of life with initiation science. They see in the patterns of the breath the exact traces of the moral or immoral conduct of that person. One's moral or immoral behavior can be seen in the steamy breath, and the breath of a person who is morally inclined is very different from the breath of a person who is inclined to immorality.

You know, with regard to various things in the human being, the more delicate qualities can be seen only in the more delicate parts of the etheric and astral aura. However, a person's moral and immoral nature, in the ordinary sense of the word, is actually visible in the etheric-astral content of one's steamy breath. The physical part of it evaporates. But what is incorporated in it does not; it contains a genie, which, in the case of steamy breath, has a physical, an etheric, and an astral part, but the physical is not earthly, just watery. Something that has an extremely differentiated form can be seen in this breath.

Actions that arise from love show something different from those done, for instance, with enthusiasm, a creative urge, or an urge for perfection. Nevertheless, in every case, the form in the breath reminds us of beings that do not yet exist on Earth at all. These beings are a preparation for the ones that will reach their human stage on Jupiter. Their forms are very changeable and will pass through further changes in the future, for these beings are the first advance shadow images of the beings who will reach the human level on Jupiter.

In a certain way we also owe our existence to the exhalation of the Angeloi on the Moon, and it is one of the moving experiences of spiritual life to know that Jupiter human beings of the future will evolve out of what we breathe out in present ages. If we turn to the Bible with such knowledge in mind, and read the opening words, we can tell ourselves: Now we begin to understand what is meant when it says that the Elohim formed earthly human beings by breathing into them.

I will confess that I would never have understood the part about the Elohim breathing the life of the human being into the mouth and nose if I had not already known that the breath of earthly human beings also contains the first seminal beginnings of the beings who will become human on Jupiter. However, Jupiter human beings can arise only from the kind of breath that owes its existence to actions that obey "you shall" and are therefore moral actions.

Thus we see that, through our earthly morality, we take a creative part in the whole cosmic order. It is indeed a creative power, and we can see that Spiritual Science gives us a strong impulse for moral action by telling us that we are working against the creation of Jupiter human beings, if we do not act in a moral way on Earth. This gives morality a very real value and makes its existence worthwhile. Our human conduct is very strongly formed by what we acquire through Spiritual Science, especially as we become acquainted with real secrets regarding the cosmos.

I have already referred to similar matters and mentioned at various times that language also symbolizes humanity's own future creativity. I do not wish to dwell on this today though, but just wanted to show you, to begin with, what significance moral behavior has in the whole of the cosmos.

You could now ask: What about immoral behavior? It, too, comes to expression in the formation of the breath. However, immoral behavior imprints a demonic form on it. Demons are born through immoral human conduct. Let us look at the difference between the demons that arise through immoral behavior and spiritual beings—spiritual insofar as they have only a watery existence on Earth—created by moral actions.*

Appendix 21
Part 3, Chapter 11

One would have found little understanding when *An Outline of Esoteric Science* was written [1909], for the things of a more moral nature that are experienced in a study of the Sun incarnation.

When we go back to the time of the old Sun, we do not find there any story of the Temptation. We find the Sun still as a planet among the seven planets; we find Venus with Lucifer as her ruler; and these two, the Sun Spirit and the Venus Spirit—in other words, Christ and Lucifer—appear at first sight to be brothers. Only by straining to the utmost our powers of perception are we able to remark the difference between them. For the difference between Lucifer and Christ, in the time of old Sun is not apparent to an observation of their external being, it requires a more inward observation and study. It is indeed extraordinarily difficult to find outward means of demonstrating wherein the difference lies. Please, therefore, take what I am now going to say as no more than an attempt to characterize, as well as may be, the difference

---

* Steiner, *Art as Seen in the Light of Mystery Wisdom*, lect. 7.

that clairvoyant consciousness can perceive between Christ and Lucifer in the time of the ancient Sun.

When we direct our gaze now to Christ, now again to Lucifer, a new perception begins to dawn upon us. Lucifer, the ruler of Venus, appears in a form that is extraordinarily full of light—I mean, of course, spiritual light. We have the feeling that all the glow and brilliance we can ever experience on Earth in looking upon a manifestation of light is weak and dim in comparison with the majesty of Lucifer in the old Sun time. But then we notice, when we begin to perceive his intentions—and we are able to see through these—that Lucifer is a Spirit endowed in his very nature with infinite pride, so great a pride that it can prove a temptation to humanity. As is well known, there are things that up to a point are not temptations for humanity but become so when they grow majestic in their proportions, and pride is one of them. When pride is majestically great it tempts humanity. Lucifer's proud greatness, Lucifer's pride in his majestic figure of light—these contain a seductive element. "Unmanifest light," light that does not shine outwardly but has immense, strong power in itself—that Lucifer has in full measure. And how does the Christ figure look beside Lucifer? The Christ figure in the time of the old Sun—the Lord and Ruler of the Sun planet—is a picture of utmost devotion, entire devotion to all that is around him in the world. Whereas Lucifer looks like one who thinks only of himself—we are obliged to clothe it all in human words, notwithstanding the fact that these are quite inadequate—Christ appears as wholly given up, in devotion, to all that is around him in the great wide world.

The great wide world was not then as it is now. If we were to transport ourselves in these days to the present Sun, then, looking outward in all directions as from the center of a circle, we should perceive in the first place the twelve signs of the zodiac. These were not then externally visible, but twelve great Forms; twelve beings were present who let their words ring out from the depths of the darkness—outer space being of course not then filled with light.

What kind of words were these? They were words (again, word is only makeshift to indicate what is meant); they were words that told of primeval times, of times that even then were in a remote and ancient past. The twelve were twelve World Initiators. Today we behold standing in the directions of these twelve World-Initiators the twelve signs of the zodiac, but from them resounds, for the soul that is open to the whole world, the original being of the Unspoken Word of Worlds, which could take form in the twelve voices. While Lucifer alone (I must speak more in pictures; human words do not suffice at all), while Lucifer had the impulse to let stream out upon all things the light that was present in him and therewith come to a knowledge of all things, the Christ on the other hand, gave himself up to the Impression of this Word of the Worlds, received It in its fullness and entirety into himself, so that this Christ Soul was now the being who united within himself all the great secrets of the world that sounded into him through the inexpressible Word. Such is the contrast that presents itself—the Christ who receives the Word of the Worlds, and the proud Lucifer, the Spirit of Venus, who rejects the Word of the Worlds and wants to establish everything with his own light.

All subsequent evolution is a direct outcome of what Lucifer and Christ were at that time. The Christ being, as we saw, received into himself the great and all-embracing secrets of the worlds. The Lucifer being, having what I can only describe as "a proud figure of Light," lost thereby his kingdom, lost his Venus kingdom. On other grounds...the other Spirits of the Planets lost also their kingdoms, or rather changed their natures.... What is important for us here is the contrast between Christ and Lucifer. It came about that Lucifer lost more and more of his reign; the kingdom of Venus gradually fell away from him. Lucifer with his light became a dethroned ruler, and the planet Venus had thenceforward to do without a proper ruler and was consequently obliged to undergo a backward evolution. The Christ, however, had received the Word of the Worlds during the old Sun time, which has the quality of kindling itself to new light in the soul that received it. Thus, from that time forward the Word of the Worlds became in the Christ light, and the planet of which the Christ was ruler, the Sun, became the center of the whole planetary system, the other planets being brought into subjection to it. The same is true also of their spiritual rulers.

We must let these scenes live before us, we must learn to see the divergence that came about during the old Sun time between the path of Lucifer and the path of Christ. Lucifer went downward; he had to remain behind in his evolution, and he remained behind also during the Moon time. Christ went forward. The Christ spirit, the Sun spirit, became a spirit evolving ever forward until at length he was able to appear on Earth in the form we have often described. Through his devotion to the World-all, through his having received and identified himself with the divinely creative, inexpressible Word, through his having rejected every sort of pride and put always in its place devotion to the Word of the Worlds—Christ, from being ruler of a single planet, as he was in the ancient Sun time, became ruler from the Sun over all the planets, the other planets being reckoned as part of the realm of the Sun. When you know this...you will not feel it as a contradiction that Christ is spoken of in those lectures as a Sun spirit of a higher kind than the spirits of the planets. For there of course we were speaking of the present day. Christ is far above the other planetary spirits. He is the spirit of the Sun. Here, however, where we are not merely describing how the individual planetary bodies are quickened to life by their spirits, but where our task is above all to describe the several states of consciousness, we have to show how Christ through his own special character and nature has, during the course of the evolution that has taken place between old Sun and the present time, passed through an upward evolution, and from having been a spirit who was of like nature with the planetary spirits has become the ruler, or regent, of the whole solar system.*

---

* Steiner, *Man in the Light of Occultism, Theosophy, and Philosophy*, lect. 10.

Appendix 22
Part 4, Chapter 5

The molecular structure of water

Based on the hydrogen molecule (H_2), one interprets the structure of the water molecule so that the electron shell of the hydrogen atom carries only a single electron, but can be saturated by two electrons. In the hydrogen molecule, the two electron shells interpenetrate, so that the shell is the bearer of two electrons. This partial overlapping of the two electron shells, through which a molecule arises, is called "covalent chemical compounding." By contrast, the oxygen atom is much more complicated in its construction. In addition to the spherically symmetrical orbit of the electrons, there are also three so-called "p orbits," two of which likewise are occupied only by a single electron. This enables these two electrons to overlap with the corresponding electrons from the two hydrogen atoms, as well. Extremely close analyses demonstrate that both the orbits of the oxygen atom, which orbits are occupied by a single electron, oppose each other at a ninety-degree angle of activity. If they in turn compound with the hydrogen atoms, both hydrogen atoms form an angle with their mass centers in relation to the oxygen atom, and at the corner of this angle an oxygen atom is situated.

Through additional mutual influence exerted by the nuclei on each other, and on the electron orbits that have no part in the bond, the mass centers shift into a position relative to one another that is different from the one they had assumed previously with the oxygen atom. The mass points of the hydrogen atoms now form an angle of 105 degrees relative to one another. Thus they form corners of a tetrahedron, whose other two corners use the pair of electrons not involved in the bonding to form the other two electron orbits of the oxygen atom. The nucleus itself of the oxygen atom sits in the middle of the tetrahedron, and the hydrogen nuclei, both of the molecule itself and of the neighboring one are located at the four corners of the tetrahedron. The bonds' pairs of electrons are all shifted toward the oxygen. This causes the inner area of the oxygen atom to have a somewhat stronger negative charge, and that of the hydrogen atoms a more positive one. Thus within the water molecule there is a relatively high electrical polarity: it is a tiny dipole.

How are these atoms connected structurally in the ice crystal? Neutron analysis of heavy-water ice shows that each single oxygen atom is bound by four hydrogen atoms. Two hydrogen atoms each are closer to the oxygen atom, and form the water molecule with a tetrahedral arrangement of the mass points. Two of the four corners of the tetrahedron are occupied by the two hydrogen atoms. The two electron pairs of the oxygen atoms, which have no part in the covalent bonding of the hydrogen atoms, then move in the tetrahedron corners' other two directions, attracting even the protons of the neighboring molecule's hydrogen atoms as they do so. So that these protons themselves are caught in the area of these electrons' cloud orbit, and so form a bonding bridge to the two hydrogen atoms of the neighboring molecule. Such a bridge is called "a hydrogen bridge." This causes each hydrogen atom to be doubly bonded, once in covalent bonding to the oxygen atom it belongs to, once through bridge bonding, via a hydrogen atom, with the neighboring oxygen atom. Thus each oxygen atom is bonded with four hydrogen atoms. By way of bridge bonding, the proton core of the hydrogen immerses itself into the electron clouds of the oxygen.

We have now shown that the oxygen atoms themselves are arranged in hexagonal rings, as a result of these complicated bonding circumstances. According to the conceptions of the mineralogists and physicists, this structure is expressed in the crystal form of ice. All hydrogen bridges are formed in the ice-state. In the gaseous vapor-state, all hydrogen bridges are dissolved and the atoms are only arranged by molecules—i.e., the molecules among themselves without matrix bonding. This means, though, that between the vapor and the ice states, that is, in water proper, both phases can be present in different quantities and in alternating circumstances.

Therefore, hydrogen-bridge bonding is a property that belongs to the sub-sensory atomic traces of the hydrogen entity. This subatomic property of hydrogen places the lightest of all substances, hydrogen at the disposal of the constitutional process of water. Water as an entity takes hold of this matrix, which comes from hydrogen, in order that it may manifest in all its physical, chemical, and biological properties as a mobile medium. By the hydrogen entity's withdrawing itself as physical manifestation, it relinquishes to water the matrix of cohesiveness, adhesion, capillarity, and surface tension. Water owes the possibility for these properties to manifest to the matrix of its hydrogen bridges.

The "oxygen atom" (what remains of the oxygen entity when it withdraws from the sensory and passes into the entity's subatomic underground) is the foundation of water's readily reactive capability—that is, for its vivacity.

Appendix 23
Part 4, Chapter 3

Researchers of the mineral realm encountered crystal forms, and thus these structures' polyhedric nature, very early on, when methods were sought for an analytic mastery of these figures. The five so-called platonic solids have been known since ancient times (tetrahedron, hexahedron, octahedron, dodecahedron, icosahedron). Crystallography was developed via the geometry of the crystal figures' symmetric structure.

The result was the seven crystal systems (cubic, tetragonal, trigonal, hexagonal, orthorhombic, monoclinic, triclinic) with the 32 classes of crystals. On the other hand, the system of the surface indices was developed. The angles formed by a crystal's surfaces were measured and were indexed according to the imaginary axes geometrically thought into the crystal and intersected by the surfaces. According to whether a surface intersects this imagined axis on the right or the left, in the front or the back, this point of intersection receives an index with a plus sign or a minus sign for the respective axis. The distance from these points of intersection between surface and axis to the center of the axis is indexed using whole numbers and with a set axis sequence. Based on the indices, it is thus possible to determine which axis is intersected by a given surface, and where. If the surface lies parallel to an axis, this axis receives the index zero. And the flatter the angle at which the axis is intersected, the larger its index. But the indexing of a surface indirectly determines all the other surfaces belonging to a certain polyhedric figure containing the indexed surface (pyramid, prism, and so on). In the case of the quartzes, four axes are projected into their ditrigonal crystals: the main axis and the three secondary axes that intersect it perpendicularly. This is how it comes that quartz crystals are assigned four indices.

Appendix 24
Part 4, Chapter 4

At this point, we must reflect once more on the nature of Apocalyptic vision. At the beginning and the end of the Bible, we have two books that deal with facts above the level of rational perception. In Genesis, the Bible begins with a suprasensory vision. Genesis springs from a spiritual retrospect; for it is not possible by outward methods to look into the ages long past—the first stages of evolution—because creation began before the material phase came into existence. To the retrospect of Genesis is now added the prophetic prevision of the Apocalypse, which reveals the secrets of the future. The retrospect of Genesis springs is nothing more than an inverted prophecy. But before the prophetic vision of the Seer John comes to the point of revealing the laws and secrets of the future in the Seven Seals and

Trumpets and Vials of Wrath, it first plunges once again retrospectively into the very beginning of evolution. It is only from this retrospect that the prophetic prevision is brought forth. We might regard the fourth and fifth chapters of the Apocalypse as a New Testament story of the Creation, a New Testament Genesis. Here the picture of the sea of glass may serve as a key. We witness a definite moment in the evolution of the world. Eons of evolution have already run their course in the spiritual sphere.

Now the first germination of physical comes, corporeal existence. Out of the all-enveloping spiritual sphere of the heavenly ocean the material world, the prima materia still pure and virginal, begins to crystallize. The world of matter is born in the form of shining crystals. In the picture of the sea of glass the Seer beholds the moment of birth, the *status nascendi* of the physical world. He is a witness of the beginning of cosmic incarnation. Why does the sight of a rock crystal or an amethyst give us such unusual delight? These starlike forms fascinate us, as if they were not of this world at all. Every crystal is, so to speak, a reminiscence of the original condition of our earthly world. Earthly, bodily existence had its origin in just such transparent crystal purity. But in the course of its evolution it has not been able to preserve its original crystal clarity. Much turbidity and loss of form has overpowered the world of earthly matter. Today every snow-crystal that we admire in its starlike structure before it melts is like a greeting from the sphere from which earthly things once rose as radiant, strong, paradisiac *prima materia*.

The moment of cosmic evolution, recognizable in the sea of glass, signifies at the same time a stage of development of the human being. Humanity already existed in the pre-physical eons, but was as yet like a drop of water in the sea, completely contained within the divine womb of higher beings. There was as yet no individuality. At the moment when the crystal heavens formed themselves from the ocean of the Spirit as the first spherical seed of physical existence, a first inkling of individual corporeality, and hence of future consciousness of self and spiritual identity, may have passed through the human soul. The sea of glass rose as a mirror. The transparent cosmos formed something corresponding to the foil behind the glass; something that turned the glass into a mirror. The very first reflection of himself, a first consciousness of his individuality, confronted humanity in the picture of the crystal. Hence a crystal speaks to us not only of the primal beginnings of the material world, but also of the first tentative sense of ego-consciousness. And it suggests that we become true bearers of an immortal Ego when the crystal clearness of spiritual thought can dwell within us, and radiate out from us like a star. Crystal clear thoughts in the human mind correspond to the crystals in Nature.

This vision of creation seen by John appeared to the poetic gaze of Novalis, the German poet and contemporary of Goethe, as the city of Arcturus, which he describes in the ninth chapter of his novel *Heinrich von Ofterdingen*. It is a wonderful poetic parallel to the Revelation of St. John. The city, with its houses and palaces and figures consisting purely of ice-crystals, lies in a milky-blue haze. "All this was mirrored in the glassy sea surrounding the mountain on which the city stood." Distant sounds were heard in the city of Arcturus, like the murmur of creation from the cosmic smithy in which the Gods were putting the world together: "Nothing could be clearly distinguished; yet strange noises could be heard over here, as if from some huge workshop in the distance."

Like the sea of glass, the rainbow that the Seer perceives around the heavenly throne is a sign of the spiritual origin of Creation. When a rainbow is formed in the sky today, it is as though the world remembers its creation out of light.*

---

*   Bock, *The Apocalypse of St. John.*

Appendix 25
Part 2, Chapter 8 and Part 4, Chapter 1

A table is shown on page 412 that contains the correspondences between various areas of existence and the creative activity of the twelve "world-initiators" (CW 137). They are the beings whose leading four spirits appear in images of the four living animals to the prophet Ezekiel and St. John, the author of the Apocalypse. They are—each accompanied by two others—the hierarchical reality of what comes to expression physically in the pictures of the fixed stars as the zodiac (the "Cherub of Leo"—accompanied by the "Cherub of Cancer" and the "Cherub of Virgo," and so on). In the table, some of the areas of the world are listed in which the creating influence of the cherubim reveals itself, as reported by Rudolf Steiner from his spiritual-scientific research. The correspondences are taken from the following sources:

1. For the precious stones, first row: Steiner, unpublished lecture of October 9, 1906 in Berlin. For the second row: The breastplate of the high priest, according to Moses.
2. For the parts of the body: Steiner, *Man in the Light of Occultism, Theosophy, and Philosophy*, lecture of Jan. 1, 1921. Steiner, *Cosmosophy*, vol. 2, lecture of Oct. 28, 1921.
3. For the senses: Contributions to the complete edition of Rudolf Steiner. Rudolf Steiner-Nachlassverwaltung, Dornach, no. 34, 1971 and no. 58 / 59, 1977.
4. For the virtues: Steiner, *Guidance in Esoteric Training*.
5. For the worldviews: Steiner, *Human and Cosmic Thought*.
6. For the speech sounds: Steiner, *Eurythmy as Visible Speech*, lecture of July 8, 1924.

The abstract concepts and designations in the table below are no more than an arid skeleton. Taking any of the individual names or concepts as one's point of departure, it is possible to work and to live

Zodiac	The 12 Stones	Human Member	Senses	Virtues	Worldviews	Speech Sounds
Aries	amethyst onyx	head	"I"-sense "I"-sense	veneration power of sacrifice	Idealism	W
Taurus	hyacinth carnelian	larynx	thought sense word sense	balance progress	Rationalism	R
Gemini	chrysoprase topaz	shoulders	word sense warmth sense	perseverance faithfulness	Mathematism	H
Cancer	gold topaz chalcedony	thorax	sense of hearing sense of taste	selflessness catharsis	Materialism	V F
Leo	beryl blood jasper	heart	sense of warmth thought sense	compassion freedom	Sensualism	T
Virgo	chrysolite emerald	abdomen	sense of sight sense of sight	courtesy tactfulness of the heart	Phenomenalism	B
Libra	sard aquamarine	hips	sense of taste sense of touch	contentedness equanimity	Realism	C
Scorpio	sardonyx amethyst	womb	sense of smell sense of hearing	patience insight	Dynamism	Z
Sagittarius	emerald hyacinth	upper arms thighs	sense of balance life sense	control of thought sense for truth	Monadism	G
Capricorn	chalcedony chrysolite	elbows knees	sense of movement sense of movement	courage redemptive strength	Spiritualism	L
Aquarius	sapphire ruby	lower arms lower legs	life sense sense of balance	discretion meditation	Pneumatism	M
Pisces	heliotrope sapphire	hands feet	sense of touch sense of smell	magnanimity love	Psychism	N

one's way ever-more deeply into the respective fields of experience in the sensory world or the spirit and soul spheres; into the respective virtues and worldviews; into the spheres of power of the speech sounds. Then, the entity of the Cherub will appear to the sensation living in the background of the mutually corresponding areas, actively shaping and enlivening within them. Only this kind of effort will import life into this scaffolding of names and concepts.

Appendix 26
Part 4, Chapter 4

"The Twelve Precious Stones: Sardonyx"
Conceptional Models of the Origin of the Agates

Water or solutions of salt and acid possess a certain dissolving power for mineral components such as SiO_2. This solubility is dependent on the solution's pressure, temperature, and composition, in particular with respect to the degree of their acidity (that is, their pH value). As a rule, it can be said that the higher the temperature, pressure, and pH value are, the higher the solubility. The influences are considerable: in a neutral solution with a temperature of 10° C, about 0.01% of SiO_2 is dissolved (= 100 milligrams per kilogram of water), at 700° C and 7 kilobars of H_2O pressure, though, about two percent.

Agate substance usually fills the available hollow space completely. It cannot come about in a single act of filling and crystallization. One must much rather expect a rhythmic process that is repeated many times: the hollow space is filled with as SiO_2-rich solution, which may have been over-saturated; through changes in the physical (pressure, temperature) or chemical (pH value, accompanying substances in the solution) conditions, over-saturation occurs, followed by precipitation; the depleted solution is then replaced by a fresh one, and the process starts over again. However, it is not the case that each filling leaves behind a layer of agate; in such case, large geodes would have to demonstrate thick layers and small ones thin layers, which also would become thinner from the exterior to the interior; and this phenomenon does not occur.

Furthermore, the layers would also be much too thin if they were deposited in a one-time filling process: a solution capable of depositing 300 milligrams of SiO_2 per kilogram of water (even this presupposes a significant over-saturation) can, in a one-time filling of a spherical hollow 1 dm in diameter, only leave behind a layer that is 2 µm thick (1 µm = 1/1000 of a millimeter). Normal agate layers are many times this thick.

Considerable quantities of fluids are necessary in order to fill in a geode: to fill completely a hollow 1 dm. in diameter, 4,700 liters of the solution mentioned above with the precipitation potential of 300 milligrams per kilogram of water would be required. That means the rock complex for the formation of agate would have to be flooded with gigantic quantities of solution if every portion of solution were expected to fill in a single geode. It is, however, almost certain that once this same solution has left the hollow it again accumulates new substances under altered chemical conditions, and is once more capable of filling hollows. Thus, the amounts of solution required would not be as great as in the calculation example above, if the repetition of the dissolving and depositing processes were not taken into account. Nevertheless, considerable involvement of fluid phases ultimately leading to a general hydrothermal transformation of the agate's origination must be expected. The original mineral components are for the most part destroyed in the process and replaced by others: and just this is what actually can be observed in agate geodes.

Thus for the process of agate precipitation the following model can be developed: Solutions containing dissolved SiO_2 (along with other substances, of course) enter the hollows of the rock. Through alterations in the physical and chemical conditions (such as decreases in temperature, pressure or pH value), these solutions reach their SiO_2

saturation point. If these changes in external conditions are drastic, the precipitation occurs as an amorphic SiO_2 suspension, which in suitable places (such as hollows) can densify to become SiO_2 gel and be deposited. Repeated phases of highly concentrated solutions lead to the formation of layers of SiO_2 gel. In calmer phases, this amorphous, watery mass is converted into chalcedony and a similar fibrous microcrystalline variety of low quartz (German *quarzin*). Through loss of water, a reduction of volume takes place, leading to the formerly compact gel layers now becoming porous, which in turn is particularly important for the coloration of the agate. It is not yet fully clear why some layers crystallize into strictly parallel-fibrous aggregates and others become a tangled confusion of rays or crystallize in grainy form. Variations in thermal balance likely play the main role here.

If the carrier of the SiO_2 components is a gaseous or a critical-state vaporous phase, the precipitation out of this phase occurs absent of the influence of the force of gravity. Not only the floor, but also the walls and the ceiling of a hollow space can be coated with the layers of gel. The precipitated layers trace the contours of the hollow. This accounts for the usually strictly concentrically shelled buildup of agates. Around the flow channels, stalactite-like studs or cones frequently form, which are hollow inside and grow through repeated layering on the outside. The entrances of such flow channels can be recognized as "spiracles" in the finished agate. If the lithotomic position is favorable, "stalactites" of this kind appear as tubular cross sections embedded in the agate mass (tube agates).

On account of their isotropic character, vapor phases (above or below the critical phase temperature) always lead to the formation of layers of this kind, which are more or less uniformly shaped on all sides. On the other hand, if a liquid is the carrier of the dissolved components, particles that precipitate in it are sedimented under the influence of the force of gravity. In this case, it is only on the floor of a hollow that a sediment consisting of gel particles precipitates when SiO_2, in suspension, concentrates to become a gel. This sediment fills in a relief that is more or less present, and forms entirely level layers, which also run perpendicularly to the direction of the force of gravity. This is how the sard layers in agates originate, which are of such outstanding significance for use as pictorial objects.

In agates displaying a buildup of concentric shell-like and level layers, both a thermometer and a level are built in: the parallel layers must have formed at temperatures below the critical temperature of the solution (in the case of pure water this temperature would be 374.1° C, but it can shift in the presence of dissolved substances), the concentric ones above this temperature. The parallel layers correspond to the orientation of the horizon at the time the depositing occurrs; if they are slanted now, it can be assumed that a tectonic shift in the rock unit took place and the movement can be reconstructed. The hollows in agate druses are frequently furnished with most recent form "crystal quartz" tips. The latter certainly never went through a preliminary gel phase, but rather crystallized directly from the fluid containing SiO_2. This is possible only if the over-saturations were not too great, that is, if the concentration of the solution was only slightly greater than that necessary for the precipitation of quartz. One almost always finds such crystals set in walls surrounding hollow spaces, which in turn point to a deposit that took place in the absence of the influence of the force of gravity. In this case, one has to do either with deposits from water vapor (which can absorb only minute quantities of SiO_2), or from weakly concentrated fluids, which must have filled the entire hollow. Either case would have been possible at temperatures in the vicinity of the critical state, but also well below it. Most agates demonstrate this temperature sequence, some even in multiple cycles, which would indicate rhythmic temperature changes caused by such things as the influx of high-temperature aqueous solutions from different hot-stone complexes.*

---

* Egon Althaus, "Agate: Its Makeup and Origin," *Lapis*, 12, Munich, 1979.

Appendix 27
Part 2, Chapter 6

One of the fundamental insights of Rudolf Steiner's Spiritual Science is the fact that the materialities and forces that are the actual bearers of everything alive within the realms of nature, are autonomous. Steiner borrows the term "etheric forces" from older terminologies, such as that of the ancient Greeks. Etheric forces are spiritually active forces of life. Their exact investigation in all phenomenological manifestations of life was initiated by Goethe in connection with the plant realm; suprasensory observations and perceptions of the activities of this world of forces lead to more detailed differentiation.

In answer to the question of what prerequisites forces of this kind must meet, it should be said that there are four of them:

These life forces must be able to permeate all material substance completely and from within, and in the course of this permeation to take hold of the substance and, in doing so, to move it in directions that run counter to the entropic law of physics, so that even inorganic substances no longer adhere to purely inorganic/chemical laws, but rather can be bundled to form the complicated materialities of the kind found in plant, animal, and human protein. This aspect of the total ability to permeate and take hold of the material world from within is the characteristic of the warmth ether.

Once matter has been taken hold of, it can be chemically united, synthesized, and transformed in a way that enables the highly complex arrangements of organic chemistry to exist next to inorganic chemical behavior. This is the activity of the so-called chemical or tone ether, which in turn subjects itself to the impulses of the living being. In this way, not only is protein created specific to species and, in the case of the human being, specific to the individual, but all other living substances are created as well.

The materiality taken hold of and transformed in this way is then differentiated and structured by means of cell growth, tissue formation, and organ formation, to become an expression of the organism, the figure and the countenance of living beings. These formative, organizing forces correspond to the so-called light ether.

Ultimately, however, life is possible only if it undergoes development, that is to say, if it receives an impulse, both from species to species and within a single living being itself, that enables its development, its build-up followed by its decline, a state of decay, and finally, the individual death of the single living being. The carrier of the forces that actually makes for the very life impulse itself in becoming and decline all the way down to the single living being—this impulse-giving force is the so-called life ether.

These four ethers form within the cosmos a realm of their own, the realm of the world-ether. And as on one hand the living entities constitute their respective physical manifestations from the sphere of the material substances, on the other hand they do so out of the sphere of the ether forces and ether substances.

Rudolf Steiner's teachings on the ether have been taken up by many of his students and verified in detail.

Appendix 28
Part 4, Chapter 4

The Natural-Scientific View of the Diamond's Origin

The origin of the diamond, this in many regards most extraordinary and most interesting of all minerals, has been disputed for many years, and remains full of riddles and mysteries even today. At any rate, it is fascinating to note that it is precisely the enclosures in diamonds that have been able to make a revealing contribution to the explanation of the diamond's origin. This is because the analysis of the syngenetic mineral enclosures and their trace elements give valuable clues to the material composition of the magma from which the bedrock was formed, which must have been an iron-poor peridotic—and hence ultra-basic—magma containing chrome and including additives of sulfur, titanium and carbon dioxide. It is in this magma's equilibrous molten state that diamond was able to grow in a hovering and stable way.

Today's generally acknowledged interpretation of the diamond's origin is based on knowledge of the fact that the genetically ideal pressure and temperature conditions of between 50,000 and 120,000 atmospheres and approximately 1,300° C are not possible at very great depths, and that they can only be expected to hold in intra-crustal areas. During a relatively early phase, that is, in the Precambium, or more than 600 million years ago, basaltic magmas ascended from the depths into sub-crustal zones and formed extended but local magma sources in which, gradually, dense olivine aggregates accumulated.

In the second and much later phase—that is, as magma mass under enormous pressure ascended within the crevices and of the actual crust of the Earth—a differentiation occurred in the proper basal depth magma, and a transformation took place in the clumps of olivine in eclogite rock containing the mineral components olivine, diopside, and anorthite. In the presence of the great pressure that held sway, the anorthite was in many places transformed into pyrope garnet. It must have been in the wake of this unusual metamorphosis of peridote into eclogite, which presumably ran its course during the Carbon era, that is, about 270 to 300 million years ago, that the formation of the diamonds took place, presumably in periodic spurts. The diamond must have crystallized out of fluid carbon dioxide, stemming from processes as yet unknown. It is possible that carbon was released from the reduction of carbon dioxide, in which process the iron sulfide pyrrhotite present in both the external and internal paragenesis of the diamond, might have acted as the reduction agent. Accordingly, the eclogite rock involved in the origin of the diamonds could be understood as the magmatic high-pressure derivatives of previously formed peridotites (olivine rock), and diamond could be understood as an accompanying product of transformation, with the minerals closest to its inner and outer paragenesis—olivine, diopside, pyrope garnet, and, as well, probably chromite—arising simultaneously with the metamorphosis as its twin brothers and sisters.

Once more, in the course of many millions of years the diamonds were transported along with their upward bedrock in sporadically triggered eruptions and catapulted above the Earth's surface in volcanic eruptions, and in the course of these events a new breccia-like clastic rock—kimberlite—developed, in which the diamonds became embedded as accessory minerals in part singly, in part preserved in remains of eclogite. These volcanic eruptions, which carried diamonds to the Earth's surface and hence into our hands, represent the third phase of the diamonds' evolution; they occurred, at least in South Africa, 140 million years ago during the Cretaceous age. Thus the diamond, with its informative mineral inclusions stemming from unattainable depths of the Earth, depths much greater than the chambers in which other precious stones were formed, arose from a foreign rock world in order by means of its mineral inclusions to bring us information about those nonrecurring processes that in times long past caused its birth.

From these times other guest minerals stem, which were created under especially high pressure, such as coesite, a variety of normal quartz. It is also from great depths that minerals containing the metal chrome come, an element characteristic of rock at great depths. Conspicuously chrome-rich minerals such as chrome diopside, chrome enstatite, chromite, and the pyrope garnet, which is colored red by chrome, are telling for diamond inclusions. But the fact that traces of chrome (0.07 percent) have also been proved in olivine contained in diamond enclosures, whereas the olivines occurring in the external paragenesis of the diamond in kimberlite are chrome-free, this fact provides further proof that the diamond can never have originated within kimberlite. The diamond is utterly devoid of vacuoles. Evidently, it originated under growth conditions that allowed no syngenetic crystallization gaps. In the deep magmatic sphere in which the diamonds were formed, there were also presumably no fluids capable of enclosure, thus possibly no water either, as the diamond's mineral relatives, as identified by its syngenetic enclosures, are all water-free minerals.

The mineral enclosures in diamonds came about in all three "generations" of enclosure formation: before, during, and after the growth of the host diamond.

However, any protogenetic enclosures have yet to be identified with certainty—with the exception of self-enclosures consisting of smaller diamonds. To be sure, these "guest diamonds" are in part syngenetic, but the majority of them are surely protogenetic—that is, they were received as "survivors" of an older generation by a descendant generation that grew in a younger phase of diamond formation. From this it becomes evident that the evolution of diamonds in the bedrock was repeated multiple times. Oftentimes, crystals of an earlier diamond formation phase were able to become seeds for the formation of larger diamonds in later crystallization sequences.

Among the guest diamonds that with certainty are also protogenetic are the ones that display traces of mechanical damage. Here one often sees otherwise well-formed small crystals—e.g. the double pyramid octahedral shape, on which a corner has been chipped off. Such damage to small and extremely hard minerals bears witness to virulent discharges of energy—of an unknown kind—in the diamond's formational environment, and are clear documentation of the fact that chipped inclusion-diamonds crystallized before the host diamonds did—thus, protogenetically.

Most inclusion minerals are syngenetic, and the quantity of these minerals syngenetically received by the diamonds is remarkably great. Those known with certainty, listed by frequency of occurrence, are:

olivine
garnet
chromite
diamondlike chrome diopside
chrome enstatite
pyrrhotite
pyrite
pentlandite
ilmenite
rutile
coesite
bronzite

These inclusion minerals grew in large part in recognizably syntactical manner on a diamond's crystal surfaces and were later grown over by it. As this happened, certain of the guest crystals' surfaces throve on preferred surfaces of the host crystal, on which the rhythm of the distance between the atoms corresponds in the crystal matrix. It often occurs that crystal surfaces of the host diamond were "settled" by numerous guests, until the host's growth caught up with, and enclosed them.

Quite often, guest minerals that settled on host crystals, syntactically during the latter's growth, display peculiar contortions in their crystal habit. For instance, after their growth on a diamond, olivines, and garnets, which normally develop into prismatic or roundish crystal figures, are stretched in directions that lie at a fully unnatural diagonal slant to their normal growth. In this crystal habit, they make a completely alien impression on the observer acquainted with their natural growth figuration. This happens most with the lattice-shaped garnets. One might say that the host diamond became a kind of Procrustes bed on which its guest lengthened abnormally (Procrustes is a mythological figure who was similarly "lengthened against his will" in his host's bed).

This peculiarity regarding mineral inclusions in diamonds is a mosaic stone that contributes to completing the picture that solves the riddle of the diamonds' origin. Due to the loss of olivine's, garnet's and chromite's natural figuration, caused by their forced elongation, they were falsely identified for a long time. The olivines mentioned above all assumed a pseudo-tetragonal crystal form that reminds one of zircon's form (zircon grows chiefly in prismatic columns with a quadratic cross section). Thus, earlier it was believed that zircons belonged to the world of diamond enclosures. But no zircons can be detected when modern methods are used.

A series of inclusions in the form of the lining of tension cracks also developed in the diamond, the most significant of which are graphite scales along with graphite, pyrrhotite and pentlandite. Furthermore, ferrous precipitations and foreign minerals occur in epigenetic cracks and crevices, which were deposited by xenophysical solutions. Important epigenetic guest minerals are calcite, goethite, hematite, quartz, kaolinite, pyrrhotite, pentlandite, rutile, sellaite, and xenotime. Finally, through erosion processes, even older syngenetic inclusion minerals were transformed epigenetically into different minerals; thus one finds accumulations of mica (phlogopite, chlorite) and serpentine, which arose out of olivine and garnet.

Finally, in addition to these recognizable inclusions of minerals from all generations, there are unknown microcrystalline substances enclosed in diamonds. Like fog, they cloud the stone's heart and seem to hover inside it like a cross. Oftentimes these fogs fill out the entire host crystal. They could be dense concentrations of sub-microscopically small olivines.*

---

*   Gübelin, *Innenwelt der Edelsteine. Urkunde aus Raum und Zeit* [The inner world of the precious stones: Primeval document in space and time].

Appendix 29
Part 4, Chapter 4

Research conducted in the 1970s, pertaining to the gold deposits of the so-called Witwatersrand Formation in South Africa, has brought completely novel aspects to bear on the origin of gold deposits on Earth.

On one of the Earth's most ancient cratons (continental bedrock), the so-called Kaapvaal craton, which makes up the southern and southeastern portion of South Africa, there lie three series of Precambrian sludge sediments. They fill flat primeval troughs or basins, 2,000 to 4,000 meters in depth, located on the crystalline bedrock. The middle one of these three series of rock is the so-called Witwatersrand Series, also known as the Witwater Reef. This trough lies approximately between Johannesburg-Delmas in the northeast and Welkom in the southwest, and Heidelberg in the southeast and Klerksdorp on the Vaal River in the northwest. Today, the Vaal River passes through it, flowing from east to west.

This ancient hollow 300 kilometers long and 80 kilometers wide is surrounded by a series of the bedrock's older granite domes, and fractured in the middle by the Vredefort Ring granite. Some of these granites are located beneath sediments. The Precambrian rock series of the Witwater Reef itself is also covered by younger deposits that filled the basin to the top. The series itself surfaces near Johannesburg as Witwatersrand. It was here that gold was discovered in 1885.

In this hollow, there was originally an inland sea, probably consisting of warm freshwater, into which mainly sands, but also clays and other substances, were washed and deposited by rapidly flowing rivers from the surrounding granite caves to the north, west and south. A distinction is made between the "lower Witwatersrand" (divided into Hospital Hill, Government Reef, and the Jeppestown Series), and the "upper Witwatersrand" (Main-Bird and Kimberley-Elsburg Series). The lower series are rock, baked hard into conglomerates and quartzites and containing uranium; the upper series are quartzites and conglomerates containing gold and uranium.

Until recently, there were two theories concerning the origin of the gold: The hydrothermal origin: the gold supposedly streamed in and was deposited in hot solutions from the volcanism of the surrounding mountains. However, this explanation is contradicted by the fact that the gold never occurs in crystallized form.

The gold was purportedly washed in by the rivers as placer gold in nuggets. But this explanation is contradicted by the fact that the gold occurs exclusively in minute structures invisible to the naked eye (particle size: 0.004–0.075 millimeters), that it never forms the nuggets worn down by rolling that are characteristic for gold found in placer deposits.

Since only geomechanical explanations were available, it was presumed that the deposits existing today were formed through mechanical transport and depositing, followed by metamorphosis.

To be sure, it was long known that at certain levels of conglomeration zones gold occurs accompanied by a coal formation consisting of tiny coal structures and called "carbon." De Kock, for instance, says (1964): "The carbon-rich seam varies in thickness from 76 mm. (3 in.) down to a mere streak. Detailed examination has shown the 'carbon' to be a form of hydrocarbon, and that it is often columnar, with the columns at right angles to the bedding" (quoted from Truswell, p. 37).

In the meantime, more advanced possibilities of examination technology have yielded entirely surprising research results. It has been shown that the "carbon" represents the charred or carbonized petrefacts of minute Precambrian plants. It revealed itself as a kind of to date entirely unknown "lichen"—that is, symbionts of fungus and algae that grew on the banks and the floor of the quartz sand deposits to become entire lawns of columnar-shaped plants. These plants took in colloidal gold existing in the warm waters of the primeval sea and secreted them organically into and around their fungal hyphae, so that the gold that was deposited replicated the forms of the plant organs all the way down to their cellular structure. The results of this most recent research were published in a summarizing article by D. K. Hallbauer, "The Plant Origin of the Witwatersrand: 'Carbon.'" Hallbauer states:

> Due to the resurgent interest in the distribution of gold value in the reef masses, in the morphology of gold particles and in the role played by the "coal" in the concentration of gold, a large portion of the work in the Chamber of Mines research laboratories has been dedicated to the examination of the peculiarity of the coal, or the thucholite, as it is often called.

Thucholite (named after the constitutive elements thorium—Th, uranium—U, carbon—C, hydrogen—H and oxygen—O) is an asphalt-like substance that is combustible and whose very abundant ash (5-60%) consists mainly of UO (UO and/or UO_2 is uranium pitchblende = uraninite; according to Klockmann 1978, pp. 545–548).

This "coal" or thucholite was then subjected to exact morphological, chemical and electron microscopic examinations. In the image portion, photos are reproduced from the aforementioned publication by Hallbauer. Plate 38 above is figure 2 of the article (under discussion here) pertaining to "carbon," and plate 41 above (taken from the same article) depicts a particle of gold magnified 120 times. Plate 40 above shows figure 7 of the article: electron microscope magnifications of the images of these "primeval lichens." In plate 39 above (figure 13 in the article), the gold replica of the fiber structures of the fungus hyphae in the gold is shown magnified 175 times, and in figure 14 of the article, the cellular structure of the gold-fiber replicas is shown under electron microscopic reproduction.

The fact that plants and animals assimilate mineral substances and can have them pass through their metabolism and deposit them out again in transformed shape is a general fact of organic life. This is how all skeletons, shells and frames are formed out of the minerals silicon and limestone. But as well, iron, sulfur and other metals or nonmetals can pass through bacterial, algal, fungal and other plant organisms. The ancient Precambrian "lichens" depicted here took silicon, gold and

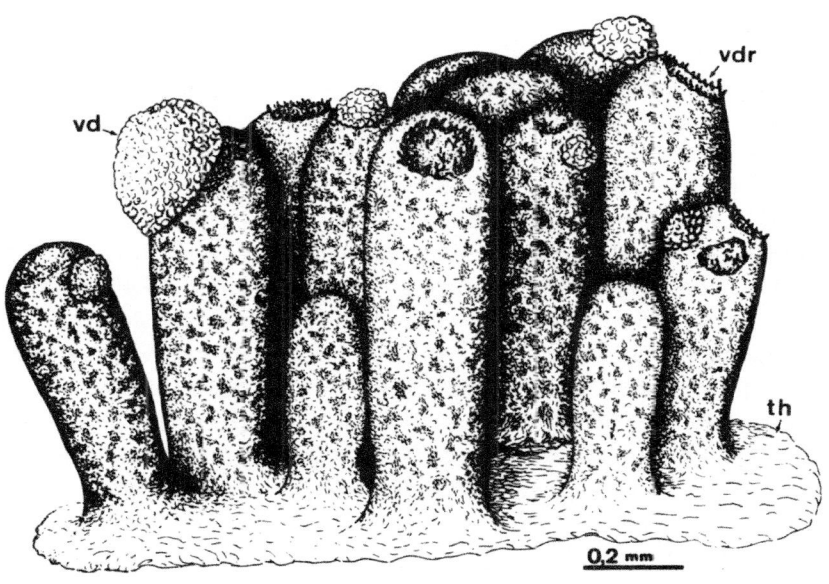

Fig. 1. *Rendering of the complete plant-vegetative diasporas on pillars, which grow from a thin sheet of basalt* (Thallus horizontalis).

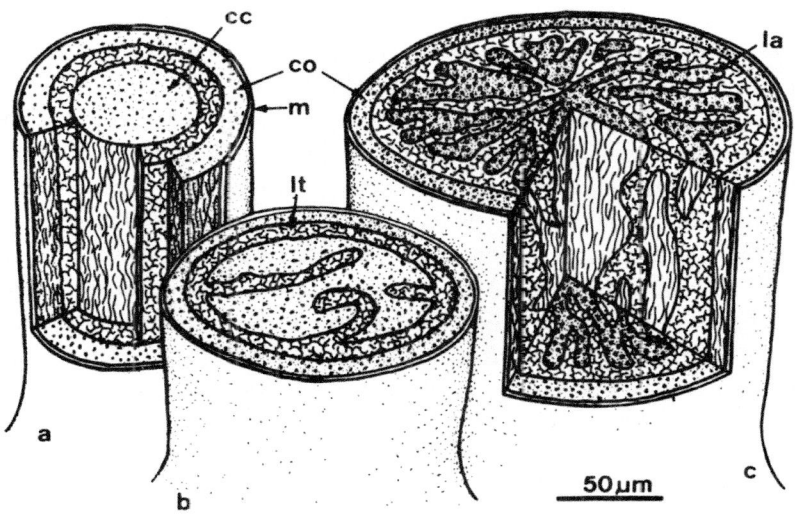

Fig 2. *Rendering of the internal structure of "younger" and "older" columns with a progressive differentiation.*

uranium ore into their metabolism, "digested" these substances, and secreted them both inwardly and outwardly. The inorganic diagenesis of the Witwatersrand Series was supplemented by the organic one. The occurrence of gold in the rock of the Witwatersrand is of organic origin. And so Hallbauer states in the article cited:

> It has been observed on polished surfaces that the coal-like material apparently "digested" eroded uranite. The large amount of gold and uranium contained in the fossilized material therefore points to a process of active assimilation of these substances, a process similar (yet today) to that of the dissolution and storage of radioactive and other minerals by lichens (according to Hale, 1967). Hallbauer and Van Warmelo therefore advanced the theory that the columnar coal-like substance is the fossil residue of a Precambrian symbiotic community probably consisting of an algae partner and fungus organism, and covering areas ranging from a few square centimeters to several square meters of naked rock or heavy mineral sand containing gold." (Hallbauer pp. 125–126)

Finally, Hallbauer states: "The age of the coal-like substance of Witwatersrand (2,300 to 2,700 million years) obviously is of little significance for the dating of the origin of life" (p. 126). And he continues:

> Ling Ong and Swanson found out that organic acids stabilize gold brine by surrounding the colloidal gold particles with protective layers that hinder their further growth and precipitation (from Ling Ong and Swanson 1974). Thus gold can be transported as an organic, protected gold colloid that remains stable over longer periods of time. Similar organic acids must have been produced by the Precambrian plants discussed above for them to be able to dissolve gold and uranium, and to redeposit them, which today appears as cell and fiber replications. And so the possibility exists that large quantities of gold were transported during the Witwatersrand age as organically supported colloids. These colloids become instable if they are introduced into different environments, such as seawater or brackish water. This transport mechanism would explain many contradictions noticed by economic geologists at Witwatersrand,

as well as the role played by primitive plants in the concentration of gold found in the Witwatersrand gold fields.*

APPENDIX 30
PART 1, CHAPTER 8

Jerusalem (Hebr., *j.ruschalem*; MT, *j.ruscoalaim*; Gr., *Jerousalem*; Lat., *Hierosolyma*), the historical capital of Palestine.

Name: The etymology of the name *Jerusalem* cannot be traced conclusively.

a. Its first mention is widely assumed to be in Eg. ostracism texts of the nineteenth or eighteenth century BC: (K. Sethe, ABA, 26, Nr. 5) = *Auschuchamem* (J. A. Wilson in ANET, 329), or *Ruschalimum* rather than *Uruschalimem* (B. Mazar, SY I, 99 and EBB III, 791). In the Amarna letters, approx. 1400 BC, the name appears as *Urusalim* (tablet 3d, Knudtzon, El-Amarna-Tablets, 285–290; RA 19, 22, 106; ANET, 487–489). The first part of the name is interpreted as "city," according to the Akkadian and Sumeric *uru*. Thus the city of Salim, whereby *salim* is understood either as "peace," or as the name of the god Salimum, *Salman,* or similarly. Likewise, the name of the municipality "Bit Ninib in the land Jerusalem" has been connected with Jerusalem itself (first P. Haupt, Jos. SBOT, 54; then J. Levy, JBL 40, 519–22; Mazar, SYI, 100 f and EBB III, 792). Albright, however, identifies this town with Bethelehem (ANET 489). Moreover, the name *U-s-li-immu* is found on Assyrian monuments of the seventh century BC (ANET, 288).

b. The Akkadian form has been retained in the Nabethean *Urischlem* (CIS II, 1, 294), pre-Islamic Arabic *Urischalumm* or similar, as well as *Schallam* (Jaqut, Ed. Wüstenfeld, I, 402 III, 315 IV, 590; LeStrange 83), and *Urischlem* in the Syrian.

---
* Hallbauer, *The Plant Origin of the Witwatersrand: "Carbon."*

c. In the MT, the name *Jerusalem* occurs some 600 times, but not in the Pentateuch (regarding references to Jerusalem in the Pentateuch, cf. M.D.U. Cassuto in Eretz Israd III, 54, 15–17, Hebr.). The consonant form is *jrwschlm*, the original pronunciation most probably *J.ruschalem* (cf. biblical Aramaic *J.ruschalem* and/or *J.ruslem*), but the Masorets vocalized *J.ruschalaim* thoroughly, in some places as *jwrsljm*, with written use of spoken vowel (BH: Jr 26_{18} EST2_6 $_1$CH3_5 2CH25_{11} 32_9). On Jewish coins from the First Revolt (AD 66–70), the name is written defectively in the first year, and full in the second and third years; on coins from the Second Revolt (132–135), exclusively defectively (A. Reifenerg, Ancient Jewish Coins, 47^2, 57–9, 60–6). The modern Israeli written version is *jrwschljm*.

d. As far as the second half of the name is concerned, the Akkadian is evidently identical with the Hebrew tradition. However, this does not hold for the first half—presumably, the name of a city. In the land of the Canaanites, it is of Canaanite rather than of Akkadian origin, so that *ura* could be the Akkadization of a Canaanitic root. In the cuneiform transliteration, weak vowels are generally adapted to the strong vowel that follows it (e.g., *edom* = *uduma*; *p.qod* = *puqudu*), so that *j.ru* or *iru* might become *unu*. However, this cannot be proven. Attempts have also been made to derive the first part of the Canaanitic name from the root *jrw.jrh* and to interpret it either as a verb, such that "He (God) throws the perfect lot" ([God] Salman throws the lot:; or, alternatively, as a noun and translated as "lot or foundation, property of safety or of the God Salman." Yet others have wanted to divide the name into *j.rusch scholem*, which would mean "hereditary seat of safety"; or into *ji'u schalem* (they will see or fear Salem) (Reland, Palestrina 1714, 1716^2, 833f; cf. Also the old Onomastic explanation of the name under 1.2a). *Jrw* has also been associated with the stem *ur* or *ir* (fire or stove), and compared with the designation of Jerusalem as ariel (Uriel?) (cf. Js $29_{1,2,7}$ with Ez 4_{15} f.; cf. Ges. B65f.), hence "stove of God" or "stove of peace [salvation, safety]" (Smith, J. II, 258f.). Albright derives Ariel = har'el, 'ar'el (mountain of God) from Akkadian *arallu*, which means both "underworld" and "mountain of gods" (JBL, '20, 139; archaeology and the religion of Israel, 53³, 151 and 219 note 85–8; cf. Vincent-Stève, 61ff.).

e. The LXX transcribes the name as *Jerousalem*, and Klearchos of Soloi appends a Gr. Ending, *Jerousaleme* (Josephus, C. Ap. I, 179). The pronunciation was originally probably unaspirated, as in *Iouda, Iordanes*, etc., hence *spiritus lenis* in Swete (LXX-edition and Introduction to the OT in Greek, '14²), Hatch-Redpath and Reinach (*Textes d'auteurs Grecs et Romains relatifs au Judaisme*, 95, 11). Others use the *spiritus asper* (incl. Niese in his Josephus edition), likely bearing in mind the aspiration of the name that obviously began even in pre-Christian times. A third group (Rahlfs LXX; the Göttingen LXX) leaves the question open. Since the second century BC, the name has also occurred in the form *Hierosolyma* (plural, with and without article), which in the end takes on general use both in the Greek and in the Latin (Aristl, 1—4 Mkk, Strabo, Josephus; Cicero, Plinius, Tacitus, Sueton). This form probably goes back to an older Greek tradition. Choirilos (end of the fifth century BC, quoted from Jos. Ap. I, 172 f) speaks of the Judean mountains as "the solymic mountains," and Mantho (third century BC) calls the Hebrews "Solymites" (Ap. I, 248). Josephus, who also uses the short form *Solyma* (fem. Sing. Indeclinable; likewise Martial and Pausanias, but neutr. Plur.), derives it from Melchisedek's *Salem* (Ant. I, 10, 2, paragr. 180f; Bell. VI, 10, 1, paragr. 438), while Tacitus has Homer's *Solimi* in mind (Hist. V, 2; cf. also Jos. Ant. VII, 3, 2, paragr. 67). The N. T. has both *Ierousalem* and *Ierosolyma* (the latter as neuter plural, with the exception of Mt2_3 and 3_5, where the name is used for the residency). The Vulgate provides the following forms: *Hierusalem, Ierusalem, Hierosolyma,* and *Ierosolyma* (fem. and neut.).

f. The Arabians call *J. Elquds* (also *el-muqaddas, el-muqaddis, Bet el-Maqdis*) "the saintess" because of its religious meaning for Islam. However, as early as the O.T., the place is called "the residence of God" and/or "of His name," '*ir haqqodesch* (Js48$_2$ 52$_1$ Neh11$_1$ Dn9$_{24}$0). The coins from the First Jewish Revolt display *jrwl(j)m (h)qdsh*, and Mt shows *he hagia polis* twice (4$_5$ and 27$_{53}$). Philo names the city Hieropolis once (Flaccus 46). The possibility cannot be excluded that the aspiration of *Hierosolyma* has its origin in the division and interpretation of the name as *Hierosolyma*, and that it was subsequently transferred to the older form of the name *Hierousalem*. The Alexandrian author Lysimachos derived the name *Hierosolyma* from *Hierosyla* (temple robbery), to slander the Jews (Jos., C. Ap. I, 311).*

APPENDIX 31
PART 3, CHAPTER 11

The Question of Technology

Today, when technical action and technical knowledge are conceived of as functioning together, one speaks of technology. An overview of human history accessible to today's consciousness provides a series of characteristic types of technology:

1. The naturalistic technology of prehistoric times: Primordial humanity derived nourishment, raw materials, and energy from the surplus of nature, without disrupting its household as a whole. Prehistoric human beings gathered, processed, and consumed the surplus of nature, while remaining a part of nature as gatherer, hunter, angler, and primitive artisan in wood, bone, and stone.

---

* This appendix is a translation of an entry from Reiche and Rost, *Biblisch-historisches Handwörterbuch* (Biblical and historical hand dictionary), vol. 2, pp. 820–822.

2. Custodial technology: The human beings of the Stone Age took plants and animals from nature, included them in the sphere of their life, developed domestic plants and animals, and isolated portions of land from the landscape, which it enclosed and cultivated. People became shepherds and planters, ultimately tenders of fields. They became sedentary. In the process, human settlements remained embedded in nature, even as they domesticated land. Wind and water were added to fire as energy sources. Craft technology gradually separated from peasantry and sheep husbandry and became autonomous. Raw materials still came from natural surplus, however. All waste products were "digested" by the circulation of nature.

3. Cultic technology: The development of religious ritual goes hand in hand with that of natural custodial technology. For today's consciousness, this is hard to understand, since people no longer know how closely human beings of the Stone Age lived with nature in a suprasensory way. Gods and elemental beings were a perceived reality. The mystery priests and initiates of the mystery sites knew that, on the level of custodial technology, humans withdrew special suprasensory life forces from nature that nature no longer has at its disposal when he consumes land, nourishment, and raw materials. Therefore, along with agriculture, the mystery centers developed rites of fertility. On the one hand, these rites served to integrate economy and technology into the rhythms of nature. On the other hand, these ancient rites replenished spent cosmic forces of life and fertility via the ritual magic of nature. The oldest of ancestral rites and cults of the dead were now supplemented with the rites of fertility and life in connection with the course of the year. (The rites having to do with the education and transformation of the soul and spiritual, but also of the bodily development of humanity itself is outside the sphere of technology proper.)

4. Exploitive technology: The transition from natural custodial technology to exploitive technology is a gradual, flowing one. The destruction of the forests surrounding the Mediterranean Sea for Phoenecian, Greek, and Roman shipbuilding was the cause of the first large-scale alteration of nature through exploitation. The same holds for coal mining in the European forests in connection with the practice of smelting in the Middle Ages. This activity was further expanded in modern times. More and more raw materials have been affected by this, especially since the replacement of the artisan's shop by factories, tools, and implements by machines. The development of synthetic materials then brought with it the problem of nonbiodegradable waste materials—in particular toxic waste—stemming from technological processes.

5. *Destructive technology:* The transition from exploitive to destructive technology was also gradual. The discovery of electricity and, from there, of the further world of subsensory forces (magnetism, atomic energy) not only interfered with the biosphere, but in its final stages also with the mineral world. This is not the place to assert sociological or political views; for now, it is purely a matter of providing a description. Destructive technology exists, has had an effect, and continues to be practiced by its advocates and carriers. In this technology, nature is put on a path of toxification, destruction, even annihilation. With exploitive technology, a problem arises that is of geological, even astronomical magnitude.

Here the reader's attention is directed to the identification of natural and artificial radiation. With respect to the whole of earthly nature, the radioactive deterioration of the heaviest elements in nature (uranium, titanium, radium) is initially a homeopathic process endowed with lengthy half-life periods: this process is a kind of redemptive process for the mineral realm. It occurs with a rhythm, a magnitude, and an intensity that are tantamount to the natural beginning of the atomization of the mineral world, loosening this world out of the ponderable realm of its bond with the subsensory forces, and preparing the essential nature of this realm for its spiritualization. This enables the mineral realm to pass over into the control of the powers of the Good in a natural way. The mineral world that flows into natural radioactive deterioration becomes capable of resurrection. Natural radiation has fermentive character.

Of all technologies, the artificial destruction of atomic nuclei is the most deeply invasive toward nature. This holds as well for the melting together of nuclei so intensively striven die today—nuclear fusion. The products of the splitting of atoms (plutonium etc.) and the waste product of fusion (tritium) are destructive toxins not only for life, but also for the mineral world itself. This technology generates substances and forces that annihilate all life in its germinal state and prevents the lifeless mineral realm from finding its way into the spiritualization of the future state of the cosmos by passing through the human being and through the world-transforming effect of the Mystery of Golgotha. This technology produces processes whose direction toward poisoning and destruction can neither be reversed nor influenced. They fall utterly out of the circulation of nature, and thus into the dominion of the adversary forces referred to in the Apocalypse of St. John. In cosmological terms, they constitute a realm for themselves for all future to come; in the language of the Apocalypse, the infernal Babylon. Thus for the rest of Earth existence, they are an element of undigested substances and forces, and for the future Jupiter evolution they are the burden of a cosmic satellite, meaning an evil moon. What in natural radioactivity has a fermentive and homeopathic effect (and frequently even has healing powers in radioactive water) becomes, in technological overdose, a corrosive toxin.

6. *Alternative technology:* The problem just described is seen and felt today by many people. The energy problem seems to stand in the foreground here. However, the energy problem is only a portion of the entire problematic. The question of alternatives arises from the full complex. The attempts to respond to them, out of the research, knowledge, and disposal over the subsensory powers are the only ones known today.

And it is within this sphere that alternatives are being sought. In truth, though, the question needs to be put differently: are the forces of nature and subnature the only ones there are, and is this sphere the only place we have to seek for alternatives? Or are there not also new powers in the cosmos that are waiting to be discovered and researched, and based on which entirely new technologies need to be developed to counter the subsensory ones?

7. *Present-day therapeutic technology:* Answers are beginning to be found—albeit unnoticed by the public—to the question pertaining to substances and forces not belonging to subnature. These technologies exist today in two areas of practical life: a) for medicine and pharmaceuticals and b) for agriculture

These fields deal with the knowledge and application of the Earth's and the cosmos's etheric substances and forces in anthroposophic terms. Pharmaceutical companies (Wala, Weleda) have been working with them since the early 1920s. And this technology is utilized on many farms and in many gardening businesses operating in different parts of the world according to the biodynamic methods of agriculture. Continuing research in these technologies goes on in different research institutes based on impulses proceeding from the School for Spiritual Science at the Goetheanum in Dornach. What these technologies promote is not merely environmental protection, but "environmental healing."

Here, I wish only to draw attention to the existence of this technology. (More detailed information on this topic can be found in authoritative literature such as Rudolf Steiner's course on agriculture or his book written with Dr. Ita Wegman, *Extending Practical Medicine: Fundamental Principles Based on the Science of the Spirit.*)

8. *The alternative technology of the future:* The therapeutic technology of the present is only a beginning. The more the suprasensory etheric and astral forces of the Earth and the cosmos are investigated, the more their technological application will be able to go beyond the therapeutic sphere. One can even envision the possibility of the development of machines capable of achieving mechanical results out of such forces. Processes of this sort take place everywhere in nature, where, in an organism's etheric life, forces cause currents of physical matter (the plants' respiratory stream, the animal and human blood circulation, the streaming of plasma in every living cell). If water, brought to streaming in a certain manner by mechanical forces, is taken hold of by etheric and astral forces, it can flow farther and provide energy out of the sphere of cosmic forces to date unknown to today's materialistically oriented natural science. But here I wish to refer to this only briefly.

In the face of prospects of this kind that may at first seem purely theoretical, the question might even arise as to whether, in a still-more distant future, the processes caused by destructive technology might be capable of being guided back into the spiritualization process of the mineral world. For now, this statement is intended merely as a thought pertaining to the future.

About the Author:
A Note from the Publisher

Most readers of Friedrich Benesch's masterly work, *Apocalypse: The Transformation of Earth, an Esoteric Mineralogy*, will have recognized that it is unique among the innumerable volumes devoted to the subject. Written from both a deep, experiential knowledge of Rudolf Steiner's Anthroposophy and a profound understanding of the esoteric meaning of Christianity and the Bible, it contains insights and wisdom that only an extraordinarily spiritually awake, accomplished person could attain. From beginning to end, in well-organized, clearly expressed thoughts, the author leads the reader from the epistemological and ontological presuppositions of his methodology into the esoteric and visionary heights and depths of St. John's Revelation and, above all, more rarely still, into the esoteric mineralogy implicit in the text's profound vision of the New Jerusalem. In this sense, this deeply spiritual book stands on its own.

However, a mystery surrounds aspects of the author's biography that demand of us—as publishers and Anthroposophists, and in the manifold interests of transparency and responsibility—a brief account of certain facts of his life, constituting at least a bare outline of author's biography.

Although every human life is a mystery, some lives, as in the case of this author, are more mysterious than others.

☙

Until 2004, the known biography of Friedrich Benesch (1907–1991) ran more or less as follows. He was a leading priest of The Christian

Community, the movement for religious renewal founded in 1922 by the noted Lutheran minister Friedrich Rittelmeyer, with the help, advice, and support of Rudolf Steiner. He entered The Christian Community Seminary in Stuttgart in late 1947 amid the confusion, chaos, ruins, and devastation of postwar Germany and the tragic events leading up to it, in which nearly everyone had been implicated, either passively or actively. At the age of forty, Benesch was already an ordained Protestant minister. He was mature, charismatic, self-disciplined, and intellectually brilliant. He also possessed a deep and living (not theoretical) knowledge of both natural science and Anthroposophy. As a result, he soon found himself teaching courses at the seminary. Very quickly, too, he was accepted as a candidate for priestly ordination and was ordained by the end of the year.

In January 1948, he was sent to lead a congregation in Coburg, a small town in Bavaria. Since the living quarters available to him made it impossible to bring his large family (his wife and six children), he was transferred in October to the much larger congregation in Kiel, in northern Germany, where he would remain for next nine years, building a strong community, and creating a vibrant and deep spiritual culture.

During that time, beyond his pastoral and priestly duties, Benesch became widely known for his exceptional work with young people, as well as for his penetrating lectures, talks, and conferences. Thus his reputation grew and, in 1957, he was invited to return to teach at the Stuttgart Seminary, where in April of the following year (1958), he was appointed its leader, a position he would hold until his death in 1991.

A striking personality, Benesch was remembered as a powerful figure and an exceptional teacher and lecturer, as well as an accomplished spiritual researcher and author of significant books.

This, in outline, is all that was known about Friedrich Benesch until 2004, when, in an obscure academic publication, Johan Böhm, published an article entitled "Friedrich Benesch: Scientist,

Anthropologist, Theologian, and Political Activist."* This article, among other things, revealed that Benesch had been a Nazi activist in the ethnic German community in Romania and a leader in the more extremist wing of the regional Nazi party. Böhm, who had been a high school student of Benesch in the early 1940s, went on to write a book on the subject.**

Clearly, such revelations needed to be faced as honestly and transparently as possible, and in 2007 Hans-Werner Schroeder, the leader of The Christian Community, published a biography that is as full and as objective as he could write. ***

Therefore, to Begin Again

Friedrich Benesch was born in 1906 to peasant stock in the country town of Sachsich-Regen in Siebenbürgen (Transylvania), then part of the Austro-Hungarian Empire. As was true of many such far-flung places then under Hapsburg rule, the inhabitants of the town were ethnically and linguistically diverse. Hungarians and Germans made up the majority of the population, followed by Romanians and Jews, as well as Gypsies, Czechs, Moravians, Armenians, Galicians, Tyroleans, and Croats. Although under Hungarian rule, in Sachsich-Regen there were German banks, two German bookstores, two German newspapers, and German schools.

It is clear that, from Benesch's earliest years, his identity as a German meant a great deal to him. As an adolescent, we find him researching his ancestry and discovering that he could trace his

---

*   *Halbjahresschrift für südosteuropäische Geschichte, Literatur und Politik*, Heft 1/2004, S. 103–119: "Friedrich Benesch: Naturwissenschaftler, Anthropologe, Theologe und Politiker."

** Johann Böhm: *Pfarrer und NS-Amtswalter: Friedrich Benesch*. In: *Hitlers Vasallen der Deutschen Volksgruppe in Rumänien vor und nach 1945*. Lang, Bern 2006,

*** Hans Werner Schroeder: *Friedrich Benesch. Leben und Werk 1907–1991*. Mayer, Stuttgart 2007. All unidentified quotations are from Schroeder's biography. Additional information has also been gleaned from the website www.Egoisten.de/

paternal line back to the thirteenth century. In fact, his family may possibly have arrived as early as the tenth century with the first group of colonizing Saxons, emissaries from Henry the Fowler, and thus constituting a first seminal manifestation of Germany's *Drang nach Osten* ("drive toward the East") in search of *Lebensraum* ("living space"). As evidence of the family's antiquity, the name of a nearby mountain is "Benesch."

The contemporary Benesch family began to rise socially during the generation before Friedrich's birth. His grandfather was a stable boy, who rose to become a wagon driver (driving as far as Russia), before marrying the daughter of a man with a small farm, thus acquiring property. This allowed his son, Friedrich's father Georg (b.1888) to attend school and university to become a teacher and to marry upward (1906). His wife brought more property with her.

Whether the family knew of Rudolf Steiner is unknown, but they may have, since Steiner gave a lecture ("Woman in the Light of Goethe's Worldview") in Siebenbürgen on December 29, 1889, at the evangelical Hospital.

The young Benesch was intellectually precocious. Serious, solitary, and a lover of nature and the outdoors, he already knew how to read and write when, in 1913, he entered school, which had apparently remained more or less untouched by the War. At school, he showed himself to be an excellent student, an independent spirit, and a natural leader. With Armistice in November 1918, however, everything changed radically and permanently. A hospital for returning wounded soldiers was installed in the school. A year later (1919), following the signing of the Versailles Peace Treaty, Siebenbürgen, without warning, became part of Romania. Intensive classes in Romanian were instituted, and all lessons were taught in Romanian. It was the end of an era. Notwithstanding, the school ethos remained German, and the German "spirit" was maintained there.

Writing about himself as a fourteen- to seventeen-year-old, Benesch cites six determining influences. First, Goethe, beginning with *Werther*, which entranced him with its focus on "human relations...nature...and love." Nietzsche's *Zarathustra* followed. Next—putting these together—came an intense engagement with nature, closely linked in his soul with a passionate study of the gods and heroes of Nordic mythology. Thus, Benesch writes that, when he experienced nature, he experienced not only the mineral, plant, and animal worlds, but also the elemental worlds of the nature gods and spirits.

All of this created within him, as his biographer notes, a deep and powerful sense of connection to, and affinity with, *Germantum* ("Germandom"), which sat, if not easily, then paradoxically, with his equally strong connection to Christianity. On the one hand, he was struck by the realization that "before the coming of Christianity, the Germans were already a people whose human experience could live fully into the world of the kingdoms of nature." On the other hand, following his confirmation, he notes: "I could experience something of Christ's love in my own heart."

However, Benesch writes further, "All these experiences remained hidden deep within my soul. I could speak about them to no one, neither to my mother nor to my schoolmates."

In 1924, he graduated from high school at seventeen. After spending a year working on his grandparents' farm, he left his homeland to study at the University of Marburg, an ancient town in central Germany, situated roughly halfway between Cologne and Weimar. Science was his first chosen field of study, but he added theology as an equal partner.

In Marburg, he soon found a home in a hostel for *Auslandsdeutsche* (Germans abroad or from other lands), run by Professor Mannhart of the "Institute for the Science of Border- and Foreign-Land-Germandom." As its name indicates, the focus of the Institute was the history, preservation, and nurture of ethnic Germans living beyond the boundaries of Germany—especially, and now particularly, as those boundaries were drawn in 1918—in countries such as Romania, Moravia, and Bohemia (now the Czech Republic).

Marburg was then at the height of its prestige. It was home to many thinkers who would subsequently and significantly mark the twentieth century, including the philosopher Martin Heidegger, the theologians Rudolf Bultman and Rudolf Otto, and the classicists Werner Jaeger and Eric Auerbach. The same was true of the student body. Heidegger's students alone included, among others, Hans Georg Gadamer, Hannah Arendt, Leo Strauss, and Hans Jonas. Despite this prestigious intellectual milieu, however, Marburg was also resolutely anti-republican, authoritarian, fervently nationalistic, and not a little anti-Semitic. In the elections of 1930, it voted overwhelmingly for the National Social Democrats.

Benesch spent three semesters studying in Marburg (1925–26). Besides his official course work, he joined "Germania," a politically oriented populist (*Volkisch*), anti-Semitic, anti-Slavic student association that was also hostile toward women (it opposed women's education). He also attended many lectures at Dr. Mannhardt's right wing, nationalist "Institute for the Science of Border and Foreign Germandom." He also went further afield, hearing many other lecturers on similar themes—such as a Dr. Gerber ("The Foundations of Minority Rights") and a Professor Bonhoff ("The Foundations of Race Hygiene and its Meaning for the Struggle for Existence of Border- and Foreign-Germandom"). This orientation or interest led him, in 1926, to attend a summer school on "European Peoples and their Folklore [*Volkstum*]."

Among the many speakers attending was Professor Hans Hahne, who was traveling with wife Magdalena, and his two daughters, Ilse and Sunhilt. Initially trained as a doctor, who became a psychiatrist, before turning to the study of prehistory—above all, German prehistory—Hahne (1875–1935), had been the Director of the Museum for Prehistory in Halle since 1912. As a prehistorian, he saw the German people as manifesting a historical and cultural continuity and destiny from earliest times into the present. This view was founded on belief in the reality of a German "race soul"—a deep-rooted spirituality in which a people, the Germans, could participate. Beginning in the 1920s, Hahne began to create a master narrative, or meta-theory, that combined prehistory, folklore, and ethnology (race) into a pseudo-science of "peoples." He was also a member of the Nazi Party, the SA or "brownshirts," and taught "race science" to the S.S. leadership. After 1933, he became rector at the University of Halle. As Hans-Werner Schroeder put it, "[Hahne] was what we call today 'an old Nazi.'" At the same time, Hahne was also familiar with Anthroposophy. He had heard Rudolf lecture at least once and had read many of his foundational works. However, he was not an Anthroposophist and never joined the Anthroposophical Society.

Benesch was immediately drawn to Hahne. Here was a preserver and nurturer of the German soul and spirit, one who was not taken in by technology and modern civilization. In Halle, members of the Youth Movement flocked to him, calling him "Father Hahne." Together, teacher and students worked to revive old German folk and peasant traditions, including, interestingly enough, the *Oberuferer Christmas Plays*, with which Rudolf Steiner also worked and that Steiner's old Goethe teacher, Schröer, had discovered in the 1880s.

At the 1926 Summer Conference, Hahn invited Benesch to visit him in Halle, but Benesch decided to continue his studies in Marburg, where he and Evangelical pastor Gottfried Schmidt became friends. In the dying days of World War I, Schmidt had been wounded and was in a hospital. He'd had a Christ experience in which he felt "higher life forces" streaming into his body, which he understood, without a shadow of doubt, emanated from the being of Christ. From that moment on, as he put it, he lived in Christ and Christ lived in him. Benesch was deeply moved by his friend's experience. He felt that he, too, would one day know the same reality—but not yet. His soul, he felt, was not yet ready to make that commitment, but one day he knew it would be. "I must still wait. I must let it ripen in my soul until it can also become ripe for my true, real, inner life." The attraction of "Germanness" was still stronger than that of true Christianity.

Another significant event at this time was Benesch's discovery, in the university library, of Rudolf Steiner's lectures, *The Mission of the Folk Souls*. It struck him like lightening. He also found a lecture by Steiner titled "The German Soul and the German Spirit." Finally, he read Steiner's book *How to Know Higher Worlds*." But, as he had said with regard to Christ, "Yes, but not yet." Likewise, with regard to Anthroposophy he said, "Yes, but not yet." Having done so, he took up Professor Hahn's invitation to go to Halle.

He spent the winter and summer semesters (1926–27) in Halle, continuing his studies in science and theology, but now he added Professor Hahne's courses on prehistory, folklore/ethnology, and race science. At the same time, he found himself growing closer to Hahne's daughter Sunhilt. During this time, too, he became a member of Artaman Society, a *blut und boden* ("blood and soil") movement dedicated to the preservation of rural life, as the word Artaman, which originally meant "agricultural man" implied, but it also carried explicit connotations of racial purity, with strong anti-Slavic undercurrents. Not surprisingly, The Artamans were later absorbed into Nazism.

With the end of the semester, it was time for Benesch to leave Halle. He was sad to leave, but he felt a powerful urge to return to his homeland, Siebenbürgen, where he could continue his studies at Klausenberg University. Arriving there, as he puts it, he experienced a deep sense of loneliness, which he was able to overcome only through intense study of Fichte's philosophy of the "I." This, in turn, led him to what he called the experience of human freedom in the "I."

Still only twenty-one, he decided to become a high school teacher. Classes were held in Romanian, which he mastered swiftly and to near perfection. He also became more overtly political during that period. In 1928, he became a member of the "Party of the Germans in Romania (PGR)," founded in 1922 by the German-Romanian Fritz Fabritius. By 1933, it would become "The National Socialist Renewal Movement for the Germans in Romania." For the next two years, while attending

Klausenberg University, Benesch devoted any spare time he had to "educating" native Germans in "Germanness."

Graduating in spring 1931, he fell ill with tuberculosis and was sent to convalesce high in the Carpathian Mountains. He took with him St. Augustine's *Confessions* and the New Testament in Greek. There, in deep solitude, the Gospels came to life as a seed within him, and he felt he began to live with Christ in a new way. In this mood, he returned to his parent's house, where, with no abatement of his work on behalf of the PGR, he began to enter more deeply his study of Rudolf Steiner, reading *Christianity as Mystical Fact*, *The Philosophy of Freedom*, and *Goethe's Theory of Knowledge*. Then, in spring 1932, Professor Mannhardt invited him back to Marburg to run the hostel in which he'd stayed before.

In Marburg, the paradox and duality, the "not-yet," in his soul (if that's what it was) continued. As the political situation in Germany intensified, he turned to the study of theology while still remaining committed to the ideology of the German soul, to German Idealism, and to the notion of a German ethnic/folk/race reality. He continued to study with Professor Mannhardt, including in courses on "The New Reich" (and similar courses by other right-wing professors), while at the same time beginning courses on Church history, as well as on the New Testament with the celebrated exegete and theologian Rudolf Bultman. Politics, however, still dominated his outlook, as evidenced by the *Hostel Newsletter* of March 1933, in which he wrote a piece on "National Socialism in Siebenburgen."

From Marburg, Benesch then returned to Halle. He was now an anomaly, since he was both a committed Christian and a committed National Socialist, which, in the pagan milieu in which he moved, meant he grew increasingly isolated. However, this was not the only change in his personal situation; in March 1933, he and Sunhilt Hahne became engaged and then married, making his mentor also his father-in-law. Marriage, of course, made the need for a career decision all the more pressing. He was qualified to become a schoolteacher. He was also now not only a Christian, but also in a position to become priest or pastor. He had already heard of The Christian Community in Marburg, which seemed to him to speak most clearly to his desire "to live with others in a Christian way." He attended services in its church in Halle. He had even heard one of the founders (Friedrich Rittelmeyer) speak and was impressed. He considered taking priestly orders in it—but still he felt: not yet.

Benesch decided he would remain Evangelical and return to his homeland, to his roots, and to the rural, peasant folk he loved. Ordained in 1934, he became Pastor in the village of Birk, a few miles south of where he was born. He was a good Pastor, well liked, able to mix well, and at home with his parishioners, building community with folk dances and festivals. He was hardworking and entrepreneurial. At the same time, he continued to maintain and promote his political views and continued to work for what had become the "National Socialist Renewal Movement for the Germans in Romania." This eventually led, in 1938, to a direct confrontation with his superiors, who thought his political activity excessive and out of place.

Asked to take a three-year leave of absence, and leaving his family behind, he returned to Halle to stay with his widowed mother-in-law. He began studying—in the spirit of his late father-in-law and mentor Hans Hahne—for a third degree, this time in anthropology, race science, and prehistory. At the same time, through his mother-in-law, he was able to deepen his political commitment by assuming a position in the SS in July 1939. A year later, he received his doctorate with a thesis on "The Fortress of Hutberg, a young Nordic Mixed Settlement near Wallendorf, in the circle of Merseburg." By now, World War II had begun. Interestingly, however, Benesch seems to make no mention of it anywhere.

In 1940, he lectured several times at SS Section XVII in Halle. Nevertheless, busy as he was, he awaited only the moment when he could return to Birk. In his heart, strange as it may seem, his avowedly deepest desire was still to live with others in a Christian way. Still, too, the

About the Author: A Note from the Publisher

work of Rudolf Steiner and The Christian Community seemed to be closest to what he sought. Thus, he again began visiting the little Christian Community in Halle, where he attended the Consecration of Man and took communion. The experience was overwhelming: "During the rite I had a direct experience of the Trinity. The pure golden aura of the Risen One, metamorphosing through each stage of the Mass—Heaven is come to Earth—such was the immediate striking content of the experience. I was shaken and moved to the depths of my being."

During Advent 1940, with his exile over, he returned to his family and parishioners in Birk. He was given a festive, even triumphant, welcome. After Christmas, he set about baptizing all the children born during his absence, as well as blessing all the couples married and visiting all the graves of those who had died. He began giving courses for young people. Many of these, as Böhm, Benesch's student, tells us, continued to be suffused with racial teachings. At the same time, he turned to a more intensive study of Rudolf Steiner. Although the Anthroposophical Society in Germany had been banned in 1935 and The Christian Community in 1941, he was able to make contact with the publishers in Dornach, Switzerland, and in this way was able to order any books he wanted. As he puts it, "I connected with Rudolf Steiner and Anthroposophy and took it ever-more intensively, wakefully, and deeply into my soul." Nevertheless, he was also appointed as a local "circle leader" of the "People's Union of Germans in Hungary" and still had "political responsibilities," which he dutifully fulfilled. There is no evidence, however, of his being involved with the deportation of Jews. Meanwhile, the reality of the war grew closer; the Red Army was approaching and life was about to become untenable.

On July 29, 1944, Benesch performed his last baptism; on August 27, the last marriage; and on September 7, the last funeral. Then, on September 11, he gathered his entire community into a column of squads of walkers and wagons and they set off westward on the long trek of more than 800 miles toward Austria and Germany.

By the time the war had ended in May 1945, Benesch had made his way back to Halle. Applying to his home diocese, he was given a new small parish in the village of Neukirchen. He was 38. What passed in his soul there—or before—we do not and may never know.

While caring for his new community, he made contact, once again, with The Christian Community in Halle. He spoke and became friends with the Christian Community priest, Rudolf Köhler, who visited him in Neukirchen several times and encouraged him to visit the priest seminary in Stuttgart. He heard other Christian Community priests speak, including Emil Bock and Rudolf Koschützski, who also encouraged him to attend the seminary. At this point, he fell seriously ill and was granted sick leave. In the silence and solitude of his sickbed, one imagines he was able to review his life. Again, we do not know what passed within him; there is no record. Nor do we know whether he spoke (or confessed) to anyone either about his past beliefs and activities or about what kinds of radical change, if any, were taking place within him.

In late 1947, Friedrich Benesch entered the Seminary in Stuttgart.

☙

Any theory, commentary, or interpretive reflection would be out of place and run the danger of seeming exculpatory or worse. One cannot tell what passes in the intimacy of another's soul. Sadly, to be a Christian does not mean that one is not also a sinner; likewise, to be an esotericist does not mean that one is also a saint. As humans, we are all all-too-human. Each of our lives is a cautionary tale. "There but by the grace of God go I." With the decease of the only witness—the inner witness of Benesch himself—there is nothing one can add to the stark facts revealed by the first part of his life. They speak for themselves and stand as a reminder of the ways one can be led astray. Therefore, we are left with only the work, within which perspicacious readers may perhaps even find some clues to the later state of the author's soul—passages such as the following, pointed out by an early reader. Here

Benesch is writing of the most precious of all stones, Jasper, in its manifestation as Heliotrope, or Bloodstone:

> The ancient authors are evidently right when they presume heliotrope to be the jasper of the Apocalypse, which with its saturated earthly dark green containing the red sprinklings of iron is an image for the workings of Christ, who sacrificed his blood for the Earth and planted seeds for the future. What must take place in the human soul so that it can develop the capacity not to succumb to petty moralizing or dogmatic sectarianism, and not to reject everything different from itself, but instead magnanimously to learn to sense and acknowledge what *must* be at work in another entity in the way of necessary errors, transgressions, and weaknesses, even if it means taking in the sacrificial fragrance created by the loss of one's own worth and given off from the depths by fallen entities who are a sacrifice unto themselves? A loss of being can lead to a becoming, and true renewal will always turn loss into gain and the greatest of misfortune into good fortune. This is what Goethe says in his *Fairy Tale of the Green Snake and the Beautiful Lily.* (pages 241–242)

In the same light, Schroeder quotes the following:

> The real truth is not the truth,
>   but error outgrown.
> And true reality is not reality,
>   but illusion outgrown.
> And real purity is not original purity
>   but impurity purified.
> And the true good is not original good
>   but evil outgrown.
>
> This is true for the whole cosmos—even for the gods.
>
> For on the paths
>   on which evil becomes transmuted
>   something can develop
>   in the good that was not originally contained in it.

> Because God has created adversaries for himself
> he has compelled himself
> to reveal his deepest being in quite other ways
> than he would have been able to do without them.

Concerning the meaning of such statements, readers must of course be the judge. Whatever the case and whatever statements or others like them may mean, the mystery of this particular human life—which is also symptomatic of the mystery the twentieth century—remains.

Select Bibliography

Bock, Emil. *The Apocalypse of St. John.* Edinburgh: Floris Books, 2005.

Cloos, Walther. *Kleine Edelsteinkunde im Hinblick auf die Geschichte der Erde* (A brief gemology in the light of Earth's history) Schaffhausen, Switzerland: Novalis Verlag, 1956.

———. *The Living Earth: The Organic Origin of Rocks and Minerals.* Sussex: Lanthorn Press, 2008.

Goethe, J. W. *The West-Eastern Divan: In Twelve Books* (tr. E. Dowden). Charleston, SC: Nabu Press, 2014.

Gübelin, Eduard J. *Innenwelt der Edelsteine. Urkunde aus Raum und Zeit* (Inner world of gemstones: Certificate of space and time). Düsseldorf, 1973.

Hadorn, Wilhelm. *Die Offenbarung des Johannes. Theologischer Handkommentar Zum Neuen Testament.* Leipzig. 1928.

Hallbauer, D. K. *The Plant Origin of the Witwatersrand: "Carbon,"* Johannesburg, 1975.

Harms, E. *Afrika: Erdkunde in entwickelnder, anschaulicher Darstellung.* Munich, 1967.

Hegel, Georg Wilhelm Friedrich. *The Philosophy of Nature.* Calgary, Alberta: Theophania Publishing, 2011.

Julius, Frits H. *Stoffliche Welt und Menschenbildung.* Stuttgart, 1965.

Julius, Frits H., and John Petering. *Fundamentals for a Phenomenological Study of Chemistry.* Fair Oaks, CA: AWSNA, 2000.

Killian, Johann. *Crystals: Secrets of the Inorganic.* London: Hanlins, 2011.

———. *Das Du im Stein. Die Sprache des Anorganischen.* Vienna, 1948.

Klockenbring, Gerard. *Geld-Gold-Gewissen.* Stuttgart 1974.

Lehrs, Ernst. *Man or Matter: An Introduction to a Spiritual Understanding of Nature on the Basis of Goethe's Method of*

Training Observation and Thought. London: Rudolf Steiner Press, 2014.

Pleiss, Hermann. *Der Kreislauf des Wassers in der Natur* (The circulation of water in nature). Jena, 1947.

Reiche, B., and L. Rost. *Biblisch-historisches Handwörterbuch*, vol. 2. Göttingen, 1962.

Rienecker, Fritz, and Cleon L. Rogers, Jr. *Linguistic Key to the Greek New Testament*. New York: HarperCollins, 1982.

Rosenkrans, E. *Das Meer in seiner Nutzung, Studienbücher Geographie für Lehrer*, vol. 14. Leipzig, 1980.

Schmidt, Philipp. *Edelstein. Ihr Wesen und ihr Wert bei den Kulturvölkern*. Bonn, 1948.

Schröder, B. (ed.). *Wasser*. Frankfurt, 1977.

Schultz, Joachim. *Sternkalender Erscheinungen am Sternenhimmel 1952*. Dornach, Switzerland: Mathematisch-astronomischen Section am Goetheanum, 1950.

Schütze, Alfred. *The Enigma of Evil*. Edinburgh: Floris Books, 2012.

Schwenk, Theodor. *Bewegungsformen des Wassers*. Stuttgart: Verlag freies Geistesleben, 1967.

———. *Sensitive Chaos: The Creation of Flowing Forms in Water and Air*. Edinburgh: Floris Books, 2010.

———. *Water: The Element of Life*. Great Barrington, MA: SteinerBooks, 1989.

Steiner, Rudolf. Agriculture Course: The Birth of the Biodynamic Method. London: Rudolf Steiner Press, 2004.

———. *Anthroposophical Leading Thoughts: Anthroposophy as a Path of Knowledge*. London: Rudolf Steiner Press, 1973.

———. *Art as Seen in the Light of Mystery Wisdom*. London: Rudolf Steiner Press, 2010.

———. *Cosmosophy, Vol. 2: Cosmic Influences on the Human Being*. New York: Clarkson Potter, 1997.

———. *The Cycle of the Year as a Breathing Process of the Earth*. Hudson, NY: Anthroposophic Press, 1984.

Select Bibliography

———. *Das Miterleben des Jahreslaufes in vier kosmischen Imaginationen*. Basel: Rudolf Steiner Verlag, 1999.

———. *Extending Practical Medicine: Fundamental Principles Based on the Science of the Spirit*. London: Rudolf Steiner Press, 1997.

———. *The Foundations of Human Experience*. Hudson, NY: Anthroposophic Press, 1996.

———. *Founding a Science of the Spirit*. London: Rudolf Steiner Press, 1999.

———. *Guidance in Esoteric Training: From the Esoteric School*. London: Rudolf Steiner Press, 1998.

———. *Intuitive Thinking as a Spiritual Path: A Philosophy of Freedom*. Hudson, NY: Anthroposophic Press, 1995

———. *Kunst- und Lebensfragen im Lichte der Geisteswissenschaft* (Questions of art and life in light of Spiritual Science). Basel: Rudolf Steiner Verlag, 2000.

———. *Man in the Light of Occultism, Theosophy, and Philosophy*. London: Rudolf Steiner Press, 1964.

———. *Mystery Knowledge and Mystery Centres*. London: Rudolf Steiner Press, 2012.

———. *The Mystery of the Trinity: And The Mission of the Spirit*. Hudson, NY: Anthroposophic Press, 1991.

———. *Nature's Open Secret: Introductions to Goethe's Scientific Writings*. Hudson, NY: Anthroposophic Press, 2000.

———. *A Psychology of Body, Soul, and Spirit*. Great Barrington, MA: Anthroposophic Press, 1999.

———. *An Outline of Esoteric Science*. Hudson, NY: Anthroposophic Press, 1997.

———. *The Riddles of Philosophy: Presented in an Outline of Its History*. Hudson, NY: Anthroposophic Press, 2009.

———. *The Spiritual Hierarchies and the Physical World: Zodiac, Planets & Cosmos*. Great Barrington, MA: Anthroposophic Press, 2008.

———. *The Temple Legend: Freemasonry and Related Occult Movements: From the Contents of the Esoteric School*. London: Rudolf Steiner Press, 1997.

———. *Theosophy: An Introduction to the Spiritual Processes in Human Life and in the Cosmos.* Hudson, NY: Anthroposophic Press, 1994.

———. *Twelve Moods of the Zodiac.* Eschborn, Germany: Verlag Gerhold, 1987.

———. *Ursprung und Ziel des Menschen* (The origin and goal of humanity). Basel: Rudolf Steiner Verlag, 1981.

———. *The World of the Senses and the World of the Spirit.* London: Rudolf Steiner Press, 2014.

Wachsmuth, Günther. *Etheric Formative Forces in Cosmos, Earth, and Man: A Path of Investigation into the World of the Living,* vol. 1. New York: Anthroposophic Press, New York, 1932.